Pentecostalism

SCM CORE TEXT

Pentecostalism

William K Kay

scm press

© William Kay 2009

Published in 2009 by SCM Press
Editorial office
13–17 Long Lane,
London, EC1A 9PN, UK

SCM Press is an imprint of Hymns Ancient and Modern Ltd
(a registered charity)
St Mary's Works, St Mary's Plain,
Norwich, NR3 3BH, UK
www.scm-canterburypress.co.uk

British Library Cataloguing in Publication data

A catalogue record for this book is available
from the British Library

978 0 334 04144 3

Typeset by Regent Typesetting, London
Printed and bound by
CPI William Clowes, Beccles, NR34 7TL

Contents

He [Jesus] will baptize you with the Holy Spirit and with fire.

(Luke 3.16)

When the day of Pentecost came, they were all together in one place. Suddenly a sound like the blowing of a violent wind came from heaven and filled the whole house where they were sitting. They saw what seemed to be tongues of fire that separated and came to rest on each of them. All of them were filled with the Holy Spirit and began to speak in other tongues as the Spirit enabled them.

(Acts 2.1–4)

For
Anthea, George and Olivia

Acknowledgements

Many people have helped directly and indirectly in the writing of this book. I'm grateful to Chris Thomas for many fruitful conversations by skype, Calvin Smith for insights into South America, Gospel Odame-Kentoe, Andrew Parfitt, Andrew Davies, Peter Kay, David Maxwell and Dave Garrard. While researching the book I travelled to South Korea, Malaysia and Singapore, and am grateful to Wonsuk Ma, Wilson Teo and Dennis Lum for their hospitality or assistance on these journeys. Allan Anderson helped me here, too. I'm grateful to him and other members of the Society for Pentecostal Studies in the United States and the European Pentecostal Theological Association in Europe. Larry McQueen, Aaron Friesen and Claudia Währisch-Oblau shared with me their unpublished doctoral work. Joe Castleberry helped me on Central America. The Flower Centre in Springfield and Darrin Rogers and the Donald Gee Centre at Mattersey provided invaluable information. Colleagues in the Glopent network likewise shared their research and may recognize traces of it in the text. The Asia Pacific Theological Association was a source of inspiration and I remember conversations with many of its members with gratitude, especially a prolonged lunch with Shane Clifton. Stephan Huber of the International Society of Empirical Research in Theology, which met at the University of Würzburg in 2008, was generous in sharing with me his research findings derived from an original survey sponsored by Bertelsmann. I'm grateful to colleagues at the School of Theology and Religious Studies at Bangor, especially Eryl Davies and Robert Pope as successive Heads of School, who supported my international conference attendance. Special thanks must be given to Anne Dyer for critical insights and her bibliographical industry, and to Andrew and Ann Parfitt for attentive proofreading. All the errors that remain are mine. There have been times when it seemed the task that I have undertaken was too vast to be accomplished in the time I had available, but I have come to understand that if academics assume that they will be able to write the perfect book during the leisurely hours of retirement, they deceive themselves. We have to do the best we can in the time that we have – an eschatological sentiment that has a very definite Pentecostal ring to it.

Introduction

This is a book about Pentecostalism, the extraordinary movement that swept through the Christian churches and beyond during the course of the twentieth century. It came into existence at about the same time as Marxism and the psychoanalytic teachings of Freud. All three movements have their roots in the nineteenth century and made a huge impact in their different ways on the twentieth. Marxism started with the economic theorizations and radical journalism of Karl Marx. It was embodied in Russia (or the Soviet Union, as it became) and spread out from there with the resources of a vast and powerful state. Freudianism began in Austria in the theoretical innovations of a gifted and restless doctor. It was transplanted to the USA in 1909, where it began to flourish. Pentecostalism's beginnings were less intellectual. It has been described variously, but the simplest and shortest definition would draw attention to its emphasis upon religious experience and particular beliefs. We might say that Pentecostalism is the marriage of a spiritual experience called 'baptism in the Holy Spirit' with evangelical doctrines, and we might add that this combination of doctrine and experience flourishes in revival meetings that translate themselves into distinctively lively forms of church life.

This book has three parts. The first and longest deals with the history of Pentecostalism from its nineteenth-century beginnings to the present day. It traces the development of doctrines and groups of churches in different parts of the world. The ten historical chapters that make up Part 1 are intended to give a global overview of Pentecostalism in North America, Latin America, Europe, Africa and Asia while tracing interconnections between these continents. (The countries in Latin America and Asia that are the focus of attention have been selected on statistical criteria that are explained in the relevant chapters.) Part 2 presents Pentecostal theology, and adds to theological themes woven into the historical chapters. Part 3 looks at Pentecostalism through the lens of two broad sociological theories. Some of this information has been touched on in the earlier chapters. Throughout the book there are references forwards and backwards to earlier or later chapters so that readers can obtain more than one perspective on central topics.

Each chapter is broken up by subheadings and at the end of each chapter are 'questions to think about', which are intended to provoke your own reflections on what you have read. At the end of every chapter are listed books for further reading, which as far as possible are all still in print. In 2004 SCM Press published *Pentecostal and Charismatic Studies: A Reader* (edited by W. K. Kay and A. E. Dyer), which contains excerpts of writings on Pentecostal themes; a few excerpts are captured here in embedded text boxes. At the end of each chapter are cross references to the *Reader* so that it can serve as a companion to the present text for those who wish to read the actual words of Pentecostals and charismatics more copiously. From time to time footnotes point to websites and YouTube clips which show Pentecostal meetings live. There will be seen contemporary examples of a movement which preaches about Jesus Christ and claims the power of the Holy Spirit of God.

PART 1

History

1

Definitions, Numbers and Historiography

Introduction

A man stands up during a Sunday morning gathering of Christians and calls out *'Euossa, Euossa use, rela sema cala mala kanah leulla sage nalan. Ligle logle lazlo loglo. Eno mino mo, sa rah el me sah rah me.'* Someone else in the congregation gives an interpretation of the words: 'Jesus is mighty to save. Jesus is ready to hear. God is love.'[1] You have just heard an utterance in 'tongues', or glossolalia as it is more technically known. The first speaker has spoken in an unknown language, unknown to himself and to any other member of the congregation, and believes that he has done so under the direct influence of the Holy Spirit. The second speaker, feeling himself to be given an interpretation by the Holy Spirit, speaks out in the common language of the hearers. In an English-speaking service interpreters speak in English but if the service is being held in Spanish or French or any other language, then the interpreter would speak in that language. In each case the utterance in tongues will sound fairly similar.

Welcome to a Pentecostal service.

Here we are on a Sunday morning in the United States in the Midwest. You drive up to one of the many small churches in this town and park your car because the noticeboard outside tells you that the service will start at 10.30 am. You get out and walk in to find a small number of people. You are given a hymn book at the door. At about 10.30 a large man walks out from the vestry at the front and announces the first hymn. The congregation shuffles to its feet and sings. The minister then conducts the service by praying aloud, directing the order of service, giving the notices, announcing the previous week's offering, reading a biblical passage and preaching on it, announcing the closing hymn, shaking your hand as you go out and, presumably, locking the door and driving away. There has been nothing out of the ordinary in the service although some

---

1 The words in italics were transcribed during a meeting convened by Charles Fox Parham and reported in the *Topeka State Journal*, 7 January 1901, p. 4. This is the start of the modern Pentecostal movement. The information comes from J. R. Goff (1988), *Fields White Unto Harvest*, Fayetteville, University of Arkansas Press, pp. 80, 202.

of the music, which seems faintly old-fashioned, speaks vigorously about the Holy Spirit. This also is a Pentecostal service.

You are on the outskirts of Nairobi in Kenya and find yourself in a shanty town composed largely of shacks built of corrugated iron. Amid this huge unplanned area of human habitation is a substantial building and it turns out to be a church. Walking inside on a Sunday morning you notice that the place is packed with people dressed in clean clothes and with their arms raised in the air in worship. There is an amplification system in action and the sound of drums and clapping are almost deafening. There are people dancing in traditional African style near the keyboard. The pastor, dressed in a suit despite the hot weather, is leading the congregation enthusiastically and singing in English but also in an African dialect from time to time. This is a communion service and there will be bread and fruit juice shared around the congregation but, more than this, this is a service about healing and the pastor is going to pray for those who are ill. He preaches for a very long time but the congregation sits in apparently rapt attention. At the end of the service he calls people forward for prayer and his elders accompany him. The first person who stands at the front and asks for prayer is an elderly woman. The pastor lays his hands on her head and begins to pray but after a moment or two she falls on to the floor though, unnoticed, one of the deacons has apparently slipped behind her to make sure that she doesn't hurt herself as she falls. And so the pastor moves along the line praying for people in direct and loud language asking God through Jesus and by his Spirit to heal those are ill. At the end, the crowd streams out blinking into the sunlight. This also is a Pentecostal service.

Now we are in south India. Again it is Sunday morning and something like a thousand people are crammed into a large low building with ceiling fans but without any other form of air conditioning. On one side of the building sit the women and on the other sit the men. The pastor calls them to pray and everybody begins to speak at once calling on God in a mixture of languages. Some people appear to be speaking in tongues and the pastor brings a prophetic utterance concerning the future of the congregation. Yes, there is blessing ahead. He invites people in the congregation to come up and share news of something that God has done for them and one or two people come to the front and tell stories about how God has helped solve their problems. This man had his bicycle stolen but it has been returned. A woman was ill but the pastor prayed for her and she is now able to move her leg. Afterwards, traditional Wesleyan hymns are sung and the pastor then begins to preach using a biblical text and involving the congregation in the dramatic retelling of a Bible story. After many exhortations to avoid idols and to trust God, the service comes to an end and everybody gathers in the courtyard outside for a large communal lunch. This also is a Pentecostal service.

And now we are in England and attending a 'Third Wave' or neo-charismatic church. The large factory-like building is situated on an industrial estate. We come in and see on our left a coffee and dough-nuts bar where people grab refreshments and mill around talking to each other. On our right is a bookstore containing all kinds of pamphlets and leaflets about lifestyle and doctrinal issues and introducing the beliefs and practices of the church. Newcomers are clearly expected. The service begins with songs projected onto a screen from a computer-controlled workstation. The words keep pace with the singing and the congrega-tion stands and faces the platform. People raise their hands and began to speak quietly in tongues. There is a smart-casual dress code here. The congregation is predominantly white but there are Asian and African people present too. The pastor on the platform is wearing a shirt and jeans and the woman next to him (his wife?) is in a dress but without any evidence of expensive coiffure. There is evidence of prophetic utterance but this comes to us from people who are clearly known to the leadership team. A young man comes to the front and speaks into the microphone giving a prophetic picture. He sees birds on the ground which take off and rise up and turn into eagles and swoop and soar. The congrega-tion will rise up and begin to have a divine perspective on its situation. Another man speaks and encourages the congregation in liturgical words of confession and then Holy Communion is served and bread is taken round the congregation with little cups of wine. There follows a sermon that is partly illustrated by pictures on the screen; it is a simple teaching message about the importance of water baptism. Later, new attenders are encouraged to attend an Alpha course or find one of the many home groups run by the church. This also is a Pentecostal service.

These different Pentecostal meetings could occur anywhere in the world. What they have in common is a willingness to be open to the Holy Spirit. There is a confidence that God is an interventionist God and that the Holy Spirit can be felt and manifested through human agency in Christian gatherings. There is a belief in charismatic gifts, whether these are gifts of healing or utterances in unknown tongues, as we shall see later.

Definitions

So, how should we define Pentecostalism? It is here that we are con-fronted by the same difficulties that face anybody who attempts to define a particular religion. We can look at the doctrine, the history, the ritual or some combination of these. There will be an overlap between doc-trine and ritual and between doctrine and history because most large religious groups have complicated historical streams and strands that subdivided them in the past. Most of the subdivisions in most religious groups occurred over doctrine. For this reason it is unsurprising to discover that the different types of Pentecostalism or different Pentecostal denominations may hold slightly different views about the work of the Holy Spirit or other aspects of their faith. This means that it is difficult to find the essence of Pentecostalism and, if we try to do this, or to isolate Pentecostal distinctives, we will end up with scholarly differences predicated on favouring one form of Pentecostalism over another. Yet, if we are going to count how many Pentecostals there are at the present time, we need *some* sort of working definition.

Walter Hollenweger's book *Pentecostalism* offers three definitions.[2] The first is his own, which he has now discarded:

> All the groups who profess at least two religious crisis experiences – 1 baptism or rebirth, and 2 the baptism in the Spirit – the second being subsequent to and different from the first one and the second usually, but not always, being associated with speaking in tongues.

Kilian McDonnell, the Roman Catholic scholar, suggests:

> Those Christians who stressed the power and presence of the Holy Spirit and the gifts of the Spirit directed towards the proclamation that Jesus Christ is Lord to the glory of God the Father.[3]

Finally, there is a definition from Eldin Villafañe quoting Vinson Synan:

> All Pentecostals agree on the presence and demonstration of the charismata [spiritual gifts] in the modern church, but beyond this common agreement there is much diversity as in all the other branches of Christianity.[4]

These definitions are progressively less specific. Over 100 years Pentecostalism has been diversifying with the result that definitions must stretch to include every variation. The first definition is specifically doctrinal, though it is doctrinal in the specialist sense that it identifies two distinct religious experiences. Here the presumption is that the Holy Spirit functions to bring about the new birth of the new Christian. This is well-established evangelical theology that equates conversion with the new birth of John 3, and both with the process of justification whereby the sinner is placed in a reconciled relationship with a holy God. The second

2 Walter J. Hollenweger (1997), *Pentecostalism: Origins and Developments Worldwide*, Peabody, MA, Hendrickson, p. 327.
3 Quoted by Hollenweger, *Pentecostalism*, p. 327.
4 Quoted by Hollenweger, *Pentecostalism*, p. 327.

experience is altogether more central to most forms of Pentecostalism. It is a *baptism in the Holy Spirit*. Baptism, for most Pentecostals, speaks of immersion. Consequently 'baptism in the Spirit' is an immersion in the Holy Spirit, a sense of the overwhelming closeness of the transcendent God, which is seen as an enduement with power for service along the lines of those discerned in the lives of the apostles in the book of Acts.

The second definition removes what might be seen to be Protestant tendencies so as to emphasize the generalized presence of the Holy Spirit for proclamatory purposes. The third simply speaks about the charismata but without any reference to their origin or purpose. Hollenweger thinks that even the widest definition fails to capture the full extent of global Pentecostalism. He proposes instead that we should think of Pentecostalism as 'a way of doing theology' related to experience, open to oral rather than literary forms of transmission, ecumenical by virtue of its plurality and 'expressing itself in the categories of pneumatology'.[5]

This last way of looking at Pentecostalism manages to combine both belief and practice. It assumes that practice *is* theology because Pentecostalism in itself is a lived expression of theology. Who can tell the dancer from the dance? Who can separate the practice from the belief implicit within the practice? So by this understanding Pentecostalism is a form and style of theology. In philosophical language it might be called a 'habitus' or a 'life world'.[6] And as Hollenweger has stressed on many occasions, it is the spoken and flexible nature of Pentecostal theology that distinguishes it from the characteristically literary and fixed theology of the West. It is a type of Christianity that doesn't depend upon liturgies, prayer books, creeds and a highly educated clergy but rather on the testimony of lay people communicating their intense relationship with a personal God. That is *one* way of looking at Pentecostalism, and a way that makes sense in a non-literary culture, the culture of the non-Western world. Yet, it is only one way because, within the West, Pentecostalism has managed to adapt itself to theological fixity and technological change. So, there is also a form of Pentecostalism that is relatively sophisticated and that self-consciously places itself alongside a whole range of other Christian expressions. We could say that Pentecostalism, like Roman Catholicism, exists both in magisterial and folk forms and is able to adapt to the grassroots of any society where it is situated. Or, again to use Hollenweger, we can refer to Pentecostalisms as well as to Pentecostalism.

In any case, whether we offer narrow or broad definitions of Pentecostalism or whether we try to define Pentecostalism by the processes

---

5 Hollenweger, *Pentecostalism*, p. 329.

6 Pierre Bourdieu (1977), *Outline of a Theory of Practice*, Cambridge, Cambridge University Press; the concept of 'life-world' is developed by J. Habermas, though it is also found in E. Husserl; see briefly Ted Honderich (ed.) (1995), *The Oxford Companion to Philosophy*, Oxford, Oxford University Press, p. 489.

through which it expresses theology, our definitions will be more or less inclusive. Inclusive definitions will be embracing and accept any kind of church that has some of the features of classical Pentecostalism as it was developed in the West. Exclusive definitions will be narrower and based upon stricter criteria allowing fewer church groups to come within its parameters. Exclusive definitions will emphasize distinctive Pentecostal doctrines connected with speaking in tongues or charismatic gifts and will be averse to any syncretistic practice. The point here is that Pentecostalism within the non-Western world will often assimilate features of traditional culture and combine these with Pentecostal distinctives. Such churches, for example, may give a vital role to the work of the Holy Spirit within their everyday practice but, at the same time, accept that ancestral spirits have a function within the life of their people as well. This means that we are left with having to decide whether a church that advances Pentecostal doctrine and experience together with traditionally non-Christian practice counts as a Pentecostal church. Or should we say that only 'pure' churches that adhere to the doctrines of the Reformation and add on top of this spiritual gifts are really Pentecostal?

These issues become not only theological but also political since African churches that incorporate an element of traditional African religion within their world view may feel aggrieved if they are excluded from larger Pentecostal affiliations. The AICs or African Independent Churches are included by most writers on the subject as being Pentecostal.[7] Walter Hollenweger, drawing on his experience within the World Council of Churches, makes a plea for 'responsible syncretism', a term that is difficult to pin down but which, in effect, signals the desire to make room for indigenous and contextual theology without jettisoning the insights of the Reformation.[8]

We could, therefore, visit another Sunday morning congregation.

We attended a service in March 1992 held on Sunday in a temporary iron structure erected on the property of the minister. The service started with congregational singing, most of the hymns from the Paris Evangelical Mission Southern Sotho hymn book, unwittingly called *Difelsa tsa Sione* (Hymns of Zion). Then a psalm was read in which the congregation gave the refrain ('his mercy endures for ever'), much as they would in an Anglican church service. During the service a few people periodically showed signs of 'possession by the Spirit' such as

---

7 Allan Anderson (2000), *Zion and Pentecost: The Spirituality and Experience of Pentecostal and Zionist/Apostolic Churches in South Africa*, Pretoria, University of South Africa Press. AIC can stand for African Indigenous Church, African Initiated Church, African Instituted Church. There is no standard formulation but the basic idea is the same.
8 Hollenweger, *Pentecostalism*, ch. 11.

jerking and jumping and falling to the ground. It is believed they had been 'carried away' by the Spirit. When they 'recovered' they were given blessed water to drink. There were six male preachers, two ministers and four evangelists, who commented on the same passage from the New Testament that had been read (John 3.1–13). A short hymn or a song interspersed the homilies. After the men had finished, four women stood to add their comments on the passage. Before and after each homily or song, the whole congregation knelt for a short simultaneous prayer. At noon a large brass bell was rung by one of the church leaders. A man was busy preaching at the time. He immediately stopped, and the congregation knelt to pray. At the end of the service, six church leaders in front of the church raised a large white banner with a blue cross and blue stars sewn onto it, and all the people had to pass under it. Ministers, evangelists and women leaders (usually wives of the ministers and evangelists) stood on either side of the banner. We were first given blessed water to drink in a small plastic container, and then the leaders laid hands on us as we passed under the banner. The banner was apparently shown to Archbishop Masango in a vision, and is therefore used in all St John churches. When we asked members what was the meaning of the ritual, they were unable to explain it – it was merely a church custom, they said. At the close of the service people brought plastic containers with water in to be prayed for by the minister. The water came from the municipal supply, but after it had been prayed for it was believed to have curative properties. The minister covered the water with a linen cloth and then encircled it with his gold staff, after which the cloth was removed and the water given back to the people to sprinkle and drink for the healing of their sicknesses. The minister called forward those who are joining the church, and those who were candidates for baptism. They were liberally sprinkled with water on their faces and on their backs, after which the minister laid hands on them. The congregation knelt in prayer to close what had been a four-hour-long service.[9]

An African variant of Pentecostalism

Here is a church service that has moved further away from the traditional position. How should we think of it?

This church treats Saturday as the Sabbath. The main services take place from Friday night throughout Saturday and Fredrick Modise the leader rejects speaking in tongues and prophecy but still gives

---

9 Anderson, *Zion and Pentecost*, pp. 153, 154.

pronounced emphasis to the Holy Spirit. There is polygyny, baptism, a church badge (a six-pointed star) and secret rules. This service was:

held on Wednesday nights in the local community hall. Visitors were ushered into the central seats in the hall, while members sat on either side separated by gender – women in red and white, and men in maroon jackets. All men wear jackets and ties in church services; women and girls wear head coverings and may not wear jewellery. In front of the huge auditorium at the church headquarters at 'Silo' [taken from the biblical Shiloh] in Zuuberkom there is a throne-like chair in front of an altar-like table on which there is a round table lamp with seven globes. Modise explained to the visitors at Silo the meaning of the lamp.[10] The centre red globe which stands higher than the others represents fire, which in the International Pentecost Church theology is the name for God. From the six smaller lamps surrounding it are the Water, the Blood and the Spirit of Truth, the Father, the Son, and the Holy Spirit. The lamp is only switched on when Modise is present at the table. Modise sits on the large chair, often dressed in his high priest-like robe. International Pentecost Church ministers at Silo wear red robes, similar to academic gowns. From sunset on Friday until Sunday morning Modise fasts and spends much of the time in the auditorium with the crowds who come to be healed. He sits behind a table with a file in which secretaries have inscribed all the particulars of each seeker before the healing service began. The secretaries give each sick person a number and then the sick proceed to Modise in numerical order. Once they reach him, they are to confess their sins to him to ensure their healing.

There is a large choir and orchestra at Silo, and music forms a very important part of the services. The taking up of various collections of money is also a prominent part of the services – only members partake in the collections. Several collections may take place during a service and members are encouraged to give liberally, even up to an entire wage. Modise himself is well provided for with several expensive cars, including a Rolls-Royce bought for him by his congregation, a Cadillac and several BMWs.[11]

These definitions of Pentecostalism and examples of Pentecostal practice have inevitably changed over the course of time. One of the things that has happened in the West (though also elsewhere), which we examine later, concerns the emergence of *charismatic churches*. These are churches

---

10 Fredrick Modise, leader of what is one of the closest examples of a messianic church in South Africa.

11 Anderson, *Zion and Pentecost*, pp. 150, 151.

that are similar to those in Pentecostal denominations except that they were founded earlier. These churches may be Baptist or Anglican, for instance, and have retained their denominational identity while accepting much Pentecostal belief and practice. The songs they sing may be the same as the songs sung in Pentecostal churches and the pattern and rhythm of church life may be very similar to that found in Pentecostal churches – there may be small home group meetings, prayer for healing, lay leadership in the congregation and attendance at the same kind of conferences that Pentecostals attend. These churches are counted within the statistics for the whole Pentecostal/charismatic movement (sometimes PCM, for short) even though they will also be included separately within denominational statistics as well.

Equally, there may be congregations that were once charismatic and have now moved out from their denominational moorings to become independent, neither formally Pentecostal nor formally denominational but existing in an independent state, perhaps relating to a distant apostolic figure. These *neo-Pentecostal* or 'third wave' churches are also apt to be included within any discussion of Pentecostalism because their beliefs and practices, while being orthodox according to Western standards, incorporate experience of the Holy Spirit and charismatic gifts. In a statistical summary these churches do not necessarily fall within recognizable denominational boundaries nor can they be counted under classical Pentecostal headings.

With this in mind, we can look at the numbers.

Numbers

Before going further we need to make several other clarifications about categories. Following Allan Anderson, this book uses the term 'majority world' to describe Christians living in what used to be called the 'developing world', 'third world' or 'two-thirds world'. I have sometimes used 'non-Western' as an adjective to describe this group although, strictly speaking, this term is itself ambiguous. In one sense 'non-Western' could refer to any country that is not in what is usually called the 'Western hemisphere', which would comprise Europe and the United States, but in another sense a non-Western country might be a country that had non-Western values wherever it was situated on the globe. Thus a country like Saudi Arabia might be non-Western in some respects even if in terms of its average per capita wealth it was Western. Conversely a country like Singapore, though it is in the East as far as European map-makers are concerned, can be called Western.

There are also times when reference is made to 'indigenous' groups. These are groups that occur naturally in a country by growing out of its own culture and customs. Although this term is generally unambiguous, there are situations when social change is so rapid or waves of immigration so large that what was once seen not to be indigenous becomes indigenous. The large, ballpark figure given for all types of Pentecostals and charismatics at the end of the second millennium AD is usually over 520 million. This amounts to around 27% of organized global Christianity and these are people found in 740 Pentecostal denominations, 6,530 non-Pentecostal, mainline denominations and 18,810 independent, neo-charismatic denominations and networks. These Pentecostals and charismatics are found in 9,000 ethnic and linguistic cultures, speaking 8,000 languages and covering 95% of the world's population. This information is provided by David Barrett and his co-worker Todd Johnson. Barrett is Professor of Missiometrics at Regent University and Johnson is Director of the Center for the Study of Global Christianity at Gordon-Conwell. Barrett has worked for many years on Christian statistics and was responsible for editing the authoritative *World Christian Encyclopedia* (published in a second edition by Oxford University Press in 2001). There are no better figures available than these, either from the United Nations or from any other source.

While it is true that Barrett has, over the course of his working life, reorganized the figures and reclassified the various groupings, there are two main tendencies that appear to have driven this process. The first has been the desire to reflect more precisely the actual nature of the different subgroups whose statistics he is compiling. This causes him to split big groups up into their constituent subgroups. The second has been to reflect the major waves of renewal and this has caused him to combine categories into megablocks of a similar kind of Christianity. Moreover, within the first edition of the *World Christian Encyclopedia* of 1985 Barrett divides his figures up country by country and regionally. He also divides the figures up according to seven ecclesiastical blocks (Anglican, Catholic (Non-Roman), Non-White Indigenous, marginal Protestant, Orthodox, Protestant, and Roman Catholic). Pentecostals appear within the Non-White Indigenous block in six subcategories and within the Protestant block in five subcategories. But in the 2001 *New International Dictionary of Pentecostal and Charismatic Movements*, the figures are reconfigured to keep pace with changes on the ground. Pentecostals/charismatics/neo-Pentecostals are presented in some 60 subgroups.[12]

Barrett and Johnson begin their presentation by viewing the Pentecostal and charismatic and neo-charismatic renewal in three distinct waves. The first wave gives rise to Pentecostalism or 'classical' Pentecostalism,

---

12 D. B. Barrett and T. Johnson (2002), in S. M. Burgess and E. M. van der Maas, *New International Dictionary of Pentecostal and Charismatic Movements* (*NIDPCM*), Grand Rapids, MI, Zondervan. Barrett and Johnson are keen to avoid double counting, and by saying there are 60 subgroups I am following their lead.

the second wave gives rise to the charismatic movement or charismatic renewal and this is followed by the third wave of 'non-Pentecostal, non-charismatic but neo-charismatic renewal'.[13] Nevertheless, they view the entire process as being one basic move of the Holy Spirit of massive world-wide proportions comprising 523 million affiliated church members, of whom 65 million are classical Pentecostals, 175 million are charismatics and 295 million are third-wavers or neo-charismatics. Of this total, 29% of all members worldwide are white and 71% are non-white. The picture is neither stationary nor simple because each wave augments the others, spreading geographically into every continent and into 236 countries.

Like all complex statistical compilations, these figures can be read in several ways. Barrett and Johnson use patterns of Christian growth over and against the predicted growth of the world's population. They calculate the number of Christian ministers compared to the total number of Christians and see the figures against a background of potential world evangelization. Also, as has already been said, they present the figures in terms of a sequence of waves of renewal. The first wave occurs from 1886 onwards with the forming of the first classical Pentecostal denomination.[14] The second wave is significantly dated after 1950 when non-Pentecostal denominations received experiences of Pentecostal phenomena, though the roots of this charismatic movement go back at least to 1907. The third wave can certainly be dated back to 1945 or even 1900 although its main impetus occurred from the 1980s onwards in the Western world. By defining the third wave in terms of non-denominational or post-denominational neo-charismatics, Barrett and Johnson can view them as predating the charismatic movement.

Other presentations of the figures may be keen to emphasize the size of the charismatic contingent in comparison with the classical Pentecostal contingent and thereby to argue that classical Pentecostalism, which is largely situated in the West, should not be understood as normative. Rather, Pentecostalism in its charismatic and indigenous form in Africa, Asia and Latin America ought to be seen as normative. In this latter form Pentecostalism is less tidy, more politically engaged – often in a left-wing way – and more syncretistic in its tendencies. In Africa it may be influenced in its praxis by traditional African religion and cultural patterns and these may be combined in endlessly changing ways with exportable parts of American culture brought in by global television and travelling preachers who emphasize the 'prosperity gospel' or spiritual warfare.

Alternatively, the term 'classical Pentecostals' can be applied to all denominational Pentecostals. If this is done then the number of classical Pentecostals grows by claiming some of the charismatics. It rises above

---

13 Barrett and Johnson, 'Global Statistics', p. 284.

14 This was the group that eventually became the Church of God (Cleveland, TN).

the 660 traditional, Western-related denominations that identify themselves specifically as Pentecostal and which are now found in 220 countries.[15] The purpose of such an exercise is not only to make Pentecostal denominations feel better about themselves but also to make their doctrines, which are generally clear cut and well worked out, more likely to be accepted as normative.

Alternatively again, it is possible to emphasize the size of the non-trinitarian component within Pentecostalism since, among narrowly defined classical Pentecostals in the United States, about 25% are 'Oneness' in their theology (see Chapter 11). This theology has affinities with modalism in the sense that God is understood to be manifested in three modes (i.e. Father, Son and Spirit) rather than three co-equal and coexistent divine Persons as outlined in the Athanasian creed. Within the global total of 523 million, however, Oneness Pentecostals amount to about 1% unless the number of the charismatic Christians in China (which is largely unknown) and developments among charismatics in the majority world adjust these figures upwards.[16]

There is a further reading of these figures that interests us, one stemming from Barrett and Johnson's discussion. They point out that the three separate waves continue to grow annually. It is not that the waves have replaced each other but that they coexist side by side. Pentecostals are increasing at 2.7% per year, charismatics at 2.4% per year and neo-charismatics at 3% per year. Consequently neo-charismatics will become even larger in comparison with the other two groups. Yet, within the pattern of growth, there are historical factors hidden away. Pentecostals are smallest in Europe because the Europeans rejected the first wave and 'because they were not prepared to leave the great state churches'.[17] But since 1970 charismatics within those churches have responded enormously, with the result that the ratio between charismatics and Pentecostals in Europe is the highest of all continents. Thus the balance between Pentecostals and charismatics will tend to vary between different continents even if, overall, neo-charismatics dwarf everybody else. Equally, the balance between Pentecostals and charismatics will vary between countries and will affect the dynamic development of each nation's Christian population.

In a discussion of the global statistics of Pentecostalism, two other considerations are important. First, the Pew Forum conducted an inter-

---

15 Barrett and Johnson, 'Global Statistics', p. 293, section 7.

16 In table 1 of 'Global Statistics' (p. 286), Barrett and Johnson give the total number of Oneness Pentecostals as 2.7 million in line 11 and 2.9 million for Black American Oneness Apostolics in line 30. Since the total number of Pentecostals, charismatics and neo-charismatics is over 523 million, the Oneness contingent only reaches 1%.

17 Barrett and Johnson, 'Global Statistics', p. 285.

national survey of the beliefs and practices of Pentecostals (see Chapters 5 and 6). This survey was not intended to find the number of Pentecostals and charismatics in the various countries where the survey was conducted. Nevertheless the findings of this material support rather than contradict the more impressionistic portrait given of Pentecostalism by other studies. Second, the Bertelsmann Stiftung Religious Monitor (used by Stefan Huber of the University of Bochum and applied in 21 nations) is able to demonstrate the centrality of religious beliefs to public practice and indices of economic development.[18] His findings demonstrate, for instance, that both in Brazil and Nigeria religion is politically relevant. This is exactly what we would expect given the numbers of Pentecostals identified by other methods and the anecdotal evidence of their political concerns. In this way the Bertelsmann data help to confirm the information given by Barrett and Johnson.

Historiography

So, having looked at examples of Pentecostalism, definitions of Pentecostalism and Pentecostal numbers, we now must consider how we tell the story of Pentecostalism. Historiography is concerned with the way history is written.

- What sort of information is counted as evidence?
- How do we interpret the evidence?
- In what way does one event cause another?
- Are historians always biased?
- Do human beings determine the course of historical events or are economic and cultural factors decisive?
- Within Pentecostal history, can we detect the hand of God or are we to presume everything can be explained naturally?

These are the kind of questions that we need to wrestle with before we can look at the story.

And, look at the story we must. The one irreducible element in history is time. Historical events occur in a sequence, as do our own lives. This means that, just as our own lives come to us naturally in the form of a narrative ('I was born in London but my parents moved to Manchester where I went to school before I got my first job as a ...'), so historical

---

18 Stefan Huber (2008), 'Leading Tone or Background Music: A Comparative Analysis of the Public Significance of Religion in 21 Nations'. Paper given at the ISERT meeting at the University of Würzburg. See also Stefan Huber (2007), 'Are Religious Beliefs Relevant in Daily Life?', in Heinz Streib (ed.), *Religion Inside and Outside Traditional Institutions*, Leiden, Brill.

events are most naturally recounted as narratives. We hear that out of the French Revolution came a brilliant young artillery man who later seized control of the army and led the French revolutionary forces in a series of victories that resulted in the control of most of Europe. This is the story of Napoleon.

As we look back on events, we can see how they turned out. We know that eventually Napoleon was defeated at Waterloo and his grand schemes came to almost nothing. But, at the time, participants looked at an uncertain future. We can investigate the story in reverse by moving from Waterloo back to the dispositions of the armies prior to the battle, and back from there to Napoleon's escape from captivity on Elba, and so on right back to Napoleon's childhood. Yet when we tell the story, we go forwards. So with the account of Pentecostalism: we know after more than 100 years roughly what happened but, when we tell the story, it is natural to begin from whatever we take to be the beginning. In doing so we will measure whatever is significant in the early stages by reference to the impact it had on the later stages. We will use the benefit of hindsight but tell the story forwards.

Hindsight sees causes

Such story-telling helps us to make sense of a random disaster. It also enables us to apportion blame. Generations of historians have toiled in this way to explain the origins of great calamities like, say, the First World War, constructing elegant narrative chains of causes and effects, heaping opprobrium on this or that statesman.

There is something deeply suspect about this procedure, however. It results in ... 'retrospective distortion'. For these causal chains were quite invisible to contemporaries, to whom the outbreak of war came as a bolt from the blue. The point is that there were umpteen Balkans crises before 1914 that *didn't* lead to Armageddon.

Niall Ferguson, *Sunday Telegraph*, 22 April 2007

What sort of information is counted as evidence?

In the case of Pentecostal history we are going to be looking at documentary accounts of events or beliefs or relationships and trying to assess how important they were in the unfolding story. We aim to interpret this evidence against the light of our knowledge of how events turned out and what we take to be the honesty of the participants. But there will be times when the evidence is inconclusive and points in two directions and, if this is so, we shall need to dig deeper into our sources. In general, historians divide their sources into those that are primary, which come directly from participants in the historical process, and those that are secondary, which are later interpretations of those events. So the contemporary historian needs to look at primary sources where possible while tentatively accepting the interpretations of previous historians. As we shall see, there are sharp divergences of opinion concerning the origins of Pentecostalism. There may not be an easy or ultimate solution to the problem of divergence since there is more than one way of interpreting events.

The question of evidence is more pressing still because Pentecostals believe, as we have seen, in the work of the Holy Spirit in their lives. They believe the Holy Spirit spoke to them, strengthened them and revealed truth to them, but from this distance in time it is impossible for us to verify such claims. There is no point in trying to write Pentecostal history that is entirely sceptical about these beliefs since we would find ourselves constantly at variance with the primary evidence in front of us.[19] If the early Pentecostals said that the Holy Spirit acted in their lives, we will have to accept their word for this since one of our tasks is to attempt to recreate the mindset of the participants in the story.[20] We are trying to enter into their life-world and to see life as they saw it even if, at another point, we may step out of that life-world into our own. So we will have to accept – or if not accept, to understand – some of the beliefs of the early Pentecostals in order to help us interpret events from their point of view. Again it has be said that this way of telling the story is complicated because, unlike the participants, we know the end whereas they did not.

In a sense we have a push–pull model of history whereby the 'pull' comes from the inner motivations and desires of the participants in the historical process. These participants have their own beliefs about each other, the society in which they live and the future. They have a life-world that we can try to enter by an act of historical imagination or by empathy. At the same time there is a 'push' factor brought about by economic circumstances or social conventions. A preacher may travel to a different part of the country because he or she has been offered employment (as was the case with W. J. Seymour when he went to Los Angeles) or because social conventions dictate a particular course of action (as when Aimee Semple McPherson had to return to the United States after the death of her first husband – she would have found it difficult to remain in China as a single woman with a child). Even so, the historian must try to see the bigger picture and to evaluate all the factors that go

19 Argued in more detail in W. K. Kay (1992), 'Three Generations On: The Methodology of Pentecostal History', *EPTA Bulletin* X.1 and 2, 58–70.

20 Following here the thinking of R. G. Collingwood (1980), *The Idea of History*, Oxford, Oxford University Press, first published in 1946, who argues we should seek to 're-enact' and so think the same thought as the historical agent.

into the decision-making of historical actors. It is not enough to take the statements of actors at face value but nor should they be dismissed out of hand, especially since they comprise genuine primary source material.

To put all this more technically, we are seeking to give an account of Pentecostal history that prioritizes the evidence of participants while accepting that an overall critical or distancing process must occur. We may or may not see this history as being shaped providentially, but we are definitely not trying to reinterpret this history entirely in secular categories. To offer an example: if we were to give an account of the Reformation using Marxist dialectical materialism, we would speak about the rise of the peasants against their exploitative Roman Catholic masters and of the eventual proletarian successes that led to severance from the Pope. We would stress the peasant origins of Luther. Yet, such an account would be deficient. It would ignore the theological heart of the Reformation and the vital role of the doctrine of justification. It would attribute motives to Luther that ignored his own wrestling with a troubled conscience and it would paint him as an agitator rather than as a scholar. Crucially, it would be unacceptable to Luther himself. Thus, if we have a rule, it is that the historian should not in some sort of quasi-omniscient way pat the participants in the story metaphorically upon the head and tell them that he or she knows better.

How do we interpret the evidence?

We interpret it in a way that takes account of the views and values of participants while seeking to find a coherence that was unavailable to them. Attempts to make history a 'scientific' discipline made much of the collection of facts.[21] The idea was that if we assemble the facts correctly, and assemble enough of them, then we would have a truly objective history that could be completely relied upon in the same way as nineteenth-century heirs of the Enlightenment thought that they could rely upon scientific progress. The trouble with this point of view is that there is not only dispute about the facts but dispute about the interpretation of the facts. We might take the death of John F. Kennedy as an example. We certainly know the fact that he was shot, but do we know exactly how many bullets were used? And when it comes to the interpretation, is there a conspiracy by the Mafia, the CIA, Russian agents, Cubans or who? So it is naive to think that we can collect a mountain of facts and thereby ensure that history is smoothly and uncontroversially written. Even simple facts like statements given out loud in a church meeting are prone to contested interpretations. A statement that everybody hears may be interpreted as a prophecy inspired by the Holy Spirit or

---

21 The most obvious exponent of this view was Leopold von Ranke.

as a manipulative attempt by an individual to change the direction of a congregation.

Yet we are helped by the sequence of events in time. We can be sure that events that come first might have an impact on events that come second; but not the other way round. So, if we discover that a particular preacher or writer offered an original idea about the work of the Holy Spirit, we may be correct in assuming that another preacher, coming after the first preacher, may have been influenced by the first preacher. In this way, when we take doctrines that are found within Pentecostalism, it is possible to track back through the nineteenth century to see how these doctrines emerged. This is a detective process and, as we shall see, has been brilliantly carried out by several writers (such as Donald Dayton, Edith Blumhofer and Mel Robeck) who put together stages by which the doctrines of classical Pentecostalism were formulated.[22]

It is true that we may have an overarching view of history by which we come to give coherence to the story. We may refuse to assume that history is simply a random collection of activities and events without any meaning. We may have a general sense that the path is upward and that there is gradual improvement both in society or the church – such would be a liberal progressive view of history.[23] Equally, we may see history as being informed by interpretations of secular society so that, for example, William Menzies' account of the development of the Assemblies of God, *Anointed to Serve*, tends to understand the progress of the denomination as a gradual specialization through the formation of separate departments.[24] This account of Assemblies of God mirrors that which might be given of a large business organization: it does not imply that the Assemblies of God was predestined to go down this road but simply that the church conforms to a rationalistic pattern that was known to work within other human organizations and that this is the best way to interpret its development. In this way we may interpret events to provide a meaning to the narrative, but the best historians will allow the interpretation to grow out of the events rather than to impose it upon them.

Are historians always biased?

This is a particularly 'postmodern' question that somehow implies that everybody is, indeed, biased, because objectivity is in principle impossible

---

22 E.g. E. L. Blumhofer (1993), *Restoring the Faith*, Chicago, University of Illinois Press; Donald W. Dayton (1987), *Theological Roots of Pentecostalism*, Peabody, MA, Hendrickson.

23 A view argued by J. B. Bury, one-time Regius Professor of Modern History at the University of Cambridge and eloquently assumed by such writers as T. B. Macaulay.

24 William W. Menzies (1971), *Anointed to Serve*, Springfield, MO, Gospel Publishing House.

and that any interpretation of events is as good as any other. It can lead to the argument associated with philosophical phenomenology, which claims that clarity can only be achieved by 'bracketing out' distorting elements in any perceptive process so as to reach a form of unassailable truth. Bracketing out, a technique advanced by the philosopher Edmund Husserl, appears to depend on a form of mental gymnastics whereby prejudices and biases can be removed by the conscious effort of the prejudiced and biased individual.[25] This idea looks like a form of elaborate nonsense since the prejudiced and biased individual is normally unaware of his or her prejudices. They are *prejudices*, pre-judgements, that come into play before anything else and function at a pre-conceptual level shaping perceptions and rationalizations. There is no fixed point within consciousness where a neutral balance can be achieved.[26] In the writing of history, one attempted solution to the issues raised by these difficulties is for the historian to admit to his or her political or social commitments so that the reader can discount these when they become intrusive. Yet, even if we know that Eric Hobsbawm is Marxist or that A. J. P. Taylor was a member of the Campaign for Nuclear Disarmament, how do we know which pieces of their historical writing are influenced by their non-rational commitments? We don't.

The subject of bias and prejudice in Pentecostal historiography may well be connected with racial, gender or denominational loyalties. As we shall see, there is evidence that Charles Parham was a white supremacist, but does this make his apparently factual account of events that have nothing to do with race unreliable? This question appears to be impossible to answer in any general way. So, we conclude that historians, simply by virtue of being human, bring to the writing of history biases and prejudices, some of which they are conscious of and most of which they are ignorant of. To complicate matters further, some prejudices belong to a particular age or epoch in the sense that they are so widely shared that it's impossible to find an example of a human being in that age or epoch who does not hold those views. All we can hope to do is to collect the facts (bearing in mind that facts are clothed with interpretive packing) and put them into a chronological sequence, wrap this sequence in a narrative framework and leave the reader (with all his or her biases and prejudices) to make a judgement.

25 See for instance, William K. Kay (1997), 'Phenomenology, Religious Education, and Piaget', *Religion* 27, 275–83.

26 See William K. Kay (2009), 'Karl Popper and Pentecostal Historiography', *Pneuma* (in press) for a more detailed discussion about neutrality and historical method.

In what way does one event cause another?

The answer to this question is a philosophical minefield.[27] In one sense we may know how cause and effect operate in the material world but, when we add human beings into the equation, there are bound to be unknowns. One line of thought is that human beings simply learn from one another and that in this way the doctrine that was partly developed in the seventeenth century might be fully or differently developed at the end of the nineteenth century (as we shall see with the notion of a 'second blessing' following conversion). So this is a form of causation that is based upon human learning. Such a view of causation might also be found in the 'historical roots' view of history, which attempts to trace every idea or theory back to an original seed.[28] Another line of thought operates using 'social facts' or sociological theory and presumes that changes within the social structure have a demonstrable impact upon human beings (see Chapters 14 and 15). For example, if there is chaos in society and human beings feel completely out of control, the suicide rate goes up; and the two things are linked as cause and effect.[29] One analysis of Pentecostalism suggested that in the nineteenth century when the American frontier was expanding and when farmers were facing the challenges of urbanization and industrialization, many of them turned to Pentecostalism as a breath of transcendence in their otherwise rootless lives. So Pentecostalism became the spiritual answer to a material need – a point of view elegantly and cogently, but not necessarily conclusively, expressed by R. M. Anderson.[30]

Do human beings determine the course of historical events or are economic and cultural factors decisive?

The answer to this question is based upon one's view of the way the whole universe operates. Most Christians have traditionally attributed enormous significance to the human will, to human decisions. This is because they have accepted that human beings can hardly be said to have moral responsibility if they are not able to act freely. If human beings can act freely, then they can change events and influence situations. Common sense would support this view. We only have to try to imagine Methodism without John Wesley to realize that human beings can

---

27 Bertrand Russell (1918), 'On the Notion of Cause', in *Mysticism and Logic*, reprinted by Penguin in 1953.

28 Augustus Cerillo Jr (1997), 'Interpretive Approaches to the History of American Pentecostal Origins', *Pneuma* 19.1, 29–52.

29 Emile Durkheim (1951), *Suicide*, New York, The Free Press. First published in 1897.

30 Robert M. Anderson (1979), *Vision of the Disinherited*, Oxford, Oxford University Press.

indeed make an impact on their generation and on the generations that follow. But this does not mean that economic and cultural factors have no importance. It is much more satisfactory to talk about human beings in the context of their own society and to show how, within society, we utilize the resources and opportunities afforded to us to make changes. Thus, after 1950 when commercial air travel became possible, Christian preachers were able to make use of international flights to preach all over the world. Social and economic factors widen rather than determine the range of choices available to human beings. On the other side of the coin, within the repressive USSR before 1989, Christian leaders were restricted in the number of choices they could make. It is much more persuasive to think of there being an interaction between human decisions and social and cultural factors.

Within Pentecostal history, can we detect the hand of God or are we to presume everything can be explained naturally?

If we can see an interaction between human beings and social and cultural factors, we can surely see a similar interaction between human beings and the Holy Spirit. And if we can see the Holy Spirit at work, then we can see God at work in human history. This, of course, is a faith statement but it follows both logically from a belief in the reality of the Holy Spirit and theologically from descriptions of the kind of thing that the Holy Spirit might do. In the past some Christians and Jews have interpreted large-scale historical events from a theological perspective. When Jerusalem fell in 586 BC, the Jewish community interpreted this as the judgement of God.[31] When Jerusalem fell in AD 70 Christian historians tended to see this as the judgement of God and the escape of the church as the providence of God.[32] Secular historians would have none of this. There is no correct answer to this question beyond the answer that is tied up with the existence of God. In other words, to answer this question leads to a completely different kind of debate, going beyond the pages of history on to the meaning of life as a whole.

What we can say is that the participants in early Pentecostalism believed that God had providentially poured out the Spirit to enable missionary work and evangelism to be strengthened. The historian is in a position to tell the story from the point of view of these participants and to show that their horizons and motivations were given by their theological understanding of Providence. The problem, however, of attributing events to Providence is that we can end up without any proper explanation at all. If there is success, this is the blessing of Providence. If there is failure,

---

31 As the book of Jeremiah makes clear.

32 Eusebius, *The History of the Church* (published by Penguin Classics) and written around AD 324. See III.5 and III.7.

this is a providential test of faith. By explaining everything, appeals to Providence are in danger of explaining nothing. One criterion that might be used here concerns the credibility of events at the time to those who held different points of view from the early Pentecostals. We can give an example here from the life of a non-Pentecostal. When Billy Graham came to London in 1954 as a young Southern Baptist preacher, not many people in the media paid attention and those who did were often hostile. Yet, after he had preached continuously for 72 nights, the final crusade meeting was packed with people and among those sitting on the platform were the Archbishop of Canterbury and the Lord Mayor of London. Winston Churchill (who was by no stretch of imagination an evangelical Christian) sent for Billy Graham to come to Downing Street and asked him how he had managed to fill Wembley Stadium. Graham answered, 'It's God's doing.' Churchill replied, 'That may be.'[33] We can argue that, when agnostic or hostile critics accept that providential events have occurred, Pentecostal assertions of Providence become far more credible.

Questions to think about

1 Read the text box on page 9. Does this describe a Pentecostal service?
2 What would happen if we defined Pentecostal groups by doctrine alone? Is it sufficient to define Pentecostal groups by practice alone?
3 List all the difficulties in collecting accurate statistical information about church attendance. Is church attendance or church membership a more useful statistic?
4 If the evidence appears to point in two directions at once, think about ways the historian should make up his or her mind about how the story ought to be told.
5 How do primary and secondary sources differ from each other? Can secondary sources ever be 'better' than primary sources? Can we ever think of history as being objective?
6 Read the text box on page 16. Is there a way to write history other than to construct 'causal chains'? Could you do this for Pentecostal history?

Further reading

Barrett, D. B. and Johnson, T. (2002), 'Global Statistics', in S. M. Burgess and E. M. van der Maas, *New International Dictionary of Pentecostal and Charismatic Movements*, Grand Rapids, MI, Zondervan.

---

33 Billy Graham (1988), *Just as I Am*, London, HarperCollins, p. 235. Other descriptions of this extraordinary series of meetings are given elsewhere in the same book.

23

Blumhofer, E. L. (1993), *Restoring the Faith*, Chicago, University of Illinois Press.

Dayton, Donald W. (1987), *Theological Roots of Pentecostalism*, Peabody, MA, Hendrickson.

Hollenweger, Walter J. (1997), *Pentecostalism: Origins and Developments Worldwide,* Peabody, MA, Hendrickson.

2

To the Brink of Pentecostalism

The story of Pentecostalism, by most accounts, needs to retrace the steps by which Pentecostal doctrine was eventually formed. So, although, as the previous chapter has indicated, the story here is told forwards, this is only possible because others have traced back the evolution of these doctrines along a number of pathways and routes. Even so, this is not only a story of doctrine. The doctrines were believed by people immersed in political and social situations in certain historical circumstances and with implicit and explicit assumptions that drew them towards their future. These factors (doctrine, society, future) provide the structure of this chapter.

There are two caveats here. First, we trace the story back to the United States with a short detour into England. This is not because Pentecostalism has nothing to do with the rest of the world or because Pentecostal stirrings in India and China were unimportant.[1] Rather the argument is that the richest raw materials of Pentecostalism were mined from the culture of the young United States. Then, when Pentecostalism had been formed at the beginning of the twentieth century, the vigour and wealth of North American capitalism enabled it to spread much more rapidly over the whole globe than would have been the case with any other geographical point of origin.

Second, there are complications caused by shifting terminology. Wesley spoke of 'Christian perfection' as the terminus of the process of sanctification. So if we speak of Christian perfection we are also referring to sanctification. Similarly the phrase 'baptism with (or in or of) the (Holy) Spirit' was used with various meanings. Most eighteenth-century and nineteenth-century preachers and writers who used the term referred to more general religious experiences than those pinned down by subsequent Pentecostals. The phrase itself is based on the promise of Jesus recorded in Acts 1.5, 'John baptized with water, but in a few days you will be baptized with the Holy Spirit', and was not simply a dramatic form of words dreamt up by religious enthusiasts.

---

1 The early twentieth-century revival in India associated with Pandita Ramabai and Minnie Abrams is recounted in the next chapter.

Doctrine

The three definitions of Pentecostalism that we gave in Chapter 1 all stress the presence and demonstration of the charismata (spiritual gifts) in the modern church. Given that the charismata had apparently been almost entirely absent from the church for 20 centuries, what happened? Specifically, given that theology as an authoritative mode of discourse had dismissed or suppressed charismatic manifestations, how was theology re-formed to justify and promote prophecies, visions, speaking in tongues, healings, and the like?

Two distinct and sometimes overlapping religious traditions are implicated. Wesleyanism, with its doctrine of a potential crisis experience of sanctification, is part of the answer and reformed theology, with its recognition of the ongoing work of the Holy Spirit in sanctification, is another part.[2] That the two traditions overlapped is evident from the existence of Calvinistic Methodism on one hand or revivalistic forms of Calvinism on the other. In a nutshell, the story is going to show how both traditions could be adapted to identify the post-conversion experience of sanctification with an immersion in the Holy Spirit along Pentecostal lines.[3] Or, to put this another way, once a theological tradition makes room for religious experience after conversion, that religious experience may be connected with Pentecostal phenomena dogmatically. This is an analytical way of expressing what happened and it might seem to imply that any experience might be dressed up in theological clothes. Obviously that's not the case. But, in principle and importantly, the Wesleyan and reformed doctrinal templates were capable of accommodating rich and vivid religious experience. Pentecostalism is the outworking of that experience within the life of the church in terms of its structure, praxis and mission. But this is to jump ahead of the story.

Methodism came to the United States in the eighteenth century and found there the early Nonconformists who had sailed to New England to escape religious persecution. There were Baptists and Congregationalists, Presbyterians and Quakers, as well as others, who comprised the old dissenting congregations. Most of these were reformed in theology. Methodism with its tradition of evangelism and discipline, with its lively

---

2 Wesley allowed for sudden as well as gradual sanctification. 'An instantaneous change has been wrought in some believers; none can deny this. Since that change they enjoy perfect love; they feel this, and this alone ... Now, this is all that I mean by perfection; therefore, these are witnesses of the perfection which I preach. But in some this change was not instantaneous. They did not perceive the instant when it was wrought.' 'A Plain Account of Christian Perfection', ch. 12.

3 See William W. Menzies (1975), 'The Non-Wesleyan Origins of the Pentecostal Movement', in V. Synan (ed.), *Aspects of Pentecostal-Charismatic Origins*, Plainfield, NJ, Logos International, pp. 81–98. William W. Menzies (2006), 'The Reformed Roots of Pentecostalism', *Asian Journal of Pentecostal Studies* 9.2, 260–82.

hymns and its travelling preachers, quickly moved westward and, meeting social conditions that were wilder and less civilized than the long-settled towns along the eastern seaboard, radicalized itself.

Wesley's doctrine of sanctification was well known but, alongside his doctrine was that of John Fletcher (1729–85), once his designated successor.[4] Fletcher had connected the crisis experience of sanctification with baptism in the Holy Spirit as described in the book of Acts. There is dispute about the extent to which Wesley himself identified sanctification with baptism in the Spirit.[5] Fletcher undoubtedly did. Fletcher's exposition of Acts found crisis experiences in the lives of the original apostles that were not only sanctifying but also equipped them with power for Christian service. So, within the theological resources of Methodism, there were texts and commentaries that made room for an interpretation of sanctification that mapped it directly onto the apostolic experience described in the history of the early church. It was not necessary to go to the Pauline epistles to explicate sanctification but here, in the vivid narrative of Acts, was an experience that was sudden (a baptism), spiritual (the Holy Spirit was involved), transformative (they went out and preached afterwards) and normative (all the apostles underwent this experience).

Fletcher and the Pentecostal baptism

Fletcher's *Last Check* is his main treatise on Christian perfection. The connection between the baptism of the Spirit and Christian perfection is frequently made in it. Wesley edited, corrected and published this work. Here is its main thesis: 'O, baptize my soul, and make as full an end of the original sin which I have from Adam ... Give me thine abiding Spirit, that he may continually shed abroad thy love in my soul ... Send thy Holy Spirit of promise to fill me therewith, to sanctify me throughout.' Although Fletcher did not literally and simply equate Pentecost and Christian perfection, he believed that the primary purpose of the Pentecostal outpouring of the Spirit was for the sanctification of the Church, which began on the day of Pentecost. Hence he made a functional equivalence between the two themes ...

Fletcher publicly testified to having been made perfect in love through the baptism with the Holy Spirit. To be sure, Fletcher believed that every day's attainment of holiness was tomorrow's aspiration. In this respect,

---

4 Wesley outlived him.

5 See the discussion between Donald Dayton and Lawrence Wood in *Pneuma* 26.2 and 27.1. Faupel argues that Wesley identified baptism in the Spirit with regeneration, *The Everlasting Gospel*, p. 81; see also Donald W. Dayton (1987), *Theological Roots of Pentecostalism*, Peabody, MA, Hendrickson, p. 54.

he did not absolutize a second crisis moment as the American holiness movement sometimes did. In this respect, Fletcher frankly allowed that this perfection is an 'imperfect perfection'. That is, it is capable of further increase in love and in grace ...

The first systematic theologian of Methodism, Richard Watson, was heavily influenced by Fletcher. Here is what he said: 'The Entire Sanctification of the soul from sin is held forth, both as necessary to qualify us for heaven, and as the result of that baptism of the Spirit which we receive in answer to prayer, and through faith in Christ.'

Here is what Joseph Benson said in an essay on 'Thoughts of Christian Perfection', in *The Arminian Magazine* in 1781: 'Allowing, what (I think) neither Reason nor Scripture forbids us to allow, that God may, and that he often does, instantaneously so baptize a soul with the Holy Ghost, and with fire, as to purify it from all dross, and refine it like gold, so that it is renewed in love, in pure and perfect love, as it never was before.' Wesley published this essay written by Benson, showing that Wesley agreed with it as a designation for Christian perfection.

Taken from Lawrence W. Wood
http://home.insightbb.com/~larrywood/index.html (13 April 2007)

The United States at the time of the Declaration of Independence in 1776 was a small group of states located on the eastern side of the North American continent. To the west, stretching from the Gulf of Mexico to what became the open land of Canada, was Louisiana, a domain that, in 1800, was ceded by Spain to France. After the defeat of the Napoleonic armies, French influence waned and the territory of the United States more than doubled. Louisiana was purchased from France and in the 1840s the United States had extended its boundaries to the Pacific. Texas broke away from Mexico in 1836 and joined the Union in 1845. The discovery of gold in California in the mid-century increased the scramble westwards. This was an era of hectic social change. The first transcontinental railway was completed in 1869, allowing a sense of national unity to be gradually consolidated. According to Faupel, the early European settlers brought with them a covenantal theology that could easily understand America as having a 'manifest destiny' towards the rest of the world.[6] Whatever subsequent reconstructions of American history might have demonstrated – and there are dark questions to ask about the treatment of North American Indians – the religiosity of the nation provided

---

6 The phrase was first used by John L. O'Sullivan in the *United States Magazine and Democratic Review* in 1845.

a self-understanding that was largely drawn in biblical terms. If America was not actually the new Israel, it was nevertheless raised up to play its part in the divine plan for humanity.

During this rapid phase of nation-building, religious revivalism took hold. Beginning in 1823 Charles Grandison Finney (1792–1875) conducted a series of highly successful meetings in towns and cities around New York. Using 'new measures' and developing a theology useful to subsequent evangelists, Finney conducted protracted nightly services at which sinners or backsliders were exhorted to repent. An 'anxious bench' at the front of the congregation was placed where penitents might come forward to receive prayer. Although Finney was said to appeal to emotion, he also appealed to human will and reason and his theology therefore ran counter to the prevailing Calvinistic mode that saw conversion as entirely initiated by God.[7]

Finney expected Christians to be sanctified after conversion or, in Wesleyan terms, to seek perfection. His great passion was revival and his letters to ministers on the subject showed impatience with critical nit picking. As he wrote in 1845:

> I have been astonished, as I have been abroad, to find how much misinformation was afloat in regard to the real views which we have entertained ... this misinformation has led a great many ministers to feel it necessary to guard their people strongly against error in this direction. And in exposing what they have supposed to be the errors of perfectionists and sanctificationists, they have practically greatly lowered the standard of gospel holiness in their own churches ... prejudice has been created against the doctrine of sanctification in the church ... and a consequent and corresponding descent in spirituality has been manifest in these churches.[8]

Rather than blame others for the decline of the church, however, he proclaimed:

> Until the leaders enter into the work, until the ministry are baptized with the Holy Spirit, until we are awake and in the field with our armour on, and our souls anointed with the Holy Spirit, it certainly ill becomes us to be looking around at a distance for the cause of the decline of revivals.[9]

---

7 There is debate about whether Finney was or was not a Calvinist because his innovative methods or 'new measures' were designed to elicit human decisions.

8 Charles G. Finney (1979), *Reflections on Revival*, comp. D. W. Dayton, Minneapolis, MN, Bethany Fellowship, p. 80.

9 Finney, *Reflections*, p. 70.

Finney's preaching contributed to the 1857 revival in the United States, the last revival, so it is said, that influenced the entire culture of the nation.[10] The most influential book of the revival was W. E. Boardman's much reprinted *The Higher Christian Life*, which presented holiness doctrines in non-Wesleyan language.[11] Connected with this revivalistic fire was an optimism for the future and a belief that the church was marching towards the return of Christ and the millennium. In Finney's theology, perfection also included a social holiness that was expressed by stern opposition to slavery.[12] Evangelicalism as represented by Finney was politically active and committed to social reform. This reformist tendency was to lead to the bloody and costly American Civil War (1861–65) which shattered optimistic hopes and resulted in the defeat of the slave-holding south, though leaving behind a bitter taste.

Charles Finney's baptism in the Holy Ghost

There was no fire, and no light, in the room; nevertheless it appeared to me as if it were perfectly light. As I went in and shut the door after me, it seemed as if I met the Lord Jesus Christ face to face. It did not occur to me then, nor did for some time afterward, that this was a wholly mental state ... but as I turned and was about to take a seat by the fire, I received a mighty baptism of the Holy Ghost. Without any expectation of it, without ever having the thought in my mind there was any such thing for me, without any recollection that I had ever heard the thing mentioned by any person in the world, the Holy Spirit descended upon me in a manner that seemed to go through me, body and soul. I could feel the impression, like a wave of electricity, going through and through me. Indeed it seemed to come in waves and waves of liquid love; for I could not express it in any other way. It seemed like the very breath of God. I can recollect distinctly that it seemed to fan me, like immense wings.

No words can express the wonderful love that was shed abroad in my heart. I wept aloud with joy and love; and I do not know but I should say, I literally bellowed out the unutterable gushing is of my heart.

C. G. Finney (1987), selections from his memoirs, in R. Lundin and Mark A. Noll (eds), *Voices from the Heart: four centuries of American piety*, Grand Rapids, MI, Eerdmans, p. 139.

---

10 Dayton, *Theological Roots*, p. 75.

11 D. William Faupel (1996), *The Everlasting Gospel*, Sheffield, Sheffield Academic Press, p. 71.

12 Donald W. Dayton (1976), *Discovering an Evangelical Heritage*, Peabody, MA, Hendrickson.

Phoebe Palmer (1807–74) and her husband Walter had been holding perfectionist meetings in their home from 1839 onwards. In the period leading up to the Civil War, she continued to teach and preach itinerantly. Her message was that it was possible to obtain sanctification now by an act of personal consecration. This was quite the opposite to the belief that sanctification was to be achieved by a slow and arduous spiritual journey. Instead, Christians who acted by faith and in obedience to the Scriptures could be holy instantaneously; in her words 'THERE IS A SHORTER WAY!'[13] So, in contrast to Wesley from whose teaching she drew, sanctification was almost invariably a crisis experience.

Palmer's 'altar theology' was chiefly influential within Methodism. Although it was accepted by some Methodist bishops, it proved divisive in the sense that it provided an argument for those who wanted to distinguish churches that were preaching sanctification and those that were not. Holiness became a watchword among segments of Methodism, a watchword that disguised socio-economic differences between disparate sections of the church. To the proponents of holiness, Palmer's teaching inspired Christians to shun lackadaisical and lukewarm Christianity and, when the National Holiness Association was set up after 1867, the collective structure necessary to carry holiness teaching throughout America began to be erected.[14] To those who came to oppose Palmer, holiness was a form of sectarianism, and particularly obnoxious because it was a 'parlour theology' that eschewed engagement with the social injustices of the day. Be that as it may, Palmer's theology and terminology took an overtly Pentecostal turn when she published *The Promise of the Father* in 1859 and equated entire sanctification with baptism in the Holy Spirit.

That year the Palmers came to England and stayed for four years promoting revival and preaching holiness. Barely a decade later the Keswick conventions began as a result of visits by other American preachers. W. E. Boardman spoke at an Oxford conference in 1874, together with Asa Mahan who was a colleague of Finney. This conference proclaimed the sufficiency of Christ for holy living. The conference gave rise to annual summer conferences at Keswick in the north-west of England. These conferences, starting in 1875, have run annually ever since.[15] The Keswick message was a holiness one. These were 'meetings for the promotion

---

13 Phoebe Palmer (1845), *The Way of Holiness*, New York, Lane and Tippett, pp. 17–18, original emphasis. Cited by http://wesley.nnu.edu/wesleyan_theology/theojrnl/21-25/23-13.htm (accessed 13.04.07).

14 Vinson Synan (1971/1997), *The Holiness-Pentecostal Tradition*, Grand Rapids, MI, Eerdmans, p. 25.

15 Charles Price and Ian Randall (2000), *Transforming Keswick*, Carlisle, OM Publishing, p. 32. The meetings have run annually apart from war-time breaks in 1917 and between 1940 and 1945.

of practical holiness'.[16] Keswick taught 'holiness by faith', by which it meant that Christians should not struggle but constantly trust Christ to overcome sin and bring about the fruit of holiness.[17] This was a form of second-blessing theology that fitted on a spectrum somewhere between radical holiness/perfectionist teaching that believed in the eradication of sinful human nature and the more revivalistic form of teaching about empowerment by the Holy Spirit that came to be associated with the evangelist D. L. Moody. Even the second-blessing pattern of Keswick was sometimes subdued and smoothed over. The Keswick message was compatible with the reformed view of holiness because it recognized both the crisis experience of sanctification and progressive sanctification. Keswick, which stressed its interdenominational credentials, taught about the Holy Spirit in a way that was arresting but without the high emotional tone of American revivalism. Consequently Keswick teaching was widely acceptable in Britain and beyond.

In short, there were two lines of holiness teaching that converged into eventual Pentecostal doctrine. A Wesleyan line ran through John Fletcher to Phoebe Palmer and a reformed line ran through Charles Finney and W. E. Boardman to Keswick.[18] The lines forced a paradigm shift within the holiness movement that moved its centre from soteriology (a doctrine of salvation) to pneumatology (a doctrine of the Holy Spirit).

The paradigm shift can be seen by comparing two hymns:

Let the water and the blood
From Thy wounded side which flowed,
Be of sin the double cure
Save from wrath and make me pure. (Augustus Toplady)

The words of Augustus Toplady's hymn are a prayer concerning the work of Christ upon the cross: 'Save from wrath' is a prayer for justification in the sight of God; 'make me pure' is a prayer for holiness.

---

16 Price and Randall, *Transforming Keswick*, p. 22.

17 Or, in the words of the hymn, 'Holiness by faith in Jesus/not by effort of your own/sin's dominion crushed and conquered/by the power of grace alone' (Frances Ridley Havergal).

18 The account given above is controverted by R. M. Anderson, who argues: 'The Keswick movement, as we shall see was absolutely crucial to the development of Pentecostalism. Thus, I find it necessary to reject the central thesis of Synan that "the historical and doctrinal lineage of American Pentecostalism is to be found in the Wesleyan tradition". To the contrary, that wing of the Pentecostal movement which had earlier connections with Wesleyanism became Pentecostal by accepting Keswick (i.e. Calvinist) teachings on dispensationalism, premillennialism and the baptism of the Holy Spirit.' See, R. M. Anderson (1979), *Vision of the Disinherited*, Oxford, Oxford University Press, p. 43. In my view Anderson overstates his case.

The second hymn is very different:

We find many people who can't understand
Why we are so happy and free;
We've crossed over Jordan to Canaan's fair land,
And this is like heaven to me.

So when we are happy we sing and we shout,
Some don't understand us, I see;
We're filled with the Spirit, there isn't a doubt;
And this is like heaven to me. (J. E. French)[19]

Here is the celebration of the joy of a Spirit-filled life.

Coupled with this emphasis upon the Holy Spirit and power for Christian service, came an emphasis upon divine healing. After all, if the Holy Spirit was present and active in the bodies of Christians, shouldn't illness automatically be driven out? We will deal at greater length in the next chapter with the earliest exponents of healing doctrine but note at this point that any doctrine that was associated with religious experience could achieve several things at once. A doctrine of holiness could quite easily coexist with or *become* a doctrine of healing. The holiness paradigm was capable of extension as well as of shifting.

Society

These doctrinal changes did not take place in a social vacuum. By 1840 Methodists were the largest religious group in America. They outnumbered Baptists by a ratio of six to ten and they outnumbered the combined membership of Presbyterian, Congregational, Episcopal, Lutheran and Reformed churches by a similar ratio.[20] By about 1850 immigration to the United States had reached a peak of 425,000 per year.[21] Between 1820 and 1840 roughly 700,000 immigrants arrived in the United States, mainly from the British Isles and German speaking areas of continental Europe. These figures escalated enormously in the next two decades. Around 4.2 million crossed the Atlantic between 1840 and 1860.[22] By 1859 the first oil well had been discovered – and all this while miles of railway line were being laid down, starting on the east coast.

---

19 Cited by Edith L. Blumhofer (1993), *Restoring the Faith*, Chicago, University of Illinois Press, p. 27.

20 Dayton, *Theological Roots*, p. 63.

21 Robert A. Divine, T. H. Breen, G. M. Fredrickson and R. H. Williams (1995), *America Past and Present*, 4th edn, New York, HarperCollins College Publishers, p. 364.

22 Divine *et al.*, *America*, p. 364.

The Civil War fractured civil society and divided the churches. Enormous efforts at reconstruction within the South took place against continuing racial discrimination: between 1889 and 1899 as many as 187 blacks per year were lynched.[23] Slavery and negro spirituals, as we shall see, left their mark upon Pentecostalism when it eventually emerged. In the 50 years after 1860 the rural population of America doubled, partly as a result of immigration, while the population of the cities went up a massive sevenfold.[24] This was an era of industrialization and urbanization. Steel production within the United States grew to the extent that by the end of the period between 1880 and 1914 it produced more steel than the rest of Europe combined. Steel enabled the construction of longer bridges and higher buildings so that iconic American cities began to appear on the map, lit by electricity (the first electric generating station opened in New York in 1882)[25] and supplied by rail and eventually the increasingly ubiquitous motor car.

The response of the churches to the Civil War, industrial expansion, materialism and social dislocation was a renewed call for holiness, though, unlike the holiness calls of Finney and the Oberlin perfectionists, a call to inner piety or, if it had an outer form, to abstention from alcohol, tobacco, gambling, gaudy clothing and even Coca-Cola and chewing gum.[26] While some commentators (e.g. R. M. Anderson) see the early Pentecostals, or those who were going to become Pentecostals, as made up from the poor displaced rural masses who had streamed into the cities, mills, mines and agrarian towns from the surrounding countryside, others (e.g. G. Wacker) saw them as indistinguishable from other Americans – shopkeepers, labourers and farmers who prized personal autonomy. In any event, the churches rode the wave of population growth and social change.

In the years from 1870 to 1890, the number of congregations in the nation rose by nearly 130% and the value of church buildings by nearly 100%. From 1880 to 1900 church membership increased at a rate faster than the population as a whole. The Methodists increased their membership by about 57% in these two decades, and added an average 800,000 new recruits in their rolls in each decade from 1870 to 1910.[27]

---

23 Divine et al., America, p. 498.

24 Divine et al., America, p. 568.

25 Divine et al., America, p. 564.

26 Charles Edwin Jones (1974), *Perfectionist Persuasion: The Holiness Movement and American Methodism, 1867–1936*, Metuchen, NJ, Scarecrow Press, p. xiv. *Word and Witness*, 20 June 1913, p. 2, quoted by G. Wacker (2001), *Heaven Below: Early Pentecostals and American Culture*, Cambridge, MA, Harvard University Press, pp. 122–6.

27 Anderson, *Vision*, pp. 29, 30. Oberlin, a college in Ohio, was founded in 1833

After the formation in 1867 of the first National Holiness Association, camp meetings, which dated back at least to 1801, began to be held in the East and then more widely.[28] At these meetings holiness teaching predominated and, such was the intensity of holiness preaching, that eventually Methodist churches, among whom holiness preachers first worked, began to break up organizationally. Holiness meetings that had originally been interdenominational now began to generate holiness churches that stood in opposition to the Methodist churches out of which they had come. Holiness denominations were started – denominations that built into their founding documents a requirement for a crisis experience of sanctification and a plain lifestyle that turned its back upon the perceived fripperies of the growing middle class.

None of this was done painlessly: 'Methodist officials lashed out at holiness believers, calling them "come-outers" and equating voluntary separation from the Methodist Church with fanaticism.'[29] Equally, some of the Methodist officials became 'put-outers'. Speaking at the General Conference of the Methodist Episcopal Church, South, in 1894, an episcopal spokesman declared:

> There has sprung up among us a party with holiness as a watchword; we have holiness associations, holiness meetings, holiness preachers, holiness evangelists, and holiness property. Religious experience is represented as if it consists in only two steps, the first step out of condemnation into peace and the next step into Christian perfection … we do not question the sincerity and zeal of their brethren; we desire the church to profit by their earnest preaching and godly example; but we deplore their teaching and methods in so far as they claim a monopoly of the experience, practice and advocacy of holiness, and separate themselves from the body of ministers and disciples.[30]

Friction between Methodists and holiness people was a sign of spiritual vitality as much as of dissent. Holiness churches, despite holding very similar doctrines, also were capable of quarrelling with each other. Typically a strong congregation would be formed and then link up with others in a loose association that became a denomination. So the Heavenly Recruit Association of Philadelphia later became the Holiness Christian Church, one of several.[31] The process produced different denominations with the same name, as with the Church of God (Anderson, IN) and the

---

and many of its staff and alumni were associated with progressive causes, especially abolitionism.

28 V. Synan, *Tradition*, refers to the Cane Ridge meetings in 1801, p. 13.
29 Jones, *Perfectionist*, p. 63.
30 Quoted in Jones, *Perfectionist*, p. 63.
31 Jones, *Perfectionist*, p. 91.

Church of God (Holiness) and later the Church of God (Cleveland, TN). This multiplication of churches and denominations in a creative ferment was carried over into Pentecostalism. For this reason, Synan speaks of the 'holiness-Pentecostal tradition' as one tradition.[32]

Future

As we have said, one of the oddities of writing history is that we know the future of the people we write about. They live within their own horizons and make the best decisions that they can with the information available to them. They have their own values and beliefs and fight the battles, intellectual and organizational, that face them. Within their life-worlds are expectations of the future and, if they are Christians as the people within our purview are, their expectations of the future will be shaped by their understanding of Scripture. The Pilgrim Fathers who sailed to what became the United States risked their lives in hazardous sea crossings to found religious freedom and communities unsullied by the political apparatus of dictatorial kings or worldly bishops. There was from that time on always a social idealism within American culture, even traces of an expectation that Christ would set up his kingdom on earth, and that it was the duty of people here and now to prepare for this glorious event. The 'puritan hope' of the Pilgrim Fathers was a positive one.[33] They certainly believed in the return of Christ, but their expectation was that glory would be given to Christ by the exploits of the church on earth. In this sense, their outlook was optimistic and, in the context of the Pentecostalism that was to develop, could be connected with the prophetically anticipated deluge of the Holy Spirit. This deluge was the 'latter rain' that would revitalize Christianity and restore the church to its miracle-working New Testament state.

Coupled with these expectations was a covenantal theology, Reformed in tone, that was capable of seeing the new America as having a special destiny within the providence of God. It is not possible to quantify exactly how many people thought in these terms or whether, in the early nineteenth century, these ideas were consciously upheld, but historians usually agree that the predominant eschatological mode among religious people in America – and most people were religious – was post-millennial. By this they meant that society would gradually improve through the arts and sciences until Christianity had been diffused throughout the earth which would then transition into the kingdom of Christ.

---

32 The title of one of his books.

33 Iain H. Murray (1996), *The Puritan Hope: Revival and the Interpretation of Prophecy*, Edinburgh, Banner of Truth.

Every social and political improvement appeared to provide evidence for the correctness of this view, which, in its secular form, was known as the 'Whig view of history', the happy tale of endless progress driven by human reason. In this sense there was a confluence of ideas from the Enlightenment and from Christianity that agreed on what the future would look like, though, naturally, rationalists wanted a tamer and less influential role for religion than Christians. In any event, part of the motivation for Christian reformers like Charles Finney was that, with every defeat of social evil, the kingdom of Christ became one step closer. The abolition of slavery was one such evil and its removal was essential to human progress: as Finney declared,

> now the great business of the church is to reform the world – to put away every kind of sin. The Church of Christ was originally organized to be a body of reformers. The very profession of Christianity implies the profession and virtually an oath to do all that can be done for the universal reformation of the world.[34]

Admittedly the expectations of William Miller, who calculated that the return of Christ would take place in April 1844, and who aroused an enormous following of people who sold their possessions and stood waiting on a hillside dressed in white ready to meet their saviour, were dashed. The credibility of eschatological prediction, let alone Adventism as a whole, was damaged by these events, but perhaps they only indicated that Miller's method of calculation was incorrect or that he had mistaken the social improvements of his time for the ultimate state of the world.

The 1857–58 revival, with its perfectionist motifs, fired religious fervour and pushed aside religious hesitation. When all the church was perfect and holy, then the millennium would begin. Indeed perfectionist holiness would be the natural state of believers once the millennium started. While waiting on tiptoe for these events to culminate, cracks began to appear. For a start it was obvious that the abolition of slavery would not occur without violence, and violence was something that belonged to the imperfect world. So how could the church move forward into the millennium without committing itself to violence? Equally, how could the church move forward into the millennium while coexisting with slavery?

When the Civil War started, the churches found themselves on different sides of the divide. Some in the South supported slavery while most in the North did not. In other ways also American society had become more complex. Lutheran immigrants were not so inclined as other Protestants to be swept up in millennial expectations, and Roman Catholics,

---

34 Charles G. Finney, 21 January 1846. Found in Finney, *Reflections*, p. 113.

who had by now come in large numbers to the United States, figured in eschatological expectations on the negative side of any calculations. It was Thomas Newton, one-time Bishop of Bristol, who had argued in a three-volume work completed in 1758 that 'Papal power would dominate for 1,260 years before being crushed' and that this event would be quickly followed by the conversion of the Jews and the return of Christ to the earth.[35] This book was first published in the United States in 1793, remained in print until 1868 and was a perpetual stimulant for eschatological speculation. In Newton's view the highly significant French Revolution of 1789 marked the end of Roman Catholicism, prophesied in Daniel 7 and Revelation 13, paving the way for the next milestone along the prophetic road.[36] Even so, holiness teaching tended to be more inward- than outward-looking in the period following the Civil War. One could say that there were extroverted tendencies towards vast social changes brought in by the irresistible hand of God and introverted tendencies towards personal purification in a world that was irredeemably evil. The extroverted camp was inspired by a series of conferences on biblical prophecy that began to reinterpret eschatology along lines that eventually culminated in a belief that the return of Christ would occur *before* the millennium. The pre-millennial return would occur just as the world was getting worse and worse, and Jesus would rescue the situation. Every social evil and wicked trend functioned as evidence to justify the belief that Christ's return was getting nearer. This was precisely the opposite way of interpreting society to that which was found in the heady optimistic days before the Civil War.

It would be a mistake to think these reversals of prophetic interpretation were brought into being simply by the pessimism engendered by the Civil War in the United States. Serious discussion of biblical prophecy can be dated back not only to Thomas Newton's book but also to the series of conferences mentioned in the preceding paragraph, the first group of which was held annually in Albury Court, Surrey, between 1826 and 1830. These conferences, organized by Henry Drummond, a British member of Parliament, brought together leading expositors of the historicist method of interpreting the book of Revelation. This method involves seeing the book of Revelation as essentially a prophecy dealing with the entire era of church history stretching from the days of the early church right through until the present. The conference members included clergy and laity drawn mainly from the evangelical wing of the Church of England and the Church of Scotland, though representatives from the Free Churches also attended. The first conference ended with all the participants agreeing that the church age was drawing to a close, that the

---

35 Faupel, *Everlasting Gospel*, p. 92.
36 Faupel, *Everlasting Gospel*, p. 92.

Jews would soon be converted and returned to their ancient homeland and that Christ would come back to the earth sometime between 1844 and 1847.[37] The remaining conferences concentrated on the practical missionary tasks needed to prepare the way for these cataclysmic events. Among those attending these conferences was Edward Irving, who later founded the Catholic Apostolic Church at which speaking in tongues and prophecy occurred. Irving was one of the most powerful and dramatic preachers of his day, so much so that fashionable London society went to hear his eloquent orations.[38] Irving was expelled from the Church of Scotland and his life ended shortly afterwards (of tuberculosis) but this did nothing to shake the confidence of the members of his circle in the truth of their prophetic calculations. Among those influenced by Albury was Lady Powerscourt who opened her stately home in Ireland for a similar series of annual conferences after 1831.

It was from Ireland that John Nelson Darby, originally an Anglican priest, came. Darby had at one stage thought of marrying the widowed Lady Powerscourt[39] and at least one commentator thought that the two of them had set up the conferences so that Darby could use 'the conferences to establish his interpretation of prophecy as the normative one'.[40] Darby came to believe that the book of Revelation should be interpreted as describing unfulfilled future events and that the return of Christ should be expected at any time. Darby's major innovation was to put forward the doctrine of the secret rapture of the church (not Israel).[41] This belief divided the return of Christ into two stages. In the first stage, Christ would come invisibly *for* the church and snatch it away from the wicked earth leaving those who remained to endure the horrors of the Antichrist's reign, a reign that would bring great pain and purificatory suffering upon Israel. In the second stage, seven years later, Christ would return *with* the church to judge his enemies and establish millennial rule.

Darby made at least six trips to the United States and Canada from the 1850s onwards and founded Brethren assemblies that propagated his dispensational interpretation of Scripture. His views were circulated in the monthly periodical, *The Prophetic Times* (established in 1863), and were further amplified in a series of annual conferences that ran from 1875 to 1900. The Niagara Bible Conferences brought together Protestant leaders and, after 1877, D. L. Moody, the leading evangelical and evangelistic figure of the day, took up Darby's views and instituted an annual

---

37 Faupel, *Everlasting Gospel*, p. 93.

38 Gordon Strachan (1973), *The Pentecostal Theology of Edward Irving*, London, Darton, Longman and Todd.

39 Tim Grass (2006), *Gathering in his Name*, Milton Keynes, Paternoster Press, p. 25.

40 Grass, *Gathering*, p. 28.

41 'Rapture' in the old sense of being seized or snatched away.

Northfield Prophecy Conference after 1880.[42] By the end of the century nearly every major American evangelist followed this method of interpreting the Bible. When the Scofield Reference Bible was first published in 1909 it incorporated the secret rapture and associated pre-millennial signs into its footnoted commentary. Nothing else could more clearly indicate how this form of pre-millennialism had become standard among holiness and evangelical people, many of whom were shortly afterwards assimilated into Pentecostalism.[43]

In summary and essence, the doctrinal changes outlined in this chapter concern sanctification and eschatology. Sanctification, through a series of metamorphoses, comes to be associated with baptism in the Holy Spirit, even if the precise dimensions and hallmarks of this baptism were unknown and only subjectively realized. Eschatology was concerned with the return of Christ and the sequence of events leading up to this great climax of history. Such events might be mapped onto the current course of history in multiple ways. The optimism of the first part of the nineteenth century gave way to something else in the second part of the nineteenth century – pessimism at one level and a renewed excitement about rapid social development (laced with the possibility of a downpour of the rain of the Spirit) at another. As a result, belief in the return of Christ at the culmination of an era of progress became less popular and it was more common, especially after J. N. Darby's reworking of scriptural interpretation, to see the return of Christ as occurring at a moment of dark crisis. While all this happened, new holiness church associations were formed and these, though they did not know it, became the receptacles into which, in many cases, Pentecostalism was poured. Such churches had a revivalistic atmosphere. Emotionalism might be seen as an indicator of a genuine spiritual experience and authentic religion might be expressed through spontaneous and non-liturgical meetings at which preaching was a key feature.

---

42 Faupel, *Everlasting Gospel*, gives a good account of these conferences and the way they were connected with each other.

43 There is a further twist to all this to be explained later. Pentecostals came to see the outpouring of the Holy Spirit as the 'latter rain', a deluge of spiritual refreshment, parallel to the rainfall in the land of Israel that fell just before the harvest. Thus, even if Pentecostals became pre-millennialists, they were optimistic ones because the outpouring of the Spirit pointed to a harvest for the church.

Cross-references to W. K. Kay and A. E. Dyer (2004), *Pentecostal and Charismatic Studies: A Reader*, London, SCM Press
(shortened afterwards to the SCM Reader *Pentecostal and Charismatic Studies*; relevant page numbers of the Reader are given in brackets)

Holiness issues in early Pentecostal circles:

6.1 Pastor Jonathan Paul, 'The Work of the Cross', *Confidence*, June 1909 (pp. 131–2).
6.2 William H. Durham, *Pentecostal Testimony*, 1907 (pp. 132–4).
6.3 G. Wacker, *Heaven Below: Early Pentecostals and American Culture*, Harvard University Press, 2001, pp. 122–6 (pp. 134–8).
6.4 International Pentecostal Church of Holiness, statement on sancification, 13 March 2003, Articles Ten and Eleven (p. 139).

Questions to think about

1 Read the text box on page 27 and note what Fletcher thought about baptism in the Spirit. Think about the argument he puts to link the experience with overcoming sin.
2 Read the text box on page 30 and note what Finney thought about baptism in the Spirit. Note the personal and emotional dimensions of this experience.
3 This chapter has connected social change with doctrinal change. Do you think this is a valid connection?
4 Think through the varied concepts of holiness that are found in this chapter.
5 Can a belief in a 'second blessing' after conversion be sustained without a strong belief in the validity of religious experience?

Further reading

Dayton, D. W. (1987), *Theological Roots of Pentecostalism*, Minneapolis, MN, Hendrickson.
Faupel, D. W. (1996), *The Everlasting Gospel*, Sheffield, Sheffield Academic Press.
Synan, V. S. (1971/1997), *The Holiness-Pentecostal Tradition: Charismatic Movements in the Twentieth Century*, Grand Rapids, MI, Eerdmans.

3

Countercultural Movements and Polycentric Ignition

How did Pentecostalism get started? How did its themes develop? These are the questions addressed in this chapter.

We have gone a long way down the historical road exploring the origins and development of Pentecostalism. We have assumed, reasonably enough, that Pentecostalism grew out of pre-existing doctrines or structures until it emerged in a fully fledged form at the beginning of the twentieth century. We might have taken a different road and examined Pentecostalism through anthropology. If we had done so we would have given greater prominence to the concept of culture, said to be the distinctive concept of social anthropological research. We might have looked more closely at the relationship between Pentecostals and their cultural contexts to see whether these were held in an unusually rich tension. At least one anthropological commentator (Joel Robbins) has insightfully pointed out that Pentecostalism appears to exist both as a type of a new Western 'cultural flow' and as a type of Christianity that embraces the indigenous and the local.[1] It is at once the same everywhere *and* locally coloured by its context. Had we gone down this path we might also have considered the role of ritual in Pentecostalism and explored the rituals of Pentecostal antecedents. Such rituals may not be consciously recognized as such (because they are seen as spontaneous behaviours) but, in the call to repentance within, say, Phoebe Palmer's 'altar theology', there is a similarity to the public profession of faith required by Finney or the later vigorous preaching of early Pentecostals in the new towns of the American West.[2] Connected with ritual is the morality of Pentecostalism and its turning against all the unrestrained delinquencies of single males who drank vast quantities of alcohol, gambled, delighted in tobacco, groped after barmaids and whores and, when in trouble, resorted to the six-

---

1 Joel Robbins (2004), 'The Globalisation of Pentecostal and Charismatic Christianity', *Annual Review of Anthropology* 233, 117–43.

2 Phoebe Palmer and Walter Palmer were friends with William Taylor, the Methodist evangelist, who did so much to stimulate 'faith missionaries' in South America, including Willis Hoover who went to Chile.

shooter. Pentecostalism domesticated these men and made them fit to be husbands and fathers living an orderly churchgoing existence with women whom they neither abused sexually nor exploited financially. So Pentecostalism, and Methodism and holiness teaching, functioned to tame small-town America, to reduce crime and to create a consensus that may, in its worst manifestations, have been the progenitor of petty bourgeois materialism but, at its best, rendered the chaotic and crime-ridden streets a safer and more welcoming environment than ever the law enforcement officer with his tin star could achieve.

Anthropology picks out facets of Pentecostalism that might be missed by the historian, and helps to expand the range of explanations for its success. When we return to the historical road, we need to keep cultural factors in mind. This confirms to us that there are many ways of telling the story of the emergence of Pentecostalism. We need, in a moment, to explain how a doctrine of healing came to the fore and was included within the panoply of Pentecostalism. We also need to explain how the doctrine of the baptism of the Holy Spirit came to be associated with speaking with tongues. Even that will not tell us the whole story. There were also existing networks and organizations that either became Pentecostal and therefore helped to spread Pentecostalism, or else (like Zion City, as we shall see) gave something to early Pentecostals that they valued and took with them on their spiritual journey. In a sense this is a story that fits together people and doctrines on one side and organizations and institutions on the other side. That said, even when all these pieces were in place, they would have remained lifeless and static without the dynamism and enthusiasm that Pentecostals attributed to the Holy Spirit. To put this in terms that the early Pentecostals would have understood, it was not until the outpouring of the Holy Spirit in different parts of the world that Pentecostalism properly came into existence. It is important to stress again that this was not purely a North American phenomenon but was replicated to a lesser extent in other locations. Donald Gee, the British Pentecostal leader who even by 1933 had preached on all five continents, wrote in 1941:

> The Pentecostal Movement does not owe its origin to any outstanding personality or religious leader, *but was a spontaneous revival appearing almost simultaneously in various parts of the world*. We instinctively connect the Reformation with Luther, the Quakers with George Fox, Methodism with Wesley, the Plymouth Brethren with Darby and Groves, the Salvation Army with William Booth, and so on. But the outstanding leaders of the Pentecostal Movement are themselves the products of the Movement. They did not make it; it made them.[3]

---

3 Donald Gee (1941), *The Pentecostal Movement*, London, Elim Publishing House.

These considerations provide a structure for this chapter (healing, speaking in tongues, organizations and revival) and take us at last to the emergence of Pentecostalism on the world stage.

Healing

As we have seen, the doctrine of sanctification was developed along more than one line over many decades in the nineteenth century. Sanctification was concerned with an essential inner experience within the heart and mind whereby wicked thoughts and habits were removed by faith, by the work of the Holy Spirit, by moral effort, by a crisis experience, by putting one's life upon the altar, by tears in public or in private, or by any combination of these. Whether this experience of sanctification was gradual or sudden and whether it eradicated sinful nature or merely suppressed it – and there were variations of this kind brought in by different theological traditions – sanctification did have an impact upon the life of the believer. He or she felt different and acted differently. It was, therefore, not by a huge stretch of the theological imagination that healing might also be called into play, and called into play by faith, the work of the Holy Spirit, moral effort, a crisis experience, and so on. So healing and sanctification were connected not only by the stages through which they might be reached but also because it was possible to attribute sickness to sin: in order to be healed, it was necessary first to be sanctified. Actually, the connection between sickness and sin was only made by the more extreme and confrontational preachers. For most, a rather different emphasis took precedence.

A crystallization of the doctrine of healing by faith is usually said to have been initiated by Dr Charles Cullis, a homeopathic physician and leader in the holiness movement, with the publication of *Faith Cures* in 1879.[4] Cullis testified to sanctification in 1862[5] and towards the end of that decade began to focus his attention on the meaning of the passage in James 5 where believers who are ill are told to call for the elders of the church who will pray for them with 'the prayer of faith'. Cullis had already begun an extensive charitable ministry and, after visiting Dorothy Trudel in Switzerland in 1873, saw 'healing homes' in action and began to set up similar places back in the United States. The healing home appears to have been a kind of guesthouse where those who were ill could stay at very low charges and where they would be cared for by

---

4 See reference to him in *The Apostolic Faith* 1.2 in the text box at the end of this chapter.

5 Kimberley Ervin Alexander (2006), *Pentecostal Healing: Models in Theory and Practice*, Blandford Forum, Deo, p. 16.

Christian staff who prayed for them regularly, and, in this atmosphere, many became better and testified to long-term cures.[6] Cullis preached at a series of conventions and influenced W. E. Boardman, a Presbyterian whose writings had spread holiness doctrines well beyond Methodism.[7] Boardman moved to England and became involved in the Keswick movement and also held an International Conference on Divine Healing and True Holiness in London in 1884 to which many of the American healing preachers were invited.[8] He had by then established a healing home where Wednesday afternoon meetings for holiness and healing were regularly held. In the United States, Carrie Judd Montgomery published *The Prayer of Faith* in 1880, a year after Cullis's book, and told the story of her own miraculous recovery from two years of illness.

Carrie Judd took over the steps in Phoebe Palmer's theology of crisis sanctification. Carrie Judd argued for healing by the 'shorter way (consecration, faith and testimony)'.[9] First it is necessary to consecrate oneself to God and then to 'act faith' by accepting healing on the basis of the written text of Scripture and, lastly, one should testify to healing. This was not a route to healing in long emotional preaching meetings but rather a quieter and less dramatic journey that required close attention to the promises of Scripture. This was healing within the life of the church or the pious individual in the context of private prayer. Carrie Judd Montgomery's growing and influential ministry was sustained for many years through the publication of *Triumphs of Faith*, 'a monthly journal devoted to faith-healing and the promotion of Christian holiness', started in 1881.[10] Like Cullis, and after her marriage to the wealthy George Montgomery, she began to set up retreats and healing homes where her teaching might be practised.

If James 5 was the main locus of healing in the New Testament in the early days of the healing movement, the tempo changed when attention was shifted to Isaiah 53. R. L. Stanton argued in 1884 that healing of the body was exactly parallel to healing of the soul and that 'the atonement of Christ lays the foundation equally for deliverance from sin and for deliverance from disease; that complete provision has been made for both'.[11] Once healing was placed within the atonement, it became natural for preachers who were holding forth the merits of the cross of Christ to

---

6 Many of the healing homes appear to have been run on the same sort of faith principles as George Muller's orphanages. Food and finance were 'prayed in'.

7 Donald W. Dayton (1987), *Theological Roots of Pentecostalism*, Minneapolis, MN, Hendrickson, p. 124.

8 Dayton, *Theological Roots*, p. 125.

9 Alexander, *Pentecostal Healing*, p. 46.

10 Dayton, *Theological Roots*, p. 126.

11 Dayton, *Theological Roots*, p. 126. The book was *Gospel Parallelisms: Illustrated in the Healing of the Body and Soul*.

crowds within evangelistic meetings also to hold forth the healing power of Christ. Both A. B. Simpson, founder of the Christian and Missionary Alliance, and A. J. Gordon, co-founder of Gordon-Conwell Seminary, argued strongly that healing was to be found 'in the atonement' and available to anyone who believed in Christ in exactly the same way as forgiveness of sin was available to anyone who believed. Simpson wrote, 'Redemption finds its centre in the cross of our Lord Jesus Christ and there we must look for the fundamental principle of divine healing, which rests on the atoning sacrifice.'[12] Both Simpson and Gordon published widely and one consequence of their teaching was to begin to raise the question of whether anyone who was trusting Christ for healing ought also to take any form of medication.[13] Belief about healing in the atonement came to be coupled with trying to act as if one were healed, which meant avoiding medicines. What had begun more gently within healing homes and in the expectation that healing might take place over a period of time now took on a sudden, public and potentially dangerous aspect.

Dayton, in his analysis of the divine healing movement, uses Captain R. Kelso Carter as an example of the way the debate twisted and turned. At first Carter, in his book *The Atonement for Sin and Sickness* (1884), argued that atonement provides the basis for pardon from all sin, the eradication of the effects of sinful human nature, and bodily healing. In this formulation the linkage between a strong holiness doctrine of sanctification and physical healing could hardly be clearer. Yet by 1897, Carter had revised his opinions and backed away from the belief that healing was automatically included within the atonement so that 'any continuing disease was a sign of continuing sin or lack of faith'.[14] Equally, he now denied that medication should be shunned. Rather, healing was evidence of God's grace that, though it could be traced back to the atonement, should be seen as a 'special favour' that might or might not be granted. Carter described the range of theological opinions that by the end of the century existed on the subject of healing and instanced his own earlier 'extreme' position of healing in the atonement and the more moderate 'special providence' position that he had now reached. He reported that Dr Cullis had never been as extreme as his followers had thought be-

---

12 Dayton, *Theological Roots*, p. 128.

13 E.g. A. J. Gordon (1882), *The Ministry of Healing: Miracles of Cure in All Ages*, Boston, H. Gannett; and A. B. Simpson (1885), 'How to Receive Divine Healing', *The Word, The Work, and The World*, July–August, 203, and cited by Paul L. King (2006), *Genuine Gold: The Cautiously Charismatic Story of the Early Christian and Missionary Alliance*, Tulsa, OK, Word and Spirit Press, p. 30. According to Blumhofer both men 'discouraged but did not denounce medical means'. Edith L. Blumhofer (1993), *Restoring the Faith*, Chicago, University of Illinois Press, p. 23.

14 Dayton, *Theological Roots*, p. 130. Carter's second book was *'Faith Healing' Reviewed after Twenty Years*.

cause he had always given medicine when necessary and that Simpson, whatever his public pronouncements, had been forced to moderate his position as a result of the death of good and faithful missionaries. Only Carrie Judd Montgomery maintained a strict line, but, as Carter pointed out, her husband had ill-health and she continued to wear glasses.

The colourful and controversial figure of John Alexander Dowie (1847–1907), born and educated in Scotland but a Congregational minister for several years in Australia, strode onto the scene at this time. Dowie received his theological training at the University of Edinburgh and it is not fanciful to assume that memories of Edward Irving, and his restorationist Catholic Apostolic Church, founded barely 40 years before, were still in the air.[15] Whether this is so or not, Dowie's personal pilgrimage led him to a ministry of healing after a plague swept eastern Australia in 1876. Visiting a young woman who was dying, he prayed for her and she instantly recovered. At this point Dowie came to preach 'the Gospel of healing through faith in Jesus'.[16] Withdrawing from the Congregational Union because of its 'worldliness and apathy' Dowie moved into revivalism despite shortages of money, the death of his daughter and marital difficulties. In 1883 he established the Free Christian Church in Melbourne and organized the Divine Healing Association while launching outspoken attacks from his pulpit on the production, marketing and consumption of alcohol. His verbal attacks provoked physical retaliation and he was thrown into jail for 30 days for holding street meetings. Yet the publicity gained by his notoriety made him a local celebrity and the number of his followers grew rapidly. In the summer of 1886 he had a vision in which he believed he was told to take 'leaves of healing from the tree of life to every nation' and so, in 1888, he and his family left Australia for San Francisco where his fame spread further.[17] After two years of itinerating the Pacific coast, he organized the (now) International Divine Healing Association of which he was president. He preached in the Midwest of the United States and in the Chicago area, and at the Chicago World Fair in 1893 competed successfully with the crowd-pulling attractions of Buffalo Bill.

Dowie was a confrontationalist. He believed that 'all forms of human

---

15 Dowie was in Edinburgh for some years around 1867 when he was 20, and Irving's church had been founded in London in about 1832, though with strong Scottish connections because Irving studied at Edinburgh and was ordained in the Church of Scotland. D. W. Faupel (2007), 'Theological Influences on the Teachings and Practices of John Alexander Dowie', *Pneuma* 29.2, 226–53, establishes the connection between Irving and Dowie almost conclusively.

16 Grant Wacker, Chris R. Armstrong and Jay S. F. Blossom, 'John Alexander Dowie: Harbinger of Pentecostal Power', in James R. Goff Jr and Grant Wacker (eds) (2002), *Portraits of a Generation*, Fayetteville, University of Arkansas Press, p. 4.

17 Wacker *et al.*, 'John Alexander Dowie', p. 4.

sickness are Satan's work'[18] and that 'the dual Gospel of salvation and healing goes hand in hand' because Isaiah 53 speaks of the atonement and Matthew 8 ties this verse to the ministry of Jesus. For this reason any recourse to medical resources was to be condemned as manifestly lacking faith in God:

> See that you fulfil the conditions of Divine Healing, and pelt away doctors and drugs for ever. 'Oh I cannot do that Doctor,' some may say. Then you cannot have the Lord as your healer, for the Lord will not enter into partnership with the homoeopath, the allopath, the psychopath, 'Mother Siegel's soothing syrup', 'Carter's little liver pills', and all that muck.[19]

This vituperation of medicine is, perhaps, more understandable in the light of the primitive state of that profession at the end of the Victorian era. Most of the great medical discoveries and advances by which whole categories of diseases became curable lay in the future. Even so, it is doubtful whether Dowie had it in his nature to compromise.

By 1894 Dowie was in a position to build Zion City, founded on holiness principles and on 6,500 acres in the Chicago area. No drugs, no doctors, no hospitals, no saloons, dance halls or brothels, no gambling, no tobacco, no pork (Dowie took this dietary requirement from the Old Testament), no racism (surprising for its time) and no unemployment disfigured 'the beautiful city of God'.[20] A huge tent city to accommodate 20,000 people was erected and 2,000 people moved in, after securing leases from Dowie's corporation. His magazine, *Leaves of Healing*, published his weekly sermons as well as testimonies of healing and exhortations to tithe. His efforts stretched beyond the United States to many parts of Europe so that, for example, 3,350 copies of *Leaves of Healing* were sold within Britain and branches were set up in the British Isles between 1904 and 1906.[21] Dowie's utopian vision was for a series of Zions in different parts of the world, each sending out a host of preachers to convert the surrounding areas, and each linked together in a grand organizational

18 J. A. Dowie (1902), 'If It Be Thy Will', *Leaves of Healing* X.20, 8 March, p. 293. Quoted in J. R. Jones (2007), 'Diving Healing in British Pentecostalism from 1900–1939', unpublished MPhil dissertation, University of Wales, Bangor, p. 60.

19 J. A. Dowie (1904), 'New York Visitation of Elijah the Restorer and the Restoration of Hosts', *Leaves of Healing* XIV.13, 16 January, p. 407, quoted in Jones, 'Diving Healing', p. 63.

20 Smokers, or 'dirty stinkpots' in Dowie's colourful phrase, merited a $20 fine in Zion City. See D. Maxwell (1999), 'Historicizing Christian Independency: The Southern African Pentecostal Movement c 1908–60', *Journal of African History* 40, pp. 243–69.

21 J. R. Jones (2007), 'Diving Healing', p. 69.

scheme with himself at the head as he waited for the return of Christ. In 1901 Dowie revealed that he was the third and final manifestation of the prophet Elijah the Restorer and, in 1904, he declared himself – without acknowledgement to Edward Irving – to be the first apostle of the Lord Jesus Christ in the Christian Catholic Apostolic Church in Zion.[22]

Dowie's theology may not have been original but his grandiose vision and bold proclamation undoubtedly were. His capacity for self-publicity and his promises of prosperity for those who tithed sounded chords that were to echo throughout Pentecostalism in the twentieth century. This did not stop financial shortages starting to make themselves heard in 1903. Despite screaming headlines in *Leaves of Healing* that 'tithing makes a vast difference in money matters; income trebled in two years; business increases every season when tithes are paid', the Zion bank began to stop paying interest in 1905 and to forbid withdrawals.[23] Dowie himself tried to borrow $7 million from the bank (perhaps to buy a large tract of land in Mexico) and in the autumn of 1905 he suffered a stroke, and his deputy, Wilbur Glenn Voliva, organized a mass meeting at which Dowie, in his absence, was removed from office. Amid these troubles there were rumours of Dowie's marital difficulties, and he died in 1907. While Zion teetered on the brink of collapse a Southern one-time Methodist preacher, Charles Fox Parham (1873–1929), arrived preaching a message about the Holy Spirit and speaking in tongues, and tried to take control of the entire concern.

Speaking in tongues

The story of glossolalia, or speaking with tongues, has been associated with Pentecostalism from the beginning. It has been its most controversial facet and its most distinctive claim. Discussion about glossolalia and its doctrinal significance in the post-apostolic age has been heated. There seems no doubt, though, that glossolalia was heard during the ministry of Edward Irving in the middle of the nineteenth century. Irving, whose concentration upon biblical prophecy made him an intense preacher, understood glossolalia to be a sign of the end of the age. His own Catholic Apostolic Church did not function as a standard Pentecostal congregation – how could it? – nevertheless it allowed individuals to give public utterances in tongues. In this respect, tongues was not seen as a matter of private prayer or the outcome of an overwrought revivalistic meeting; tongues belonged within collective worship.

---

22 The similarity between the name chosen for his church by Dowie and the name of Irving's is surely more than a coincidence.

23 Wacker *et al.*, 'John Alexander Dowie', p. 9.

We do not know exactly what these tongues sounded like but reports indicated that hearers thought them to be speech in foreign languages.[24] Irving's Catholic Apostolic Church and his theology passed into relative obscurity after his death in 1834 and had, as far as we can tell, no impact on the re-emergence of tongues at the end of the nineteenth century. There is a historical problem here: given that tongues sounded like foreign languages (fluently or stutteringly spoken) they may have occurred in revivalistic meetings without their being recognized as such. At least from the time of the Wesleys deep emotion in revival meetings had resulted in cries, groans, shrieks and tears, and among these noises may have been utterances in tongues. Without a theology of tongues these noises would not have been identified as having had any value.

The story of the acceptance of tongues and their theological significance is slightly different, therefore, from the story of the actual prevalence of tongues in revivalistic atmospheres. Only after a theology of tongues had been formulated could preachers remember back to earlier meetings where they could now identify the phenomena they had previously discounted. We have no way of checking exactly what went on in the heady proto-Church of God holiness revivals in small communities in the United States at the end of the nineteenth century.[25] What we do know is that once tongues emerged as a distinctive mark of Pentecostalism, various preachers were keen to claim credit for the rediscovery of the gift.

The attribution of tongues as *the* sign of baptism in the Holy Spirit is usually credited to Charles Fox Parham, but the story is not quite as simple as that. Frank Sandford (1862–1948), some 11 years older than Parham, was himself making a spiritual journey. Sandford, a natural leader, had become a Free Baptist pastor before embracing holiness teachings on sanctification.[26] As a result of contact with A. B. Simpson (1843–1919) and D. L. Moody's summer conferences, Sandford came to accept divine healing and pre-millennial eschatology. After his denomination asked him to travel widely overseas to assess the viability of Christian missionary work, he returned convinced that the methods then being applied were simply inadequate to meet the enormous needs of the world. He came to believe that the evangelization of the world could

---

24 There is a description of Irvingite tongues given by William Goode (1934) in *Gifts of the Spirit Stated and Examined*, see http://books.google.co.uk/books?hl=en& id=pprGxmz5SfQC&dq=william+goode+gifts+of+the+spirit+stated&printsec=frontc over&source=web&ots=TMs4vgWWV5&sig=Pna_Rw-mehBVnPC8CwjbqKxNMD g&sa=X&oi=book_result&resnum=1&ct=result#PPA11,M1.

25 R. G. Robbins (2004), *A. J. Tomlinson: Plainfolk Modernist*, Oxford, Oxford University Press.

26 D. W. Faupel (1996), *The Everlasting Gospel*, Sheffield, Sheffield Academic Press, p. 136.

only be achieved by training a special group of missionaries empowered by the Holy Spirit.

In 1893 he founded Shiloh, a community near Durham, Maine, and started the Holy Ghost and Us Bible School as well as a periodical, *Tongues of Fire*. He also engaged in roving evangelistic campaigns, visiting Topeka, Kansas, where Parham was located, in June 1899. Impressed by Sandford's religious vision and tangible success, Parham took the northbound train to Chicago to investigate Dowie's Zion City, A. B. Simpson's work at Nyack, New York, and, from there, to Maine (probably in the summer of 1900) where he spent six weeks at Shiloh, Sandford's bustling complex. Jenny Glassey received a vision in which she believed she was taught to read an African language.[27] By 1895 she had received what would now be identified as glossolalia, a story that was reported in the *Amherst (Nova Scotia) Daily News* for 9 December 1895.[28] When Sandford received the newspaper reports he republished them in *Tongues of Fire*. Here the purpose of tongues was allied with missionary work. These were 'missionary tongues' designed to speed up the evangelization of the earth by cutting out the laborious process of language school while, at the same time, ensuring that Spirit-filled missionaries spoke to their would-be converts with miraculous effectiveness.[29] Parham recounted the story of Jenny Glassey's miraculous tongues in his newspaper, *The Apostolic Faith*, on 21 June 1899. At the watchnight service on 31 December 1899, speaking with tongues occurred at Shiloh and was reported by the local press. Moreover, Sandford reported to the local newspaper that he was astonished to count 120 people present when the gift of tongues descended – astonished because 120 was the number of people present in the Jerusalem upper room on the original day of Pentecost reported in Acts 2.[30] Prayer of this kind must have become part of the normal practice of Shiloh because Parham heard glossolalia for the first time while he was present in the late summer of 1900.

Parham returned to Kansas with a desire to emulate Sandford's work. He surrendered control of the healing home he had previously started and opened up a new Bible School in a large mansion outside Topeka. Some 34 students registered and Parham was their lecturer and principal. To his existing battery of doctrines he now added emphasis upon the life

---

27 She was a young woman with a Scottish Presbyterian background, born in c. 1877.

28 G. B. McGee (2004), *People of the Spirit*, Springfield, MO, Gospel Publishing House, p. 47.

29 Speaking with tongues understood by the hearer but not the speaker is technically known as 'xenolalia'.

30 S. and R. Nelson (2002), 'Frank Sandford: Tongues of Fire in Shiloh, Maine', in Goff and Wacker (eds), *Portraits*, p. 53. They cite the *Lewiston (Maine) Evening Journal*, 6 January 1900.

of faith as exemplified by Sandford and the baptism of the Spirit as a spiritual experience eschatologically necessary for world evangelization. The narrative of what happened next has passed into Pentecostal mythology, as Parham intended. From this distance in time, though, it looks derivative and selectively told.

Parham continued teaching his students until December 1900 when, in own his words,

> We had reached in our studies a problem. What about the 2nd chapter of Acts? ... having heard so many different religious bodies claiming different proofs as the evidence of their having the Pentecostal Baptism, I set the students at work studying out diligently what was the Bible evidence of the baptism of the Holy Ghost ... leaving the students for three days at this task, I went to Kansas City for three days services [and returned] to the school on the morning preceeding [sic] Watch night services in the year 1900. About 10 o'clock in the morning I rang the bell calling all the students into the chapel to get their report on the matter in hand. To my astonishment they all had the same story, that while there were different things [which] occurred when the Pentecostal blessing fell, that the indisputable proof on each occasion was, that they spake with other tongues. About 75 people beside the school[,] which consisted of the 40 students, had gathered for the watch night services. A mighty spiritual power filled the entire school. At 10:30 p.m. sister Agnes N. Ozman, (now La Berge) asked that hands might be laid upon her to receive the Holy Spirit as she had to go to foreign fields. At first I refused, not having experience myself. Then being further pressed to do it humbly in the name of Jesus, I laid my hands upon her head and prayed. I had scarcely repeated three dozen sentences when the glory fell upon her[,] a halo seemed to surround her head and face[,] and she began to speak in the Chinese language, and was unable to speak English for three days.[31]

Leaving the main body of students for a preaching engagement on 3 January, Parham went to a Free Methodist Church in Topeka and there announced what happened to the assembled congregation. When he returned that night he found scenes that, to his mind, even more closely resembled the original outpouring of the Spirit in the book of Acts. Not only were there many people speaking in different glossolalic languages, but also there was an unnatural brightness in the room. Among those present were 12 ministers from a variety of denominations, and Parham himself, feeling that God was asking him to be willing to accept perse-

---

31 Quoted from *Apostolic Faith* (Baxter) 2, July 1926, by J. R. Goff (1988), *Fields White Unto Harvest: Charles F. Parham and the Missionary Origins of Pentecostalism*, Fayetteville, University of Arkansas Press, pp. 66, 67.

cutions and hardships as a condition of Spirit baptism, accepted, and then began, according to his account, to worship God in Swedish and other languages. Other members of the community underwent similar experiences while Agnes Ozman now began 'writing in tongues', though what has been preserved amounts only to scrawls and scribbles.[32] Such unheard-of exploits attracted journalistic attention, ensuring newspaper reports spread the story far and wide.

Parham's account, as Sandford's, is written so as to parallel the original Pentecostal events. In Sandford's account there are 120 in the room. In Parham's there are 12 ministers from different denominations. These are biblical numbers and, when we add the unnatural brightness in the room and its description as 'an upper room', the vocabulary appears deliberately designed to resonate with the biblical text. This was a new Pentecost, a repetition of the first great event that signalled the start of the church. Such a high view of what happened in Shiloh and Topeka appears to be in line with Sandford's evaluation of himself and Parham's evaluation of himself. Sandford went on to make increasingly grandiose claims about his own status in end-time revival. He claimed to be the restored biblical Elijah and the Davidic Prince and his followers had to sign a pledge saying as much. Parham pushed forward his ministry as a healing evangelist and Bible teacher while casting himself as the 'Projector' of the burgeoning Pentecostal movement.[33] As 'Projector' he seems to have believed he had a quasi-apostolic authority over other non-denominational aspects of Pentecostalism. This is partly why he tried to take over Zion City and why, later, he went to Los Angeles, attempting to take charge of the revival there.

Parham's doctrine of tongues was precise and vigorously expressed. Like other early Pentecostals he believed in the pre-millennial second coming of Christ, but he combined this doctrine with his doctrine of the Holy Spirit. He continued to believe in sanctification as a second work of grace and accepted that those who are sanctified know the presence of the Holy Spirit in their inner lives, what he called 'the anointing that abides'. The baptism in the Holy Spirit was eschatologically important because it marked out those who would be carried up in the rapture when Christ returned. These people were not simply the church but an elite subsection of the church that would spearhead missionary conquest by virtue of their special gifts of the Holy Spirit. So, to Parham, the baptism in the Holy Spirit was both a sign of being among the elect of the elect and also a practical gift enabling the propagation of the gospel in any country of the world. This is why the baptism in the Holy Spirit was indissolubly

---

32 See for instance McGee, *People*, p. 54. It is also worth pointing out that Ms Ozman had studied previously under the auspices of A. B. Simpson's Christian and Missionary Alliance.

33 Goff, *Fields*, p. 106.

linked with speaking in tongues. There was no point in having any other gift of the Spirit to fulfil this role since no other gift could make the gospel known and understood in foreign lands.

To those who stand 100 years away from these events, it seems odd that early tongues-speakers thought they knew which languages they were speaking. Parham said he was speaking Swedish when he received the gift of tongues but no objective evidence of this was ever provided and Parham himself made no attempt to go and preach the gospel in Sweden. As we shall see, other Pentecostals *did* go overseas to the country where they thought their own tongues language would be understood, but those who followed Parham in the Kansas area tended to remain where they were while, for the next year or two, he pressed on with his multifaceted ministry.

Tongues and the baptism of the Holy Spirit

Now we want to say to private individuals or to schools, that the speaking in other tongues is an inseparable part of the Baptism of the Holy Spirit distinguishing it from all previous works; and that no one has received Baptism of the Holy Spirit who has not a Bible evidence to show for it. As pardon is received as a result of sincere repentance, restitution and surrender; sanctification received as a result of entire consecration; so the speaking in other tongues is received as a result of this Baptism. The Holy Spirit, thru witnessing to the work of Calvary wrought in our lives, in justification and sanctification, reserves the speaking in other tongues as the evidence of His own incoming. Many say, 'Oh, I have the gift of healing or discernment or some other gift that is as good to me as the speaking in the other tongues as evidence that I have the Holy Spirit.['] Yet in spite of the rebellious toss of the head and seeming disregard for the Word of God, the fact is the gifts of wisdom, knowledge, faith, healing, working of miracles, prophecy, discernment of spirits, and interpretation of tongues were fully manifested in Old Testament prophets, and New Testament disciples before the day of Pentecost; and many have received inspiration, teaching and anointing, for holy men of old spake as they were moved by the Holy Ghost; (2 Peter 1:21), yet His personal Baptism was not ministered.

Charles Fox Parham (c. 1910), *A Voice Crying in the Wilderness*, Baxter Springs, 4th edn, 1944, p. 35.

Organizations

Many early Pentecostals were highly resistant to any form of organization. They saw it as preventing the free flow of the Holy Spirit and being likely to lead to ecclesiastical bureaucracies or hierarchies. 'Organization' was a dirty word. And yet, undeniably, early Pentecostals could see that there were churches in the New Testament and these churches did show signs of organization. There were obviously different ministries and functions within the congregations. So, once it was admitted that the local church was ordered, and once it was admitted that local churches might need to work together, the vestiges of organization could be justified. Even so, it took about a decade for Pentecostals to make the transition from disorganized and independent-minded beginnings to the type of organizational forms that are typically found within denominational structures.

Equally influential was the pressure of missionary work. Pentecostals understood themselves to be part of a great new outpouring of the Spirit that was given by God to enable the evangelization of the world. Missionary work might occur without organization as individuals travelled from one country to the next. Yet, the experience of these travelling preachers and their families soon provided practical reasons why organization should be set up. There was the need to send money overseas; there was a need to communicate between the missionary thousands of miles away and the supporting churches; there might be a need for the missionary's family to return home in emergency; there might be a need for further missionaries to join the earliest pioneers. So, missionary organizations began to be forged in the fire of revival or through the pentecostalization of existing missionary societies.[34]

Having said this, it has to be admitted that a few irresistibly dominant individuals, and Dowie and Sandford were among them, bulldozed their way through early Pentecostal hesitations. While the majority of Pentecostals might show an instinctive aversion to organization, there was a large minority that looked up to successful preachers. Here an implicit mental equation could be found: if this autocratic person is successful, he or she must have the blessing of God; if this person has the blessing of God, then whatever he or she does must be right – including the establishment of an organization. Dowie was certainly successful in terms of the size of his following (over 250,000 internationally) and the people

---

34 See, for instance, Michael Bergunder (2007), 'Constructing Pentecostalism: On Issues of Methodology and Representation', *Journal of the European Pentecostal Theological Association*, 27, 55–73. Allan Anderson (2007), *Spreading Fires: The Missionary Nature of Early Pentecostalism*, London, SCM Press.

who claimed to have been healed under his ministry.[35] The same, on a lesser scale, could be said of Sandford.

So, in one way or another Pentecostal organizations came into existence. One of the earliest to be 'pentecostalized' was the CMA. A. B. Simpson set up the Christian Alliance and the Evangelical Missionary Alliance, which in 1897 became the Christian and Missionary Alliance (CMA), an interdenominational umbrella for missionary work that eventually became a denomination in its own right. The CMA preached sanctification and divine healing and, as we have seen, early Pentecostals like Parham held it in high regard. There were clearly Pentecostal phenomena in CMA meetings, including healings and glossolalia, ensuring that the theological significance of tongues was debated within CMA ranks.[36] They eventually agreed a 'forbid not, seek not' policy that was intended to allow tongues to occur within the Alliance without making them a touchstone for membership. Before this policy was reached, a considerable number of preachers and churches left the CMA to join the ranks of growing Pentecostalism with the result that the CMA suffered losses and those who remained behind were largely cold towards the claims of this new spiritual upstart. It is arguable that a pro- and anti-Pentecostal struggle took place in the CMA after the death of Simpson in 1919.[37]

After the Pentecostal events in Topeka, Parham held a series of thriving healing campaigns in booming Southern towns. He now had enough followers and congregations to make organization essential if he was going to sustain what he had built up. Yet he, like other early Pentecostals, was temperamentally and theologically opposed to organization. He recognized the wider scandal of disunity in the church. In *A Voice Crying in the Wilderness* he fulminated, 'your narrow sectarian individualism and fanaticism destroyed my Lord's body [i.e. the church]'. He argued, 'unity is not to be accomplished by organisation or non-organisation. Unity by organisation has been tried for 1900 years and failed. Unity by non-organisation has been tried for several years and resulted in anarchy.'[38] Whatever organization Parham was going to establish had to be loose enough not to look like an organization.

Goff, Parham's best biographer, points out that 'of primary concern was the training of Pentecostal evangelists and the retention of those followers who attended churches hostile to his innovative endtime theology'.[39] So Parham set up support groups for 'assembly meetings' that

---

35 McGee, *People*, p. 63. See also Faupel, 'Theological Influences', 226–53, where the figure of 250,000 is cited.

36 King, *Genuine Gold*.

37 King, *Genuine Gold*.

38 Parham, *Voice*, p. 65.

39 Goff, *Fields*, p. 117.

resembled the class meetings used by Methodism. Parham presumed that these groups would meet on weeknights for prayer or discussion in the homes of members. Each group was to have an elder and Parham hoped that these groups would convert 'all of Christendom to a worldwide evangelistic effort within a generation'.[40] The March 1906 issue of *Apostolic Faith* set out the new scheme with rules about the support groups, the names of elders in the major towns and listed the three state directors, one each for Texas, Kansas and Missouri. A general secretary of the Apostolic Faith movement, Parham's sister-in-law, was also announced and Parham claimed the title of 'Projector'

Within a year disaster struck. Early in 1907 rumours began to circulate of Parham's immorality. In July, the *San Antonio Light*, a local newspaper, reported that Parham had been arrested. The charge was never pressed and the case was dismissed a month later.[41] Even so, Parham's prestige was damaged beyond repair and his organization, already infected by power struggles, began to break up. Within ten years many of its remaining fragments found their way into newly formed denominations.

Parham gave to Pentecostalism a distinctive stance on speaking with tongues. He explicitly associated speaking with tongues with the Pentecostal baptism and, by this means, removed imprecision from the terminology. Until that point the Pentecostal baptism might have been used metaphorically for any special spiritual experience. Equally, the Pentecostal baptism might have been claimed 'by faith' without any obvious outward indication that faith had secured its objective. Parham made connections between the objective sign of tongues and Spirit baptism and between tongues and missions, and it is partly as a result of his insights that early Pentecostalism developed a strong missionary drive. This drive was expressed through travel, conventions, revival meetings and, yes, through organization. During his period in Houston, Texas, as the principal of the Bible School, Parham admitted W. J. Seymour, the son of a freed slave and a black man, to his classes. Because of the discriminatory laws Seymour had to sit outside the classroom and could not be taught in the same room as the other students. This did not prevent Seymour learning Parham's doctrine of tongues and becoming convinced that the crowning moment of sanctification occurred when Spirit baptism was realized through glossolalia. We shall shortly examine Seymour's role in the Azusa Street revival.

---

40 Goff, *Fields*, p. 118.

41 Parham was charged with sodomy, then a felony in Texas. Parham's defence was that he had been the victim of an elaborate hoax arranged by his rival for the remnants of Dowie's Zion City, Wilbur Voliva. No evidence against Parham was ever presented in court. See Goff, *Fields*, pp. 128–46.

Revivals

Religious revivals have a long history within the church. The term 'revival' is problematic in the sense that it literally refers to the revivification of something that was once alive. Since it is normally argued that the early church was constantly alive in the power of the Spirit, it is difficult to argue that there are revivals present within the pages of the New Testament. It makes even less sense to go back to the pages of the Old Testament to speak about Christian revival because of the fundamental covenantal differences between the church and the people of Israel. Consequently there is no obvious biblical pattern for revival. As a result revival has to be studied historically and, from these historical accounts, revivals can then be placed into different categories, a placement that is slightly arbitrary.

The best-known and most thoroughly studied revivals are those of the eighteenth century involving Jonathan Edwards (1703–58) on the east coast of the United States, John Wesley (1703–91), the founder of Methodism, and their contemporary George Whitefield (1714–70). All three men preached in the United States and the revivals in which they participated could be classified as revivals of preaching. The centre of the revival was a meeting at which preaching took place and at which warm, excited, fearful, tearful and occasionally uncontrolled emotions surfaced. These were revivals that affected whole communities and resulted in bulging church attendance. Wesley left behind him the highly organized Methodist Church.[42] Whitefield's preaching, which was probably more dramatic and to larger crowds, was hardly accompanied by any organization outside that which already existed within the participating churches. Edwards, the most philosophically acute of the three, saw in response to his somewhat cerebral preaching the stirring of his community in New England. Edwards, more than the other two, attempted to distinguish the necessary and genuine marks of revival from those that were peripheral and incidental. He wanted to discern those elements of the revival that were brought about by the activity of the Holy Spirit and those elements that were merely the froth of human emotionalism.[43]

Revivals that follow passionate preaching are associated with religious experience and religious emotion. It is in revival that the beliefs and practices of Christianity come home to men and women with renewed force. Church attendance that has been perfunctory or dutiful now becomes urgent and exciting. Patterns of behaviour change. There

---

42 Note the place given to Wesley in *The Apostolic Faith* 1.2 in the text box at the end of this chapter.

43 Edwards's *Distinguishing Marks of a Work of a Spirit of God* was delivered at Yale College in 1741 at the height of 'the great awakening'.

may be less emphasis upon theatre-going, drinking, dancing, gambling, horse racing, and instead, social life is caught up in and around the church. There may be reconciliation between families that have been broken by years of ill-feeling. It is the excited, emotional side of revival that is the most visible to the dispassionate observer. Connected with revival, there is a spontaneous element. The revival takes on a life of its own. It begins, perhaps, with the preacher and religious services but spreads outside the church into the town or city and onto the streets. Spontaneity causes religious behaviour to overflow into secular situations. The workplace changes its character and personal prayer intensifies. At the same time, the spontaneous nature of revival may lead to disorganization and a breakdown of social habits. Church services may be prolonged indefinitely. People may, within church services, behave unpredictably by standing up to pray without warning, sing, speak and in other ways to participate. This ensures that revivals are often outside the control of professional clergy and led by laity. The revival becomes an opportunity for untrained and theologically unsophisticated individuals to 'share what is on their heart' or to confess to wrongs they feel they have committed. All these characteristics may occur within a small limited community like a fishing village or a mining area or, by different social mechanisms, may be part of an urban society brought about by transport to a central point. In the community revivals, news of religious excitement or conversion spreads rapidly by word of mouth. In the urban revival, people travel to the scene of spiritual excitement as they would to a theatre or a sporting event, and it is often the local press that stimulates the initial interest.[44]

Pentecostalism is revivalistic. Patterns of revival behaviour became part of Pentecostal worship. There was lay leadership, emotion and unpredictability and there might or might not be preaching at the centre of worship. In effect, Pentecostalism normalized revival behaviour and could claim to be a 'revival movement', as well as a movement that opened the way for women to take an active role in preaching and ministry and, as we shall see, for mixed-race meetings to occur in the United States at a time when churches were largely segregated upon racial lines. The impetus provided by creative and bold women as well as the enormous contribution of African Americans enabled Pentecostalism to advance with great energy, crossing gender and racial barriers.

We now turn to revivals that can be specifically connected with the start of Pentecostalism.

---

44 See W. K. Kay (2003), 'Revival: Empirical Aspects', in A. Walker and K. Aune (eds), *On Revival: A Critical Examination*, Carlisle, Paternoster Press, pp. 185–204, as well as other chapters in the collection.

Korea

Roman Catholic missionaries reached Korea as early as 1592. The first resident Protestant missionary, a medical doctor, settled in Korea in the autumn of 1884.[45] Other missionaries, mainly Presbyterians and Methodists, continued their Christian work concentrating on medical activities, like building hospitals, and educational activities, like building schools. Between 1897 and 1906 Korea was caught between the militaristic rivalry of Russia and Japan, and the churches were one of the few places where Korean national feeling could flourish. The Presbyterians trained Korean church leaders. Since Presbyterians govern churches through presbyteries, or collections of local church elders, Korean Christians began to organize themselves without having to be answerable to foreign missionary control. By the start of the twentieth century Christianity had spread over the whole Korean peninsula and a good Korean translation of the New Testament was published in 1900.[46]

In August 1903 a group of seven Methodist missionaries, convened by Miss Mary White, came together for a week of Bible study and prayer. Their theme was the Holy Spirit and their meetings led to public confession of sin and a vitalization of spiritual life that touched churches in all the major cities. A year later at a similar gathering a similar response to the Holy Spirit led to more than 700 converts in Pyongyang, especially as Bible teaching on the second coming of Christ raised the spiritual temperature. In 1906 Howard Johnson, who had visited the Welsh and Indian revivals (see below), told of what he had seen – leading the Korean revival to reach its climax in 1907. The short-term Bible schools now attracted 1,500 people every night and the Korean preacher, Sun Joo Kil, urged his listeners to open their hearts to receive the Holy Spirit.[47] There were miracles of healing, exorcism and other supernatural signs, as well as the emergence of a group of Korean leaders. The Korean Presbyterian Church was impressed and amended its by-laws to admit the possibility of contemporary miracles. By 1910 'there were nearly 30,000 communicants of the Presbyterian and Methodist Churches, with a much larger number of believers and adherents'.[48]

---

45 Allen D. Clark (1971), *A History of the Church in Korea*, Seoul, The Christian Literature Society of Korea, p. 88.

46 Clark, *Church*, p. 151f.

47 Yeol Soo Eim, 'South Korea', in S. M. Burgess and E. van der Maas (eds) (2002), *New International Dictionary of Pentecostal and Charismatic Movements*, Grand Rapids, MI, Zondervan, p. 240.

48 S. Neill (1990), *A History of Christian Missions*, London, Penguin, p. 291.

Wales

The revival in Wales that took place between the autumn of 1904 and the late summer of 1905 began in the yearnings and warnings of the preachers a few years before.[49] Among the young people in a Calvinistic Methodist congregation at New Quay and among the Baptists in Aberdare, spiritual excitement started to rise from December 1903. Aberdare and New Quay are in west Wales, in a strongly Welsh-speaking area, and, though the chapels in which the revival began belonged to different denominations, the enthusiasm the members felt was exactly the same. Their feelings were widely shared. The Wesleyans at their Regional Meeting in May 1904 had held a conference on 'the Spirit and His work': in other words there was a spiritual thirst, widely manifested, among Welsh people and Welsh clergy. Events took on a new momentum after Seth Joshua preached at Newcastle Emlyn on 29 September 1904. Joshua prayed, 'Humble us, our Lord!' and his prayer had a dramatic effect on a young man who fell down sighing, 'Humble me! humble me!'.The young man, a trainee for the Calvinistic Methodist ministry, was the 26-year-old Evan Roberts.

Roberts became the public face of the revival. He travelled back along the railway to his home chapel 50 miles away, preached to young people there and brought them to commitment to Christ, was invited by other ministers to other nearby chapels on successive nights and, almost before he knew it, was busy holding lengthy meetings far into the night in one Welsh town or village after another. Wales was then a land of Nonconformist chapels, which were the centre of social and spiritual life. There may have been numerous denominations, and denominations may have squabbled with each other reducing spiritual harmony but, when the revival came, the chapels forgot their differences and opened their pulpits to Roberts and other travelling evangelists. Roberts is unusual in that he was not a classical evangelical preacher. The meetings he convened seemed to have little or no leadership and Roberts might or might not speak. Sometimes he would pray and at other times would walk up and down the aisle addressing individuals, exhorting them to repent or putting his arm round a shoulder giving encouragement. Women might read a verse of Scripture aloud or lead in prayer and congregations would sing together without hymn books from music they had known since childhood. Roberts tearfully encouraged people to confess their sins publicly

---

49 The best composite account of the revival, and the one followed here, is given by R. Tudur Jones (2004), *Faith and the Crisis of a Nation: Wales 1890–1914*, Cardiff, University of Wales Press. The Welsh edition was published in two volumes in 1979, and the English edition in one volume, edited by Robert Pope, was published in 2004. See also Robert Pope (2006), 'Demythologising the Evan Roberts Revival, 1904–1905', *Journal of Ecclesiastical History* 57.3, 515–34.

and this had emotional impact. News of the revival spread through the *Western Mail*, the main newspaper of south Wales, and the newly laid railways enabled people to reach the meetings wherever Roberts was.

He preached almost every night until Christmas and, because the meetings might go on with singing and praying until after midnight, he became physically exhausted. When he reached the mining areas of the Rhondda the revival impacted those close-knit communities and nearly closed some of the pubs. In the new year Roberts continued his preaching tours until he was attacked by a letter published in the *Western Mail* from Peter Price, another clergyman, who accused him of bringing a 'sham revival, a mockery, a blasphemous travesty of the real thing' to Wales.[50] The accusation obviously hurt Roberts, but he never publicly answered it. Going north to a Welsh community in Liverpool Roberts's already unpredictable behaviour became worse. In one meeting he refused to preach because he said a hypnotist was present. In another he accused one of the churches of being 'not founded on the Rock'.[51] After being examined by doctors and recommended a period of rest he continued preaching a lighter schedule until tapering off in the spring of 1906. Although he spoke occasionally in public meetings, his ministry was to all intents and purposes over. He retired to Leicester, to the home of Mrs Jessie Penn-Lewis, 'a powerful and domineering woman', where he stayed until 1925.[52] He died in 1951.

The revival continued sporadically without Roberts but, by 1906, after a general election was held, it had finished. Emotions had subsided, public interests turned elsewhere and church attendance in many chapels dropped back to its old pre-revival level. Women who had led congregations found themselves relegated to the margins and clergy reasserted their control over religious life. Yet, it would be a mistake to think of the revival as having left no trace behind. Other Welsh communities in England were affected after the revival had stopped in Wales. In England – in Leeds, Bristol and London where there were Welsh congregations – powerful religious meetings were held. In Scotland there were also evidences of revival, and further afield, among the Welsh mission in the Khasi hills in India, Pennsylvania and Norway, revivalistic meetings took place at the same time as, or just after, what was happening in Wales.[53]

---

50 Jones, *Faith*, p. 313. The lengthy letter was dated 31 January 1905. It can be found on the CD-ROM, *The Welsh Revival*, published by The Revival Library (see www.revival-library.org) in the history written by J. V. Morgan.

51 Jones, *Faith*, p. 324.

52 Jones, *Faith*, p. 332.

53 Jones, *Faith*, pp. 337–48. The Khasi mission started in 1841 by Welsh Presbyterians who needed help and so the Revd D. E. Jones was sent in 1897, and revival began in January 1904: soon after that John Roberts returned from Wales with the news of the revival there; matters escalated into thorough revival. Revival and Mission

Theologically, it seems that the aftermath of the revival saw speaking in tongues and healing, and, if Evan Roberts's insight into the minds of individuals is equated with the occasional bursting out of charismata in the form of 'a word of knowledge', then there were indeed Pentecostal phenomena present.[54] It is arguable that the revival in Wales would have continued longer had a more robust Pentecostal theology been available to Roberts to help him understand what Pentecostals later formulated into an approach that balanced a respect for spiritual gifts with an appreciation of the need for discernment.

Among those in contact with Roberts were believers living in Los Angeles on the West Coast of the United States.

Los Angeles, Azusa Street

The most direct contact between the Welsh revival and the outpouring of the Spirit on the West Coast of the United States was made by Joseph Smale, one-time pastor of the First Baptist Church at Los Angeles. After theological education at Spurgeon's College, London, Smale had emigrated from England around 1895. Then, leaving for the United Kingdom for a period of rest in about 1904, Smale developed a friendship with Evan Roberts that allowed him to observe the revival first-hand. On returning to Los Angeles, Smale attempted to start a revival there by holding a series of daily meetings for 19 straight weeks. His church board objected to this unusual practice. Smale parted company with them in September 1905 to start a new congregation which he named the First New Testament Church. His new constitution made the Pentecostal gift of the Holy Spirit central to sanctification and Christian service.

At roughly the same time Frank Bartleman, an itinerant evangelist and preacher as well as a writer of tracts and occasional journalist, had also heard of the Welsh revival through written accounts that had now reached America.[55] Bartleman, deeply moved, wrote to Evan Roberts asking the people of Wales to pray for the people of California. Roberts replied:

> My dear brother in the faith: many thanks for your kind letter. I'm impressed of your sincerity and honesty of purpose. Congregate the people together who are willing to make a total surrender. Pray and

---

– http://mizoramsynod.org/synfo.php?article&read_article&article_id=16 (accessed 3/04/2008).

54 Jones, *Faith*, pp. 324, 335.

55 Frank Bartleman (1925), *How 'Pentecost' Came to Los Angeles – As It Was in the Beginning*, reprinted in 1980 under the title *Azusa Street* and introduced by Vinson Synan. The accounts that reached Bartleman about Wales were those of S. B. Shaw and G. Campbell Morgan. Roberts' letter is taken from p. 15 of the reprint.

wait. Believe God's promises. Hold daily meetings. May God bless you, is my earnest prayer. Yours in Christ, Evan Roberts.

Bartleman in his impulsive way visited Smale's congregation, sometimes noting the wonderful spontaneity of the services, at other times judging that overwrought human orchestration appeared to be the driving force.

It is here that we need to be careful in giving an account of what happened. Bartleman was prone to exaggerate his own importance in the events that followed. He also had a profound detestation of organized religion and so only praised spontaneous religious occurrences. Quite independently of Bartleman, a Mrs Hutchins invited William Seymour to Los Angeles. On the recommendation of one of its members she invited Seymour to become the pastor of a holiness congregation while she prepared to go as a missionary to Liberia. Seymour seemed a good candidate for the post. He was a holiness preacher and had been recommended for his Bible teaching ability as well as his gracious demeanour. She was specifically looking for someone who was not 'harsh and denunciatory'.[56] Seymour arrived by train from Texas on 22 February 1906 and began his preaching duties.

For Seymour, of course, this was a bold new beginning. He knew no one in the city and he had no money for the train journey home.[57] This was his first ministerial appointment of any consequence. He preached over the next few days and conveyed the substance of the teaching that he had learned from Charles Fox Parham, namely that after justification and sanctification there was a 'third work' of God in the baptism of the Holy Spirit that was evidenced by speaking with other tongues. This was unorthodox, especially to the ears of the classic holiness Christians who believe that after justification (or conversion) all Christians should go through a stage of sanctification. Whether this stage was called, at its crisis moment, the baptism in the Holy Spirit, was unimportant. What was not acceptable was the notion that an entirely new stage beyond sanctification was possible and, even more, that this new stage was glossolalic. Mrs Hutchins called the president of the Holiness Church Association to confront Seymour. A discussion took place and Seymour refused to back down. Speaking with tongues was essential and not optional – a position that Seymour took even though he himself had not, at that stage, undergone the experience.

Seymour was locked out of the building and, returning to the people with whom he was staying, launched into extensive prayer at their home. When the prayer meeting grew large, it transferred to North Bonnie Brae Street, a short distance away. The core of the group comprised about 15

---

56 Cecil M. Robeck Jr (2006), *The Azusa Street Mission and Revival*, Nashville, TN, Nelson Reference and Electronic, p. 61.

57 He told the story in *The Apostolic Faith*, 1.1.

African Americans and some children.[58] At the beginning of April there was an outbreak of the longed-for speaking with tongues and the congregation moved to Azusa Street in time to open their services for Easter. The building they chose had originally housed a church that met upstairs, while the downstairs area held stables for horses. A fire had gutted the building a year before, with the result that the downstairs area was still dirty and damaged. Yet the new congregation enthusiastically prepared it for worship. Straw and sawdust were scattered on the floor, benches and an assortment of chairs were put in lines, and the pulpit, such as it was, was made from a commercial wooden packing case used for shipping shoes. The seats and benches were arranged on three sides of a square to accommodate about 40 people.

On Easter morning, a woman stood up in Joseph Smale's First New Testament Church and told everyone she had spoken with other tongues. The congregation reacted with surprise and excitement and many of them now began to attend the Azusa Street mission, if only on an irregular basis. Later that week a reporter from the *Los Angeles Daily Times* attended the Tuesday evening service on 17 April and his report appeared the following day under the headline 'Weird Babel of tongues', noting that the congregation comprised 'coloured people and a sprinkling of whites'.[59] The mocking report, the first of many, was barely noticed because of the dramatic news of a huge earthquake in San Francisco, the next major city further up the coast, on 18 April. Large swathes of the city were destroyed and, since both Los Angeles and San Francisco rested on the same geological fault line, what had happened in one place threatened to happen in the other.

Preachers reacted to the earthquake either by announcing that it was nothing whatever to do with the loving God of the Bible or, as Frank Bartleman unhesitatingly did, hearing it as the voice of the Almighty crying against human sinfulness. Bartleman quickly wrote a tract on the subject, had it printed and gave it to members of the First New Testament Church for handing out across the city. Further printings were made so that by May 125,000 copies had been distributed. Whether it was because the earthquake raised levels of religious anxiety or as a result of the zeal of the congregation, the Azusa Street mission grew. By mid-July between 500 and 700 people were regularly in attendance, although not all at the same time because the building would not hold them. People came to the mission at all times of the day and night and services ran almost continuously. The secular press reported on the revival in a mocking tone that must have worried the Los Angeles Church Federation: they did not want all the churches to be contaminated by the same ridicule. Joseph Smale

58 Robeck, *Azusa*, p. 65.
59 Robeck, *Azusa*, p. 75.

wrote to the Federation's members who, after consultation, decided to copy aspects of what they had seen in Seymour's mission. The Federation agreed to implement a programme of street meetings, prayer meetings and prepare for a city-wide evangelistic campaign. It is clear that the Azusa Street revival was now making an impact in secular and ecclesial circles.

Meanwhile the revival continued unabated. This does not imply that it was without leadership. Cecil Robeck has traced out the transport links in Los Angeles to show where and how evangelistic groups fanned out from the central point.[60] So successful was the Azusa Street mission that other missions opened up nearby with the same or slightly different beliefs and practices. People would switch allegiance from one mission to another, and through all this Seymour himself began to receive invitations to travel that caused him to be away from his base. There was a properly constituted church board and a famous photograph of leaders of the Azusa Street mission showing them to have been both male and female and black and white.[61] This racial integration and gender equality was fostered by Seymour whom several accounts agree to have been a humble and gracious man. Seymour saw the matter theologically, believing that the church was the *undivided* body of Christ.[62] In other words the racial mix, including Hispanics, Latinos and all kinds of Caucasians and African Americans, was deliberate and, at the height of the revival when spontaneous singing in tongues, prayer, healing and testimony flowed in an unforced rhythm, expressed an underlying spiritual harmony.

Behind-the-scenes complications came and went. One challenge to Seymour's leadership occurred in November 1906 when Parham arrived, detested what he saw, and tried to take control of the mission in a way that would today be seen as a grotesque breach of ministerial ethics. Parham reacted viscerally against the mixing of races and the sight of blacks and whites praying fervently together. After vitriolic denunciation of what he saw, Parham set up in opposition to Seymour by establishing a rival congregation nearby. This drew away a small number of people, presumably mainly whites, until Parham left to meet the nemesis of his alleged moral failure. More important than Parham's uncalled-for intervention was what happened with Florence Crawford and Clara Lum. Both these women were involved in the leadership of the mission. Crawford, a feisty and autocratic woman, was separated from her husband, and Seymour disapproved of this.[63] Clara Lum, who functioned as a secretary and editor, invested time and skill in *The Apostolic Faith*,

---

60 Robeck, *Azusa*, p. 204.

61 Robeck, *Azusa*, p. 100.

62 *The Apostolic Faith* 1.4.

63 For an account of Crawford, see C. M. Robeck (2002), 'Florence Crawford: Apostolic Faith Pioneer', in Goff and Wacker (eds), *Portraits*, pp. 219–35.

a newspaper published by the mission to proclaim its teachings as well as attract funds for its work. The newspaper amplified the impact of the mission's vision and doctrine but in 1908 the publication suddenly transferred to Portland, Oregon. Numerous explanations have been offered for what happened, but the most convincing is that Clara Lum together with Florence Crawford took the newspaper to Oregon to help them found an alternative mission. Whether they 'stole' the newspaper, as much of the evidence indicates, is impossible to resolve conclusively; Robeck's authoritative recent account speculates that Lum might have left because she had wished to marry Seymour and he chose someone else.[64] By 1909 attendance at the Azusa Street mission had tumbled and, though it peaked again in 1911 when William Durham, a compelling preacher, ministered there for two and a half months, he also challenged the three-stage doctrine that Seymour had by now established. To Durham, sanctification and baptism in the Holy Spirit belonged to one stage – in other words, he telescoped stages two and three on the basis of 'the finished work of Christ'. Seymour disagreed and so Durham made an exit, taking a following with him that made the original congregation dwindle back into its African American core.

These difficulties have only been uncovered by diligent historians. At the time, with the constant ebb and flow of people, with arrivals from all over the world, with men and women determined to seek 'their Pentecost' in the hallowed precincts of Azusa Street, the impact of the mission was felt widely. One calculation suggests that about a third of those who attended were already missionaries or ministers who came for a few days or weeks, received a new experience of the Holy Spirit, and then returned to other parts of the United States or other parts of the world.[65] Both the duration of the revival and its accessibility through transport links enabled it to function in this way. Spirit-filled personnel from Azusa Street went out all over the United States and also to India, China, Africa, South Africa, Israel, Sweden, Ceylon (now Sri Lanka) and other countries of the world, with the result that many formal Pentecostal groupings can trace their roots back to those decisive events in Los Angeles.[66]

If we are to question the reasons for this outburst of activity, the most obvious answer lies within the unique Pentecostal configuration to be found in the revival. There was certainly healing (as the discarded crutches and other medical impedimenta in the mission building amply demonstrated); there were abundant manifestations of speaking with tongues, which were interpreted as signalling the baptism in the Spirit,

64 Robeck, *Azusa*, p. 310.

65 An Englishman, Cecil Polhill, who came from a wealthy family and who had worked as a missionary in China, gave £1,500 in 1908 and this cleared off the debt. Robeck, *Azusa*, p. 289.

66 Robeck, *Azusa*, pp. 235–80.

and, in the early days, as an ability to speak missionary languages; there was fervent belief in the impending return of Christ. The combination of missionaries who thought they could speak all kinds of languages at the miraculous prompting of the Spirit and of evangelists who believed that they now had a 'full' healing gospel to preach, was potent.

It is this urgent evangelistic and missionary programme that makes Azusa Street so important in the spread and formation of Pentecostalism.[67] Part of the influence of the revival there was mediated through pre-existing denominations and societies, with the result that the effects of Azusa were indirect as well as direct. We know, for instance, that in 1907–09 Frank Bartleman 'crisscrossed urban America' taking a Pentecostal message, and that 'the great majority of his meetings took place in … [Holiness] missions and camps and Christian and Missionary Alliance Churches'.[68] A proportion of the impact of the revival was brought about by its strategic position in the United States and by the relative freedom with which ethnic groups could intermingle in the new city. Equally, the dynamic American economy and its capacity to utilize English-language communication pathways were important to the revival's spread. The British Empire was still in existence and English was widely spoken across the globe. Travel for English-language speakers in most of Africa and India was relatively straightforward, and even China, which was a different proposition altogether, had not yet been damaged by atheistic communism. There are still questions to be asked about the role of other revivals and of ordinary men and women who, without the quasi-celebrity status of missionaries, worked hard to spread the full gospel. For now, we turn to India and an extraordinary religious outpouring there.[69]

India

The outpouring of the Holy Spirit in India was in the context of the ministry of Pandita Ramabai (1858–1922) and Minnie Abrams (1859–1912). Although born as a high-caste Hindu, Ramabai had converted to Christ-

---

67 Dale T. Irvin (2005), Pentecostal Historiography and Global Christianity: Rethinking the Question of Origins, *Pneuma* 27.1, 35–50, offers the concept of 'double consciousness' whereby 'Pentecostals experience the Holy Ghost infusing this world with a sanctifying presence in a way that does not require them to evacuate the modern world'. In this way Pentecostals can ride the 'globalizing tides of modernity' while breaking 'its totalizing hold'.

68 Augustus Cerillo Jr (2002) 'Frank Bartleman: Pentecostal "Lone Ranger" and Critic', in Goff and Wacker (eds), *Portraits*, pp. 105–22.

69 This outpouring of the Spirit was known about by Pentecostal historians from an early date. *The Apostolic Faith* reported it within a few months of its occurrence and both Stanley H. Frodsham, *With Signs Following*, Springfield, MO, Gospel Publishing House, first published in 1926, and Donald Gee's *Wind and Flame*, Nottingham, Croydon, Assemblies of God Publishing House, mention it.

ianity and, after visits to England and the United States, set up a rescue home near Pune, not far from Bombay (now Mumbai), named Mukti (or Salvation) for young Hindu widows. Although essentially an orphanage, it rapidly became a large community with training and farming facilities. Minnie Abrams was an American Methodist holiness missionary with a strong evangelistic drive. She joined Ramabai and her daughter Mano-ramabai who had worked hard – although without startling evangelistic success.[70] After hearing of revival in Australia and Wales, and realizing the crucial importance of preparatory intercession, Ramabai started to gather the young women together for daily prayer. About 70 girls joined 'this praying band' and studied the Bible. The band of 70 grew to 500 and they prayed for six months and committed many passages of Scripture to memory. The girls, however, were still timid and unwilling evangelists until one night one of the girls felt herself to be on fire, 'a baptism of fire' so it seemed. The following day there were visions of Jesus. Extensive prayer continued and the numbers of worshippers increased.

> It seemed as though God sent a wave upon wave upon us of confession and repentance. He baptized a great many others with fire; demons were cast out, the sick were healed and God wrought in marvellous power just in our own midst, and then he sent us out to the churches. God wrought in the churches round about, and gave us blessed times.[71]

Following these experiences in Mukti, a group of workers went out to an Anglican station at Aurangabad in April 1906 and it is here that speaking with tongues was added to the other phenomena.[72] The importance of the date is that it occurs at the same time as the outpouring of the Holy Spirit in Los Angeles. In other words, it cannot be argued that the Azusa Street revival was a cause of the revival in India. The two events occurred in parallel, both related to the Welsh revival as well as other revivals taking place earlier in the century. By July 1906 there were further outbreaks of speaking with tongues at the Anglican school in Bombay and by December 1906 the same thing happened at Mukti itself. As Minnie Abrams wrote:

> God sent another wave upon us with the gifts of the Spirit, that was some two years after the first mighty out-pouring. He sent the mighty spirit of prayer upon our people, and how they pleaded for salvation and the outpouring of the Spirit upon the children of God and upon the

70 Minnie Abrams (1909), 'How the Recent Revival was Brought About in India', *Latter Rain Evangel*, 6–13 July, says that 'when I went to Mukti there were just five Christians in place, only five; four besides Pandita Ramabai'.

71 Abrams, *Latter Rain Evangel*, July 1909, 11.

72 G. B. McGee (2002), 'Minnie F. Abrams: Another Context, Another Founder', in Goff and Wacker (eds), *Portraits*, pp. 87–104.

heathen. God poured out upon us a mighty wave of speaking in other tongues, and the mighty wave of interpretation; He used the Spirit of prophecy in witnessing to the heathen. He sent us out on several occasions a hundred at a time.[73]

Only in January 1907 did missionaries from Azusa Street arrive in India, and they caused theological dispute by insisting that the baptism of the Holy Spirit was only evidenced by speaking with other tongues – the line that Seymour had learned from Parham.[74] Abrams had already written a booklet, *Baptism of the Holy Ghost and Fire* (which was in its second edition by December 1906 and, significantly, found its way to Chile), in which she had referred to the restoration of speaking with tongues. But her view was that speaking with tongues denoted prayer to God rather than a special sign of Spirit baptism. The difference between the Azusa Street revival and the Mukti revival revolves around such theological variations. Ramabai and Abrams believed that the outpouring of the Holy Spirit in India was appropriate to an Indian context – Ramabai argued that Christianity in India should be expressed through Indian culture rather than pre-packaged in a form handed down from colonial masters.[75] The two revivals were similar in their evangelistic effects and in the fervour and humility they generated. Both understood the Holy Spirit to have been powerfully manifested and there were instances in offshoots of the Indian revival where speaking with tongues did, apparently, result in utterances in English by girls who could only knowingly speak Indian languages.[76] So there was a belief that tongues *could* be real languages but there did not appear to be a belief that these real languages were intended to speed up world evangelization by enabling preachers to bypass language school, nor did they identify tongues as the infallible sign of the baptism of the Spirit.

We need to add one other emerging factor that speeded up the spread of Pentecostalism. This is illustrated both by Minnie Abram's book and Seymour's newspaper. Printing enabled information to be rapidly disseminated, particularly in countries where mass literacy was now one of the benefits of universal primary education. More than this, as David Maxwell pointed out, the introduction of a Universal Postage Union in

73 Abrams, *Latter Rain Evangel*, July 1909, 11.

74 The missionaries were Alfred and Lillian Garr.

75 M. Bergunder (2005), 'Constructing Indian Pentecostalism: On Issues Of Methodology and Representation', in A. Anderson and E. Tang (eds), *Asian and Pentecostal: The Charismatic Face of Christian Asia*, Oxford, Regnum, and Baguio City, APTS, pp. 177–213, provides an extensive account of Indian Pentecostalism, though complicated by methodological discussion. See also S. Neill (1990), *A History of Christian Mission*, London, Penguin, for an account of Mukti in the context of wider Christian work.

76 McGee, 'Minnie F. Abrams', p. 98.

1875 and the system of flat-rate postage, as well as subsidies from the US Congress to steamship companies, linked North America to Europe and the rest of the world.[77] The postal service was the internet of its day and the flow of information around the world increased abundantly.

The Pentecostal Baptism Restored
The Promised Latter Rain Now Being Poured Out on God's Humble People

All along the ages, men have been preaching a partial Gospel. A part of the Gospel remained when the world went into the dark ages. God has from time to time raised up men to bring back the truth to the church. He raised up Luther to bring back to the world the doctrine of justification by faith. He raised up another reformer in John Wesley to establish Bible Holiness in the church. Then he raised up Dr. Cullis who brought back to the world the wonderful doctrine of divine healing. Now He is bringing back the Pentecostal Baptism to the church.

God laid His hand on a little crippled boy seven years of age, healed him of disease, and made him whole except his ankles. He walked on the sides of his ankles. When he was fourteen years of age, he had been sent to college and God had called him to preach. One day as he was sitting reading his Bible, a man came for him to go and hold a meeting. He began to say to the Lord: 'Father, if I go to that place, it will be necessary for me to walk here and yonder, just put strength into these ankle joints of mine.' And immediately he was made whole and leaped and praised God, like the man at the beautiful gate. He has since been in evangelistic work all over the United States, seeing multitudes saved, sanctified and healed.

Five years ago, God put it into this man's heart (Bro. Charles Parham) to go over to Topeka, Kansas, to educate missionaries to carry the Gospel. It was a faith school and the Bible was the only textbook. The students had gathered there without tuition or board, God sending in the means to carry on the work. Most of the students had been religious workers and said they had received the baptism with the Holy Ghost a number of years ago. Bro. Parham became convinced that there was no religious school that tallied up with the second chapter of Acts. Just before the first of January 1901, the Bible School began to study the word on the baptism with the Holy Ghost to discover the Bible evidence of the baptism that they might obtain it.

Taken from W. J. Seymour's newspaper, *The Apostolic Faith* 1.2, October 1906

---

77 David Maxwell (2006), *African Gifts of the Spirit: Pentecostalism and the Rise of a Zimbabwean Transnational Religious Movement*, Oxford, James Currey, pp. 27–32.

Summing up

In this long chapter we have looked at the historical components that came to make up Pentecostalism. We have looked at the people involved, their cultural milieu and the differences among the nations where similar revivals broke out. We have shown how Pentecostal doctrine grew out of existing holiness doctrines in the nineteenth century and how the combination of these doctrines with revivalism eventually gave birth to Pentecostalism. We need to add that on top of a belief in healing and sanctification Pentecostals understood that their new religious life had arrived at a foreordained point on God's calendar. Pentecostalism was believed to be the prophetically anticipated 'latter rain' and not merely a series of sporadic and disconnected revivals scattered across the world. The crystallization of a new pattern of beliefs joined to revival experience at a point in modern history when methods of communication, printing and transport were breaking out in new directions, to create a religious movement that, over the twentieth century, would change much of Christianity and therefore the world.

Cross-references to the SCM Reader *Pentecostal and Charismatic Studies*

2.1 Charles F. Parham, 'The Latter Rain', *Apostolic Faith*, December 1950–January 1951, pp. 3 and 15, abridged (pp. 10–13).
2.2 W. J. Seymour, in *Apostolic Faith*, September 1906, p. 1 (p. 13).
2.3 F. Bartleman, *Azusa Street*, Plainfield, NJ, Bridge Publishing, 1925, ch. 3 abridged (pp. 14–17).
2.4 A. A. Boddy, 'Whitsun Convention Sunderland', *Confidence*, May 1910 (pp. 17–18).
2.5 Guy Shields, *Camp-Meeting Special*, Amarillo, TX, Nebraska District Council, 1953, pp. 10–14, abridged (pp. 18–19).
2.6 George R. Hawtin, Latter Rain *'Letter to Wayne Warner'*, Flower Pentecostal Heritage Center, Springfield, MO, 65802, 15 December 1987 (pp. 19–21).

Questions to think about

1 Why did speaking in tongues become a vital part of Pentecostalism?
2 In what ways might healing and speaking in tongues be connected?
3 Do you think it is important to understand how early Pentecostals understood themselves? Or is it just as valid to understand them only in our own terms? Or should we try both kinds of understanding?

4 Can we think of the early inter-racial religious revivals as a model for modern Pentecostalism?

5 Why were many Pentecostals unhappy about religious organization? Should religion be organized or is it better if it is 'free'?

6 How should we contrast Charles Fox Parham and W. J. Seymour? From what has been said in this chapter, which man might have the better claim to be 'the founder of Pentecostalism'? Or should we think of them both as founders? Or would it be better not to think in these terms at all?

Further reading

Alexander, Kimberley Ervin (2006), *Pentecostal Healing: Models in Theory and Practice*, Blandford Forum, Deo.

Goff Jr., J. R. and Wacker. G. (eds) (2002), *Portraits of a Generation*, Fayetteville, University of Arkansas Press.

Maxwell, D. (2006), *African Gifts of the Spirit: Pentecostalism and the Rise of a Zimbabwean Transnational Religious Movement*, Oxford, James Currey.

Robeck Jr, C. M. (2006), *The Azusa Street Mission and Revival*, Nashville, TN, Nelson Reference & Electronic.

4

Consolidation

Introduction

Black and white Charlie Chaplin silent films give us an impression of
West Coast America before the 1914–18 war and at the time of the Azusa
Street revival. Authority represented by the policeman on the beat chases
the comic tramp in a cameo of stratified society. Black and white photographs of the Football Association Cup Final in London at the same time
show large crowds standing obediently around the pitch with hardly a
policeman in sight. These were the men who, in response to a patriotic
call, marched off to the trenches to be gassed and machine-gunned. In
South Africa, a mixed British and Dutch colonial society grew wealthy on
trade and, as in the United States, a large impoverished black population
served. These were different times from those we live in today. Nevertheless, the similarities between the past and present are sufficient to allow
us to reconstruct the choices faced by early Pentecostals. As today, the
law allowed religious freedom: religious groups could buy land, preach,
evangelize, publish and attract crowds. As today, religious groups faced
a measure of opposition and scorn, and new groups very often found
themselves socially located among the poor.

The story of Pentecostalism has been told in terms of doctrinal development and missionary endeavour, but in this chapter we examine a crucial element in the survival of the movement. Looking at examples from
among the many that could be chosen from all over the world, we look
at the formation of denominations in the United States, South Africa,
Norway and Britain.

From revivals to denominations

Pentecostals were resistant to organization – at least at the beginning of
the twentieth century. It is easy to see why someone who had found their
faith in the hot excitement of revival reacted against the idea of enforce-
able practices or dampening authority. Yet, the trouble with revival was
that it did not know what to do with the crowds it attracted. If a revival

74

was to endure, then, to use the biblical phrase, 'new wine must be put into new bottles', new congregations must be put into new structures. There would have to be arrangements for paying for structures and ministers, of deciding when a congregation should meet, which missionaries it might support, what it believed, and which visiting preachers to welcome or to shun.

Organization was unavoidable. We have already noted that Charles Parham began to organize his Apostolic Faith movement in the Texas area in the years preceding the Azusa Street revival. He appointed state directors of groups of congregations and, in this, he was following the long-established notion of installing bishops.[1] The bishop, from the early centuries of Christianity, was a minister with authority over more than one congregation and, typically, each bishop held jurisdiction over his diocese, with several parishes in each diocese. Even if the terminology of 'dioceses' and 'parishes' was not used, the same idea was widespread: there would be a religious authority over a large geographical area and that large geographical area would be divided up into smaller geographical areas, each of which contained one or more congregations looked after by local ministers. So the organization of Christianity in its Roman Catholic, Orthodox and Protestant forms included this kind of tiered leadership. Charles Parham, when he registered in Texas, may or may not have consciously been copying historic Christian organizational patterns. More likely, he believed himself to be copying the pattern of the book of Acts within the New Testament. Here apostles travelled over wide areas but left behind 'elders' to look after local congregations. It was not difficult to equate apostles with bishops or to equate elders with local ministers.

The point of Parham's organization, and of most denominations, is that there is authority within the system. Bishops are senior to local ministers and expect to carry weight in matters of doctrine and organization. But there is another kind of religious organization that is less dependent upon a tiered structure with authority flowing down from above. This is the 'association' that members join because they share common beliefs or values and wish to support each other in the expression of them. The holiness associations of the nineteenth century were like this, as were the camp-meeting associations.[2] In each case an association draws up membership criteria, aims, a written constitution and, usually, the requirement that members make a financial contribution. Associations will often hold annual gatherings where decisions are made and, since associations

---

1 J. R. Goff (1988), *Fields White Unto Harvest: Charles F. Parham and the Missionary Origins of Pentecostalism*, Fayetteville, University of Arkansas Press, p. 118.

2 Cf. Charles Edwin Jones (1974), *Perfectionist Persuasion: The Holiness Movement and American Methodism, 1867–1936*, Metuchen, NJ, Scarecrow Press, p. 47.

are voluntarily entered into, they tend to be democratic. They also have one other indispensable feature: people or congregations can be members of more than one association at a time. By contrast, denominations almost invariably insisted on exclusivity: you could not simultaneously be a Baptist and a Methodist.

Many early Pentecostals, or people who became Pentecostals, would previously have been members of religious associations as well as of religious denominations. Even if they did not analyse precisely how these social groupings operated, they would have been aware of the advantages such arrangements offered. When we look at the three revivals – in Wales, in Azusa Street, in Mukti – it is clear that the protagonists in each case, Evan Roberts, W. J. Seymour and Minnie Abrams, belonged to religious denominations or, at any rate, had at one time belonged to them. Roberts was training for Calvinistic Methodist ministry, Seymour had received some Methodist training and had been a member of the organization set up by Parham, and Abrams was also a Methodist. Even those not involved in revivals, like Alexander Dowie or Frank Sandford, had also once been ordained in recognized denominations. It is not surprising that these people in one way or another wanted to establish their own religious groupings, whether these were associations or denominations.

Within the United States and within most other Western countries there were legal and financial advantages in belonging to a religious organization. Within the United States there were advantages connected with cheaper rail travel for ministers. Within Britain, religious organizations could own buildings and benefit from the tax exemptions given to charities. In each country the practical benefits of religious organization were slightly different but important enough to be an incentive for the setting up of a denomination with its own name and its own support system for ministers. Most of the denominations that came into existence contained the following elements: a process whereby their own ministers were inducted and credentialled (ordination); a process for unifying the aims and activities of the ministers (often a magazine or annual conference); a training school for their ministers (which might be residential, or non-residential and part-time); a set of cherished beliefs that marked out the denomination from other similar groups.

The denomination had several serious advantages for Pentecostals. First, the denomination provided clarity over what its members actually and in detail believed. Second, it provided a sense of belonging, coherence and security to its members, especially by enabling dispassionate authoritative rebuttals of anti-Pentecostal invective. Third, it provided a back-up system in case something went wrong at the local level. Fourth, it provided continuity over time allowing a congregation, if it lost its minister, to replace him or her by someone who was trained, recognized and recommended. Fifth, it provided social status for its ministers. Sixth, if the denomination provided annual conferences or camp meetings, there was a chance to meet up with other like-minded believers from different parts of the country.

The denomination, as an organization and regardless of the actual religious beliefs of its members, had a durability that enabled it to adapt and survive in a variety of social environments. The creation of a denomination was like the founding of the town or the setting up of a commercial business. It would attract men and women with complementary skills and talents who, together, would be able to achieve more than they might achieve separately. Someone might be a good accountant, another person might be a good children's worker and a third person might have a good understanding of how to put up or repair buildings. Together these people shared their expertise and, across the breadth of the denomination, enabled it to grow and prosper.

In terms of sociological theory, religious groups were often thought to start as sects with hostile attitudes to the surrounding culture.[3] Sects typically drew sharp boundaries around themselves so as to distinguish their activities and beliefs from those of the culture in which they found themselves. Then, gradually, over time, sects came to moderate their views and to see the surrounding culture and other religious organizations as legitimate entities. So there is a well-known transformative path from sect to denomination. The denomination is relativistic in its acceptance of other denominations. A Methodist will accept a Baptist and each will acknowledge the validity of the beliefs and lifestyle of the other. So once Pentecostals began to organize themselves into groups they were, particularly if they took on the features of a denomination, going down a road that would lead them to accept organizational variations and alternative systems of belief. For this reason, some tough-minded Pentecostals were unwilling to compromise and wished to retain their own sectarian attitudes, but others, especially those who had originated in other church backgrounds, could see Pentecostalism as the culmination of (for instance) Methodist or holiness beliefs. It is not that Methodist or holiness beliefs were wrong but simply that they had not finally been crowned with Pentecostal experience.

Four examples

Assemblies of God in the United States

The formation of Pentecostal denominations is best documented in the United States. In the period between the Azusa Street revival and the formation of what became the largest denomination, Assemblies of

---

3 B. R. Wilson (1966), *Religion in a Secular Society*, London, Watts and Co.

God, in 1914, Pentecostalism was found within independent missions and churches all over North America.[4] 'One can find almost any practice in the "free" Pentecostal assemblies.'[5] These assemblies encouraged non-credential itinerant ministers and allowed unlicensed missionaries to solicit funds. The unlicensed missionaries then wasted much of their time travelling backwards and forwards between one country and another without doing anything useful.[6] There were also idiosyncratic private Bible schools that relied upon prophecy and interpretation of tongues for the teaching of students – a practice bound to lead to doctrinal disaster.

By 1913 thoughtful leaders came to realize that unless attempts were made to bring order out of Pentecostal chaos the effects of the early revivals would soon be dissipated.[7] E. N. Bell, after his Spirit baptism, came into contact with a group of preachers in Texas who had broken free of Charles Fox Parham. When Bell and those now connected with him began to work with a loose association of preachers that called itself the Church of God in Christ, the beginnings of a denomination were visible. Bell called a meeting in April 1914 to discuss the way forward and, despite verbose criticism from 'free' Pentecostals on one side and evangelicals on the other, about 300 people, of whom a third were ministers and missionaries, met in Hot Springs, Arkansas, to discuss five things: unity, stabilization, missions, the legal chartering of the movement, and the setting up of Bible schools. The Hot Springs participants accepted voluntary co-operation and did not, at first, adopt a statement of faith. They agreed to meet the following year and, in the interim, appointed 12 men to act as an Executive Presbytery. Arrangements were made to credential worthy ministers and two Bible schools were recommended. The meeting was deemed a success. Several hundred ministers transferred their existing credentials to the new body, which called itself 'the General Council of the Assemblies of God'.

Within a short time contradictory doctrinal beliefs ruffled the smooth surface of the new grouping. There was dispute over whether believers should expect an intermediate stage of sanctification prior to their baptism in the Spirit. This was relatively easily dealt with: everyone could

---

4 The account has been taken from E. V. Blumhofer (1985), *The Assemblies of God: A Popular History*, Springfield, MO, Radiant Books.

5 Blumhofer, *Assemblies*, p. 34.

6 G. B. McGee (2004), *People of the Spirit: The Assemblies of God*, Springfield, MO, Gospel Publishing House, p. 111.

7 Although, as we have said, many early Assemblies of God ministers were influenced by Wesleyan Holiness thought, it is also true that prominent individuals were influenced by A. B. Simpson and the Christian and Missionary Alliance. Simpson and the college at Nyack were reformed in theology, and so this stream of spirituality also contributed to what became the largest Pentecostal denomination in the USA.

agree that what mattered was sanctification itself rather than the stages by which it was reached. A more serious challenge to the new group took place over the mode of water baptism that Pentecostals should adopt and, ultimately, over the nature of God. In 1915 Pentecostal preachers at a camp meeting in California believed they had received a new revelation that water baptism should be in the name of 'Jesus only' rather than in the more usual name of 'the Father, the Son and the Spirit' given in Matthew 28.19. This baptismal formula came then to be associated with the belief that God was manifested in successive modes as Father, as Son and then as Holy Spirit or, rather, that 'Father, Son and Holy Spirit' were titles for *one* person, that is, Jesus. To many believers this teaching appeared to sanction a form of Unitarianism that contradicted the historic doctrines of mainstream Christianity. At the 1916 General Council meeting, after a complicated debate covering both religious doctrine and decision-making procedure, the majority voted for a statement of fundamental truths expressing trinitarian evangelical theology. The Oneness believers, as they came to be called, left to form their own organization.

The General Council became the supreme decision-making body for its remaining trinitarian Pentecostals, a centre of authority. This council comprised all the ministers – all those holding credentials – within the churches (or 'assemblies', as they were called) belonging to Assemblies of God. So, in essence, the denomination organized itself democratically because anybody could speak at the annual conference and decisions were made by voting. The General Council chose an Executive Presbytery by voting a few of its members into office. In other words, there was no ecclesiastical rank between one member of the council and another. All members were at the same level but, by a vote, one minister could be placed on a Presbytery (or committee) that was given a leadership role. It is easy to see how this system provided stability based on an adaptable consensus of opinion. Wild practices or contested teachings could be discussed in an agreed forum and rationally assessed.

Although the General Council was the supreme body within Assemblies of God, individual congregations were given the right to govern themselves. It was this combination of local self-government and a national authoritative body that particularly appealed to many of the early Pentecostals. Within his or her own congregation the minister was firmly in charge; but some distance away, both geographically and psychologically, the General Council existed for advice, inspiration and identity. Nearer to home, local congregations might band together into separate districts or regions and function co-operatively. Whenever a national question arose, it could be debated at the General Council. Whenever missionary strategy was questioned, again the General Council was the forum for decisions about funding and credentials, though relatively permanent subcommittees were eventually spun off from the council for such specialist purposes. By contrast, the day-to-day running of the congregation was in the minister's hands and he or she could buy buildings, preach whatever he or she wanted (as long as it agreed with the *Statement of Fundamental Truths*) and negotiate pay and holidays in line with local customs.

This was a model for denominational life that could, and was, transplanted to other countries. The *Statement of Fundamental Truths* ensured doctrinal unity while at the local level there was operational flexibility. Over time the centralizing structures gradually inflated, using the money sent in by each congregation to fund full-time national officers who, after a generation, came to be situated in a large office block from where publishing interests were directed. The disorganized revival solidified into an organized denomination.

Apostolic Faith Mission in South Africa

Pentecostal denominations were formed in a variety of ways. The formation of the Assemblies of God in the United States resulted from the drawing together of separate independent ministers and churches. The formation of the Apostolic Faith Mission in South Africa followed a different pattern.

We can go back to three separate factors that prepared the way for its formation. First, there was a large revival in the Dutch Reformed Church in the 1860s and this was followed by smaller revivals in 1874 and 1884. These revivals, like all revivals, loosened formality in church life and prioritized religious experience.[8] Second, Andrew Murray, one-time moderator of the Reformed Church in South Africa, emphasized the importance of holiness. He propagated teachings on holiness similar to those found in holiness circles in the United States; just as holiness doctrine was preparatory to Pentecostalism there, so it was in South Africa. The South African War of 1899–1902 between Britain and the Dutch settlers also had an indirect effect. It created intense hardship in the Afrikaans-speaking population, and when during the war Afrikaner prisoners were interned in prison camps, holiness teaching reached them and predisposed them to powerful religious experiences, including speaking with tongues and apocalyptic visions.[9]

Third, the powerful voice of Alexander Dowie was to be heard in

---

8 The Dutch Reformed Church agreed at its synod in 1857 that there would be separate church buildings for black and for white Christians. See A. Smit (1945), *After Two Hundred Years*, Cape Town, UCT Publications, p. 304. The revivals did not alter this practice, and even Andrew Murray accepted racially separate congregations. All that can be said was that this was at least a better conclusion than the earlier one adopted by the DRC which forbade gospel preaching to blacks.

9 David Maxwell (2006), *African Gifts of the Spirit*, Oxford, James Currey, p. 39.

South Africa – not in person to be sure, but through the extensive reach of his printing press. Zion-type congregations were formed and these cultivated links with Zion City in Chicago. Among those who did so was P. L. le Roux who worked with large congregations situated near the Johannesburg gold mines and with the urban poor. Meanwhile, among those who belonged to Zion City in Chicago were John G. Lake and Tom Hesmalhalch. Both these men left Zion around the time of its collapse and they and their wives soon afterwards received Spirit baptism at the Azusa Street revival before leaving to spearhead missionary work in South Africa. They disembarked in May 1908 and, not unnaturally given their background, soon got in touch with the Zion work in the Johannesburg area.[10] An African Pentecost followed as Lake developed an impressive ministry of healing. There were numerous extraordinary miracles, which resulted in the expansion of Pentecostalism into buildings formerly owned by Zion churches. As was the case in the United States and elsewhere, Pentecostalism then spread rapidly along communication pathways which, in the case of South Africa, had been created through Zion teaching.[11]

Among its converts were impoverished blacks who in many instances turned out to be outstanding evangelists, particularly as they were able to speak African languages as well as English and often Afrikaans. The Afrikaners themselves found Pentecostalism appealing after they had been impoverished by war and disorientated by the destruction of their traditional way of life. Gambling, promiscuity and drunkenness were countered by Pentecostal holiness teaching.[12] And the Afrikaans lifestyle, with its trekking and ox wagons, made Afrikaners excellent evangelists, spreading the Pentecostal message wherever they went.

Pentecostalism was inter-racial in its earliest days. Lake had learned from Seymour in Los Angeles. In September 1908 the Apostolic Faith Mission (AFM) was formally constituted with an Executive Council of seven men, which in 1909 was made up of five Americans and two Afrikaners. A year later the proportions were reversed.[13] Seymour had used the name 'Apostolic Faith', which of course Parham had also used. By adding the word 'Mission' to the title, Lake and others were showing that this was not a denomination but a missionary outpost from the Azusa Street revival: they identified with its zealous beliefs in the baptism in the

---

10 Lake was from America rather than Britain or the Netherlands, that is, he was not from one of the colonial powers. This must have made him all the more welcome to South Africans.

11 I have only used the term 'Zionist' sparingly because it is frequently applied to the quest associated with Theodore Herzl to find a homeland for the Jewish diaspora.

12 Maxwell , *African Gifts*, p. 41.

13 Allan Anderson (2007), *Spreading Fires*, London, SCM Press, p. 171.

Holy Spirit and divine healing. Indeed, Lake and the others could hardly have made their position clearer:

> Who are we? And what do we teach and practice? We are known as the Apostolic Faith Movement of Johannesburg, SA, which is included in the great world-wide Holy Ghost Revival which has taken its impetus from the work of the Azusa Street Mission, Los Angeles, California.[14]

The mission in Johannesburg appears to have grown out of the mother church set up in the former Zion building that was the centre of Lake's powerful ministry. Later, and again copying the Azusa Street pattern, the AFM began to credential its ministers by issuing certificates very similar to those that had been issued by Seymour. In the earliest days there was a reciprocal relationship between the AFM and the Zion congregations. Each supported the other and there were common practices and beliefs, especially divine healing and clapping during worship. But, when Lake and his colleague Hesmalhalch had to return to the United States in 1912, le Roux became president of the AFM in 1913, a post he was to retain until 1943. After about two years the relationship between the AFM and the largely black Zionist movement began to deteriorate. AFM black leaders were sidelined and only whites were given positions of authority. The mixture between paternalism and racism gave black leaders little choice but to work in their own way inside the Zion churches or within their own branch of the AFM.[15] Pentecostalism within Southern Africa was only partially protected through the establishment of denominations. The early founders of the AFM deliberately avoided denominational thinking and constituted themselves as a limited company, that is, on a commercial basis rather than as a church.[16] Yet, in the period after 1915 during le Roux's tenure, defensive organizational patterns emerged in response to the hostility shown by mainline clergy.[17] Pentecostalism was tamed and damped down – some would say perverted – and, although doctrine was preserved, the fault lines that ran through African society were replicated.[18] The AFM, led by whites, curried favour with the Dutch Reformed Church and so identified all too closely with the ruling white

---

14 Quoted by Cecil M. Robeck Jr (2006), *The Azusa Street Mission and Revival*, Nashville, TN, Nelson, p. 278.

15 Japie LaPoorta (1999), 'Unity of Division: A Case Study of the Apostolic Faith Mission of South Africa', in Murray W. Dempster, Byron D. Klaus and Douglas Petersen (eds), *The Globalization of Pentecostalism: A Religion Made to Travel*, Carlisle, Paternoster Press, pp. 150–69.

16 Maxwell, *African Gifts*, p. 42.

17 Maxwell, *African Gifts*, p. 42.

18 See a discussion of Pentecostalism fighting against oppression in Amos Yong (2006), 'Justice Deprived, Justice Demanded: Afropentecostalisms and the Task of World Pentecostal Theology Today', *Journal of Pentecostal Theology* 15.1, 127–47.

elite. Pentecostal doctrine was conserved in a more precise form within the AFM and in a more Africanized version within the Zion churches, both of which survived through the rest of the twentieth century.

Pentecostalism in Norway

From a sociological point of view, the formation of Pentecostal groupings in Norway is interesting. Essentially, the movement started by attempting to maintain an interdenominational stance towards Methodists and Baptists while cultivating friendly connections with Lutherans as well. This became impossible to sustain. Pentecostals then attempted a loose association that eventually gave way to a tighter and more precise organization. These relational changes were partly driven by the refinement and hardening of Pentecostal doctrines.

The story can be told by looking at the life of Thomas Ball Barratt (1862–1940), an Englishman whose father emigrated to Norway. The young Barratt, who came from a strong Methodist family, became fluent in both English and Norwegian, a factor that was later to facilitate his extensive travels. Sources for Barratt's life can be found in the 60 or so pamphlets and books he published in English and Norwegian as well as numerous articles in the newspaper *Byposten*, which he founded in 1904. He also published an autobiography in 1927, *When the Fire Fell and an Outline of My Life*, and this provides an insight into his spiritual development but without giving details of all the doctrinal and institutional changes he passed through.[19]

Barratt was clearly a gifted and passionate young man. He started preaching when he was about 17 and by 1882, when he was 20, he passed the Methodist examination as a local preacher for the Methodist Episcopal Church of Norway. From 1885 he was a preacher in the second Methodist church in Christiana (Oslo), the capital city. In 1889 he was appointed pastor of the third Methodist church in Oslo. The vast majority of the population of Norway was Lutheran, and Methodists, as dissenters, felt themselves undervalued and denied their religious rights. Barratt made contributions to local political elections and wrote in favour of dissenters and the local temperance society (which campaigned against the selling and drinking of alcohol).[20] Even at this early point in his life Barratt was socially engaged. He proclaimed an evangelistic message coupled with a concern for the poor. He had good relations with the Lutheran Home Mission.[21] His move to Oslo, by far the largest city in Norway, relocated him in the centre of population where there were

---

19 Thomas Ball Barratt (1927), *When the Fire Fell and an Outline of My Life*, printed by Alfons Hansen and Sonner.

20 Barratt, *Fire*, p. 72.

21 Barratt, *Fire*, p. 73.

around 225,000 inhabitants. The demographics of Norway are such that the whole country could be affected by evangelistic meetings in the capital. After all, any meeting involving, say, 2,000 people was reaching nearly 2% of the urban population, whereas in London or New York, a meeting of the same size would have touched a much smaller percentage of the total. The result was that when in 1903 Barratt launched an impassioned plea for the setting up of an independent Oslo City Mission this made a considerable impact.[22] Barratt had already become the superintendent of the Methodist Church's welfare work in the city, but he wanted something more substantial from which to launch his gamut of activities. The Methodist Conference allowed Barratt to become the city missionary but refused to pay him any salary or any housing allowance.[23]

From this distance in time it is impossible to analyse exactly what was happening, but it appears that the Methodists had Barratt marked down as an up-and-coming man but also as a firebrand. The decision to allow him to function as a city missionary without a salary smacks of internal politics and plain meanness. Barratt, however, grasped the opportunity and, with the help of one or two supportive Methodist bishops, was able to begin his new role in 1902.[24] He launched into a series of meetings in concert halls, student halls, hotels, theatres and in the open air and took up philanthropic work of many kinds as well as going out to other parts of the country to hold meetings. Newspaper reports spread accounts of his activities and he was seen as leading a 'forward movement' within the church. It was in this context that he began *Byposten*, the paper that publicized his activities and provided theological articles and news.

Barratt's early efforts to organize the Mission, which still did not have a proper building of its own, took place across a broad front. Significantly, people could join the Mission *without leaving the state church*, so that it was possible to remain a Lutheran while dabbling in Methodism. At that time the law in Norway allowed the formation of 'a mission' but did demand that anybody who joined other churches should leave the state church.[25] In other words, everybody was presumed to be a member of the Lutheran state church unless he or she actively and consciously left it. This made it difficult for non-Lutherans to grow their churches since there was always a residual reluctance to leave Lutheranism behind. Eventually, to raise funds, Barratt decided to go to the United States where there was a large Methodist community as well as an expatriate Norwegian community. He left with episcopal letters of recommendation

---

22 Barratt, *Fire*, p. 87. Dated 1903, though by some accounts the Mission started a year earlier.

23 Barratt, *Fire*, p. 77.

24 Barratt, *Fire*, p. 79.

25 Barratt, *Fire*, p. 95.

in his pocket and every hope that he would be able to persuade the rich Americans to support his beloved Oslo City Mission.

But things did not turn out as he had hoped and, according to David Bundy, he was caught up in internal misunderstandings between the Methodist Mission Board and the Methodist bishops: 'The Mission Board actively hindered his efforts.'[26] As a result, Barratt found himself stranded in New York, 'penniless but forbidden to return to Norway by the Methodist bishops'.[27] He was separated from his wife and children for about a year and his careful plan for very small but regular financial contributions from large numbers of churches came to nothing. It was at this time that he heard about the outpouring of the Holy Spirit in Azusa Street and read a copy of *The Apostolic Faith*, published in September 1906. He immediately corresponded with Azusa Street and began earnestly to search for his own Spirit baptism. His autobiography details the extensive spiritual experiences he underwent, especially as, at the urging of the Azusa Street correspondents, he was unsatisfied with any experience that did not result in speaking with other tongues. After prolonged prayer and fasting, and while he was staying at A. B. Simpson's Christian and Missionary Alliance house, he began to feel that he had received the Holy Spirit, though only some time later did he actually speak in tongues. His experience helped to shape his later doctrine and he understood the 'full' baptism in the Spirit to be accompanied by tongues, whatever other wild surgings of spiritual fire he had previously felt in his heart.[28]

He informed his readers in Norway about his experiences through *Byposten*. He then sailed home via Liverpool with a party of Azusa Street missionaries on their way to Africa with whom he had presumably consolidated his Pentecostal views. Barratt's return and the subsequent Pentecostal revival hit the front pages of the newspapers in Norway. Queues formed outside the services and for two or three weeks there were all kinds of typically revivalistic phenomena, including trembling, jumping, dancing, glossolalia and visions. There was also exorcism and 'holy laughter'. The Methodist Church rapidly made up its mind about all this and stood firm against the revival. One of its bishops wrote to Barratt telling him that he was dividing the church and that, if he persisted, he would have to resign from the Methodist Conference and drop down to the status of local preacher. So, Barratt resigned.

During 1907 Pentecostalism spread to at least 51 different places in Norway and attempted to operate on inclusive ideals similar to those

---

26 David Bundy (1992), 'Spiritual Advice to a Seeker: Letters to T. B. Barratt from Azusa St, 1906', *Pneuma* 14.2, 159–70.

27 Bundy, 'Spiritual Advice', p. 160.

28 The decisive meeting took place on 26 December 1906. See N. Bloch-Hoell (1964), *The Pentecostal Movement*, London, Allen and Unwin, p. 67; this book gives the best overview of Barratt's life.

used by the Christian and Missionary Alliance. This did not work, however, because a considerable number of those who were Pentecostals had originally been Baptists who insisted on baptizing by total immersion all those who joined the Pentecostals – even if they had previously been baptized as infants. This dispute over baptism was to cause rancour within the spreading Pentecostal movement. Barratt had initially opposed baptism by immersion since this allowed Lutherans and others to move much more easily into the Oslo City Mission without undergoing rites that would incense the state church. After a short time Barratt set out on his travels again. Within a year or two he spread Pentecostalism, or aided its spread, to England, Finland, Switzerland, Germany, the Netherlands and, later, to India, Syria and Palestine.

But, by 1909 Barratt was back in Norway and starting to impose order on Pentecostal believers. He quickly realized that outrageous doctrines were being circulated – some believers apparently thought that they had 'the gift of damnation' (whatever that meant) – and so Barratt set up a process whereby preachers were only accepted on the basis of reliable recommendations, which was the first step towards some form of denomination. Meanwhile, Barratt changed the name of his newspaper to the *Victory of the Cross* (*Korsets Seier*), secured new premises for his own headquarters in Oslo and presided over regular meetings which came to be less unpredictable and charismatic in their character. In 1910 Barratt set out 'general principles for the preservation and promotion of the Pentecostal brotherhood'. He proposed an alliance of independent Pentecostal assemblies that allowed preachers who were recommended to the group by one to be accepted by all. The emphasis was still interdenominational: 'We don't work for an assembly or a denomination but for Jesus!'[29] In 1912 Barratt, again issuing a statement concerning Pentecostalism, stressed missions and social welfare, though he also strengthened his generally biblical and evangelical statement of gospel beliefs. What had the effect of bringing Pentecostals into unity more than anything written down was a series of international conferences. The first of these was held in June 1911 when Pentecostals from the United States, England, Germany, Finland, Sweden and Denmark came, and about 2,000 people gathered. A year later another conference was organized, and, according to Bloch-Hoell, Barratt appeared to have left revivalism and moved in the direction of more orderly conduct in Pentecostal meetings.[30]

In 1913, Barratt finally came down on the side of water baptism by immersion, a move that immediately estranged him from large numbers of people who were friendly to the Pentecostal movement but retained a commitment to infant baptism. In 1916, he officially established his own

---

29 Bloch-Hoell, *Pentecostal Movement*, p. 70.
30 Bloch-Hoell, *Pentecostal Movement*, p. 72.

independent Pentecostal congregation in Oslo, and stipulated that adult baptism by immersion was enjoined upon all believers after 1919. Surprisingly, this step resulted in the expansion of Barratt's mother church from 200 members to more than 1,700 by 1933.[31]

The open interdenominational period of Pentecostalism ran for about ten years, from 1906 to 1916, but once Barratt stipulated that water baptism and other Pentecostal distinctives were incumbent upon the membership of his church, he had effectively built doctrinal walls around his Pentecostal sheep. He had established a denomination that was intended to preserve Pentecostal life and belief and, although revivalistic phenomena occurred from time to time when visiting evangelists and healing preachers came for special meetings, it appears that Pentecostalism settled down into the normal rhythm of church life and mission. By 1933 the mother congregation supported more than 40 evangelists in addition to a permanent staff – an indication not only of its intent but of its stable organizational features.[32]

There is one other perspective on what happened here. Discussions took place as early as 1912 at the International [Pentecostal] Council at Amsterdam about whether the Pentecostal outpouring should be seen as a movement within existing denominational structures or should be an organization separate but running alongside denominations.[33] Some of the delegates instinctively regarded any new ecclesiastical entity as undesirable. Others, like Barratt, came to regard free-standing Pentecostal churches as a necessary consequence of the revival and were prepared to fight to achieve their ends. It is arguable that the pugnacious Barratt was more clear-sighted than the delegates who, with the best motives, wanted a conciliatory solution to the innovations that Pentecostalism brought. Barratt's group is called *Pinsebevegelsen* (the Pentecostal movement). It is the largest Pentecostal denomination in Norway and now has some 30,000 members and about 300 autonomous churches.[34]

Elim in Great Britain

The Elim Pentecostal Church became a denomination in answer to the organizational needs of the revivalism of George Jeffreys and the congregations associated with his ministry. Simple interdenominational beginnings and ideals gave way to a central organization stamped with Jeffreys' personality and functioning as a new religious movement.

By common consent George Jeffreys was the greatest British evangelist

---

31 Barratt resigned completely from the Methodist Church in 1916.
32 Bloch-Hoell, *Pentecostal Movement*, p. 73.
33 See *Confidence*, December 1912, pp. 283, 284.
34 I am grateful to Geir Lie for this information.

of the twentieth century.[35] Born in 1889 in Maesteg, South Wales, his conversion and early religious life was interfused with the Welsh revival of 1904–05. He learned to preach in the open air, came to appreciate the interplay between spontaneous revivalistic phenomena and ordered church services, and, as Pentecostalism was taking shape, he looked for and found the baptism with the Holy Spirit accompanied with speaking in other tongues. He probably received the experience in Bournemouth in 1910.[36] In 1911 he and his brother were baptized in water by immersion. In 1912, George, whose fees were paid by the wealthy Cecil Polhill, entered the Pentecostal Missionary Union's (PMU) school in Preston run by Thomas Myerscough.[37] Meanwhile George's older brother, Stephen, conducted a mission in Swansea that was so successful that George left the school to help. The two brothers, referred to in *Confidence* as 'the Welsh revivalists',[38] preached wherever they were invited to go and undeniably stirred the embers of revival in South Wales. Unannounced, Alexander Boddy visited them in March 1913 and was impressed enough to invite them to speak at the Sunderland convention. *Confidence* regularly thereafter reported the progress of the brothers, so we can trace their steps to Llanelli, Plymouth, Ireland, Hereford, London and Belfast.[39] The Sunderland conventions appear to have had an entirely beneficial impact upon the Jeffreys brothers.[40] They introduced the two young men to a much wider circle of Christians than they were accustomed to and helped them understand the role of the Pentecostal movement in relation to the rest of the church and, by extension, the rest of the world.

As a result of the 1913 Sunderland convention a delegate from Belfast invited George to Ireland. George hesitated, wondering whether he should take ship for the United States or if the call to Ireland was the will of God.[41] In the end Ireland won and he set out to plant a group of

---

35 D. W. Cartwright (1986), *The Great Evangelists: The Lives of George and Stephen Jeffreys*, Basingstoke, Marshall Pickering; Donald Gee (1980), *These Men I Knew*, Nottingham, Assemblies of God Publishing House; W. J. Hollenweger (1972), *The Pentecostals*, London, SCM Press.

36 Malcolm R. Hathaway (1998), 'The Elim Pentecostal Church: Origins, Development and Distinctives', in K. Warrington (ed.), *Pentecostal Perspectives*, Carlisle, Paternoster Press, p. 10.

37 *Confidence*, October 1913, p. 205.

38 *Confidence*, March 1913, p. 47. They joined forces with Dan Roberts, the brother of Evan, at one point.

39 *Confidence*, May 1914, April 1915, May 1915, August 1915, October 1915, November 1915, January 1916, and frequently thereafter.

40 Although they were both invited, only George is mentioned as preaching at the 1913 convention. Stephen did, however, join George for a mission in Silksworth near Sunderland once the convention ended. *Confidence*, December 1913, p. 244.

41 James Robinson (2005), *Pentecostal Origins*, Milton Keynes, Paternoster Press, p. 120.

churches and follow in the steps of John Wesley.[42] He preached at a Belfast convention, crossed briefly to England and then returned to Ireland in 1914. By January 1915 George had formulated a fourfold message of Jesus as saviour, baptizer in the Spirit, healer and coming king. He met with the Irish friends who had invited him to their still-undivided land and they formally proposed that

> George Jeffreys, of South Wales, who was present with us, be invited to take up a permanent evangelistic work in Ireland and that a centre be chosen for him for the purpose of establishing a church out of which evangelists should be sent into towns and villages, and that a tent be hired, for the purpose of holding a Gospel Mission during the month of July to commence the work in Ireland.[43]

They also decided that every worker should be financed 'on faith lines', which in practice meant that they shared whatever came through the offerings. The workers were called the Elim Evangelistic Band. A photograph dated 1915 shows there were five people in the original team. That year the first substantial Elim congregation was established in Belfast with Jeffreys as its pastor.[44]

Little by little and campaign by campaign, they began to plant Pentecostal congregations in the more English part of Northern Ireland (especially in areas where the Anglican Church of Ireland was strong) and in the more Scottish part between Belfast and the northern coast, a zone that was strongly Presbyterian.[45] Although the Band was notionally interdenominational in outlook, the hostility that Pentecostal converts experienced when returning to their own assemblies was such as to ensure that specifically Pentecostal churches were needed. By 1920 there were 15 new Pentecostal congregations in existence.[46] By 1921 the Elim Evangelistic Band had grown to no fewer than 22 members.

Shortly after this, a generous act had unforeseen consequences. In her will a widow left £5,000 to George Jeffreys personally, to advance his evangelistic work. The family challenged this legacy and, after legal wrangles, Jeffreys only received £1,000. Jeffreys was advised, probably by the lawyer John Leech who was by now a leading supporter of the group, to create a charitable trust to function as a property-holding body.

---

42 E. C. W. Boulton (1928), *George Jeffreys: A Ministry of the Miraculous*, London, Elim Publishing House, p. 22.

43 Quoted by A. W. Edsor (1989), *'Set Your House in Order'*, Chichester, New Wine Ministries, p. 30. Ireland was partitioned in December 1920.

44 Hathaway, 'Elim', p. 12.

45 Robinson, *Pentecostal Origins*, maps B and C.

46 D. N. Hudson (1999), 'A Schism and its Aftermath: An Historical Analysis of Denominational Discerption in the Elim Pentecostal Church, 1939–1940', PhD dissertation, King's College, London, 158, p. 2. Robinson, *Pentecostal Origins*, photograph D.

So, in 1918, the Elim Pentecostal Alliance Council was formed and this covered the three separate branches of the work: the Elim churches, the Elim Evangelistic Band and Elim mission.[47] 'Governing power was no longer in the hands of local church officers, but in the hands of the Council', a result that started a centralizing direction Jeffreys later regretted.[48] From the beginning, appointment to the Council was in Jeffreys' hands, a situation that was further tightened by constitutional changes in 1923.[49]

Whatever happened behind the scenes within the growing administrative machinery, Elim enjoyed astonishing success from 1925 until 1934. Jeffreys preached all over mainland Britain and huge crowds gathered in the halls he hired. There were accounts in the religious and secular press of conversions, healings, baptisms in the Holy Spirit, and, almost without fail, wherever Jeffreys went, he left behind thriving congregations. In 1927 on Easter Monday and right up until 1939, he hired the Royal Albert Hall in London and held a massed rally at which he would baptize 1,000 people. Members of Elim could travel up and revel in the extraordinary spiritual power on display as well as the sense of community and unity that was engendered by these gatherings. A visitor to Britain in 1934 conveyed the mesmeric impression:

> I saw through my opera glasses a strong face with a rather soft mouth, dark curly hair and a fine presence in which there was nothing calculated to play upon the emotions … the moment Jeffreys began to speak the impression of impersonality disappeared … the voice was strong … it was baritone, and full of the melody which we are accustomed to find in a Welsh voice … I did not doubt that the strong and sincere tone of the voice of Jeffreys was responsible for much of the veneration in which his followers held him.[50]

Even Donald Gee, who by no means saw eye to eye with Jeffreys, was to write:

> George Jeffreys' rise to fame became almost meteoric through his evangelistic and divine healing campaigns that soon filled the largest public halls in the country … his ministry could truly be described as that of an apostle for he not only won thousands of converts, and healed the sick, but he established churches that stand to this day … he presented his message with a logical appeal and a note of authority that was compelling.[51]

---

47 Boulton, *Jeffreys,* p. 41.

48 Hathaway, 'Elim', p. 13.

49 Hathaway, 'Elim', p. 14.

50 Robinson, *Pentecostal Origins*, p. 91, quoting R. Landau (2008) in *God is My Adventure*, Landau Press.

51 Gee, *These Men*, pp. 49, 50.

Elim came into existence, as Gee pointed out, through the ministry of one man. Centralization existed at two levels. At one, the massed rallies created a sense of identity and this was reinforced by the *Elim Evangel* (a religious periodical started in 1919) which almost invariably featured photographs of Jeffreys and reported glowingly on his campaigns. At another level, centralization existed within the constitution. Although ministers met annually, they had no right to institute change. In 1934 Jeffreys drew up the revised constitution that partially limited his authority while making him President of the Executive Council for life and allowing him to nominate three of its other eight members. By this means Jeffreys had a huge stake in the decision-making process and, since the Council controlled the *Evangel*, set the salaries of ministers, appointed and dismissed them, and was able to make binding rules for the whole organization, Jeffreys appeared to have imprinted his will upon the whole enterprise.

Although Elim saw itself as being part of the Pentecostal movement, the changes that were taking place could be interpreted according to sociological theory.[52] Jeffreys was the charismatic founder of Elim but E. J. Phillips, the Secretary-General of the Executive, was the voice of the growing bureaucracy. Nearly all the lines of communication passed through Phillips, and he – and the other ministers – became increasingly infuriated by the demands Jeffreys made, particularly when Jeffreys began to reverse some of the constitutional arrangements he had already imposed. According to Hudson:

> Phillips became the Secretary-General of the work [in 1923], a post he held until 1 September 1957. He had entered the Movement at a time when there were 'no accounts, no list of properties, the situation was hopeless' and developed the infrastructure of the Movement to the extent that it survived the loss of its founder and became a stable denomination.[53]

So the struggle between Jeffreys and Phillips could be seen as one between fire and water, between charismatic leader and bureaucratic leader. At the end of an acrimonious dispute, Jeffreys resigned from Elim in 1940 and left to found another, smaller and less successful organization.[54]

---

52 This is how B. R. Wilson (1961), *Sects and Society: The Sociology of Three Religious Groups in Britain*, London, Heinemann, understood Elim. His account is still one of the best available.

53 Hudson, *A Schism*, section 3.1.

54 The dispute concerned (a) Jeffreys's desire to allow individual Elim congregations to own their own buildings, and (b) the concern that, by reducing central control, Jeffreys would be free to go round Elim propagating the doctrine of British Israelism which he had acquired from John Leech. Jeffreys argued for (a), which the rest of Elim rejected on the grounds of (b). The church Jeffreys left to found was called the Bible-Pattern Church Fellowship.

Reflection

We can analyse the reasons or factors leading to the formation of these denominations in the table below:

Reason/factor	AG	AFM	Norway	Elim
Unity among Pentecostal believers	✓		✓[55]	
Stabilization of doctrine	✓		✓	
Missions	✓		✓	
Legal chartering	✓			✓
Setting up Bible schools	✓		✓	✓
Early interdenominational ideals	✓	✓	✓	✓
Hostility from other churches	✓	✓[56]	✓	
Single founding ministry		✓	✓	✓
Retention of people			✓	✓
Property considerations				✓
Evangelism		✓	✓	✓

The analysis is not exact because the situation surrounding the formation of these different denominations changed over time. There is also an overlap between the factors in the sense that 'Retention of people' and 'Early interdenominational ideals' are connected: where there are interdenominational ideals, people will float between one church group and another. Equally, where there is 'Hostility from other churches', it is difficult to maintain interdenominational ideals. Yet, what the analysis shows is that there are certain features that appear to be common to all the groups. The early stages of Pentecostalism in all four instances contained hopes for the whole church, hopes that the whole church across the entire Christian spectrum would be renewed and revived; and they expressed this hope by the formation of associations of various kinds. No one seems to have started off with the idea that Pentecostalism would result in brand-new denominations.

In nearly every new denomination there was a 'single founding ministry', and even when there was not, as in the case of Assemblies of God in the United States, it took only a very small number of people to call the meeting together that led to the formation of the General Council. The

---

55 This is shown by Barratt's 'general principles for the preservation and promotion of the Pentecostal brotherhood'.

56 Hostility was intensified once Barratt insisted on baptism by immersion for believers.

founding minister(s) must possess the capacity to seize the moment of revival and enough stamina to build a new organization against the odds. All of those who founded new denominations seem to have started with less grandiose plans. In each case the tipping point came with the building up of vibrant congregations: *congregations are the building blocks of denominations*, and, once congregations band together under the authority of an exclusive spiritual leader (or council), the denomination has been formed in all but name.

And when denominations *were* founded, influential Pentecostals remained vigilant about the consequences. For these Pentecostals the enforced compliance that they considered to be the consequence of denominational structures was characteristic of a false church. Such Pentecostals distinguished between a false church that coerced its members into uniform belief by fear and threats – and they had at the back of their minds the harlot church in Revelation 17 – and the true church where brotherly kindness and liberty were present. They sometimes expressed this difference by saying that the true church was not an organization but an organism, not an institution but a body.[57]

The situation in the United States was different from elsewhere because there was a large number of quasi-Pentecostal people in separate parts of the country. This is a consequence of the enormous religious vitality of the United States at the beginning of the twentieth century and of the impact of the holiness movement at the end of the previous century. Parts of England, Wales and Germany generated similar conditions, but the United States dwarfed them all in the scale and turbulence of its religious diversity.

Norway and Britain were alike in that each had a state church with certain privileges, but whereas in Norway Lutheranism had a near monopoly of the population, in Britain there was a strong Nonconformist or dissenting constituency. Consequently, the obstacles that Barratt had to overcome in Norway were unique to that country. In other respects the work of Jeffreys and Barratt was similar, and the same might have been said for the AFM in South Africa, apart from the fact that Lake, who was a powerful preacher in the same mould as Barratt and Jeffreys, returned early to the United States after the death of his wife.

In each of the countries hostility from other churches arose once Pentecostals began to be successful. This was definitely so in Norway and in the United States. In South Africa the situation looked different because the AFM was started by the missionaries whose revivalist preaching reminded others of the religious renewals experienced some years before by the Dutch Reformed Church. In Ireland, which was already a community divided between Protestants and Catholics, there were further

---

57 See Dale M. Coulter's discussion of Frank Boyd in D. M. Coulter (2005), 'Pentecostal Visions of the End: Eschatology, Ecclesiology and the Fascination of the *Left-Behind* Series', *Journal of Pentecostal Theology* 14.1, 81–98.

complicated subdivisions between the Protestants, so that at first an extra group appeared insignificant. Yet, when the Pentecostals began to muster support, the other churches tended to gang up on them, making the Pentecostals defensive and digging a ditch between Pentecostalism and the surrounding religious and social culture.

But did the formation of Pentecostal denominations preserve Pentecostalism? Here the answer must surely be 'Yes'. Pentecostalism might have drifted into the shadows and become an elusive spiritual experience within existing mainline denominations – much as happened in the 1970s when the charismatic movement began to slow down. Without the formulation of doctrine, the creation of denominational structures, the establishment of conferences, journals, Bible schools and recognized ministers, it is difficult to believe Pentecostalism would have stood through the twentieth century and remained as a force to be reckoned with. Although there were idealists and dreamers who wanted Pentecostalism to have nothing to do with humanly made committees, structures, rules and traditions, it is almost impossible to imagine repeatable spiritual experience being continued without some of these features.

Cross-references to the SCM Reader *Pentecostal and Charismatic Studies*

2.2 A. J. Tomlinson, 'Brief History of the Church that is Now Recognized as the Church of God', in A. J. Tomlinson, *The Last Great Conflict*, Cleveland, TN, Press of Walter E. Rodgers, 1913 abridged, p. 184 (pp. 7–9).

8.1 *The Constitution of the Apostolic Church UK*, 3rd edn revised, originally published in 1937, abridged (pp. 168–70).

Pacifism

11.2 Minutes of the General Council of the Assemblies of God, held 21–27 September 1920 in Springfield, Missouri (pp. 243–4).

Generations

12.1 J. Roswell Flower, 'The Present Position of Pentecost', *Redemption Tidings* 3.10, 1927, pp. 4–6 (pp. 245–8).

Questions to think about

1 Is the creation of denominations inevitable after revivals that spread across previous denominational boundaries?

2 Does a strong leader make the difference to the creation of that new denomination or cause more problems?
3 How long would an amorphous group of believers last without organization?
4 Is it realistic to distinguish between a coercive organization and a non-coercive organism, between a church that is strongly hierarchical and a church that is fundamentally an association of equals?

Further reading

Anderson, Allan (2007), *Spreading Fires*, London, SCM Press.

Blumhofer, E. L. (1985), *The Assemblies of God: A Popular History*, Springfield, MO, Radiant Books.

Goff, J. R. (1988), *Fields White Unto Harvest: Charles F. Parham and the Missionary Origins of Pentecostalism*, Fayetteville, University of Arkansas Press.

McGee, G. B. (2004), *People of the Spirit: The Assemblies of God*, Springfield, MO, Gospel Publishing House.

5

Asia

Like Confucianism, Christianity seeks righteousness and reveres learning. Like Buddhism, Christianity seeks purity and promises a future life. Like shamanism, Christianity teaches that God answers prayer and performed miracles. (Yong-Hoon Lee)[1]

Introduction

Pentecostalism in Asia is a vast, diverse phenomenon scattered over numerous countries, cultures, language groups and ethnicities. Depending upon one's definition of Asia, it is arguable that Christianity is an Asian religion. Church tradition identifies St Thomas, one of the original disciples of Jesus, as the apostle who took Christianity to India.[2] The introduction of Christianity to the eastern part of Asia goes back at least to the seventh century and was reasserted in the thirteenth century before receiving further impetus from the pioneering work of the Roman Catholic Francis Xavier, who reached India in 1548, Japan a year later and who died in China in 1552.

In the nineteenth century, Protestant missions made their own impact. In terms of its geo-political structure, Asia differs from Africa in size and in its inclusion of thousands of offshore islands. The Philippines is composed of over 7,000 islands, there are 3,000 islands comprising Japan and over 17,000 islands comprising Indonesia. This means that religious development may take place differently on adjacent islands and also that it is difficult for a single unified political power to dominate nations where transport is broken up by seas, straits and waterways. For instance, the island of Timor, which is part of the Indonesian archipelago, maintains a strong Christian presence despite the numerical dominance of Islam nearby. Additionally, large numbers of islands caused differential linguis-

---

1 Yong-Hoon Lee (2001), 'Korean Pentecost: The Great Revival of 1907', *Asian Journal of Pentecostal Studies* 4.1, 73–83, taken from p. 79.

2 Roman coins have been discovered in South India, showing that St Thomas's visit was technically possible. See S. Neill (1990), *A History of Christian Missions*, London, Penguin, p. 46.

tic development with the result that dialects and sub-dialects emerged over time, putting barriers in the way of national government and missionary work.

Sprawling empires emerged within Asia, often facilitated by concentrating governmental power within an increasingly important capital city; both India and China harboured imperial ambitions. Japan, partly because of its militaristic culture, periodically enforced its will by conquering parts of China and all of Korea. As we shall see, the West could be viewed either as an alien power bringing an alien religion or, in the case of the countries subdued by Japanese force, a liberator to be welcomed with open arms. It was the United States that rescued the Philippines from Japanese domination during World War Two and that enabled South Korea to retain its freedom in the face of Chinese Communist aggression in 1950. In all these historical twists and turns, there is a barrage of propaganda – nationalistic, communistic and capitalistic – that floats like a fog over the unfolding of historical events and obscures their outlines.

According to the best available statistics, the total number of Pentecostals and charismatics in China amounts to 54 million, in India 33 million, in the Philippines 20 million, in Indonesia 9.45 million and in South Korea 7.5 million.[3] There are also Pentecostals and charismatics in Japan (1.76 million), in Vietnam (about 0.8 million) and in Thailand (about 0.8 million).[4] When we look at the statistics for the top five countries we find that 4.1% of the total population of China appears to be connected with the Pentecostal and charismatic movement, 2.9% of the total Indian population, 22.2% of the population of the Philippines, 3.9% of the population of Indonesia and 15.3% of the population of South Korea. The Philippines and South Korea are the most strongly affected by Pentecostalism but there is a surprisingly high impact in Indonesia, China and India. *The countries used to illustrate Asia in the sections that follow are based on the number of Pentecostals and charismatics they have.* We take the countries with the largest percentage of Pentecostals in descending order.

---

3 According to the Pew Forum statistics, http://pewforum.org/surveys/pentecostal/ Pentecostals and charismatics amount to 5% of the Indian population (56.6 million), 20 million higher than the figure we have used. The figure for South Korean renewalists is around 5.6 million.

4 I have followed the statistics given in S. M. Burgess and E. van der Maas (eds) (2002), *New International Dictionary of Pentecostal and Charismatic Movements* (*NIDPCM*), Grand Rapids, MI, Zondervan. In each case I have used the 'total renewal' figure for the country concerned.

Five Asian countries

Philippines

Spanish governance of the Philippines ended in 1898 with the defeat of the Spanish fleet by the US navy. Spanish territories were transferred to the United States with the result that the Philippines was opened up to extensive Protestant mission. Classical Pentecostals, including especially those from the United States, arrived to preach and teach. In 1926 the first of these missionaries belonged to the Assemblies of God and they were supplemented by large numbers of Filipinos who had taken advantage of opportunities to emigrate to the United States earlier in the century and who, now with educational qualifications and having received experience of baptism in the Spirit, returned to their native land with a desire to evangelize. The first Filipino leader of Assemblies of God was appointed in 1944. Despite the imprisonment of missionaries during Japanese occupation, the churches continued to grow, often by the conversion of ex-Catholics, so that when liberation came in 1940 a further phase of expansion rapidly followed. By 1979 Assemblies of God had 1,195 ministers and 383 churches, as well as 16 training schools. By 1999 there were 2,357 local churches and around 3,200 ministers/workers and a membership of over 130,000. A similar story could be told about the Church of God (Cleveland, Tennessee) which by the end of the twentieth century reached over 60,000 members with 631 local churches. The Foursquare Gospel group, first founded by Aimee Semple McPherson, is about the same size, and there are other classical Pentecostal groups as well.[5] To these should be added many indigenous charismatics, though the word 'indigenous' is imprecise because of multicultural identities. These charismatics were founded and led by Filipinos, and one, Jesus is Lord Fellowship, which began with 15 students in a polytechnic in 1978, now has at least 500 congregations, two Bible schools and, more especially, a TV station that is willing to engage in political debate.[6] In this way the charismatic movement in the Philippines resembles Latin American Pentecostalism, and it is possible that in the future charismatics – including Catholic charismatics – will not only endorse political candidates but also found political parties.[7] There is room for such radical innovations because politics in the Philippines has been marred by bribery scandals and the wealth of the nation is in a disproportionately small number of

---

5 Wonsuk Ma (2002), 'Philippines', in Burgess and van der Maas (eds), *NIDPCM*, pp. 201–7.

6 Joseph Suico (2005), 'Pentecostals in the Philippines', in A. H. Anderson and E. Tang (eds), *Asian and Pentecostal: The Charismatic Face of Christianity in Asia*, Oxford, Regnum and Baguio City, APTS Press, pp. 345–62.

7 A point echoed by Mathew Clark (2001), 'Asian Pentecostal Theology: A Perspective from Africa', *Asian Journal of Pentecostal Studies* 4.2, 181–99.

hands. The Pentecostal and charismatic movements bring a globalized dimension to internal debates within the country, and, in addition, the flow of finance for charitable enterprises is a valuable resource for what is still essentially a poor country. If the prevalent theology is predominantly of a health-and-wealth type, this is hardly surprising.[8]

South Korea

As we saw in Chapter 3, Korean Pentecostalism grew out of Methodist and Presbyterian renewal before ever the Azusa Street revival began. By 1907 a huge revival was in full swing and it laid down new and unique traditions in the Korean church: early-morning prayer meetings, congregational prayer when every member of the congregation prayed out loud at the same time, Bible studies, generous offerings, and co-operation between the disparate churches.[9] Presbyterians and Methodists together took part in planning an ineffective Declaration of Independence in March 1919 after Korea had been taken over by Japan in 1910.[10] The fanatically militaristic Japanese remained in charge until their defeat in 1945. The churches helped to nurture Korean identity in the period of occupation. They also promoted a dualistic mindset about the evil of this world and the true hope of another world. The atomic bombs brought Japan to its knees and a new democratic constitution was imposed by the Allies as part of the price of peace. Japan was forced to give up its overseas possessions. With the departure of the Japanese, rampant and communistic North Korean armies attempted to control the entire Korean peninsula, and South Korean forces were driven back until the US army came to the rescue. In 1953 there was an armistice and the refugee South Koreans set about rebuilding their homes, their economy and their hopes. Pentecostal Christianity became part of the nation-building solution.[11]

Early on, Pentecostal preachers understood the God of the Bible as one who could change their material circumstances. There was plenty in the Bible – especially the parable of the talents – to encourage believers to self-improvement and energetic business enterprise; the blessing of God, spoken of in the Old Testament, could be theirs in the present age. When a country has been trampled on by an invading army and then rescued by the forces of a 'Christian' nation, it becomes easy to believe in miracles.

---

8 According to the Pew Forum statistics, http://pewforum.org/surveys/pentecostal/ p. 30, as many as 90% of Pentecostals in the Philippines believe 'God grants material prosperity to all believers who have enough faith'.

9 Lee, 'Korean Pentecost', 73–83.

10 Lee, 'Korean Pentecost', 82.

11 Other Christian denominations – especially Methodists and Presbyterians – had also suffered and made massive contributions to the recovery of the nation, but this book is about Pentecostals.

Among those who believed was a young Buddhist who had been dying of tuberculosis. He prayed to the God of the Christians, recovered, read the Bible, bought a small plot of land, started a church, bought another plot of land and began his plans for a congregation that would eventually become the largest in the world. David Yonggi Cho (b. 1936), starting his ministry in 1958, retired at the point when his congregation had reached a massive 800,000 people, all living in Seoul, South Korea's capital city. It is an astonishing story and Cho's insistently upbeat message of a gospel of blessing, together with his exceptional organizational abilities, resulted in a positive Pentecostal Christianity sustained by numerous home groups led by women.[12] Cho taught that the imagination of believers could be spiritually inspired to picture future scenarios of blessing and that, by faith, these scenarios could be brought into concrete existence (see Chapter 15). Giving money was one way to trigger such dreams. The generous financial giving of church members resulted in the building of a large congregational complex, a university, printing facilities, a television studio, a welfare town for the elderly, the purchase of a prayer mountain and a vision for worldwide revival.

The exceptional growth of Pentecostalism in Korea has been attributed by its critics to shamanism. The shaman is a holy person who mediates between this world and the world of spirits. It is argued that the place of shamans in Korean culture was exploited by Cho, who has simply re-dressed the concept in Christian clothes. Cho's power to heal and to hear the voice of God is an adaptation of ancient shamanistic claims. This interpretation of Korean Pentecostalism has been repeated by Western scholars and frequently rebutted by Korean ones.[13] As Wonsuk Ma points out, Pentecostals have sharply distinguished themselves from animistic beliefs and practices, sometimes to the point of being disowned by their families for turning their backs on ancestor worship.[14] The accusation of shamanism rings hollow when one considers that Pentecostalism has been effective all over the world and in a variety of cultures. It is more rational to attribute the success of Pentecostalism in Korea to unique national circumstances faced in the South after 1953, to the fervour and ability of Korean Pentecostals and to the far-sightedness of its leadership.

12 An examination of David Yonggi Cho's theology has been made by Wonsuk Ma, William W. Menzies and Hyeon-sung Bae (eds) (2004), *David Yonggi Cho: A Close Look at his Theology and Ministry*, Baguio City, APTS Press.

13 W. J. Hollenweger (1972), *The Pentecostals*, London, SCM Press, p. 474f. Even W. J. Hollenweger (1997), *Pentecostalism: Origins and Developments Worldwide*, Peabody, MA, Hendrickson, pp. 100, 105, says, 'Christianity also, in its Catholic, Protestant and Pentecostal versions, has borrowed much from Korean shamanism.' Harvey Cox (1996), *Fire from Heaven*, London, Cassell, p. 219, makes a similar point.

14 Wonsuk Ma (2005), 'Asian (Classical) Pentecostal Theology in Context', in Anderson and Tang (eds), *Asian and Pentecostal*, p. 61.

Indeed, a detailed recent study argues that classical Pentecostalism was transformed into *sunbogeum* Pentecostalism after about 1953, a style of Pentecostalism that is rooted in Korean prayer and devotion coupled with an American capitalist orientation towards goals and achievement. Cho became the prime exemplar of this innovation, combining traditional Korean virtues with American dynamism.[15] It would, of course, be misleading to equate Korean Pentecostalism with one man: it is far bigger than that, and Cho has simply been chosen to illustrate a wider canvas.

Indonesia

The Dutch influence over the Spice Islands lasted for at least 400 years and made Indonesia, as it became, a valuable colony right up until the Japanese invasion of 1942. Early Dutch Pentecostals travelled to Indonesia soon after Pentecostalism was established in Amsterdam before World War One. These early Pentecostals preached divine healing and were far more successful than other missionaries had been. Pentecostal groups were registered by 1924 in the name of the Pentecostal Church of Indonesia – though the registered name was first in Dutch and then in Indonesian. Most Pentecostal groups trace their roots back to this original set of churches after a series of schisms from the parent body. *Pinskter Zending* was formed in 1931, *Gereja Gerakan Pantekosta* in 1932 and United Pentecostal Church in 1938. Further schisms produced further growth by further subdivision. Prior to 1942 the church had been partially indigenized, but during the Japanese occupation when missionaries were absent or imprisoned Indonesian leaders stepped into their shoes. They were ready to take charge of their own spiritual affairs. In 1945 the Indonesian peoples declared independence and despite attempts by the Dutch to wrest back control, by 1949 the country was freed. Despite its large Muslim population (still over 85%), the Constitution adopted was secular.

Without Dutch government control or hardship brought about by the Japanese, the period after 1949 was one of rapid Pentecostal growth. Many new Pentecostal denominations were founded, a consequence partly of the island geography. There was economic and national turmoil as communists were hunted down, and this must have contributed to the fervent prayers of Indonesian Christians who were caught up in the turbulence. 'It is estimated that over 2 million Indonesians, particularly Javanese and Timorese, joined evangelical and Pentecostal churches during the political and economic instability of the 1960s.'[16] During rapid

---

15 Ig-Jin Kim (2005), 'History and Theology of Korean Pentecostalism: Sunbogeum (Pure Gospel) Pentecostalism', doctoral dissertation, University of Utrecht, see p. 305.

16 Mark Robinson (2005), 'The Growth of Indonesian Pentecostalism', in Anderson and Tang (eds), *Asian and Pentecostal*, p. 335.

cultural and social changes that occurred in the modernization of the country, the middle class emerged ripe for the charismatic movement. The Catholic charismatic renewal gathered strength in the 1970s, while the Pentecostals pressed forward despite opposition. 'During the period 1965–98 there were 514 churches which were closed, vandalised, destroyed or burnt down.'[17] Because of their aggressive evangelism, Pentecostals were often targeted by hardline Islamic groups. Overall, the church continued to grow, sometimes metamorphosing through cell structures or in one case by revival on Timor between 1965 and 1971, which saw the Evangelical Christian Church grow from 375,000 to 517,000 in seven years, accompanied by gifts of the Spirit, revelations through visions and dreams, speaking with tongues, divine healing and numerous miracles. In 1999, East Timor, with a mainly Christian population of 1.1 million, voted to secede from Indonesia, a point of religious contention.

Indonesia's economy continues in a state of crisis, with endemic poverty, unemployment and starvation affecting as many as 80 million people. The adaptability and transformative nature of the Pentecostal message as well as its cultural fit with Indonesian life has contributed to growth, as have mass crusades by well-known healing evangelists such as Morris Cerullo (b. 1931) and Reinhard Bonnke (b. 1940).

China

Historians and theologians disagree about whether Pentecostal and charismatic renewal in China can be attributed to direct missionary influence or whether emphasis on the Holy Spirit arose spontaneously within well-established Christian groups of Chinese.[18] Both Catholic and Protestant forms of Christianity existed in China in the nineteenth century and, after Protestant missions took Christianity to the rural interior, simple patterns of church life became deeply rooted in the culture. Among those who adopted Chinese clothes, customs and food were members of the China Inland Mission (CIM), and their incarnational approach helped

---

17 Gani Wiyono (2005), 'Pentecostalism in Indonesia', in Anderson and Tang (eds), *Asian and Pentecostal*, p. 320.

18 Edmond Tang (2005), '"Yellers" and Healers – Pentecostalism and the Study of Grassroots Christianity in China', in Anderson and Tang (eds), *Asian and Pentecostal*, pp. 467–9. See also Luke Wesley's letter to the editor of *Pneuma* 29, 2007, 365–6, which questions the interpretation of events. According to Wesley, 'the experience of persecution in the house churches and the lack of it in the TSPM is the single most significant factor in shaping the outlook of these two, distinct groups'. TSPM is the Three-Self Patriotic Movement which is government-recognized. See also Gotthard Oblau (2005), 'Pentecostal by Default? Contemporary Christianity in China', in Anderson and Tang (eds), *Asian and Pentecostal*, p. 428.

foster indigenous forms of Chinese Christianity.[19] In favour of the notion that Pentecostalism came from outside Chinese culture is the date of the arrival of the first missionaries from Azusa Street, Alfred and Lillian Garr. They reached Hong Kong in 1907 and Garr's interpreter, Mok Lai Chi, effectively became the leader of the work and started the first Pentecostal newspaper in Chinese, *Pentecostal Truths*, in 1908.[20] They were followed by members of the British Pentecostal Missionary Union (PMU) which modelled itself upon the CIM and in 1912 sent its workers to the Yunnan province where churches and children's work were initiated. The PMU fostered belief in speaking with other tongues as an indication of baptism in the Holy Spirit, and its missionaries also practised healing through the laying on of hands.[21] Evidence that Pentecostalism arose spontaneously in China is provided by the highly successful evangelistic ministry of the native Chinese John Sung (1901–44), whose style of preaching and emphasis on the Holy Spirit went way beyond his Methodist upbringing. According to one recent estimate, 'all Christian churches in China practise some form of healing' and 'according to some surveys, 90% of new converts cite healing as a reason for their conversion'.[22]

The experience of the church in China during the twentieth century is disfigured by extremities of violence and tragedy. During the early part of the century, when Chinese nationalism was on the boil and especially after the Boxer uprising of 1899–1901 that targeted foreigners, diplomats and especially missionaries, Chinese Christians broke away from most foreign influence. The Assembly Hall was founded by Watchman Nee in the 1920s and the True Jesus Church in 1914.[23] When the Communist Party took power in China in 1949, and again when Mao launched the Cultural Revolution in 1966, Christians, including Pentecostals in China, were maltreated. The Communists pursued their standard policy for dealing with religion: they insisted on registration of each minister and building and, if they could, manipulated religious leaders to control or destroy their own religious groups on the pretext of 'purifying' these

---

19 Founded by J. Hudson Taylor in 1865 to prioritize reaching inland provinces of China.

20 D. H. Bays, 'China', in Burgess and van der Maas (eds), *NIDPCM*, p. 59.

21 See especially Peter K. Kay (1995), 'The Four-Fold Gospel in the Formation, Policy and Practice of the Pentecostal Missionary Union (PMU) (1909–1925)', unpublished MA thesis, University of Gloucester. See also John Andrews (2004), 'The Regions Beyond', unpublished PhD dissertation, University of Wales, Bangor.

22 Tang, 'Yellers', p. 481.

23 It accepts the deity of Christ, Saturday as the Christian Sabbath, speaking in tongues, foot-washing as a sacrament and salvation by faith. See Deng Zhaoming (2005), 'Indigenous Chinese Pentecostal Denominations', in Anderson and Tang (eds), *Asian and Pentecostal*, p. 444.

churches.[24] Once the leaders had fulfilled this perverse ideological function, they were disposed of by death or imprisonment.[25]

The procedures for registration ran across the desk of the Chinese Christian Council (CCC) and the Three-Self Reform Movement (TSRM).[26] Later visitors to China had the impression that all the churches identified with these two organizations were phoney and compromised by the state.[27] But more recent analysis has shown this simplistic picture to be questionable. There are still arguments about the extent to which registered churches have been true to the gospel and a recent commentator argues that it is helpful to differentiate 'between a charismatic structure from below and a bureaucratic structure from above'.[28] The charismatic structure from below is made up of local networks of believers in simple free-standing congregations or in relational connectedness. The bureaucratic structures from above emanate from major provincial cities where liberal forms of Protestantism were entrenched. A recent empirical study of religion in China shows that approximately 10% of Han Chinese people hold a religious faith and of these about one third, or 3.3% of the total, are Christians of various kinds, some of whom are also members of the Communist Party.[29]

We could say that the Chinese church suffered three waves of persecution: one during the Boxer rebellion, one during the initial seizure of power by Mao in the late 1940s, and one in the 1960s during the so-called Cultural Revolution. The effects of persecution and the inevitable betrayal by some Chinese Christians of others, as well as the long-term impossibility of investing in the training of ministers, have created a fragmented Christian picture.[30] Recent accounts are given of villages that have benefited from the presence of loving Christian communities and of the commendations by Communist officials of the effects of village harmony.[31] Equally, resistance to persecution has produced intransigence and a tendency to isolationism. Research on Pentecostalism within China from Chinese universities appears to have been of questionable

---

24 The same policy was used in Soviet Russia. See T. Beeson (1974), *Discretion and Valour*, London, Fount.

25 Zhaoming, 'Indigenous', p. 449.

26 Bays, 'China', p. 63.

27 E.g. Arthur Wallis (1985), *China Miracle*, Eastbourne, Kingsway.

28 Oblau, 'Default?', p. 418.

29 See Xinzhong Yao and Paul Badham (eds) (2007), *Religious Experience in Contemporary China*, Cardiff, University of Wales Press, pp. 72 and 75.

30 Groups include: Mentu Hui (Apostolic Church/Disciples), Huhan Pai (Yellers or Shouters), Yesu Jiating (Jesus Family), Kupa (Weepers), Beili Wang (Established King), Quan Fanwei (All-Scope), Kuangy Hui (Wilderness) and Congsheng Dao (Way of Rebirth). See Anderson and Tang, *Asian and Pentecostal*, pp. 429, 439.

31 Oblau, 'Default?', pp. 413–15.

value in the past.[32] What is noticeable about Pentecostal, or Pentecostal-style Christianity, within China is that it has come into existence without TV evangelism, evangelistic crusades, high-profile ministries, extensive literature or innovative music. In this respect it resembles strong holiness groups in other parts of the world. It has become a religion of deep piety, and 'Jesus is pictured as a parent and educator for his followers in many Chinese sermons and testimonies'.[33] Once periods of persecution ceased, surviving churches grew rapidly, as was the case with the True Jesus Church. Others, however, remained stunted. The Jesus Family, a communitarian Protestant group, was not even allowed to reorganize itself after the Cultural Revolution, so that the 'relationship between indigenous churches and the *lianghui* (CCC and TSPM) remains tense and problematic'.[34] The hope must be that, as China is opened up by economic reform, its churches will benefit. Certainly, there are large and thriving Pentecostal-type churches in Hong Kong, which, because of the unique history of the place as a British dependent territory from 1842 until 1997, escaped the anti-religious ravages of Chinese Communism.

It is worth noting at this point the huge Chinese diaspora. There are Chinese people all over the world (as their restaurants demonstrate!) but it is in Asia itself that Chinese minorities have the longest history. There are Chinese in Thailand, Malaysia and Singapore, and their Pentecostal churches in these countries are impressively organized and fervent. Both City Harvest Church and Trinity@paya Lebar, Singapore, reach many thousands of people with a wide range of educational and religious activities in several languages. Travel to and from China by members of the diaspora brings benefits to the churches in both locations.

India

India's incorporation within the British Empire laid it open to Protestant mission. Baptists, Anglicans, Methodists and others arrived in the eighteenth and nineteenth centuries. There were revivalistic phenomena in South India matching the British revivals between 1857 and 1859. As we saw in Chapter 3, Pentecostalism arrived in Mukti before emissaries of the Azusa Street mission could reach them, and when Alfred Garr did arrive his insistence that speaking with tongues was a sign of baptism in the Spirit caused controversy. Although church tradition maintains that Christianity reached India before it reached Europe, most of India is Hindu. New missionaries, many of them American from classical Pentecostal backgrounds, arrived from 1915 onwards and the Indian Pentecostal Church (IPC) was formed in 1930. The southern part of India was

---

32 Tang, 'Yellers', p. 469.
33 Oblau, 'Default?', p. 427.
34 Zhaoming, 'Indigenous', p. 464.

more amenable to Christianity than the north, which was both poorer and disturbed by Hindu–Muslim tensions. As a condition of its new nationhood when India became independent of Britain in 1947, it adopted a secular or neutral constitution that favoured none of the religions held by its peoples. This was mainly to prevent further bloody conflict between the two largest groups, the Hindu majority and the Muslim minority, whose hard-headed refusals to live together resulted in the partition of Indian territory and the parcelling out of what became Pakistan and later Bangladesh. The small Christian minority was protected by the terms of the Constitution, although the status of missionaries, once an Indian Parliament had been elected, became more precarious.[35] Moreover, rampant Hindu nationalism was prepared to use anti-conversion laws against Christians, as well as to be obstructive in the granting of planning permission for new church buildings.

The size of India, its numerous languages (22 are currently recognized by its Constitution) and its deeply rooted but illegal caste system resulted in local variations. The Anglican Church of South India had concentrated on prestigious educational institutions and made some inroads into the higher echelons of Indian society.[36] Roman Catholics were also notable. Among the British Pentecostal missionaries to India was Lawrence Livesey, who left England in 1935 and lived on a subsistence income with little initial success among the impoverished population south of Coimbatore.[37] When anyone from a Hindu village converted to Christianity, he or she was likely to be disowned by the family and therefore unable to work or eat. Livesey and his wife Margaret opened their own home, such as it was, to one of his converts and over 30 years a powerful new ministry was built along lines that were later repeated by others. The convert became the pastor of the church, which opened up a tailoring and carpentry school and offered apprenticeships for boys, worked among lepers and hill tribes, and established an orphanage and Bible School until a spectrum of enterprises had been built up from the original point of ministry.

Indian Pentecostalism now matches the forms found across the world elsewhere. There are classical Pentecostal denominations, charismatic fellowships, mercy ministries, old or new groupings brought about by splits and fusions, megachurches and, with India's increasing wealth and its access to North American and European markets, the emergence of superstar ministries, as well as the appearance of apostolic networks within the

---

35 In 1976 the word 'secular' was added to the preamble of the Constitution so there is no 'state religion'. About 80% of India is Hindu, 14% Muslim and about 2.5% Christian.

36 For instance, St Stephen's College, Delhi, where Muhammad Zia-ul-Haq, a President of Pakistan, was educated.

37 Andrews, 'Regions', passim.

sprawling urban jungles of the great cities.[38] Where Indian Pentecostalism may differ from its counterparts elsewhere is its appeal to the people
of the very lowest caste. To be born into a caste is to be pre-assigned a
place and a status in society. The lowest caste are in the lowest place, and
must remain so. Christianity does not recognize castes because it is predicated on a belief that Christ died for everyone regardless of their colour,
gender or social origin. Among those who have become Pentecostals are
Dalits, who were originally not even allowed to enter Hindu temples. At
least one Dalit has established a Pentecostal denomination.[39] Given that
the Indian population is due to exceed the Chinese population later in
the century and, in the expectation that Indian economic power grows
and utilizes the global advantages given to it by command of the English
language, the churches in such a climate have the capacity to prosper by
reaching out to poor and rich.

Reflection

Although this account has provided an overview of Pentecostal and charismatic churches within five Asian countries, the actual style of Pentecostalism in each country may vary considerably. Korean Pentecostalism,
for example, has been criticized for being formulaic. Particularly in the
larger churches, Christians will be expected to carry out their prayers
and Bible study almost according to a routine. Many of the churches will
hold to a rigid weekly pattern that admits of almost no variation. The
pastor, or associate pastors, will be seen as those who possess charismatic
gifts, and the body of the congregation, despite a belief in the power of
the Holy Spirit as the birthright of all Christians, may find themselves
excluded from any form of ministry. Charismatic utterances are likely
to be highly controlled and critics would point to a certain machine-
like regularity in the programmes of churches. These criticisms may have
force, although in any organizations of the size of the Korean churches it
is difficult to see how personal spontaneity could prevail in the same way
as is to be found in much smaller Western congregations. Moreover, in
Korea huge importance is given to prolonged prayer where individuals
can 'pour their hearts out' to God. In short, the ordered nature of church
services in Korea does *not* imply that Korean Pentecostals are inactive or
spiritually passive.

The division between the official, registered churches in China and the

---

38 Newfrontiers, a British apostolic network led by Terry Virgo, has over 30
churches in India. See W. K. Kay (2007), *Apostolic Networks in Britain*, Milton Keynes, Paternoster Press.

39 Paulson Pulikottil (2005), 'Ramankutty Paul: A Dalit Contribution to Pentecostalism', in Anderson and Tang (eds), *Asian and Pentecostal*, pp. 245–57.

unofficial, house churches is a perennial bone of contention. Those who have been imprisoned and beaten for their Christian beliefs are unlikely to be impressed by the claims of Christians who have managed to avoid the fire of a governmental dragon.[40] Those who belong to the house churches feel that *they* are the real Christians, and, at some points in the last 50 years, their demands for religious freedom are intransigent and powerful enough to have been seen by the Communist Party as a threat to its monopoly of power. The registered churches are more compliant and more liberal in their views and it is possible that inter-church rivalry has been expressed by attempts to manipulate the sympathies and antipathies of the Chinese government. How better to get rid of a group you consider to be heretical than by informing on them to the police? It will take many years for the whole church in China, registered and unregistered, to be reconciled.

Although the Pentecostal and charismatic movements do not constitute a majority in any of the Asian countries, they do comprise a well-established minority in all of them. In nearly every case, Christianity has appealed to the poor or the dispossessed while the ruling elite in each country adheres to a non-Christian religion. This is especially so in India but also in China, if one classifies communism as religion, and Indonesia. Consequently Christianity, in working among the poor, brings welcome gifts. Where any members of the middle class in any country accept Christianity, they find themselves alienated from ancestral traditions and pressed to conceive of the church as one voice among many. Liberal Christianity much more easily adapts to a pluralist regime than conservative Christianity. As Jenkins points out, 'Asian theologians commonly hold that Christianity needs to engage in a triple dialogue – with other religions, with other cultures, and (throughout the process) with the poor.'[41] But Pentecostals find themselves not just dialoguing with the poor but representing the poor. And, as a consequence of their theology, Pentecostals are almost bound to regard their non-Christian neighbours as religiously wrong, if not damned, and not people with whom dialogue should be held.

It remains to be seen whether Pentecostals will continue to confront their cultures. In the Philippines, where their numbers are higher, the confrontation takes a distinctly political shape informed by ethical standards. In South Korea, where their numbers have grown impressively since

---

40 Brother Yun (2004), *The Heavenly Man*, London, Monarch, pp. 111, 112, speaks of the torture of a house-group leader. At one point the torturers say, 'If you admit your crimes against the government, we'll release you if you agree to attend a Three-Self Church. We can even let you become the Chairman of the regional branch of the Three-Self Patriotic Movement!'.

41 Philip Jenkins (2006), *New Faces of Christianity*, Oxford, Oxford University Press, p. 86.

1953, Pentecostals have forged a new theology that incentivizes capitalistic activity while helping to fulfil national economic goals. This is not
so much a theology of confrontation as a theology of material transformation. There are traces of such a theology in parts of China where
Christian communities can help to make a rural economy more produc-
tive. In India, too, Christianity serves a purpose in bringing education
and employment to those who would fall outside the circle of privilege.
In all the Asian countries, though there is a deep respect for Western
technology and rationalism, there may be an underlying and animistic or
spiritual world view. None of the Asian countries underwent a process as
profound as the eighteenth-century European Enlightenment when centuries of authoritarian religious teaching were intellectually attacked, and
when a new scale of values based on human beings with morality but
without God was erected. So, if we view the Asian countries as places
that jumped from the pre-modern era through to the globalized world
of today, we can understand how different they are from Europe. Moreover, if we see the Asian countries as essentially driven by centuries of
trade and if Christianity in its Pentecostal form creates networks of trust
as well as communities of hope, we may begin to understand the niche
that middle-class charismatics might seek to fill.

Cross-references to the SCM Reader *Pentecostal and Charismatic Studies*

9.8 Yoido Full Gospel Church, http://davidcho.com/NewEng/bd-1.asp
   (pp. 208–10).

Questions to think about

1 Find out more about Yonggi Cho's church in Seoul. There is plenty of
   material on the internet and in printed form.
2 Is it reasonable to argue that an Asian world view is conducive to
   Pentecostalism?
3 Find out about Asian understandings of extended family responsibili-
   ties and work out whether these might have helped the spread of Pentecostalism. For instance, if families are close-knit we would expect
   Christianity to spread through family relationships.
4 Summarize the effects of government crack-downs on Pentecostals in
   China.
5 How far is Asia homogenous? Is it sufficiently homogenous in culture
   to find an overriding cultural or political context as a cause for the
   spread of Pentecostalism?
6 Do you think 'signs and wonders' rather than prosperity teaching is a
   better explanation for the spread of Pentecostalism?

Further reading

Anderson, Allan and Tang, E. (eds) (2005), *Asian and Pentecostal: The Charismatic Face of Christianity in Asia*, Oxford, Regnum, and Baguio City, APTS.

Brother Yun (or Liu Zhenying) with Paul Hattaway (2004), *The Heavenly Man*, London, Monarch.

Jenkins, Philip (2006), *New Faces of Christianity*, Oxford, Oxford University Press.

The Pew Forum statistics, http://pewforum.org/surveys/pentecostal/

Yao, Xinzhong and Badham, Paul (eds) (2007), *Religious Experience in Contemporary China*, Cardiff, University of Wales Press.

6

Latin America

The social composition of Pentecostalism seems to vary from place to place and church to church, as well as over time. Its appeal is not univocal, and marginal differences in liturgy and message can meet subtly different social demands. (Paul Freston)[1]

Introduction

Latin America, a long single landmass stretching all the way from the hot, dry US–Mexican border in the north to the windy desolation of Cape Horn in the south, first knew Christianity from the Spanish *conquistadores* arriving after Columbus in 1492. The Spanish had organized themselves into aristocratic and knightly bands, mixing Catholicism with nationalism, to drive out Islam from Spain. Once this combination of religion and military force had been successful, the promise of wealth across the ocean to the west beckoned. Overseas expansion in this direction was only possible because of improved shipbuilding, naval gunnery, more certain navigation and a better understanding of the dimensions of the globe. The Spanish aims might be summed up in the words of the Bernal Diaz del Castillo giving his reasons for going to the Indies: 'to serve God and his Majesty, to give light to those who were in darkness, and to grow rich, as all men desire to do'.[2] When the New World came within the reach of the two Iberian powers, Spain and Portugal, competition between them was minimized by Pope Alexander VI in 1493 who drew a line down a map of the Atlantic ceding the western part to Spain and the eastern part, which included Brazil, to Portugal.[3]

---

1 Paul Freston (1998), Pentecostalism in Latin America: Characteristics and Controversies, *Social Compass* 45.3, 335–58, 342.

2 Quoted by J. McManners (1990), 'The Expansion of Christianity', in J. McManners (ed.), *The Oxford Illustrated History of Christianity*, London, Guild Publishing, pp. 304, 305.

3 'Portuguese historians have discovered an almost fabulous character, Prince Henry of Portugal, "the Navigator"... for some forty years from about 1420 till his death in 1460, Prince Henry, we are told, sat at Sagres, on the Atlantic tip of southern Portugal, surrounded by his cartographers and scientists, devising ever new and

The Spanish empire was swiftly established, beginning with the seizure of the West Indies, and soon afterwards with the destruction of the Aztec empire in what became Mexico, and the Inca empire in what became Chile. Once treasure had been looted and silver mines had been manned, economics dictated a policy of farming that required indigenous peoples to pay tribute to individual Spaniards. Had the Roman Catholic Church not intervened, the native Indians would have been reduced to slavery. Dominicans outraged the settlers by appealing back to Spain, with the result that a colonial code was published in 1512 and the Indians were classified as free men, not slaves, though they could be required to work, a requirement that was to lead to their later endemic poverty. It would be a mistake to think that no Protestants arrived until the Pilgrim Fathers came to Massachusetts. On the contrary, there were Protestant soldiers in the Spanish army of Charles V and the Spanish Inquisition in Mexico arrested and tried its first Protestant as early as 1531, only ten years after Mexico had first become a Spanish colony.[4] The very fact that the Inquisition was at work in Latin America is evidence enough that Protestantism began its evangelism early. Even so, the overwhelming religious power at work within that part of the world was the Roman Catholic Church. By the mid-sixteenth century there were eight Catholic dioceses in Mexico and three in South America.[5] But according to McManners, the Spanish conquest was hardly a matter of military brutality given the relative size of the Spanish and Indian populations. The main force used by Spain was directed towards the desecration and destruction of idols and temples, many of them places of human sacrifice. Mass conversions – and we are told of Catholic missionaries who baptized over 14,000 people in a single day – could hardly allow for teaching and instruction to take place.[6] Catholicism was built on a barely assimilated folk religion and displayed with great pageantry and pomp, but the lack of Mexican or South American priests in the mid-sixteenth century is indicative of the superficiality of aspects of the missionary process.[7]

The Portuguese empire in South America, centred on Brazil, utilized coastal lands and largely ignored the tropical interior. Where the Portuguese attempted to make a profit out of their sugar plantations by enslaving the indigenous population, particularly the population from the interior, production was hampered by the high mortality rate of the slaves. Only when stronger African slaves were imported by Portuguese

---

longer journeys.' H. Trevor-Roper (1967), *The Rise of Christian Europe*, London, Book Club, pp. 182, 183.

4 Manuel J. Gaxiola-Gaxiola (1991), 'Latin American Pentecostalism: A Mosaic within a Mosaic', *Pneuma* 13.2, 107–29.

5 McManners, 'Expansion', p. 309.

6 McManners, 'Expansion', p. 310.

7 McManners, 'Expansion', p. 310.

entrepreneurs did the sugar plantations begin to show a profit, and by the end of the seventeenth century a lucrative trade was plied with a large mercantile fleet. Conversions under the Portuguese were slower than in the Spanish colonies because there was no settled and uniform social structure by which the native population could be treated as a single group. Jesuits in Brazil attempted to protect their converts by organizing them into villages built around churches, though with less success than in areas under Spanish control. 'Brazil developed a feudal system of large holdings run by regional bosses and a cismontane hierarchy (more loyal to the crown rather than to the papacy) heading a church whose practices were those of folk Catholicism.'[8] The arrival of African slaves as well as European immigrants, and the later removal of the taboo of intermarriage, have led to a rich and vibrant Brazilian nation. While the early Portuguese empire was repressive, later Portuguese emperors, particularly after they had tasted defeat at the hands of Napoleon and had relocated themselves in Rio de Janeiro, were more enlightened, and this led to the founding of polytechnics (later becoming universities).[9] Religiously, African animism or spiritism (*Macumba*) might coexist with South American versions of the same phenomenon (later *Umbanda*) and all this be overlain by unreformed Roman Catholicism. As events were to demonstrate, the ground was well prepared for the arrival of Pentecostalism at the start of the twentieth century.

The involvement of the United States, largely a Protestant power, in the affairs of Latin America began early. In the period after the defeat of Napoleon, the European colonies in Latin America began to seek independence. Mexico and Colombia were recognized by the United States in 1822, Chile and Argentina in 1823, Brazil in 1824 and Peru in 1826. A more active strong-arm policy pursued by President Roosevelt led to the construction of the Panama Canal in land that originally had been part of Colombia. When Colombia refused Roosevelt's overtures, he recognized Panama as a separate country, paid the Panamanians for the canal and opened it in 1914. Before 1920 the United States was to intervene or exert pressure upon other Central American countries, including Cuba, the Dominican Republic and Nicaragua, sometimes through trading links and at other times through military power. This situation led all the way to the United States policy enacted by President Reagan in the 1980s, when the Americans found themselves either having to support repressive right-wing regimes or trying to undermine communistic left-wing ones. Pentecostals in Latin American countries were often caught up in the crosswinds of political argumentation when liberation theology, which

8 E. A. Wilson (2002), 'Brazil', in S. M. Burgess and E. van der Maas (eds), *New International Dictionary of Pentecostal and Charismatic Movements* (*NIDPCM*), Grand Rapids, MI, Zondervan, p. 36.

9 Escola Politécnica was founded in 1792.

could be described as a mixture of Roman Catholicism and Marxism, clashed with Christian capitalism.[10] Events in Nicaragua displayed the contention most sharply.[11]

The 13 countries of Latin America contain a vast number of Pentecostals and charismatics. The largest absolute number of these is in Brazil (80 million), followed by Mexico (13 million), Colombia (12.5 million) and Argentina (8.4 million). When we turn to the percentage of a nation's population that is Pentecostal-charismatic, about 43% of Brazilians are Pentecostal in some way or another and the corresponding figure for Chile is 33%, for Columbia 28.4% and Argentina 20.6%.[12] In the account that follows we take the countries with the largest percentage of Pentecostals in descending order.

Four South American countries

Brazil

The truly astonishing growth of Pentecostalism within Brazil can be gleaned from a large number of statistics. A 40-metre-high concrete statue of Christ stands with outstretched arms over the picturesque city of Rio de Janeiro. In Greater Rio, 61% of all congregations are Pentecostal and 'in one Catholic diocese there were over twice as many Protestant places of worship as Catholic, and in the poorest districts the ratio was seven to one'.[13] According to figures given by Everett Wilson, Assembleias de Deus could count 85,000 congregations in the country as a whole and, when other Pentecostal groups are added, this figure rises to a staggering 121,135.[14]

The beginnings of this religious transformation can be dated back to the start of the Pentecostal outpouring. Two Swedish immigrants to the United States, Daniel Berg (1884–1963) and Gunnar Vingren (1879–1933), were instrumental in the founding of the Brazilian version of Assemblies of God. Berg had come into contact with Pentecostalism while visiting Sweden in 1909, and after his return to the States he met Vingren during a conference sponsored by the First Swedish Baptist Church in Chicago. After attending Pentecostal churches, including that of William H. Durham,

---

10 My characterization of liberation theology may offend some scholars but I take the view that the visionary dimension of Marxism comes from Marx's transposition of the eventual triumph of the biblical elect and their millennial victory into a secular key where the proletariat replace the elect. Marx came from a Jewish family that converted to Christianity and Marx's early writings are religiously romantic.

11 The situation is expertly explained by C. L. Smith (2007), *Revolution, Revival and Religious Conflict in Sandinista Nicaragua*, Leiden, Brill.

12 Calculations made using statistics from Burgess and van der Maas, *NIDPCM*.

13 Freston, 'Pentecostalism', 338.

14 Wilson, 'Brazil', p. 38.

the preacher who had caused such controversy by his 'finished work' doctrine,[15] both Berg and Vingren received a prophecy that they should go to Pará and, although they did not know where in the world Pará was, they consulted a map and, after being dedicated by Durham, set off for Brazil in November 1910. They began working in a Baptist Church but, because of their Pentecostal teaching, were asked to leave, and they took with them 18 church members. They first called their church Apostolic Faith Mission, presumably following the name used by Seymour at Azusa Street, and Vingren became their pastor. Shortly afterwards they registered themselves under the name Assembly of God and over the next 18 years, aided by Swedish and North American finance, this congrega tion and others connected with it grew. They were no doubt influenced by their strong belief in the autonomy of the local church. Though the Assemblies of God in the United States and Swedish Pentecostalism made considerable play of the need for local churches to be autonomous, in Sweden, far more than in the United States, steps were taken to prevent the building up of a centralized denominational bureaucracy. Once local church autonomy is emphasized, growth is in the hands of enterprising local leaders rather than denominational officials at a headquarters a long way away. These local leaders became formidable figures in their own right: autocratic *pastores-presidentes* with many daughter churches connected with their largest congregations. In 1930, when their first national conference was held, 16 pastors attended but these pastors had between them more than 300 congregations and 40,000 people under their care. Berg was associated with the churches until 1961.

The other large early Pentecostal church in Brazil was begun by Luigi Francescon (1866–1964) among the Italian community in São Paulo. Originally the preaching and the services were in Italian, but in the mid-1930s Portuguese was adopted and native Brazilians began to attend. Currently Congregação Cristã has around 15,000 congregations and 1.5 million members, but in contrast with other Brazilians its clergy are not full-time or paid. Its resources are devoted to charitable giving so that there is a weekly distribution of finance to the poorest worshippers who, in the services, follow traditional practices and set prayers. Women wear veils and are separated in the seating arrangements from men. The church does not engage in street preaching or broadcasting, neither are members required to tithe their income. All this makes its growth remarkable and, though in recent years it has sent out missionaries to Italy and Portugal, its conservative morality and dress code, as well as its lack of interaction with other churches, makes it seem exclusive.[16]

The early development of Pentecostalism in Brazil was well adapted to

---

15 See Chapters 3 and 13.

16 A. H. Anderson (2004), *An Introduction to Global Pentecostalism*, Cambridge, Cambridge University Press, p. 71.

the culture. Although the beginnings were associated with foreign missionaries, the church rapidly adjusted to Brazilian customs and became to all intents and purposes indigenous. Many of the Brazilian Pentecostal churches were both morally rigorous and orientated towards charitable activity, while at the same time keen for missionary work directed at the interior of their own country. It might be argued that the congregations, with their strong demands upon members, created a sense of family unity at the expense of natural kinship ties. Yet the moral rigour of Brazilian Pentecostalism might also be seen as an extreme response to the laxity of traditional Catholicism. David Martin compares Pentecostalism to early Methodism, which discouraged immorality, organized working people, educated them, and brought them out of the cycle of poverty and ignorance.[17] By the 1950s, however, the beginnings of the charismatic movement were visible. The house churches of Brasil par Christo came into being through tent meetings conducted by Manoel de Mello, a former Assemblies of God evangelist. Similarly, the Irgeja do Evangelho Quadrangular (Foursquare Gospel Church) was launched through public mass evangelism. Here the tempo and values changed. The new churches were more entrepreneurial, inclined to political involvement and modelled on the pattern of the divine healing evangelists in the United States. They were also less exclusive and sought good relations with Catholic charismatics and the World Council of Churches. By the mid-1970s the Universal Church of the Kingdom of God (UCKG) started up. It was even more flamboyant than the other groups and acquired a TV channel, radio stations and stressed the use of sacred objects like water, or oils in healing.[18] The UCKG confronted Brazilian spiritism head-on and regularly conducted exorcism services for its members who for the most part were drawn from the poorer sections of Brazilian society. The huge Cathedral of Faith in Rio de Janeiro seats 10,000 worshippers. Although its founder Edir Macedo has been arrested and imprisoned for illegal financial dealings, his rejection of the legalistic morality that is common among most Brazilian Pentecostals has made his churches, which have now reached as far north as US Hispanics, much more like postmodern charismatic congregations elsewhere in the world.

The impact of Brazilian Pentecostalism was recognized by holding the World Pentecostal Conference in Rio de Janeiro in 1967. It was here that the Korean Yonggi Cho preached about small groups as the building blocks for much larger congregations. Cho's advocacy was heard by Latin Americans, and cell groups in Latin America can probably be dated from this time. Yet, methods alone are not enough to explain what happened: Brazilian Pentecostalism seems to be in a class of its own.

Of all the features of Pentecostalism within Brazil that astonishes most

---

17 E.g. David Martin (2002), *Pentecostalism: The World their Parish*, Oxford, Blackwell, p. 7.

18 Anderson, 'Global', p. 72.

readers, the political inroads made by Brazilian Pentecostals is the most arresting. This is especially surprising in light of the fact that liberation theology advanced by liberal Roman Catholics made great play of the belief that, just as God came to rescue the Hebrew slaves from Egypt, so there was a divine purpose in rescuing the poor from the exploitation of capitalism. Pentecostals were simpler: they saw politics in terms of integrity – leaning on the words of Jesus about salt (preventing corruption) and light (good deeds) – and a bias towards the needs of the poor. Moreover, Pentecostals and evangelicals tended to select their politicians at the ballot box by reference to moral issues like abortion and to favour any politician who took a moral stance whatever his or her actual political affiliation might be. From the late 1980s the 'personalization of politics' occurred. By this, 'the political leader achieved credibility and legitimacy with a certain segment of society not by the content of his political acts or his political programmes but by the type of man he shows himself to be'.[19] In using popularity gained through gospel singing or preaching, a number of high-profile pastors began to garner votes in city elections and, later, in national elections. The most politically sophisticated Pentecostals/charismatics belonged to the UCKG (Universal Church of the Kingdom of God), which used its influence to ensure the election of the largest number of its endorsed candidates but spread these candidates across a range of political parties.[20] Once elected, the candidates worked together in Parliament and were answerable to their church. Despite fierce criticism at the start of this strategy, UCKG began to make inroads into the political scene: 'In 2002 the UCKG caucus did grow by about 30%, electing twenty-two members of Congress out of a total of about sixty evangelicals elected.'[21]

In his assessment of the success of evangelical and Pentecostal involvement with politics in Brazil, Fonseca argues that economic inequality will not be removed by policies that improve procedures but otherwise serve the interests of the national elite. In his view, only more egalitarian and traditionally left-wing policies will make the difference necessary to remove violence from the streets. In short, he sees Pentecostal involvement in politics as having only entered a preliminary phase.[22]

19 Alexandre B. Fonseca (2008), 'Religion and Democracy in Brazil: A Study of the Leading Evangelical Politicians', in Paul Freston (ed.), *Evangelical Christianity and Democracy in Latin America,* Oxford, Oxford University Press. Fonseca is quoting D. Saes (2001), *Republica do capital: capitalism e processo politico no Brasil,* Sao Paulo, Biotempo, p. 71.

20 Though M. Bergunder (2002), 'The Pentecostal Movement and Basic Ecclesial Communities in Latin America: Sociological Theories and Theological Debates', *International Review of Missions* 91.361, 163–86, draws attention to findings that 'Pentecostal deputies did not, as might have been expected, reveal right wing or neo-liberal tendencies ... the Pentecostals showed a rather centre-left tendency'.

21 Fonseca, 'Brazil', p. 195.

22 Fonseca, 'Brazil', p. 204.

Sociological and theological attempts to account for the booming Pentecostal churches across Brazil have advanced a variety of suggestions, few of which are empirically testable and most of which are plausible.[23] First, a Pentecostal world view of the primacy of the spiritual is compatible with the typical working-class world view of poorer Brazilians. Spiritism was endemic, sophisticated and wide-ranging, and Pentecostalism offered the power of Christ and the Holy Spirit for casting out demons and breaking the power of the devil. It was no longer necessary to speak to the spiritist (*Umbandan*) priest in the hope that he might lift the curse or cast a spell. Instead, by faith in Christ the spirit of bondage could be dramatically expelled, allowing the believer to enjoy blessed liberty.

Second, sociological explanations reiterated the interpretation that was intended to account for the early growth of Pentecostalism in the southern part of the United States.[24] Rural migration to growing towns had created rootlessness and disorientation. By coming into a strong and supportive Christian community, the new arrivals could find a fresh sense of purpose and thereby resist crime and debt. Pentecostal Christianity offered an antidote to the secularization of urbanization. Pentecostal congregations could be set up all over growing towns without complicated parish boundaries or building programmes, and, if the family had connections with the Roman Catholic Church, the move to the city made it much easier to sever these. Third, Pentecostalism was progressive in the sense that it could offer answers to the practicalities of life. Pentecostalism was not only a religion for Sunday but encompassed the whole of the person's life including employment, family and the future.[25] The prosperity gospel gave energy and hope to those within the slums: God does not want you to be poor because he loves you too much. And it is not too fanciful to see the appeal of Brazilian football in a similar light. Here barefoot boys playing on the street might dream one day of becoming world superstars with untold wealth. Football and religion mingled in Brazilian culture, each making the individual part of a team, each requiring dedication and discipline, each promising glory.

Fourth, there were those who criticized Pentecostalism. There were certainly Catholic critics who routinely denounced Pentecostals as emotional sects, but there were more sophisticated sociological detractors who saw Pentecostals as replacing one form of bondage (to the plantation owner) by another (to the pastor).[26] A more positive version of the

---

23 Freston, 'Pentecostalism', discusses a range of sociological theories.

24 See the brief discussion in Chapter 1 of Robert M. Anderson (1979), *Vision of the Disinherited*, Oxford, Oxford University Press.

25 For a discussion of the theme of 'progressive Pentecostalism', see D. E. Miller and T. Yamamori (2007), *Global Pentecostalism: The New Face of Christian Social Engagement*, California, University of California Press.

26 See Freston, 'Pentecostalism', 344. A different criticism might argue that in

same account focused on the role and position of women. Pentecostalism met the needs of women either by giving them power within their
congregations and home groups or by educating them or by turning their
drunken and feckless husbands into disciplined providers for their families. Men were socialized out of the irresponsible machismo tradition into
a role that honoured women and valued monogamy.[27] The Pew Foundation survey found that 72% of Brazilian Pentecostals thought that drinking alcohol was 'never justified' (though admittedly only 37% thought
the same about divorce). Equally, 83% of Brazilian Pentecostals thought
'God grants believers prosperity' and 89% that 'God grants believers
health'.[28]

Chile

Methodism became established in South America in the 1880s and 1890s
through 'soldiers, sailors, migrants, traders, civilisers, and colonial governors'.[29] Among those who tried to improve Methodist mission was
William Taylor, an itinerant evangelist who wanted to revive St Paul's
missionary methods. Taylor, in his *Pauline Methods of Missionary Work*
published in 1879, argued for self-supporting missionaries who would
establish self-supporting, self-governing and self-propagating churches.
Self-supporting missionaries could function independently of a controlling mission board and the churches they founded could operate without
foreign interference; in other words, they would be properly indigenous.
Willis C. Hoover (1858–1936), who trained as a medical doctor, applied
to Taylor's self-supporting mission in 1889, and was sent as a teacher to
a school in northern Chile where he worked for four years. Disappointed
with his evangelistic results, he dedicated himself to street preaching and
quickly formed two congregations outside Iquique where he worked.
Already proficient in Spanish – he was often the official translator for
Methodist annual conferences – he was made pastor of the Spanish-
speaking church where he lived. While on furlough in the United States

---

Latin America, a regional or communal authoritarian figure is known as the *caudillo*, who exercises power, dishes out favours and services, and demands service,
leading some sociologists to liken local, powerful pastors to the *caudillo*. There are
certainly some similarities, though paradoxically Latin American Pentecostalism also
displays strong collectivist tendencies (based, of course, on its theology vis-à-vis spiritual gifts, congregational participation, and so on). I am grateful to Calvin Smith for
this insight.

27 Bernice Martin (2001), 'The Pentecostal Gender Paradox: A Cautionary Tale
for the Sociology of Religion', in R. K. Fenn (ed.), *The Blackwell Companion to Sociology of Religion*, Oxford, Blackwell, pp. 52–66.

28 http://pewforum.org/surveys/pentecostal/

29 David Hempton (2005), *Methodism: Empire of the Spirit*, New Haven, Yale
University Press, p. 158.

he saw pre-Pentecostal churches in Chicago that reaffirmed his spiritual yearnings.

In 1902 he was made the pastor of the Methodist congregation in Valparaiso where he found fervent believers searching for an Acts 2 experience of the Holy Spirit. A devastating earthquake of 1906 destroyed the church building and forced members to worship in their own homes under the care of lay leaders. The underlying quest for revival continued, and in 1907 Mrs Hoover received a booklet written by Minnie Abrams describing the revival at Pandita Ramabai's girls' home at Mukti, India. The booklet described a 'clear and distinct baptism of the Spirit, as a complement to justification and sanctification which we had hitherto believed to comprise the whole of Christian experience'.[30] Hoover corresponded with T. B. Barratt and A. A. Boddy about the new outpouring, while his congregation continued to meet in a large tent and in homes during the reconstruction of their church building. By 1909 the new building was complete and could seat 1,000 people. This was a prelude for a further intensification of the spiritual life of the congregation. Lay leaders pressed for daily study groups and all-night prayer meetings, with the result that revivalistic phenomena occurred. In Hoover's words:

> Laughing, weeping, shouting, singing, foreign tongues, visions and excesses during which the individual fell to the ground and felt himself caught up into another place, to heaven, to Paradise, in splendid fields, with various kinds of experience: conversations with God, the angels or the devil. Those who experienced these things profited greatly and generally were changed by them and filled with praises, the spirit of prayer and love.[31]

Methodist officials frowned upon these goings-on. Matters came to a head with the visit of Nellie Laidlaw, a new convert who was recognized as a prophetess in the city despite her previous life as a drunkard and a prostitute.[32] When, on 12 September 1909, Laidlaw visited the church in Santiago, the pastor refused her permission to speak and so she went out into the courtyard to give out her revelations. As a result of the conflict, arguments broke out and during the evening service the police were called, and arrested Ms Laidlaw. This is often regarded as the day on which the Chilean Pentecostal Church began. Members went back to holding meetings in their own homes until the matters could be investigated by the annual Methodist Conference in February 1910.

30 Juan Sepúlveda (1999), 'Indigenous Pentecostalism and the Chilean Experience', in A. H. Anderson and W. J. Hollenweger (eds), *Pentecostals after a Century*, Sheffield, Sheffield Academic Press, p. 114.

31 Quoted by Sepúlveda, 'Chilean Experience', p. 116.

32 W. J. Hollenweger (1997), *Pentecostalism: Origins and Developments Worldwide*, Peabody, MA, Hendrickson, p. 121.

Later that month disciplinary proceedings were inaugurated against Hoover, who defended himself by extensive quotations from Wesley's writings. The Conference attempted a compromise by suggesting Hoover return to the United States while the charges against Nellie Laidlaw were passed, and a formal declaration made that the baptism in the Holy Spirit and speaking in tongues were 'anti-Methodist, contrary to the Scriptures and irrational'.[33]

This virtual excommunication resulted in the formation by the revivalist group of a separate church, first called the Iglesia Metodista Nacional (National Methodist Church), but then, after Hoover himself resigned from the Methodist Church in April of that year, the Iglesia Metodista Pentecostal (Pentecostal Methodist Church or IMP). By this means a new indigenous and fully Pentecostalized Methodist Church came into existence in Chile independently of the Azusa Street revival and with a doctrine of the Holy Spirit that was carefully fitted into Wesleyan theology. It did not insist upon glossolalia as evidence of baptism in the Holy Spirit. It did insist upon bishops and it continued to employ the other features of Methodist ecclesiastical polity. Hoover's leadership had resulted in a church that was Chilean in essence and with the capacity to fund and organize itself, make decisions, survive the loss of one new building and then set about buying or constructing others. As a result, the oldest Pentecostal congregations in Latin America are to be found in Chile, and Hoover, because he threw in his lot with the new Chilean breakaway group rather than with the established Methodist Mission, earned the respect and love of the nationals – and this was particularly so because the Methodists had him arrested and tried to force him to leave the country.

The IMP led by Hoover provided a framework for incipient Pentecostalism. It grew rapidly, welcoming important roles for women and encouraging evangelism. There were a limited number of early conflicts over liturgy that led to the formation of other groups under Chilean leaders. But after 1925, when the Chilean constitution separated church and state, persecution of Pentecostals stopped. This, unfortunately, paved the way for further disagreements among Pentecostals themselves. In 1933 Hoover was ousted from the IMP, and so he and his supporters formed a new group, Iglesia Evangelica Pentecostal (IEP). Pentecostalism continued to multiply by internal division, an unedifying process but one not too dissimilar in practice from evangelistic growth by planned church planting. Between 1930 and 1955 over 20 new Pentecostal denominational groups burst into existence.

By and large Chile avoided the switchback ride caused by the ups and downs of political and military coups. Like other Latin American

---

33 The beginnings of Chilean Pentecostalism are well documented and told by Hollenweger, *Pentecostalism*, and D. D. Bundy (2002), 'Chile', in Burgess and van der Maas (eds), *NIDPCM*, pp. 55–8.

countries Chile was ethnically diverse, being composed of descendants of the original Spanish settlers, descendants of the original native inhabitants and, most numerous, mixed-race individuals or *mestizos*. Spanish descendants tended to retain positions of political leadership and land ownership in a society that still carried the marks of its original stratification. Persistent disempowerment of sections of the population resulted in dynamic political confrontations between the conservatives, wedded to social stasis, capitalism and the free market, and left-wingers embracing redistributive policies designed to share wealth, education and opportunity more evenly. The old Spanish elite were almost uniformly Roman Catholic in education and outlook, while the disadvantaged poor found in Protestantism – and in Pentecostalism – a faith that spoke to their political aspirations as well as to their spiritual needs. Pentecostals became leaders of rural labour unions or neighbourhood social service associations organized by the Christian Democratic government of the 1960s.[34]

Between 1970 and 1973 the rightist Christian Democrats were locked in conflict with the coalition of the socialist Salvador Allende, with Pentecostals more likely to support left-wing parties. It may be that one reason why Pentecostals moved in this direction was because they did not wish to support the Christian Democratic Party that was associated strongly with the Catholic Church. Protestants were included in the annual Te Deum prayer service held in honour of Chile's independence, a public recognition that Catholics did not have a monopoly of religious authority. During the three years after 1970 at least one survey showed that Protestantism in Santiago increased from 5.5% of the population to 8%.[35]

In 1973 a military coup installed Augusto Pinochet. Later justifications of Pinochet's regime argue that he 'saved the country from communism'. Quite quickly Catholic bishops fell out with Pinochet and, as a result, he invited Protestants to work with his government. The Bishop of the Methodist Pentecostal Church (IMP) invited Pinochet to the inauguration of a new cathedral, and in 1975 the IMP took over the traditional role of hosting the Te Deum service.[36] Yet, while Methodist Pentecostal leaders worked with Pinochet, other Pentecostals demonstrated against the regime and were exiled or killed. A survey in 1990 showed that the

---

34 Much of the information on Chile in the paragraphs that follow comes from http://pewforum.org/surveys/pentecostal/countries/?CountryID=41 (accessed 30.07.08).

35 Paul Freston (2004), 'Contours of Latin American Pentecostalism', in Donald M. Lewis (ed.), *Christianity Reborn: The Global Expansion of Evangelicalism in the Twentieth Century*, Grand Rapids, MI, and Cambridge: Eerdmans, pp. 221–70.

36 The IMP were not the only Pentecostals to work with Pinochet. According to Bergunder, Jimmy Swaggart, before his disgrace, 'made no secret of his anti-communist bias and had no objection to being welcomed by dictators like Pinochet', 'Pentecostal Movement', p. 171.

majority of Pentecostals evaluated Pinochet negatively – not surprisingly, given the repressiveness of his regime and his capacity to destroy legitimate opposition with his vile secret police.

In 1989 a new president supported a bill to sponsor religious equality and in 1999 one Pentecostal bishop stood unsuccessfully for the presidency. By 2006 Pentecostals were in a strong enough position to call on the government to support evangelical religious education in public schools and this led to the setting up of a Presidential Advisory Council that included two Pentecostal bishops.

The collaboration between the IMP hierarchy and Pinochet and, equally, the resistance to Pinochet by many other Pentecostals, especially those Pentecostals working with the urban poor, has resulted in a public perception of Pentecostalism that is contradictory.[37] The IMP is still viewed with suspicion because of its support for a repressive regime, while those Pentecostals who resisted Pinochet were often the ones who worked with the World Council of Churches.[38] In effect the Pentecostal constituency now straddles the social and political spectrum. It has 'moved from a persecuted sect to an official church'.[39] The subtle dilemma that confronts Christian leaders is this: should they support a political regime that is unjust in order to secure (as they perceive it) advantages for the gospel or should they oppose a wicked regime and risk the wrath of the secret police?

Colombia

Colombia secured independence from Spain in the early nineteenth century. Its first years were marred by civil war and then the loss of what became Ecuador and, early in the twentieth century, Panama. War with Peru followed so that it was not until later that the country settled into peaceful equilibrium. A Danish couple, the Larssons, arrived in 1936 with a Oneness Pentecostal message. Shortly afterwards, Trinitarian Pentecostals arrived.[40] Although the country entered into a period of political turbulence known as 'the violence', Pentecostal congregations were gradually established. Other missionaries arrived in the late 1940s, including Southern Baptists, but political violence was fierce during this period also. 'People were pouring from mountain areas ... [they were attacked by] bands of killers hired by the Conservative government to wipe

---

37 Anderson, *Introduction*, p. 67.

38 The World Council of Churches held a consultation with a significant Pentecostal attendance in Santiago in 2003 and reported in *International Review of Mission* 93, 407–12.

39 Hollenweger, *Pentecostalism*, p. 130.

40 D. D. Bundy (2002), 'Colombia', in Burgess and van der Maas (eds), *NIDPCM*, pp. 65–6.

out the Liberals, who were over 60% of the total population.'[41] Some of the refugees from the mountains came to Pentecostal services where they were converted. Flora attributes the subsequent success of Pentecostalism to the social conditions of the time that created a 'highly solidarity movement' as a result of 'social dislocation'.[42] Solidarity 'implies a focused and universal world view present in a given group'. Her explanation, while interesting, is only one of a number that might be offered and is a strictly sociological description without any theological freight: in other words, it is not an explanation that is derived from the lips of Colombian Pentecostals themselves. In a review entitled, 'Who Speaks for Latin American Pentecostals?', Everett Wilson notes how analyses of Latin American Pentecostalism either patronize Pentecostal people by assuming that they are unaware of the significance of their actions or criticize them for failing to address social issues in their pursuit of individual salvation. He notes:

> Many publications – among them some with excellent insights and claims to legitimacy in speaking for Latin Americans – imply that the bulk of Latin American Pentecostals are susceptible to paternalistic manipulation, are compromised by foreign influence and resources and have betrayed their own peoples ... but it seems especially desirable that Latin American Pentecostals speak for themselves.[43]

Pentecostal groups, both Oneness and Trinitarian, grew despite opposition from municipal authorities at the behest of Catholic priests.[44] Further missionaries arrived after 1945 with the result that there was a range of denominational groupings, some with their origins in the United States and others in other Latin American countries. This wave of Pentecostalism was further supplemented by the outbreak of the charismatic movement in Bogota after 1967. The resulting breadth of Pentecostalism is wide, including both middle-class charismatics and working-class classical Pentecostals drawn from the difficult beginnings in the 1930s. Social and theological attitudes among Pentecostals cover a spectrum from, on one side, the collaborative and ecumenical and, on the other, to hardline and semi-sectarian. The Latin American Evangelical Pentecostal Commission (CEPLA) has co-operated with the World Council of Churches, whereas the powerful G12 cell churches of Cesar Castellanos are altogether more

---

41 Cornelia Butler Flora (1976), *Pentecostalism in Colombia: Baptism by Fire and Spirit*, London, Associated University Presses, p. 36.

42 Flora, 'Colombia', pp. 22, 23.

43 Everett A. Wilson (1994), 'Who Speaks for Latin American Pentecostals?', *Pneuma* 16.1, 143–50.

44 Bundy, 'Colombia', p. 66.

exclusive.[45] Yet, as even its most sympathetic commentators would admit, Colombian society is blighted by drug-related crime to the extent that the government is unable to control large sections of its own territory. The guerrilla factions, an expression of Marxist revolutionary zeal, are symptomatic of the polarization of Colombian opinion.[46] Against this background the hardline G12 cell churches appear less extreme.

Pentecostal churches in Colombia stand against the power of drug cartels.[47] These cartels are alleged to protect their interests by routinely bribing the police, judiciary and government officials. A strong church structure is needed to support the converts and in 1983 Cesar Castellanos launched a form of cell church that became known as G12, standing for 'Government of 12'.[48] Each cell was expected to grow to 12 people and each member of the cell was expected to pioneer his or her own cells. By this means one cell ought quickly to multiply to 12 cells and then to 144 cells. Each person would continue a deferential relationship with his or her own cell group leader as well as an overseeing relationship with the people in the cells which he or she led. Congregations were organ ized around these pyramidical principles and great credit was given to individuals who managed to enlarge the size of their own cells. Castellanos claimed that this vision for the church was universally applicable and began to travel to other countries propagating its adoption.[49] Within Bogota, his results were astonishing and his success can be gauged by the fact that at least one assassination attempt was made upon him by the drug barons he was challenging.

During the 1980s Protestants believed the Catholic Church was becoming more conservative and more supportive of heavy-handed state-sponsored crackdowns. Capitalistic right-wing Colombians found themselves in sharp conflict with left-wing activists. In 1991 Colombia adopted a new constitution that introduced greater religious freedom and thereby facilitated Protestant church growth. When an economic crisis struck in the mid-1990s, the middle classes were badly affected and many turned to the prosperity gospel preached by Pentecostals.[50] Around 50% of Protestants are Pentecostal.[51] Among these Pentecostals, or neo-Pentecostals, the G12 group has a membership of about 90,000 (some reports go as

45 See   http://www.oikoumene.org/en/member-churches/regions/latin-america/cepla.html and http://www.g12europe.com/about-g12/ (accessed 29.07.08).

46 http://www.cnn.com/SPECIALS/2000/colombia.noframes/story/reports/kidnapped/index.html (accessed 29.07.08).

47 I heard Castellanos preach to this effect.

48 http://www.g12europe.com/about-g12/ (accessed 29.07.08).

49 'Church-Growth Strategy Goes Global', *Charisma Magazine*, September 2003.

50 http://ipsnews.net/news.asp?idnews=37295 (accessed 29.07.08).

51 http://www.oikoumene.org/en/member-churches/regions/latin-america/colombia.html (accessed 29.07.08).

high as 300,000). The influence of Castellanos reaches to the very top of Colombian politics: his wife was a senator and represented Colombia as ambassador to Brazil from 2004 to 2006. The tight cellular church structure advocated by Castellanos makes sense in the light of the dangers of Colombian society. Reports indicate that there were 571 new kidnappings reported in 2007 alone, with a peak of 2,917 in 2001. Even a presidential candidate, Ingrid Betancourt, was kidnapped and held for six years for speaking out once too often against guerrillas and their cocaine barons. Betancourt's rescue, it is hoped, heralds a new era for the region.[52]

Argentina

Argentina, like Colombia, had to fight against Spain for its independence. Taking the opportunity created by Spain's struggle with Napoleon, the Argentinians declared themselves independent in 1816. Military force had colonized Latin America and military force freed it. As a result, the indigenous military elite was closely identified with nationalism, an identification that, as we shall see, later impacted Pentecostalism. When Argentina broke free of Spain, three elements of the colonial era remained: the Spanish language, Roman Catholicism and social stratification.

Emerging into the turbulence of the twentieth century, Argentina steered a neutral course during the 1914–18 war and became prosperous through its agricultural exports.[53] It was into this peaceful and prospering country that early Pentecostal missionaries came. As part of a wider wave of immigration, Alice Wood, a Canadian Methodist with the Christian and Missionary Alliance, arrived in 1909.[54] In 1914 she joined with the Assemblies of God and led her congregations into the Pentecostal fold.[55] Italian missionaries Louis Fracesconi, Giacomo Lombardi and Lucia Menna also reached Argentina in 1909; Danish missionaries came four years later and Swedish missionaries arrived in 1920. Chilean Pentecostals, once their own congregations were established, also made a pioneering contribution. Little by little Pentecostal churches grew, especially when they became thoroughly Argentinian in language and outlook, so that by the 1950s there were five or six major groups.

A major Pentecostal breakthrough occurred in 1954 when the revivalist Tommy Hicks preached at a two-month crusade in Buenos Aires.

---

52 *Telegraph Magazine*, 2 August 2008, pp. 22–6.

53 Daniel K. Lewis (2001), *The History of Argentina*, Basingstoke, Palgrave Macmillan, ch. 5.

54 See http://www.oikoumene.org/en/member-churches/regions/latin-america/argentina.html (accessed 25.07.08). For details about Alice Wood, see G. B. McGee (2004), *People of the Spirit*, Springfield, MS, Gospel Publishing House, pp. 94, 95.

55 For further details of the early years of Pentecostal mission, see Allan Anderson (2007), *Spreading Fires: The Missionary Nature of Early Pentecostalism*, London, SCM Press, pp. 200, 201.

The Atlanta Football Stadium with a capacity of 45,000 was hired, the churches came together in an ecumenism of the Spirit, divine healing and salvation were preached, people of all classes attended and after a month over 100,000 people were packing the stadium nightly. There is good authority supporting the story that the Argentinian President Juan Perón was healed of a skin disease and gave permission for the revivalists to use radio and television.[56] By the end of the revival over 200,000 people were attending the meetings and numerous new congregations had been established throughout the country and in its dominant capital city. Co-operation between the churches, particularly the Protestant churches, gave respectability to the Pentecostals. The number of Spirit-filled congregations trebled so that by the start of the 1960s the total number of Pentecostals was estimated to be around 60,000 adult baptized members, a figure that translates into attendance levels of at least 100,000.[57]

Politically Argentina remained moderate during most of these years although military power gradually increased until the armed forces took control in 1976. Human rights were suppressed (which damaged the churches) and the economy declined. In an effort to win patriotic approval and to divert attention from internal repression General (or President) Galtieri made the mistake of invading islands that had been in British possession at least since 1833. The Falkland Islands, or Malvinas, appear to have been of little strategic, economic or military value, but the British under Margaret Thatcher dispatched a small naval task force, which, assisted by intelligence from US satellites, fought with skill and bravery. The Argentinian military collapsed, the islands were recaptured, Galtieri was disgraced and democracy was restored in 1983. The humiliation of the military government could be seen as a providential event by Argentinian Christians.[58] Those who had grown up under the military dictatorship were delighted to have their liberties restored and, although the Argentinian economy was not immediately cured, the churches found themselves in a position where they could once more freely and passionately evangelize.[59]

At the start of the 1980s evangelicals accounted for about 2.5% of the Argentinian population, but by the end of the decade they made up around 10%.[60] Evangelicals became Pentecostalized. While it is simplistic

---

56 David Bundy (2002), 'Argentina', in Burgess and van der Maas, *NIDPCM*, pp. 23–5. Perón's wife, Evita, passionately advocated the rights of the poor, never forgetting where she had come from.

57 Bundy, 'Argentina', pp. 23–5, quoting Walter Hollenweger.

58 http://forerunner.com/forerunner/X0274_Revival_Surges_in_Ar.html (accessed 25.07.08).

59 Cf. Ruth Padilla DeBorst's comments in http://www.christianvisionproject.com/2007/08/liberate_my_people.html (accessed 25.07.08).

60 Wes Richards (2005), 'An Examination of Common Factors in the Growth of Global Pentecostalism', *Journal of Asian Mission* 7.1, 85–106.

to attribute all this to the ministry of one preacher, Carlos Annacondia, who began his public preaching in 1982, is credited with being at the cutting edge. His evangelistic campaigns followed the Tommy Hicks model but his theology was more radically Pentecostal. He became a proponent of spiritual warfare and saw himself as a priest of God with the power to destroy the curses of the past or of paganism (see Chapter 13). All-night prayer meetings to 'bind the strongman' preceded street preaching and vigorous forays into the slums.[61] Annacondia did not forget his own underprivileged origins and, like the independent healing evangelists within the United States, saw his power as emanating from the special anointing of the Holy Spirit that allowed him to fight against the encroachments of the devil. The title of his book *Listen to Me, Satan!* encapsulates this aggressive drive.

Annacondia's ministry is often mentioned in the same breath as that of Omar Cabrera.[62] The emphasis of the two ministries is distinct in the sense that Cabrera appears to be more concerned with prosperity than spiritual warfare; he started the Foundación Visión de Futuro which is linked with Asociación Iglesia de Dios Argentina and now has over 85,000 adherents.[63] In the same group is placed Hector Giminez, a church planter with a congregation, or set of congregations, with between 70,000 and 120,000 members.[64]

These public protagonists for Pentecostalism need to be located among numerous other minor ministries of a similar kind and among numerous social welfare ministries. One runs in a large prison, part of which has been revolutionized by a sustained operation of the Holy Spirit. One entire floor of the 4,000-strong prison has become Christian, and violence there has been largely eliminated. This section of the prison has been cleaned up and those who serve their sentences find that they are able to give up crime and integrate into the community on their release, many of them fitting in to congregations drawn from the urban poor.[65] Converts to Pentecostalism, despite the comments of its critics, should not be seen as passive recipients of an irresistible message (brainwashing) but as men and women who have chosen to follow Christ because they believe, upon the testimony of the preachers, that he empowers them to overcome all

---

61 http://www.godtube.com/view_video.php?viewkey=345d20e9287be1b6d7e0 (accessed 25.07.08).

62 http://www.necf.org.my/berita/berita_nov_dec1999/argentine.htm (accessed 25.07.08).

63 Bundy, 'Argentina', p. 25.

64 http://www.grmi.org/Richard_Riss/history/argentina2.html (accessed 25.07.08). The lower figure was given to me by Andrew Parfitt.

65 http://www.grmi.org/Richard_Riss/history/argentina2.html (accessed 25.07.08). Successful prison ministry is also reported by Miller and Yamamori, *Global Pentecostalism*, pp. 110–12.

their social and educational disadvantages.[66] The consequences of Argentina's unequal society, an inequality that dates back to the aristocratic landowners of the nineteenth century, are that the poor must look for answers to their predicament either in a political philosophy or in an intensely practical Pentecostal Christianity. The fact that many Argentinians prefer Christianity to Marxism surprises sceptical left-wing intellectuals but it makes perfect sense to many men and women within the shanty towns along the banks of the river Riachuelo.

Reflection

Attempts to explain the advance of Pentecostalism within Latin America go back at least to the 1960s. Most of these attempts have been driven by sociological theory and some have been tinged by critical colours. Some of the theories have been supported by small-scale research projects in individual countries, but in these cases it is very doubtful whether variables unique to one country can be applied across the whole of Latin America. And, according to recent theoreticians, empirical sociology is approaching its own crisis.[67]

The best-known large-scale theories include studies by C. Lalive d'Epinay, which argued that Pentecostal congregations provide psychological or social security within conditions of rapid and disorientating social change.[68] The basis for this account goes back at least as far as Emile Durkheim (1858–1917) and has plausibility, though the theory does not explain why people should go to *Pentecostal* churches rather than to any other kind of church, or why they should join churches rather than other organizations like trade unions or political parties. The theory presumes that individuals need supportive social relations (which is probably true) but cannot predict which agencies will provide those relations in times of uncertainty. The theory is formulated on the basis of late nineteenth-century or early twentieth-century psychology and on the basis of an explanation of religion that sees any understanding of God as a projection of the highest social values of a group or community. Thus the theory is intellectually imperialistic in the sense that it uses sociological discourse to swallow up theological discourse.

An alternative account by E. Willems sees Pentecostal communities as standing in sharp contrast to ancestral feudal societies.[69] Pentecostal

---

66 David Bundy (1998), 'Pentecostalism in Argentina', *Pneuma* 20.1, 95–109.

67 M. Savage and R. Burrows (2007), 'The Coming Crisis of Empirical Sociology', *Sociology* 41.5, 885–99.

68 C. Lalive d'Epinay (1969), *Haven of the Masses: A Study of the Pentecostal Movement in Chile*, London, Lutterworth Press.

69 E. Willems (1967), *Followers of the New Faith: Culture Change and the Rise of Protestantism in Brazil and Chile*, Nashville, TN, Vanderbilt University Press.

communities emphasize brotherly and sisterly love rather than deference to a feudal boss. Those who lost their feudal identity found a new identity within the Pentecostal family and, taking hold of a new Puritan work ethic, learned to better themselves economically in environments that rewarded hard work and entrepreneurialism. In this respect Pentecostalism is seen as actively encouraging the modernization of society.

David Martin parallels Pentecostalism with early Methodism.[70] The early Methodists in the eighteenth century provided mechanisms for increasing adult literacy and opportunities for learning and education and thereby created a social space for democracy to flourish. If Pentecostals do not concern themselves with political matters, this is quite in keeping with their search for personal freedom. As a rider to this theory one can add reference to 'social capital'. Bordieu proposes that 'social capital' provides intangible resources for individuals just as financial capital provides material resources.[71] Social capital exists in two forms: membership of a Pentecostal community gives individuals capital in both its bridging (into other sectors of society) and bonding (emotional solidarity) forms.

What has surprised many scholars is the willingness of the poor to embrace Pentecostalism rather than Catholicism's ecclesial communities.[72] According to Mariz:

The Catholic Church opts for the poor because it is not a Church of the poor. Pentecostal churches do not opt for the poor because they are already a poor people's church. And that is why poor people are choosing them.[73]

Questions to think about

1 How plausible do you find sociological explanations of the boom of Pentecostalism in Latin America?
2 Should Pentecostals be involved in politics? What are the dangers?
3 Should Pentecostals be involved in broadcasting? What are the dangers?

---

70 D. Martin (1990), *Tongues of Fire: The Explosion of Pentecostalism in Latin America*, Oxford, Blackwell.

71 Pierre Bordieu (1977), *Outline of a Theory of Practice*, Cambridge, Cambridge University Press.

72 See also the discussion in Edward L. Cleary and Hannah Stewart-Gambino (eds), 1992, *Conflict and Competition: The Latin American Church in a Changing Environment*, London, Lynne Rienner.

73 C. L. Mariz (1994), *Coping with Poverty: Pentecostals and Christian Base Communities in Brazil*, Philadelphia, Temple University Press, p. 80.

Further reading

Freston, P. (2004), 'Contours of Latin American Pentecostalism', in Donald M. Lewis (ed.), *Christianity Reborn: The Global Expansion of Evangelicalism in the Twentieth Century*, Grand Rapids, MI and Cambridge, William B. Eerdmans.

Hollenweger, W. J. (1997), *Pentecostalism: Origins and Developments Worldwide*, Peabody, MA, Hendrickson.

Martin, D. (1990), *Tongues of Fire: The Explosion of Pentecostalism in Latin America*, Oxford, Blackwell.

Smith, C. L. (2007), *Revolution, Revival and Religious Conflict in Sandinista Nicaragua*, Leiden, Brill.

Wilson, E. A. (2002), 'Brazil', in S. M. Burgess and E. van der Maas (eds), *New International Dictionary of Pentecostal and Charismatic Movements*, Grand Rapids, MI, Zondervan.

7

Africa: The Cases of Ghana, Congo and Zimbabwe

When the missionaries came to Africa they had the Bible and we had the land. They said, 'Let us pray.' We closed our eyes. When we opened them we had the Bible and they had the land. (Desmond Tutu)

Before Azusa Street

I imagine this book in the hands of an African Pentecostal or charismatic Christian. In academic circles there has been heated discussion about colonialism and post-colonial studies. One writer describes colonialism as a 'variety of fascism' and inevitably 'racist'.[1] Others are more measured and reflective, taking in both the pluses of colonialism as well as the minuses. It has been said that the British were to India what the Romans were to Britain: both brought a unity to formerly disparate and warring peoples and, when they departed, left a legacy of roads, buildings and, in the case of the British, railways.[2] Some of my colleagues consider that the missionary zeal of nineteenth-century Protestantism disgracefully replaced African culture and religion; others, even if they are African, are only too pleased to see the worst aspects of African culture (cannibalism and feudal poverty) removed. This is not a matter about which people easily agree because ethnic pride is at stake.

Moreover, when we look at the present religious and economic situation in Africa, there is evident poverty and a form of government that builds upon African kinship obligations. Parliamentary democracy in the West functions through a neutral civil service, and government power is counterpoised by free institutions – the press, the judiciary, public corporations, charities, professional associations, and the like – whereas African democracy is riddled with nepotism, which European eyes see as a

---

1 http://www.english.emory.edu/Bahri/Memmi.html Albert Memmi describes colonialism as 'one variety of fascism'.

2 An insight attributed to Tom Stoppard.

form of corruption.[3] It is therefore easy for African leaders to blame their problems on the colonial epoch, even when these problems are of their own making. One only has to read about Ghana's Kwame Nkrumah to find completely contradictory judgements: for Martin Meredith, he is an impractical dreamer, a man who suppressed opposition, robbed his country, mismanaged it, and infused all his grandiose schemes with a pan-Africanism that those African leaders he tried to undermine found contemptible; for others, he is a hero and the first African president in the post-colonial era whose leadership and vision inspired others along the same path.[4] Such considerations lead David Maxwell, in his account of the growth of churches in Zimbabwe, to argue that the same stringent criteria by which colonial governments were judged should be applied to African leaders of all kinds.[5] Otherwise, we create double standards: foreign missionaries might be castigated for patronizing Africans while African leaders, displaying haughty disdain for their own people, benefit from uncritical acclaim.

Africa is a continent, a vast mass of land comprising many types of climate and geography, and rich in gold, diamonds, copper and other mineral resources (later oil), as well as highly prized ivory. Along its northern coast, once within range of Imperial Rome, Christianity quickly took root and grew. Augustine of Hippo lived on the North African coast across the Mediterranean sea from Rome. After the rise of Islam, all the countries along Africa's northern shore were rolled up into a new Islamic empire and the Christian population either converted or burdened with heavier taxation. Inland, the Sahara Desert forms a natural and almost impenetrable barrier between the northern countries and the tropical interior of Africa. It is for this reason that contemporary Africa is roughly divided between the northern, Islamic sections in Morocco, Algeria, Tunisia, Libya and Egypt and the more southerly equatorial or sub-equatorial Christian blocks of countries.

The eastern 'horn' of Africa is across the water from Arabia and vulnerable to its raiding parties and the slave trade that grew up in the eighth and ninth centuries. The history of slavery is full of tragedy and irony, fuelled by cruelty and greed, and often susceptible to horrible twists as African betrayed African to the slaver's iron shackles.[6] The trade lasted

---

3 See the discussion in Paul Gifford (1998), *African Christianity: Its Public Role*, London, Hurst and Co., ch. 1.

4 Martin Meredith (2006), *The State of Africa*, London, Free Press. For more flattering comments on Nkrumah, see Wikipedia.

5 David Maxwell (2006), *African Gifts of the Spirit: Pentecostalism and the Rise of a Zimbabwean Transnational Religious Movement*, Oxford, James Currey, p. 4.

6 According to Robert Hughes writing in *Time* magazine, 3 February 1992, 'The African slave trade as such, the black traffic, was an Arab invention, developed by traders with the enthusiastic collaboration of black African ones ... The image

for about 1,000 years and it is to the credit of the British Parliament that it first voted for the abolition of slavery from Africa's west coasts in 1807, a vote that became effective wherever the British ruled from 1833.[7] If we are looking for one reason for the spread of the British Empire, it must be in the refusal of the British to allow slavery, and consequently the elevation of the rule of law. Freetown in Sierra Leone became a British colony in 1808 and was a place of refuge for escaped slaves. The British Navy, supreme at sea after the defeat of the French at Trafalgar in 1805, enforced anti-slavery legislation. If we are judging the morality of imperial adventures in Africa, we need to take into account those who opposed and those who accepted slavery.

The British Navy enabled the enlargement of the British Empire, both in Africa and India, but, of course, the British government was by no means altruistic in all that it did. It was concerned with material gain and advantageous trade; and unfair trading conditions stacked against Africa continue to this day. The Gold Coast in West Africa was attractive because of its mineral wealth. Yet among the first missionaries to begin work there were those from the Basel Mission in Switzerland in 1828. The story of the Mission has been told by Jon Miller who has shown, using the immense archival resources at Basel, how those German Swiss worked hard and long to spread the Protestant gospel in a place where many of them were ill-adapted to the diseases that were not to be found in Europe.[8] Malaria, until the discovery of quinine, struck missionaries down with awful regularity so that at one point dead missionaries easily outnumbered live converts. Large-scale use of quinine did not take place until after about 1850.

The Gold Coast (now Ghana), along with other West African territories, was evangelized first in the 1840s and 1850s. David Livingstone famously walked from the Atlantic coast of Africa to the Indian Ocean, a trek of around 2,000 miles, between 1852 and 1856. He wanted to open up Central Africa to Christianity and civilization, a conscious pairing of religious and civil duties, and was driven by anti-slavery motives

---

promulgated by pop-history fictions like *Roots* – of white slavers bursting with cutlass and musket into the settled lives of peaceful African villages – is very far from historical truth.'

7 However, an African friend of mine commented: 'The British liberated the people from slaving in the form of people being no longer chained and shipped away, the slavery continued in mental slavery and domination. The feeling is that the African was made to occupy the position of a second class human being, and was treated as such by their colonial masters. To many Africans, it was a new approach to slavery.' Thus the impact of slavery remains.

8 Jon Miller (2003), *Missionary Zeal and Institutional Control: Organizational Contradictions in the Basel Mission on the Gold Coast, 1828–1917*, Grand Rapids, MI, Eerdmans.

as a way of expressing his cooling evangelical fervour.[9] He was the first European to see many of the great African rivers – the Zambezi, the Nile and the Congo – as the way to open up the heart of the continent.[10] Where the missionary explorer went, the trader followed. And where the trader went, the colonial administrator was not far behind. And where the colonial administrator set up office, slavery faced the rigour of the law. All this was made easier by the opening of the Suez Canal in 1869 since the journey to East Africa became shorter.

The Christian voices which view Africa as a continent needing the gospel were in competition with other voices that saw the theory of evolution as applicable to clashes of culture. If one civilization destroyed another, this was an example of the survival of the fittest. Belief in evolution, becoming part of common intellectual currency after the publication of *The Origin of Species* in 1859, appeared to support the replacement of a technologically inferior civilization by a technologically superior one.[11] Yet it is simplistic to see European engagement with Africa as motivated by competition between Christianity and evolutionary theory. African civilization had a far longer history than is normally credited to it, as archaeological remains in parts of the continent indicate.[12] African culture may have been tribal, but it was also communitarian by virtue of polygamy, a feature which rendered it compatible with Islam and often incompatible with Christianity. If a man became a Christian, what was he to do with his second and other wives? Was he to divorce them, and, if not, was he to be admitted to Holy Communion? These questions were not theoretical in West Africa, especially as the Anglican Church Missionary Society, led by the far-sighted Henry Venn, urged the formation of indigenous African churches, a plea that was paralleled by the appointment of indigenous evangelists by the Methodist Church, the first of whom worked in Ghana before 1816.[13]

---

9 Peter Hinchliff (1990), 'Africa', in John McManners (ed.), *The Oxford Illustrated History of Christianity*, Oxford, Oxford University Press, p. 460, tells of the formation of the Africa Civilisation Society in 1839. Among those present was the young David Livingstone. Livingstone literally gave his heart to Africa. It was buried in Africa, while his body was interred in Westminster Abbey in London. See R. Mackenzie (1993), *David Livingstone: The Truth Behind the Legend*, Eastbourne, Kingsway, ch. 21.

10 Stephen Taylor (2000), *Livingstone's Tribe: A Journey from Zanzibar to the Cape*, London, Flamingo.

11 Hinchliff, 'Africa', p. 463.

12 Egyptian archaeology is well known, but more recently excavations or discoveries in Somalia, Zimbabwe, Nigeria and Mali (Timbuktu) show the extent of the heritage. See http://wordpress.com/tag/african-cultural-heritage/ and http://archaeology.about.com/od/tterms/qt/timbuktu.htm

13 David L. Edwards (1997), *Christianity: The First Two Thousand Years*, London, Cassell, pp. 537, 538.

The Cape of Good Hope at Africa's most southern point had to be navigated by sailing ships taking the long voyage from northern Europe to India. The seafaring nations, first the Portuguese and then in the seventeenth and eighteenth centuries the Dutch, established settlements in the Cape area and the Dutch settlers eventually fought with the local black population of Hottentots at about the same time as Bantu-speaking Xhosa arrived from the north. Shortly after this, the British seized Cape Town and in 1806 established a colony which, because diamonds and gold were discovered a couple of generations later in the Transvaal, expanded rapidly northwards. The Dutch brought with them the Calvinism of the Reformed Church and the British their moderate Anglicanism (in an Anglo-Catholic form), with the result that in most of the major South African cities there are large imposing cathedrals with fine buildings around them and long-established episcopacies.[14]

French resurgence at the end of the nineteenth century, as well as the partial unification of Germany, led directly to the 'scramble for Africa' that took place roughly between 1880 and 1902. The tempo and aims changed: gone was the Livingstonian ideal of Christianity and civilization. Bismark, 'one of the few authentic geniuses among nineteenth-century statesmen', wanted to 'sow dissension between Britain and France', and saw Africa as the ideal arena.[15] At the 1884–85 Conference of Berlin the European powers divided Africa up using lines of longitude and latitude, swapped countries and lands with each other, and in this way demarcated their own zones of influence – often in ways that ignored the ancestral territories of nomadic tribes. *Realpolitik*, politics stripped of any ethical content, prevailed and it did so at a time when the earliest machine guns came into production. The maxim gun was in use after 1884 and could fire 600 rounds a minute. No African army could resist it, and the European colonies were soon founded. Germany had colonies in Togoland, Cameroon, Rwanda, Burundi, Tanzania and Namibia.[16] The Americans gained a foothold in Liberia, the French took parts of North Africa, Senegal, Guinea, Mali, Côte d'Ivoire, Benin, Niger, Chad, the Republic of Congo and, after the defeat of Germany in 1918, some former German colonies. The Belgian king, Leopold II, gained much of central Congo as his personal possession. The Portuguese took Angola to

---

14 For more details, see Peter Hinchliff (1964), *John William Colenso*, London, Nelson.

15 N. Ferguson (2004), *Empire: How Britain Made the Modern World*, London, Penguin, p. 234.

16 There are difficulties here. The spellings of names of countries have been Africanized over the years, the countries themselves have changed and there are also variant spellings. Thus Ruanda or Rwanda are variant spellings and Tanzania was called Tanganyika because Zanzibar was not part of the German territory, although it is included in Tanzania today.

the west and Mozambique to the east.[17] The British took Egypt, the Cape area and what became South Africa, and a line of countries stretching northwards through what became Zambia and Kenya, as well as its West African possessions of Nigeria and Ghana.

Roman Catholicism, in the first instance supported by 'secular' France, was represented by the 'White Fathers', founded by Archbishop Lavigerie in Algiers in 1868 and also stoutly anti-slavery.[18] This community of priests and lay men bound themselves to lifelong missionary work and were soon followed by 'White Sisters', who, eventually penetrating the Sahara, reached Uganda by the 1880s. As the colonies grew and as the European powers flexed their political and military muscles in the pursuit of new territory, missionaries, whether Roman Catholic or Protestant, might find themselves given favoured status – if they were Protestant then the British would favour them and if they were Roman Catholic then the French would favour them.[19] In Central Africa, where the arm of the colonial power hardly reached, there could be competition between Christian groups representing different colonial powers; and all this was complicated by Islamic encroachments from the east.

In short, not all missionaries were the same and not all parts of Africa shared a common history. If a simplified pattern is to be found it is this: first came the fervent missionary societies, both Protestant and Roman Catholic, with little colonial pressure behind them. Then, after the real-politik scramble for Africa when colonial rule was firmly rooted and connected to governments in London, Paris, Berlin, Lisbon or Brussels, national churches set up parallel structures to those at home. As a result, the religious culture of Britain or Germany or Portugal was transplanted to Africa and a range of versions of Christianity, some ritualistic and some evangelical, came into being. In countries like Kenya a variety of religious groups was to be found. In others, like Mozambique, the Portuguese territory, Catholicism and the Portuguese language were predominant. A hundred years later Brazilian Pentecostals took advantage of this and planted fresh congregations almost identical to those that were so successful in Brazil.[20]

Finally, Ethiopia, as readers of the book of Acts will know, is the country from which Queen Candace's treasurer travelled up to Jerusalem

---

17 Originally the Portuguese claimed land running right across Africa from west to east, but the British resisted by the threat of war and the Portuguese backed down.

18 'White' because of their robes, not their race.

19 Though the British did sometimes favour those who were not Protestant. For instance in Kenya the British supported the Roman Catholic presence.

20 Paper given at the Glopent conference at the University of Heidelberg, 1–2 February 2008.

(Acts 8.27f).[21] On his return journey, and while reading from a scroll of the prophet Isaiah, he met Philip the evangelist and was converted to Christianity. Presumably his interest in the prophet Isaiah was prompted by an acquaintance with Judaism – perhaps he had been to worship at the Temple. The account of this man's remarkable conversion tallies with the long-standing presence of Christianity in Ethiopia. Churches have existed there from at least the fourth century onwards and, within a mountain kingdom, its peoples developed their own Christian tradition and held out against the pressure of Islam for more than 1,000 years. Only recently have the Ethiopian churches begun to be open to charismatic and Pentecostal spirituality and welcoming to preachers who fly in from Europe and elsewhere to give well-attended seminars.

Patterns of Pentecostalism

The size of the Pentecostal and charismatic movements in Africa sky-rocketed from the 1980s onwards but their deep beginnings go back many years before.[22] In each country – though early land boundaries did not follow the lines they follow today – a unique pattern of missionary enterprise occurred among tribal groups, some large, some small, some coastal, some inland, some warlike and some given to trade, farming or herding and nomadic migration. In every place a typical African world view incorporated belief in spirits, demons, an afterlife, animal sacrifice and the significance of dreams. Social stability and tribal continuity were enhanced by the veneration of ancestors. Social integration and population growth were stimulated by polygamy. Even so, there were elements of this world view that almost exactly accorded with Pentecostal and charismatic Christianity; we could say that Africa was prepared for Pentecostalism in a way that the rationalistic West was not.

The three countries that follow have been chosen for their contrasting nature. Ghana is in the west, Congo is central and Zimbabwe is in the east. While Ghana and Zimbabwe are anglophone, Congo is francophone. Their pre-Pentecostal experience of Christianity differs greatly, but each country by the end of the twentieth century enjoyed a similar abundance of Pentecostal activity.

---

21 Although I have identified Ethiopia in the Bible with Ethiopia today, this may be incorrect. Biblical Ethiopia was Cush, which is anywhere above the second cataract on the Nile. That is today's Sudan.

22 I am indebted to David Garrard for his comments on an earlier draft of this chapter.

Ghana

A great empire, the 'centre of an elaborate trading network', radiated out from Ghana as early as the tenth century.[23] Portuguese traders appear to have reached that part of the world in the fifteenth century. An early missionary foray was made in 1751 by Thomas Thompson who had met black slaves in New Jersey. Thompson's five-year stint was largely unfruitful but he sent three African boys to England for education and one of them, Philip Quaque, was baptized in 1759, became an Anglican priest in 1765 and worked for more than 50 years in the Gold Coast, as it was then called, dying in 1816 having served as 'missionary, schoolmaster, and catechist'.[24] In 1828 the Basel Mission, a Swiss Protestant society, began its work and gradually fostered Christianity, schooling, the study of African languages and the development of agriculture and commerce.[25] When the missionaries arrived, they found Ghana plagued by the slave trade and consequent poverty, and their work over many years, including the introduction of cocoa, helped reverse the situation. Methodists overlapped with Basel, and Thomas Freeman (1809–90), of mixed African and English parentage, contributed to steady Methodist growth and to the training of lay preachers who were later to make a notable impact in the region.[26] Roman Catholics appear to have reached Ghana in 1880 and settled inland where malaria ravaged missionary personnel.[27]

So Christianity was present in Ghana by the end of the nineteenth century. One of the most dramatic demonstrations that Africa had taken Christianity to its heart came through William Wade Harris (1865–1929), a prophetic figure who would have been at home in the company of John the Baptist. Harris had been raised and educated in the home of a Methodist minister in Liberia and became a Methodist lay preacher with a good command of English. His early life was occupied with a series of jobs as a seaman, bricklayer, schoolteacher and government interpreter, but he was imprisoned after supporting plans to make Liberia a British colony. Harris pulled down the Liberian flag and planted a British flag and then led an uprising of the Grebo people.[28] Had this been the full extent of Harris's life, he would have remained a footnote in the colonial struggle, but during his time in prison he saw a vision of the angel Gabriel who commanded him to preach 'as a prophet of the last

23 Hinchliff, 'Africa', p. 455.

24 S. Neill (1990), *A History of Christian Missions*, Harmondsworth, Penguin, p. 203.

25 Neill, *Missions*, p. 260.

26 Neill, *Missions*, p. 261.

27 K. E. Larbi (2001), *Pentecostalism: The Eddies of Ghanaian Christianity*, Accra, Ghana, Centre for Pentecostalism and Charismatic Studies, p. 147.

28 A. Anderson (2007), *Spreading Fires: The Missionary Nature of Early Pentecostalism*, London, SCM Press, p. 163.

times, to destroy the fetishes that were part of the region's traditional African religions [and] to baptize all who would receive this Christian sacrament'.[29]

After his release from prison, Harris left Liberia and moved eastwards to the Ivory Coast where in July 1913 his impact was dramatic. Thousands responded to his mission. He and his two female companions would approach a village singing songs, gather a crowd, preach passionately and command them to renounce their African religious traditions and to put their faith in the one true God. He baptized penitents in the name of the Father, Son and Holy Spirit and placed a Bible on their heads, and on occasion miracles happened. Harris was a 'proto-Pentecostal' who believed that the Spirit had come upon him as on the day of Pentecost and that he had spoken in other tongues.[30] Harris's own itinerant ministry barely left time for the founding of independent congregations. He encouraged his converts to attend mission churches, whether Protestant or Catholic, though eventually Harris Churches were founded. He appeared to accept polygamy (and may indeed have practised it himself). His own churches were largely in unevangelized places and he left his congregations in the charge of 12 apostles whom he appointed. The followers of Harris were by no means anti-missionary and Harris himself, as his approval of the British government showed, was by no means anti-colonial. But it was the French administrators, probably prompted by the Catholic Church in the Ivory Coast, who eventually imprisoned him towards the end of 1914. Over the next ten years, Harris's believers were persecuted and their prayer houses were burnt. He died in 1929.

What was astonishing about Harris, apart from the huge crowds he drew and the immense success he enjoyed during an intense public ministry – sometimes baptizing 300 people a day – was that he showed how an African form of Pentecostal Christianity could run like wildfire through rural areas. Harris, dressed in a white robe and carrying a staff and Bible, impacted Liberia, the Ivory Coast and Ghana with his authoritative proclamation of God's power over traditional African fetishes and spirits, and blazed a trail for later charismatic radicals.

Christianity continued to grow slowly within Ghana in the first part of the twentieth century. Nationalism began to bubble up after 1945 and, like Christianity, helped unite the 75 tribes that make up the modern Ghanaian population.[31] British colonial rule included a Legislative Council and it was to this that Kwame Nkrumah was elected in 1951. By 1957 the country had gained independence and Nkrumah had become

29 Mark A. Noll (1997), *Turning Points*, Grand Rapids, MI, Baker Books, p. 289.

30 Anderson, *Fires*, p. 163.

31 This section relies heavily on Gifford, *African Christianity*.

the first prime minister.[32] He remained in power until 1966 when he was overthrown in a military coup, which, within a few years, descended into corruption and inefficiency. Flight Lieutenant Jerry Rawlings took power in 1979, and after executions of previous rulers made way for a republic that only lasted until 1981, when Rawlings again took power. Although an admirer of Castro and Qaddafi, Rawlings realized the bankruptcy of socialism and turned to the World Bank for aid. Money flowed in, the country transitioned to civilian rule, the infrastructure was improved and Rawlings won the popular presidential vote in a 1992 election.

In 1960 43% of the population were Christians, but by the end of the century this number had risen to 60%, which shows that the boom in Christianity took place in the last third of the twentieth century.[33] Muslim numbers appear to have remained static at about 16%, although the figures are disputed. The public impact of evangelical and prosperity-orientated Christianity is exemplified by the slogans painted on buses, cars, houses and offices. Preachers can be heard on the public transport system, on Ghana's TV, and the local newspapers are full of Christian metaphors and references. Rawlings's 1981 coup was referred to as his 'second coming'. In 1986–87 the Ghana Evangelism Committee surveyed the whole country, counting those attending Sunday services. A similar survey, carried out five years later, revealed the underlying trend. The mainline Protestant churches held steady: the Anglicans dropped by 2%, the Presbyterians rose by 17% and the Methodists grew by 2%.[34] The really big losers were to be found among the traditional African Initiated Churches (AICs), which almost all declined by between 17% and 23%. By contrast, the winners were the Pentecostal and charismatic churches: Assemblies of God grew by 87%, the Church of Pentecost by 31%, the Apostolic Church by 27%, and the Christ Apostolic Church by 36%. Other apostolic churches grew by similar amounts and Paul Gifford interprets the figures as showing that Ghana is 'experiencing something more complex than a "Pentecostal explosion"'. Moreover, despite claims to the contrary, traditional African religion appears to be losing ground and mainly exists as a submerged set of attitudes within Christianity and Islam.[35] The largest single Christian block remains the Roman Catholic Church, which has gained credibility over many years for its bold

---

32 He ran a one-party state at election time. See Martin Gilbert (1999), *A History of the Twentieth Century*, vol. 3, London, HarperCollins, p. 333.

33 An interesting discussion of the way film and television make magic plausible is given by Birgit Meyer (2003), 'Ghanaian Popular Cinema and the Magic in and of Film', in Birgit Meyer and Peter Pels (eds), *Magic and Modernity*, Stanford, Stanford University Press, pp. 200–22. This inflation of magic is said to be compatible with the teachings of Pentecostal preachers.

34 Gifford, *African Christianity*, p. 67.

35 Gifford, *African Christianity*, p. 63.

denunciations of the abuse of political and police power. Additionally, the Catholic Church has been involved in health and education initiatives.

Gifford's more extensive analysis of Ghanaian churches considers the economic and cultural influence of Pentecostal and charismatic Christianity. He senses a paradigm shift whereby the new globally aware churches are a conduit for foreign money as well as a sounding board for prosperity economics. Here Christians are encouraged to give to the church and give money to God on the grounds that if they do so God will enrich them. This 'trading with God', which can have complicated connections with deliverance ministry through the casting out of 'spirits of poverty', is hammered home by extravagant preaching (see Chapter 13). Preaching normally lasts an hour and is preceded by choirs, rousing congregational singing, energetic and skilful instrumental playing and not a little dancing.[36] The preachers are powerful verbal communicators with their own individual styles and preferences, most of them serving as lifestyle exemplars for their huge congregations. TV broadcasting covers the whole country and channels will often carry big American charismatic names like Benny Hinn or T. D. Jakes. The Pentecostal and charismatic churches sink their money into broadcasting while the traditional mainline churches put their funds into education or development.[37] Christian radio amplifies the often repeated assertions about Christianity being the road to blessing, health, financial success, successful marriages and the solving of every personal problem: 'I wasn't born successful – I *became* successful. No one gave me a break; I broke the forces of darkness.'[38]

So powerful is the Pentecostal and charismatic movement that it impacts the political scene. Rawlings has been bathed with the glow of sacral kingship in the discourse of Pentecostal preachers; if he is a believer (and he has attended religious rallies), then ultimately all that he does is open to the blessing of God.[39] Such a theology extracts the teeth of social critique and makes a cosy relationship with the government all too probable. While the government benefits from Pentecostal adulation, Pentecostals benefit from tacit government support for their activities – this is Gifford's charge. Moreover, he sees the consistent spiritual warfare, deliverance and prosperity cocktail as ultimately detrimental to the economic progress of the country. Whereas earlier revivals in Britain and the United States resulted in a stress upon hard work and honesty as the indispensable ingredients of material advance, the present West African theology of personal gain is ultimately unrealistic. Instead of working hard at their farms, businesses and offices, Ghanaians are exhorted by

---

36 Paul Gifford (2004), *Ghana's New Christianity: Pentecostalism in a Globalising African Economy*, Bloomington and Indianapolis, Indiana University Press, p. 28.

37 Gifford, *New Christianity*, p. 33.

38 Gifford, *New Christianity*, p. 53, and quoting an African preacher.

39 Gifford, *New Christianity*, p. 40f.

their pastors to attend overlong and repetitive services, with the result that normal commercial activity suffers. Only one African preacher, Mensa Otabil, appears to stand out against the prevailing trend. Otabil's voice, while accepting the label of 'prosperity preacher', argues that what the African needs is not a car to be sent from heaven or a house built by angels but wisdom to enable the believer to create wealth for him- or herself.[40] Equally, his take on witches and spirits is more relaxed than that of his contemporaries:

'Maybe there are witches; maybe there are even some here today to hear me preach. In that case welcome! You are most welcome!' This is typical; he does not confront the issue directly, but deflects it with some humour, quietly moving on to another plane where witches simply have no place. He may not directly address the issue of the existence of witches, yet he is totally dismissive of the power and significance attributed witches in so many charismatic churches: 'you want to be a success, with family, houses, job, education finances, wealth ... you don't become a failure through witches, wizards or juju; you become a failure because of choices made by you or on your behalf. We must take full responsibility for how our lives turn out.'[41]

The phenomenal William Wade Harris in the early twentieth century can be seen as a forerunner of the later Pentecostal and charismatic wave of churches. There is evidently a compatibility between an African world view and a Pentecostal/charismatic world view, and this compatibility must be part of the reason for the success of pentecostalism in Africa. We can also offer two other explanations. The first is that the missionary work of the eighteenth and nineteenth centuries laid a foundation for Christianity within Ghana. Churches, after 200 years, had become part of the landscape, and, because their influence was largely benign, Ghanaian people accepted the gifts that Christianity could bring. And, second, the prevalence of English opened Ghanaian Christianity up to Britain and, more significantly, to the United States. This openness to American Pentecostal and charismatic styles provides a reason for the rush to religious broadcasting. In Britain the Pentecostal and charismatic churches hardly have a broadcasting profile, but in the United States, both on radio and on television, they are heard and seen by all who want to switch on. No one could have predicted the impact of charismatic Christianity on Ghana after 1960, though the relative peace of the country and its willingness, after flirting with socialism, to turn in a Western direction for inflows of finance can, with hindsight, be seen to have signalled an orientation towards capitalism. Indeed, the overthrow

---

40 Gifford, *New Christianity*, p. 120.
41 Gifford, *New Christianity*, p. 121.

of Nkrumah is thought to have been supported by the CIA.[42] Prosperity teaching, whatever else can be said about it, has affinities with entrepreneurial materialism.

Congo (The Democratic Republic of Congo)

'The Congo's origins as a state were different from any other African country. It began life not as a colony but as the personal property of Leopold II, an ambitious, greedy and devious monarch.'[43] Leopold was determined to gain a big slice of the African cake (his own words) and so sent Henry Morton Stanley to sign 'treaties' with African chiefs up and down the Congo River. In 1885 Leopold gained international permission for a personal territory that he called the Congo Free State, an area of nearly 1 million square miles that was one-thirteenth the size of the African continent, which was reachable through numerous tributaries by steamboats that could ferry out the huge resources of the interior – ivory, palm oil, timber and copper. Leopold set about amassing a vast fortune by authorizing his company agents to raid villages, press-gang porters, collect ivory and, using a sun-dried hippopotamus whip, beat the inhabitants into submission. In addition to ivory (treated as a commodity) was rubber, which rapidly shot up in value in response to the invention of motor cars. By 1901 Congo was exporting 6,000 tons of rubber in an operation that was managed by a small group of administrators in Brussels. The Catholic Church was responsible for education and moral welfare. Huge mining and business corporations were responsible for extracting the country's resources and selling them at a profit on the international market; ploughing back finance into Congo was not a priority. The scandal of Leopold's regime was exposed by Edwin Morrell, a shipping clerk in Liverpool, and Roger Casement, the British Consul in Congo. The cruelty of the Belgian sovereign was hardly believable. Women were tied to stakes as hostages so that their men folk would be forced to collect rubber, and Belgian soldiers had to account for every bullet they fired by bringing back the severed hand of a Congolese man.[44] These atrocities raised an international outcry that forced Leopold to surrender control of his personal fiefdom to the Belgian Parliament in 1906.

It was to this huge country that a group of Pentecostal missionaries, two English, one American and one South African, arrived after travelling by steamboat, train and on foot in 1915. Their leader, W. F. P. Burton (1886–1971), was a gifted artist, linguist, map-maker, Bible teacher, builder and leader. During the journey upriver the oldest member of the party died of malaria and they buried him under a palm tree on the river-

---

42 Gifford, *New Christianity*, p. 1.
43 Martin Meredith (2006), *The State of Africa*, London, Free Press, p. 94.
44 Gilbert, *A History*, p. 94.

bank. Advised to return, Burton paced up and down through the night praying, and, remembering the thousands of young men engaged in the trench warfare of World War One, resolved to press on: 'Death there might be, but that was no worse than thousands of men were facing in the trenches of Flanders for an earthly king. Surely he could face it for the King of kings?'[45] Arriving in Congo in 1915 one of their party turned round and went back to South Africa:

> Messrs Burton and Salter were left with very few stores and no money, in a leaky shed whose walls threatened to collapse. They were among the people of whose language they knew practically nothing, and with their nearest friends over 2,000 miles away.[46]

These inauspicious beginnings were matched by the state of the people they found. There were inter tribal tensions and rampant animism, as well as some cannibalism. The work began slowly. The missionaries built their huts, held meetings for Bible study and prayer, walked 80–100 miles per week and preached two or three times a day, gradually making converts.[47] After about two years nearly 200 people attended the chapel near Mwanza where they began. They followed the pattern of the New Testament by preaching in the villages and praying for those who were ill. In one village a man with a withered arm was healed and the rest of the village demanded to hear the gospel.

Having read Roland Allen's *Missionary Methods: St Paul's or Ours*, Burton was determined to nurture an indigenous church that systematically covered the area of mission, a huge territory estimated in 1933 as being 400 miles from north to south and 200 miles from east to west and including over 1,000 villages. In 1973 it was estimated as being larger still: 600 miles by 350 miles.[48] By 1918 they had trained six native evangelists who were paid enough money to allow them to preach every day without being tied to the normal tasks of village life. The ministry steadily expanded in the 1920s and came to include mission stations, outstations, schools and medical clinics. A major spiritual breakthrough occurred at the beginning of the decade when a new Pentecost rained down on a specially convened conference of missionaries and Africans. Old tribal rivalries were dissolved, stolen property was returned, people spoke in tongues and new evangelistic ventures were launched. By 1929 the mission was under threat of closure, however, partly because Burton

---

45 W. F. P. Burton (1933), *God Working with Them*, London, Victory Press, p. 11.

46 Burton, *God Working*, p. 11.

47 Burton, *God Working*, p. 46.

48 Burton, *God Working*, p. 94; David Womersley (1973), *Wm. F. P. Burton: Congo Pioneer*, Eastbourne, Victory Press, p. 84.

found himself overworked to the point of exhaustion and partly because its success had provoked Roman Catholic opposition that was reflected in the withholding of government certification of various kinds. And, most cruel of all, his young son had died. He wrote to a friend in England: 'Our little David, after being with us for just ten days has fallen asleep in Jesus ... we do not understand it ... pray for my poor wife. She is terribly cut up.'[49]

Organizationally, the mission vested control and direction firmly on the field and not with a council in England. Burton took care to make his mission's representatives in England interdenominational, especially involving Assemblies of God and Elim, and adopted the equal distribution system that ensured that all missionaries on the field received exactly the same payment. Burton, as the Congo Evangelistic Mission's (CEM's) director, took no greater salary than the youngest volunteer. In addition, Burton implemented his ideals for an indigenous church by supporting African converts as full-time evangelists. His book about Shalumbo, who once worked in partnership with slavers, is a true and touching story of a man who exchanged a whip and a spear for a Bible so as to bring the gospel to his own people.[50] The continuing success of this and the other policies of the mission was evidenced by its results. Astonishingly, by 1972 the mission had planted over 2,100 churches and had 2,500 workers.

The depredations of Leopold had made him one of the richest men in Europe at the expense of the lives of perhaps half the native population.[51] The cruelty and avarice shown by these early twentieth-century European imperialists, as well as the less-than-honourable record of the Roman Catholic Church, came back to haunt the Congo. At independence in 1960, when the Belgian king gave his address to the assembled officials in Leopoldville, the newly elected Prime Minister, Patrice Lumumba, became agitated as the king praised his great-uncle. Lumumba, incensed by what he heard, denounced the

humiliating slavery that was imposed on us by force ... we have seen the law was quite different for a white man than for a black: accommodating for the former, cruel and inhuman for the latter ... who can forget the volleys of gunfire in which so many of our brothers perished, the cells where the authorities threw those who would not submit to a rule where justice meant oppression and exploitation.[52]

---

49 Much of this section is gratefully taken from John Andrews, 'The Regions Beyond', unpublished PhD thesis, University of Wales, Bangor, 2003.

50 W. F. P. Burton (1937), *When God Changes a Man*, London, Victory Press. A similar account is also given in W. F. P. Burton (1947), *Mudishi: The Congo Hunter*, published privately.

51 Meredith, *State*, p. 96.

52 Meredith, *State*, p. 94.

The Belgians were offended by this breach of diplomatic niceties but, for our purposes, what is notable is that Lumumba's speech came more than 50 years after the hated Leopold's death. The pain Leopold inflicted and the socio-economic system that he supported were remembered long after he had disappeared from the scene. When independence came to the Congo, as it did soon after Ghana had gained its independence, the transition was sudden and disjointed. The Congolese could not wait to kick the Belgians out.

The disordered and confused political process in the Congo assumed the proportions of crisis. The Belgians supported their mining by commercial firms in the rich Katanga area while elsewhere other political parties tried to gain control of other regions. Lumumba demanded that the United Nations expel Belgian troops and used as leverage a threat to call in the Soviet Union. Eventually the Soviets, the Belgians, the United Nations and groups supported by the CIA were struggling for control of the whole country. Lumumba was eventually beaten up and executed by a Belgian military policeman, though his anti-colonial rhetoric had sown the seeds for further dissension.[53] The Pentecostal churches were caught in the turmoil, although they were as well prepared as possible because the original missionaries had handed over control to national leaders prior to independence. The large network of CEM churches eventually subdivided, a fragmentation exacerbated by the civil war that was fought between 1960 and 1964 and the break-up of the country. The Belgian Congo became the Democratic Republic of Congo (at one time also called Zaire), and during this political turmoil two of the southern provinces where many Pentecostal churches were situated fought for and gained, but then lost, their own independence.[54] After 1964, missionaries returned to found Bible schools and continue their work. Different parts of the Congo region were occupied by different denominational groups – a legacy of the licensing system imposed by the Belgians during their period of dominance.[55] Comity systems of dividing nations between missions were common until the later decades of the twentieth century.

Other agencies such as the British Assemblies of God established mission stations and churches in the north east of the country, though their work was hampered by lack of money and sporadic massacres of Christians by anti-government rebels. Such civil violence also provoked dissension within the churches. Norwegian, Swedish, Finnish and

---

53 Meredith, *State*, p. 112.

54 This country should not be confused with the smaller French Congo that became the Republic of Congo (or Congo-Brazzaville).

55 David J. Garrard (2002), 'Democratic Republic of Congo', in Stanley M. Burgess and E. M. van der Maas (eds), *The New International Dictionary of Pentecostal and Charismatic Movements*, Grand Rapids, MI, Zondervan, pp. 67–76.

American Pentecostals also worked for many years in the Congo area and left behind churches, Bible schools and an orphanage.

Zimbabwe

As a land-locked country bordering on South Africa, the history of Zimbabwe is indissolubly connected with its larger neighbour to the south. In 1888 Cecil Rhodes gained mining concessions from the African chiefs in an area later recognized by the British government as belonging to Rhodes's British South Africa Company. Rhodes gained similar concessions in adjacent territories and then promoted colonization that enabled the white settlers to take control over the African labour force and the precious metals they extracted. After pitilessly crushing an African rebellion, Rhodes established his powerful administration, so that by 1900 further settlement and distributions of land displaced the indigenous peoples. Southern Rhodesia, as the country was then called, became a British colony in 1923 and government was firmly in the hands of the minority white population. From about 1950 onwards when 'an overweening, contemptuous attitude towards "munts" developed among whites',[56] African resistance was organized and British rule was challenged. In 1965 the Rhodesian Prime Minister, Ian Smith, declared independence from the United Kingdom without British consent. About a quarter of a million whites now expected to rule about 12 million blacks for ever. It had been British policy to prepare the ground for the independence of its colonies by establishing elected councils that could gradually take over the functions of government. Smith's action brought this transition abruptly to a halt.

International economic sanctions failed to persuade Smith to back down and two African guerrilla movements, the Zimbabwe African National Union (ZANU) under Robert Mugabe, and the Zimbabwe African People's Union (ZAPU), infiltrated the country from bases in Mozambique to plant landmines, attack white homesteads and force the unilateralist regime to concede a new political settlement. The official death toll exceeded 15,000. In 1978, Smith was forced to negotiate a constitution allowing multi-racial government. A Methodist Bishop, Abel Muzorewa, became the country's first black prime minister and made room for Africans to play a subordinate role in government while failing to dismantle white control over the police and armed forces. This unsatisfactory situation was resolved at a meeting in London in 1979. By now the guerrilla leaders, soaked in nationalist emotion with an admixture of Marxism, were hardened and unwilling to make any concessions to the whites. Free elections were held and Mugabe, hailed as a hero, gained an overwhelm-

56 Stephen Taylor (2000), *Livingstone's Tribe: A Journey from Zanzibar to the Cape*, London, Flamingo, p. 195.

ing victory. Within two years he had ousted his ZAPU rival and retained his grip on power without a serious challenge for many years.

As with all British colonies, the pattern of religious life established by the expatriate whites echoed Britain's. There were Methodist, Roman Catholic and Anglican churches within the white community and their influence spread out to the African population through relatively high (perhaps as much as 60%) church attendance. The traditional churches concentrated on education. Robert Mugabe, for instance, received his teaching at the hands of Jesuits and then became a teacher, eventually amassing four bachelor degrees and two more masters degrees.

Salisbury, the colonial capital (now Harare), became a sprawling conurbation whose population grew rapidly after 1945 to meet the demands of the manufacturing sector. Migrant labour was drawn in from East Africa and created a multi-racial city with numerous sporting and cultural societies as well as a diverse range of churches.[57] Within this religious complex a black middle class gradually formed, supported by ethical values of self-reliance, economic frugality and the avoidance of gambling, drunkenness, prostitution and unemployment. Even so, the African middle class were usually shunned by the white middle class and white churches mostly refused to integrate African fellow believers. African nationalism was at first infused with Christian piety; nationalist meetings in 1960 began with prayers and hymn singing.[58] Only a year later the piety was gone and bombs were being thrown. Social distances between whites and blacks, even Christian whites and blacks, grew and removed the black population further from the levers of power.

Pentecostalism arrived in Zimbabwe through several channels. First, the Assemblies of God and the Pentecostal Assemblies of Canada had reached all the main towns before independence but were mainly white. Second, many black Rhodesians and Malawians who had travelled down to work in the South African mines had been converted and returned to evangelize by holding meetings on Rhodesian farms and in the townships. Third, the Apostolic Faith Mission planted an assembly in Salisbury in the early 1930s, though there was a Pentecostal mission in Bulawayo as early as 1914.[59] While the Pentecostals naively attempted to remain apolitical during the long years that followed, the ecumenical churches – especially in the lead-up to independence – became conduits for liberationist theology and revolutionary Marxism.[60] This had the effect of making these churches popular after independence while inhibiting their capacity to stand against the brutal state that Mugabe later created.

---

57 Maxwell, *Gifts*, p. 63.

58 Maxwell, *Gifts*, p. 64.

59 Anderson, *Fires*, p. 173. Today the Zimbabwean branch of AFM has more than 1,000 churches.

60 I am indebted to Mathew Clark of Regents College for this information.

To say that the Pentecostal churches attempted to remain apolitical was not the end of the matter. During the 1950s the AFM missionaries were almost entirely white, so that, although they approved in principle of inter-racial church activities, in practice they supported the pro-Christian white government that backed law, order and economic growth. When black Pentecostals began to evangelize and plant churches without seeking missionary permission, there were bound to be conflicts within the Pentecostal churches. The white missionaries saw the black Pentecostals as acting in a way that might lose the approval of the colonial government.[61] More than this, they noted that the black Pentecostals were apt to combine Christianity with a zealous regard for aspects of the law of Moses. The love of ecclesiastical robes, rituals and food laws was contrary to the Protestantism of the AFM heritage. When the black Pentecostals, who had now split off from the old white missionary patriarchy, found their own position threatened by a new generation of recent graduates from Bible colleges, they introduced hierarchical church government. In this way African leaders created a type of church government that was as restrictive as that against which they had rebelled.[62]

Post-independence Harare was a seething city. Borders had been opened and restrictions lifted as the whole of Zimbabwean society travelled in a new direction. Assemblies of God from South Africa, the great Zulu evangelist Nicholas Bhengu (who died in 1985), the Pentecostal Assemblies of Canada, American Assemblies of God and independent Pentecostal ministries, many of them American, arrived and stimulated more crusading and church planting. There were power struggles, winners and losers, as uncompromising Spirit-filled preachers, each utterly convinced of his own divine calling, fought for control of the major black areas of the city. By the late 1990s the AFM had over 1,000 churches and more than 87,000 adherents, and other groups such as the Apostolic Faith Church (Portland, Oregon) attracted over 13,000. More astonishing was the success of Ezekiel Guti, originally of the Apostolic Faith Church and later associated with Bhengu's South African Assemblies of God, who formed his own Assemblies of God, African (AOGA) in 1968.

The story of Ezekiel Guti's eventual dominance is threaded through with self-advertisement and tactical astuteness. The aspiring urban poor flooding into the city in the late 1960s were all desperate for work while trying to avoid the trap of destitution caused by a lifestyle of beer halls and petty crime. Guti offered a new disciplined way of life that encouraged saving money, building families and harnessing the craft skills of women. By 1969 Guti could make modest claims for his denomination, which now had a presence in the capital as well as the countryside. It

---

61 During white minority rule it was illegal for black Africans to have control of missionary societies.
62 Maxwell, *Gifts*, p. 68.

owned a few buildings but most of its congregations met in the open air. And so things remained until Guti went to America for further education. In 1971 he studied with Christ for the Nations in Dallas, Texas, a college founded by Gordon Lindsay. The education he received was strongly in the faith-and-prosperity tradition but his exposure to American abundance opened his eyes to the possibilities of organizational growth and gave him a range of financial contacts in the United States. He was to capitalize on these over the coming years, without in most cases revealing the sources of his income flow. He returned to Zimbabwe with a capacity to draw money into his organization – which had remained faithful to him – and with a determination to evangelize. By 1977 membership had increased to 40,000, there were 185 branches across the country and 15 buildings were now in his possession. Not only did he evangelize within Zimbabwe but across the border in Malawi (1961), Mozambique (1972), Botswana (1974), Zambia (1976), Congo (1981), Tanzania (1985), Rwanda (1986), Kenya (1990), and, alongside this, was international expansion to London (1983), Glasgow (1996) and Germany (1999).[63] Preaching tours in Texas and Australia followed. Guti was building a transnational religious movement that managed to survive the desperate poverty that blighted Zimbabwe in the late 1990s. When Zimbabwe fractured economically, international resources could come to the rescue: as the Zimbabwean currency lost value, international donations became even more precious. All the while the stress upon healing, family, careful use of money, sexual morality, spiritual gifts, faith and modern living continued. Guti took the elevated title of 'Archbishop' and his place within the history of his own denomination was firmly secured by obliterating reference to the contributions of his co-workers in the early days.[64] He moved comfortably in a circle of international Pentecostal charismatic preachers and his growing personal wealth could be seen as a validation of the message that he preached. Even Robert Mugabe admired the pro-African self-reliance of this preacher who had broken free from the control of white missionaries. Only as Guti began to lose confidence in the Mugabe regime and turn his support towards the Movement for Democratic Change (MDC), led by Morgan Tsvangirai, did the government start to withdraw its favour. Given that Guti has as many as 400,000 adherents in Zimbabwe, he is a man the politicians will listen to.

Reflection

In each of the three African countries considered here, Christianity arrived in the nineteenth century. In one case, Ghana, missionaries had

63 Maxwell, *Gifts*, frontpiece.
64 Maxwell, *Gifts*, p. 117.

begun to make contributions to the welfare of the people. In another, Congo, the imperialism of Leopold was ruthlessly exploitative. When Pentecostal missionaries penetrated the interior of the vast country by boat they found entrenched African religion. In Zimbabwe the traditional churches, Anglican, Roman Catholic and Methodist, were involved in education, and Pentecostal fire spread by outreaches from South Africa. Indeed South Africa, because of its transport links and the prevalence of the English language, proved to be the launching pad for Christianity into the anglophone countries of Zambia and Malawi as well, reaching even as far as Kenya in the process. Wherever it went, Pentecostal mission proved to be multi-functional: it was successful when it worked in Christianized populations, as in Ghana, or as a potent force against the worst aspects of animism, as in Congo. It could adapt itself to the needs of displaced and impoverished workers, as in Zimbabwe.

In Ghana and Zimbabwe white missionaries may have started churches but black converts, especially after independence, took the churches to a new level. If white missionaries attempted to retain control over the churches, the black converts and their congregations simply split off, and in this way racial divisions were embodied in the divisions between churches. Pentecostalism, with its emphasis on an experience of the Holy Spirit, healing, visions, miracles and speaking with tongues, gave to African converts a power that more sacramental forms of Christianity denied them. The African who had been healed or had spoken in tongues could evangelize his tribal village with a boldness that astonished the local elders.

In both Ghana and Zimbabwe, African Pentecostal churches after 1945 quickly drew financial resources from the worldwide Pentecostal community and started missionary travels beyond their own borders; they even began re-evangelizing the countries from which their own missionaries had first come. Ghanaian Christians sent preachers to London where they worked among expatriate Africans, and Zimbabwean Christians went wider still. Transnationalism became the norm. The old colonialism, whatever it stole from Africa, gave it European languages. By the 1980s, in an era of global travel, European or American communities were hosts to migrant African churches. African self-government, after the cheering had died away and the colonial flags had been hauled down, rarely delivered on the high hopes that it had inspired. The reasons for this are still contested but appear to be nothing whatever to do with the practice of Christianity.

Questions to think about

1 How do you assess the imperialist and colonialist past?
2 Do you think Pentecostalism and African world views are especially compatible?

3 Should Pentecostal churches try to keep out of politics or are they better to become involved?

Further reading

Anderson, A. (2007), *Spreading Fires: The Missionary Nature of Early Pentecostalism*, London, SCM Press.

Gifford, P. (1998), *African Christianity: Its Public Role*, London, Hurst & Co.

Gifford, P. (2004), *Ghana's New Christianity: Pentecostalism in a Globalising African Economy*, Bloomington and Indianapolis, Indiana University Press.

Kalu, O. (2008), *African Pentecostalism: An Introduction*, Oxford, Oxford University Press.

Maxwell, D. (2006), *African Gifts of the Spirit: Pentecostalism and the Rise of a Zimbabwean Transnational Religious Movement*, Oxford, James Currey.

8

Latter Rain and Religious Broadcasting

As we shall see, Pentecostalism spread through broadcasting. Religious broadcasting in the United States and in Europe moved at different speeds. Conflicts over patents delayed American developments, but during the 1920s radio broadcasting in America expanded rapidly. In 1920–21 eight stations served a few thousand listeners, but by 1928 there were more than 700 stations with 40,000 listeners.[1] Among the very first religious broadcasters was the flamboyant Aimee Semple McPherson who was invited to speak on radio during a revival meeting in San Francisco in 1922. Rapidly grasping the potential of the new technology, she raised funds for her own radio station and began broadcasting on Kall Four Square Gospel (KFSG) in 1924.[2] Symbolic of her extensive reach were the 250-foot radio towers that she placed on the roof of the newly built Angelus Temple. Although she broadcast her own weekly sermons, she realized that listeners needed a varied diet and so live music, organ recitals, black gospel singers, Sunday school lessons and other talks quickly followed. She used radio to propagate her socio-political views by denouncing the evils of dance halls, evolution and political corruption. Over time she helped to shape the psychological profile of the American Right by establishing its cultural identity. What she imprinted on the American psyche remained in place until the end of the twentieth century, as the followers of Pat Robertson well illustrate.[3]

---

1 Philip T. Rosen (1979), 'The Marvel of Radio: Review Essay', *American Quarterly* 31.4, 572–81.

2 M. A. Sutton (2007), *Aimee Semple McPherson and the Resurrection of Christian America*, London, Harvard University Press, pp. 78–81.

3 Gregory S. Pastor, Walter J. Stone and Ronald B. Rapoport (1999), 'Candidate-Centred Sources of Party Change: The Case of Pat Robertson', 1988, *The Journal of Politics* 61.2, 423–44.

Premillennial Signal Towers

Our Newspapers have been carrying strange headlines recently! Strange phenomena, peculiar signs and signals, supposedly from the planet Mars, have been picked up by Government Signal Towers and Radio Stations in New York, Canada, England and Australia ...

'Ta-da-da-Da-da-da-da!' came the signals from the sky. Where were they coming from? Millions asked the question.

The origin of these signals I know not, whether they came from Mars (which I doubt), or whether they originated from some static condition of the air (which is more probable).

But this I do know – strange flashes and signals are being received by the Church of Christ today from the Signal Towers of Heaven. These signals come in code. Only the believer has the key. To all others these dots and dashes from Heaven's Signal Towers are meaningless and uninterpretable.

'Why, Sister McPherson, what do you mean? What are you getting at? Signal Towers! Where–what–why–when?'

Heaven's Signal Towers speak by the Word of God, by the witness of the Spirit, and by prophecy fulfilled. The Signal Towers of the Church speak to Heaven by way of prayer, obedience, watchfulness, and relay the message which she receives to the world by means of preaching, exhortation and warning.

Oh, I love the Old Time Religion! I love the old time power! What we need today is a great movement back to God, back to the Bible, back to the faith of our fathers, back to the Old Time Religion ...

'Nation shall rise against nation, kingdom against kingdom.'

Here again we have lived to see the World War, the most bloody carnage that was ever known to mortal man. Yet, 'tis but a shadow of the great tribulation that is to come.

'There shall be blood, and fire, and vapours of smoke.'

Blood! They fought knee-deep in it in the trenches.

Fire! For the first time in the history of the world, men fought each other during the late war with curtains and barrages of liquid fire. Vapours of smoke! For the first time in the history of the world, men fought each other with smoke, vapours, poisonous gasses, and curtained in the ships at sea and the ships in the air behind smoked screens ...

'Ta-da-da- -da-da!' Premillennial Signal Towers spake loudly that day, saying, 'Behold, the Lord is near – He is even at the doors. Know, oh church, that the cup of the Gentiles is almost full – the Christ is coming back.'

Wake up, wake up, wake up! Work for the night is coming when man's work is done! Work now. Roll up your sleeves and go at it! Stop preaching mere politics! Stop cooking up oyster suppers and fixing strawberry festivals! Stop putting on bridge parties and trivial things! Stop showing moving pictures on Sunday night when you should be preaching the Gospel and getting people saved! Stop fighting other preachers and lifting up the sword to pierce the heart of other ministers! Whether we see eye to eye with them or not, the time is at hand – let us stop squabbling and fighting over little doctrinal differences. Let us stop fighting each other. Let us join hands, join hearts, voices and forces, and turn to fight the enemy – modernism, higher criticism, agnosticism and worldliness.

'In fundamentals – unity! In non-essentials – liberty! In all things charity!'

We are relay stations for Christ. Let us speed the message out and away till it leaps the sea and girdles the globe, and all men hear the cry – 'Behold, the Christ is coming! He is even at the door!'

From 'The Bridal Call Foursquare', Aimee Semple McPherson's sermon from Angelus Temple, 24 August 1924, in the SCM Reader *Pentecostal and Charismatic Studies*, p. 32.

The commercial genius of the United States was applied to radio. Broadcasts were funded by advertising, and advertisers would pay higher rates for larger audiences. As a result radio stations networked together so that programmes broadcast in one locality could be heard in another. This created nationwide networks carrying enterprising shows (and advertising jingles) across the time zones of North America. In Britain, which began regular broadcasting in 1922, the situation was always different. The British Broadcasting Corporation (BBC) was formed in 1926 as a single agency to serve the whole nation. From the start the political power of broadcasting was understood and so the Corporation was made independent of the government and regulated by a high-minded charter monitored by worthy governors. Broadcasting costs were covered by funds generated by licences that listeners had to buy yearly. Consequently for the first decade, the radio set, enclosed in a wooden case to blend in with the furniture, was a luxury item. Yet, by 1939 as many as 34 million people could receive the BBC's broadcasts.[4]

The distinctions between network commercial radio in the United States and a public Corporation independent of commercial pressure in Britain resulted in two different broadcasting cultures. In America the preacher could hire air time for a hot gospel message. In Britain the preacher was hemmed in by the need to be inoffensive; licence payers complained if preachers challenged time-honoured customs – indeed, if they were 'too

---

4 John Stevenson (1984), *British Society 1914–45*, Harmondsworth, Penguin, p. 408.

American'. John Reith, the first Director-General of the BBC, was the son of a Scottish clergyman. He valued Sunday worship and dynamic Christianity but realized he needed advice if he were to avoid choosing unrepresentative preachers.[5] Setting up a committee that contained Anglicans and Nonconformists, he started broadcasting church services featuring recommended speakers. Anglican and Roman Catholic services were thought to be suitable for broadcasting because they were full of music, whereas the Nonconformists were thought to be too wordy. Although the services were valued by non-attending Christians, among the least supportive of broadcasts were the clergy. They felt that the radio was competing with what they could offer and putting their own preaching and musicianship in a bad light. 'Throughout the late 20s, Reith was still conscious of opposition to broadcast religion by the general run of the clergy and criticized them for their conservatism and timidity' because 'in his view they were more anxious about the possible ... diminution of their own congregations than the spread of a religious message over 15 million people.'[6] When religious broadcasting was combined with the educational aims of the BBC, listeners benefited from a two-pronged policy: first, longer Christian acts of worship were offered on Sundays with a shorter act of worship during the working week, and, second, there were talks or discussions on religious topics that attempted to keep a balance, sometimes a balance between humanistic and Christian views but more often a balance between different Christian views. Pentecostals, however, were never part of any of this.

Religious broadcasting in Britain was led by clergy and primarily featured simple Protestant acts of worship – though Roman Catholic services were appreciated by listeners. There were meditations in Lent, and the service of nine lessons and carols from King's College, Cambridge, became a Christmas tradition. Emotional preaching or preaching intended to drive the listeners to 'make a decision to be saved' was absolutely avoided, and fundraising was forbidden.[7] The Christianity of the BBC was liturgical, musical, thoughtful and moral. Amazingly this situation continued almost unchanged into the twenty-first century. There is still a mid-morning daily service on BBC radio and there are radio broadcasts of services every Sunday of the year, and all of this is funded by the annual licence fee.

5 Kenneth M. Wolfe (1984), *The Churches and the British Broadcasting Corporation 1922–1956*, London, SCM Press, p. 5.

6 Wolfe, *Churches*, p. 19.

7 This is not completely true. Money could be solicited for 'the week's good cause' or for children in need during Comic Relief.

Consolidation and diversity

Pentecostal denominations consolidated their positions in the United States and the rest of the world during the 1930s. Benefiting from the large American population and its relative prosperity, American Pentecostal denominations grew fastest. A denomination could accumulate money to buy a printing press and set up a publishing house; it could also invest in radio programmes and advertise through them; in a virtuous circle, print media could support radio stations and radio stations could promote printed materials. Although Pentecostal denominations in Europe could draw large crowds at special meetings, they were unable to break into the world of broadcasting because legal barriers prevented them from doing so. The most that a British Pentecostal denomination might hope for was that its services would be attended by the BBC and broadcast on a Sunday morning, something that did not happen until 1952.[8]

American Assemblies of God began a radio ministry in 1933 through a single-station outlet, and in 1936 it extended this across Missouri.[9] In 1943 a radio department was established and a 34–station network carried programmes on the West Coast. Three years later, a 15-minute service was carried over a network of 72 stations. In 1950 the broadcast *Revivaltime* was initiated, still only with a 15-minute broadcast, but available in Europe from Luxembourg and popular across the United States. By 1969 *Revivaltime* was aired on 601 stations in the United States as well as 97 worldwide. Postbags of more than 10,000 letters a month rolled in, showing that the preachers' voices were heard. *Revivaltime* may have been modelled on Charles Fuller's *Old-Fashioned Revival Hour*, which had the largest network audience in America in 1942 and 1943. Fuller ended every sermon with a call to repentance and salvation, as well as commending Jesus as the friend who 'strengthens, cheers, comforts, guides, and directs'.[10]

Fuller was an independent radio evangelist and knew Harold Ockenga since both were 'leaders in the world of transdenominational fundamentalism'.[11] While Fuller set about establishing a new neo-evangelical seminary, Ockenga founded the National Association of Evangelicals (NAE) in 1942 to provide an evangelical counterbalance to the more liberal Federal Council of Churches.[12] The NAE was itself an answer to

8 See W. K. Kay (1989), 'A History of British Assemblies of God', PhD dissertation, Nottingham University, p. 225.

9 William W. Menzies (1971), *Anointed to Serve*, Springfield, MO, Gospel Publishing House, p. 254.

10 Gary Dorrien (1998), *The Remaking of Evangelical Theology*, Louisville, KY, p. 50.

11 Dorrien, *Remaking*, p. 51.

12 http://www.nae.net/index.cfm?FUSEACTION=nae.history (accessed 15.04.08).

the much more fundamentalist American Council of Christian Churches. Once founded, the NAE was offered a choice between throwing in its lot with the American Council of Christian Churches or with the Pentecostals. The American Council of Christian Churches berated Pentecostals and its founder claimed that 'tongues is one of the greatest signs of the apostasy'.[13] Ockenga made his choice and turned to the Pentecostals, the holiness churches, Free Methodists and Nazarenes and accepted their membership. This enabled Pentecostals to benefit from the negotiating leverage the NAE was able to exert on the owners of radio networks.[14] This was just as well, so Pentecostals thought, because when liberal–conservative disputes turned nasty in 1956, the liberal National Council of Churches lobbied Congress (unsuccessfully as it turned out) for a ban on the sale of broadcasting time for religious purposes.[15]

The healing revival

So we enter a period in the 1940s in the United States when, while at war, there were voices raised in defence of political and religious freedom. While American forces turned against the dictatorships of Europe after Pearl Harbor, it was natural for religious broadcasters to see their own messages as examples of the freedom that was allowed in the United States but denied elsewhere. Pentecostal denominations had grown from their rickety and uncertain beginnings into substantial and impressive organizations. They knew what they believed and they knew how to propagate their beliefs. At the same time the dead hand of bureaucracy – as the old Pentecostals saw it – rested upon their evangelistic efforts. Despite all their newly impressive respectability, old Pentecostals felt that the fire was going out. By now there were a number of Pentecostal evangelists who had quarrelled with denominational officials and found themselves forced to stand on their own.[16] Instead of collapsing into poverty or creeping away into obscurity, these evangelists found a niche for themselves by going back to the old ways of tent campaigning and transdenominational meetings.

---

13 C. M. Robeck (2002), 'National Association of Evangelicals', in Stanley M. Burgess and Eduard M. van der Maas (eds), *New International Dictionary of Pentecostal and Charismatic Movements (NIDPCM)*, Grand Rapids, MI, Zondervan, p. 923.

14 The National Religious Broadcasters group was formed in 1944 in response to concerns to protect 'free and complete access to the broadcast media'. See Robeck, 'National', p. 925.

15 David E. Harrell (2001), 'Healers and Televangelists after World War II', in Vinson Synan (ed.), *The Century of the Holy Spirit*, Nashville, TN, Thomas Nelson, p. 331.

16 David E. Harrell (1975), *All Things are Possible*, Bloomington, Indiana University Press, pp. 69, 71 and *passim*.

Separate from this band of independent Pentecostals was a 'Latter Rain' movement that began in Canada in 1948 and emphasized the rediscovery of apostolicity. The belief that apostles had been restored to the church ran completely counter to the mindset of denominational ecclesiastical bureaucracy. For sure, apostles were not going to be tied up in legal knots by administrators. Apostles felt themselves to be free of constraint and able to go where the wind of the Spirit took them. This was attractive to revivalistic Pentecostals who, after all, believed firmly in the twentieth-century restoration of charismatic gifts. If charismatic gifts were restored to the church as part of the outpouring of the Spirit, then why not expect modern apostles?

The stock-market crash of 1929 and the Great Depression that followed reduced many Pentecostals to poverty. They belonged to the class of tenant farmers or blue-collar workers who found the 1930s hard going.[17] Several preachers who were to emerge in the 1940s had grown up through the Depression era and had taken their first pastorates when small congregations were hardly able to pay their ministers. In 1946, as the post-war boom began, William Branham reported that he had been visited by an angel with the dramatic news that he would take 'a gift of divine healing to the people of the world'.[18] Branham, born in 1909, grew up in a dirt-floor log cabin on a little farm in Kentucky. He was among the poorest of the poor because his father drank heavily. After ordination as a Baptist minister Branham began revivalistic preaching in 1933.[19] He lost his wife and child when the Ohio River flooded in 1937 and was so poor that his easy chair was repossessed by a finance company. After his angelic visitation Branham began to preach and pray for those who were ill, and started a ministry that took him all over the United States and five times round the world.

By 1947 Branham attracted large crowds in a series of crusades in four cities with only a small amount of advertising. These were second-generation Pentecostals in the main who had heard of the Azusa Street revival at the beginning of the century but who had never themselves seen any kind of miracle. Branham's ministry astonished them and when Gordon Lindsay took over the management of Branham's itinerary and began to publicize it through his new magazine, *The Voice of Healing*, invitations flowed in from all over the country in a way that would have allowed Branham to blaze a Pentecostal trail across North America. Branham used to spend many gruelling hours praying in his crusade meetings

---

17 Robert M. Anderson (1979), *Vision of the Disinherited*, Oxford, Oxford University Press.

18 Harrell, *All Things*, p. 28.

19 Branham, despite his Baptist ordination, did have connections with Oneness Pentecostals who supported him early in his ministry and whose doctrines he began to advocate towards the end of his life; Harrell, *All Things*, p. 163.

for those who were ill each night and the effort damaged his health just as he appeared to be ready to make a quantum leap into national prominence. He took a break from ministry. On his return five months later, he conducted a series of successful campaigns in the early 1950s; on one occasion in 1951, in Los Angeles, a former United States Congressman who had been crippled for many years was enabled to walk again. Branham became a living legend in Pentecostal subculture and there were reports that he raised the dead.[20]

Among the extraordinary signs that marked Branham's meetings were his 'words of knowledge'. He appeared to know what was wrong with people before they told him and even discerned their inner secrets. People would walk forward to the front, and he was able

> to tell the suffering many of the events of their lives from their childhood down to the present time ... the great audience hears all this over the public address system. Brother Branham actually sees it enacted and pushing the microphone away so the audience won't hear it, he tells the patient any unconfessed and unforesaken sins in their lives which must be given up before the gift will operate for their deliverance. As soon as such persons acknowledge and promise to forsake the sin ... their healing often comes in a moment before Brother Branham has time to pray for them.[21]

Later historians of Pentecostalism agreed that Branham's insights were 'remarkably accurate'.[22]

By 1955 Branham began to stumble. He was, by all accounts, a humble and simple man, with little head for finance, organization or business, and when the Internal Revenue filed a tax-evasion suit against him in 1956 he was saddled with the huge debt. He never seems to have fully recovered.

Among those who revered Branham was Oral Roberts, a young preacher who grew up in the Depression era in his father's Pentecostal holiness church. Again, the family were poor and, in Roberts's case, were partly of Indian extraction, which gave him a capacity to empathize with marginalized groups. Roberts was a tall athletic young man yet he collapsed during a high-school basketball game and was discovered to have tuberculosis. He was ill enough to face the fact that he might be a perpetual invalid. Taken by his sister to a tent crusade meeting, a travelling evangelist prayed for him and Roberts was instantly healed – a story that he told many times over during his long ministry.

---

20 Later reports of Branham questioned his orthodoxy, especially as he cited angelic revelation for some of his beliefs.

21 Harrell, *All Things*, p. 38, quoting F. F. Bosworth.

22 Harrell, *All Things*, p. 38, quoting Donald Gee.

Where Branham was naive, disorganized and unbusinesslike, Roberts was astute, capable of building a complicated evangelistic organization and financially resourceful. Where Branham was inclined to become ever more unorthodox with his claims of further angelic revelation, Roberts managed to broaden his appeal beyond the Pentecostal subculture. To start with, Roberts concentrated upon a crusade ministry with the use of a vast and expensive tent. The tent could be pitched anywhere there was open farmland and seated more people than the biggest indoor auditoria in the main cities. At the same time Roberts began radio broadcasting; he was on 20 stations in 1949 and 70 in 1950. A year later he was on 100 stations, by 1953 he had reached 200, and for the remainder of the decade he fluctuated between 300 and 500 stations in the USA and Canada. His ministry became widely known and his preaching was passionate, direct and powerful. Although he needed to raise money to secure airtime on the radio stations, he could also use the radio stations to appeal for money so that the programmes could be sustained. And, when people had heard Roberts on radio, they were more likely to attend his tent meetings.

Roberts' restless and perceptive mind early on appreciated that television was likely to replace radio. He began buying airtime on TV stations in 1954, even though the cost of filming and production was many times greater than radio. Roberts was a man to exercise the faith that he preached and was never satisfied with small successes. Though his TV programme was groundbreaking, he scrapped it after six months because it was too stilted. He wanted to convey the atmosphere of the big-tent meetings on television but was told that this was impossible because the lighting conditions within the canvas arena were unsuitable for filming. In those days television did not have the facilities for live outside broadcasts and depended instead on filmed newsreel footage. Roberts bought expensive fast film, shot his own crusade meetings in Ohio and then showed them on television in 1955.[23] The immediacy and quality of the material succeeded where studio-bound broadcasts had failed: the new programmes permanently changed religious broadcasting on television. In 1955 Roberts was on 31 stations and soon doubled this to include the big population centres in New York, Chicago and Los Angeles. He was reaching across the whole of the United States of America and his gamble paid off. The high cost of airtime was met by high levels of financial support, often in a very large mailbag with many small gifts.

It was here that Roberts showed his astuteness. He also obtained sponsorship from businesses and so avoided debt. He was instrumental in the launching of the Full Gospel Business Men's Fellowship Inter-

23 D. E. Harrell (1985), *Oral Roberts: An American Life*, Bloomington, Indiana University Press, p. 126f.

national.[24] Pentecostalism moved out of the lower-income groups and began to touch the commercial and country club classes. Even so, television ate up money at a frightening rate and Roberts realized that he needed a big support base to sustain his ministry. He instituted the 'blessing pact' whereby donors were asked to contribute to the ministry and promised that if they did not receive money back following their gift, Roberts would refund them. He based his prosperity teaching on the biblical verse 'give and it shall be given unto you' (Luke 6.38) and developed this into a complicated and central doctrine. Jesus came to save you from your sins but also to save you from poverty. On the cross Jesus was stripped of all possessions and became poor so that we might become rich. Healing was only one aspect of the blessing that God came to give human beings. The generosity and optimism encouraged by Roberts's teaching often resulted in expanding businesses. He taught people to 'expect a miracle' because 'God is a good God'. His constant attempt through television was to reproduce the effect of his crusade ministry where he, like Branham, spent endless hours laying hands on terribly ill people and praying with energy and compassion for them. His first book *If You Need Healing – Do These Things!* encouraged people to 'use a point of contact for the release of your faith', by which he meant that faith would be focused on the moment when he laid hands on the sick person and prayed. The point of contact between the evangelist and the individual was the point at which healing was possible if faith was 'released'. Roberts took this teaching further when he encouraged viewers to lay their hand on the television set while they watched his programme and believe that the television set was as meaningful a point of contact as his own hand placed upon their head.

We could interpret the 'point of contact' as a theological idea that sacralized secular space. Television, if it was a point of contact, stopped being an unholy purveyor of vulgar entertainment and commerce and became a holy object transformed by the power of the Holy Spirit. Pentecostalism was colonizing the airwaves and investing objects of everyday culture with religious significance. It was projecting itself into the hearts and homes of millions of Americans and turning their living-rooms into miniature crusade venues. Roberts managed to combine the roles of sawdust trail preacher and stardust-sprinkled celebrity. Early black and white photographs show him as a large man in a business suit or, when praying for those who were ill, with his jacket off, his face contorted and covered in sweat. Later colour photographs show an altogether better groomed man looking like a television journalist in an expensive suit, with a silk tie and fashionable haircut.

---

24 The FGBMFI was founded by Demos Shakarian, a wealthy dairy farmer, in 1951. Roberts spoke at the inaugural meeting.

Roberts was by no means the only tent evangelist who made the transition into broadcasting: T. L. Osborn, Jack Coe, A. A. Allen and Tommy Hicks also moved in this direction. The *Voice of Healing* magazine founded by Gordon Lindsay was also an association that held an annual convention in an attempt to maintain harmony between the many independents.[25] At one point Lindsay had about 50 evangelists on his list, and he would only support those who retained their moral and financial integrity as well as those who avoided high-flown rhetoric attacking denominational officials. Lindsay himself had been an evangelist with Assemblies of God and appreciated the good intentions of denominational mechanisms as well as the perspectives of ordinary pastors who, if they were not careful, might find themselves envious of the superstar evangelists. By 1952 *Voice of Healing* had a new headquarters in Dallas and was a substantial force in co-ordinating cutting-edge Pentecostalism while maintaining peace between the roving evangelists and the denominations.

Lindsay's efforts could not hold the line. Jack Coe, one of the most aggressive and colourful of the evangelists, needled the other evangelists by questioning their claims (he said that his tent was bigger than that owned by Oral Roberts, who had claimed the largest gospel tent in the world!) and he added to his circle of critics by embarrassing Assemblies of God, the denomination that had ordained him, to the extent that it expelled him in 1953. A bitter public row followed and Coe seemed ready to begin a rival denomination to be called Fundamental Assemblies of God, with the implication that the original was not fundamental enough. Three years later Coe was taken to court and accused of practising medicine without a licence. The main ministers who initiated the charge were from churches with views similar to those of the Brethren, and after a tense couple of days the judge dismissed the charges. Although some commentators saw the court case as a clash between the more refined sensibilities of the middle class and the rougher Pentecostal intransigence of the working class, others viewed it as entirely a religious dispute.[26]

By the end of the 1950s the healing revival was beginning to subside. The most organized of the evangelists, particularly T. L. Osborn and Oral Roberts, began to campaign overseas each year. Osborn, who in 1958 decided to cease his radio broadcasts so as to concentrate on overseas crusading, already had an impressive track record in holding big meetings outside the United States. He was in Jamaica in 1948, Puerto Rico in 1949, Venezuela in 1950, Guatemala in 1953, and by 1969 he had reached 40 countries including Kenya, Indonesia, Formosa, Japan, Java, Holland, Chile and Switzerland.[27] His Association for Native Evan-

---

25 Harrell, *All Things*, p. 55.

26 Harrell, *All Things*, p. 62.

27 R. M. Riss (2002), 'Osborn, Tommy Lee', in Burgess and van der Maas (eds), *NIDPCM*, p. 950.

gelism took American dollars and funded local preachers. In Kenya he bought bicycles for local pastors and in other places he would pay a pastor for a year so that the man might have a chance to work full-time to build up a congregation. Oral Roberts also travelled abroad, although, as with all the tent evangelists, the practical matter of transporting a vast tent and all its amplification equipment was daunting; shipping everything from America around the world might cost $40,000 but there was no choice in the matter because the evangelists attracted crowds that were too large for any indoor location. Huge crowds attended Roberts in South Africa in 1955. In 1956 on his way to Australia, he stopped off to hold a large meeting in the Philippines, and then landed in Sydney where, because his broadcasts had been seen in that country, further success was anticipated. How wrong he was. Despite the attendance of 75,000 people at the opening services, the hostility of the Australian press was beyond anything that Roberts and his team had experienced before. In Melbourne the newspapers were unrestrained in their attacks and there was open heckling and intimidation of those who responded to Roberts's invitation to conversion. The heckling turned into scuffling and meetings had to be cancelled; after further attempts at holding services the campaign was cancelled. 'Louts and hooligans defiled my consecrated tent', were Roberts' parting words.[28]

After a period of introspection the Australian press and the Australian churches re-evaluated what happened. Religious freedom was evidently threatened and the churches were determined that Billy Graham would not run into a similar barrage of criticism and disruption when he came the following year. Roberts, hurt by the experience, compared it to the occasion when the apostle Paul was stoned on his first missionary journey (Acts 14.19).

Roberts returned to the United States to continue his work. The healing evangelists had publicized the Pentecostal message in the non-Pentecostal churches. In fact, the healing evangelists of the 1950s had performed a crucial service to Christianity: they both stimulated worldwide Pentecostalism in an era when America was still viewed as the moral leader of the free world and they prepared the way for the charismatic outpouring that took the mainline churches by surprise.[29] Nearly all the places Roberts, Osborn and Tommy Hicks (who held revival meetings in Argentina) visited in the 1950s subsequently enjoyed booming Pentecostal churches and produced their own pastors and evangelists with big dreams and plentiful congregations. Equally, the charismatic movement, which seemed to come from nowhere – though there were clearly interdenominational

---

28 Harrell, *Roberts*, p. 77.

29 According to D. E. Harrell (1987), *Pat Robertson: A Personal, Political and Religious Portrait*, San Francisco, Harper and Row, p. 110, Roberts noted that 'thousands of people from mainline churches were attending his tent meetings' in the 1950s.

prayer meetings and ecumenical initiatives with which the name of David du Plessis is associated – was stimulated by the religious broadcasting of the healing evangelists.[30] Roberts, whose TV show was successful, surprised everybody by launching a completely different style of religious broadcasting in 1968. He offered a weekly series on Sundays after four one-hour specials in prime time. The format was that of the chat show, with a series of interviews, songs, talks and miscellaneous items, strung together by a host or hostess sitting on a sofa in the studio. Gone was the tent and serried ranks of the big crusade meeting; in its place came a flexible, friendly and televisually digestible style that mixed religion and entertainment. Roberts's early Pentecostal supporters were critical of his apparent turn to worldliness – some of the singers wore dresses that were well above the knee – but Roberts's judgement turned out to be accurate. The new style of religious broadcasting attracted a large supportive mailbag (always an indication of success) and was quickly copied by other religious personalities. Indeed, Roberts pioneered a new form of religious broadcasting, even of broadcasting itself. It had the advantage of variety but could still, in an American context, make appeals for money, discreetly advertise books and records, and offer personal prayer, especially when viewers could phone into a bank of telephones staffed by trained counsellors who were visible in the studio. Roberts's doctrine of the 'point of contact' could easily be translated into this sort of interactive television, and viewers obviously liked seeing the phone being picked up in response to their requests for help.

Summing up

The emergence of religious broadcasting at the beginning of the twentieth century came to be important in the spread of Pentecostalism. The legal and financial framework encasing broadcasting varied from country to country. In the United States, where the regulation was lightest, airtime could be bought by commercial organizations and by churches. In Britain and in much of the rest of the world, airtime was monitored by a variety of agencies designed to prevent the politicization of the airways, which, as it happened, also prevented free access to radio for churches. Although religious voices might be heard in radio programmes outside the United States, the context was almost entirely non-evangelistic.

Pentecostal denominations solidified during the 1930s and 1940s. In the United States they amassed sufficient financial muscle to allow

---

30 P. D. Hocken, in a magisterial article on the charismatic movement in Burgess and van der Maas (eds), *NIDPCM*, p. 477, also realizes that the healing evangelists 'produced a following of Spirit-baptized believers who could not all be classified as pentecostal', which is essentially the point I am making.

them to broadcast by radio. The more inventive broadcasters, however, turned out to be those independent Pentecostals who may once have been ordained by Pentecostal denominations but now felt themselves to have outgrown their origins. At first, independent Pentecostal healing evangelists held crowded tent crusades and campaigns. These later gave the evangelists access to radio and, in a leap of faith, to television. The most successful early religious television was film of the great tent meetings. By the 1960s the format had been broadened and softened into the familiar chat show that included snippets of entertainment as well as short friendly interviews.[31] Yet the power of healing evangelists within American society and their energetic travel was such as to give an enormous boost to little Pentecostal groups in the English-speaking world – in South Africa, in the Caribbean, even in the Philippines and elsewhere where Pentecostals were welcomed. At the same time, on the American scene, the healing evangelists prepared the ground for the interdenominational charismatic movement of which they were unwitting heralds.

Cross-references to the SCM Reader *Pentecostal and Charismatic Studies*

3.4 Aimee Semple McPherson, *Pre-Millennial Signal Towers: Sermon delivered at the Angelus Temple, 24 August 1924*, abridged (pp. 32–4).
5.10 T. B. Barratt, *In The Days of the Latter Rain*, London, Elim Publishing House, 1928, pp. 108–9, 112–14, abridged (pp. 116–17).

Questions to think about

1 What would countries outside the United States look like if broadcasting were freely accessible to religious groups?
2 Does radio encourage a different kind of religion from television?
3 Do you think religious broadcasting strengthens or weakens the traditional congregational religion?

Further reading

Harrell, D. E. (1985), *Oral Roberts: An American Life*, Bloomington, Indiana University Press.
Sutton, M. A. (2007), *Aimee Semple McPherson and the Resurrection of Christian America*, London, Harvard University Press.

---

31 Pat Robertson's CBN network became the third largest cable network in America and features *The 700 Club*, its longest-running programme, which makes use of the chat-show format.

9

The Charismatic Movement

Here we describe the emergence of Pentecostalism in traditional, non-Pentecostal churches. These churches might be Baptist, Methodist, Anglican or any other type of Christian denomination that had come into existence through the revivals and reformations that marked the path of nearly 20 centuries of church history.

First phase

It is convenient to divide the European churches into three groups. First, there are the established churches that are in some way linked with the government of the country. The Anglican Church in Britain is the most obvious example of this since the Queen is also the temporal head of the church; the monarch's supremacy dates back to the Reformation when Henry VIII took over many of the functions that had been claimed by the Pope. A certain number of Anglican bishops have seats by right in the second legislative chamber of Parliament, the House of Lords, and therefore have a direct influence on law-making. Since the French Revolution the Roman Catholic Church in European countries has been ostensibly weakened, although in Belgium for instance Catholicism is close to the heart of national identity, a position that also applies in countries like Luxembourg. Second, there are churches that are not directly related to the government but form the majority church in a particular area. After the Reformation and the religious wars that followed it, Germany found itself roughly divided between Protestant and Roman Catholic areas according to the religious convictions of aristocratic landowners. In Germany and Switzerland, and possibly other countries, money paid to the church was collected through the normal tax system, which gave these churches some of the rights of establishment. Taxpayers could opt out of the payment of this amount as well as deciding, if they did give it, whether it should go to Lutheran or Roman Catholic churches. The effect of this stream of tax revenue was to make the receiving churches extremely wealthy but also to push these churches into providing social services that were appreciated by the population.[1] To be a minister of the main Lutheran or Roman Catholic Church was to have a recognized status within society and also a secure income and housing. Third, there were the Free or Nonconformist churches that received no tax income at all and depended on the gifts of local people in their congregations. These churches were obliged to pay for everything out of the pockets of their parishioners – buildings, ministerial stipends, theological colleges, and so on. These Nonconformist churches were the poorest ecclesiastical groups in much of Europe, though, in Britain as well as in parts of Eastern Europe, long-standing groups like the Baptists gradually accumulated a respectable name and financial stability.

At what might be called the top end of the system, in the established churches, but also where particular churches held the allegiance of the majority of the population, bishops and theologians engaged in public debate, were concerned with politics and might even influence the outcome of general elections. Such churches invested heavily in schools and expressed themselves in solemn convocations with major debates on topics of theological interest like the reform of the prayer book or the extent to which the trainee ministers should recognize rationalistic forms of biblical criticism.[2] At the lower end, among the Nonconformists, there was a struggle to survive and almost always a concentration on the individual's relationship with God, with the meaning of biblical text and with the training of preachers; the Nonconformists in the main had no hand in law-making or politics and so focused their attention on the Sunday-by-Sunday business of preaching and teaching their flocks. Yet, there could be a diffusion of spirituality across the Christian spectrum and there might be movements that crossed over ecclesiastical boundaries. Pietism as a way of expressing one's religious commitment through inner prayer and simplicity of lifestyle might be attractive to members of an established church or to Nonconformists. Even Methodism, the newest arrival on the religious scene as a result of the prolonged ministry of John Wesley and his preachers in the 1700s, located itself initially within the Anglican Church: Wesley himself never left Anglicanism and appears – at least initially – to have seen Methodism as a renewal movement rather than as a separate denomination. By stressing the evangelical gospel, a social conscience and the consequent duty to show compassion to other human beings, evangelicalism became a broad orientation that crossed over religious boundaries and it is this that allowed the formation of the Evangelical Alliance in London in 1846. At first, Pentecostalism in Europe might

1 I believe the Protestant and Roman Catholic churches between them are the biggest employers in Germany.

2 Revisions of the Anglican 1662 Book of Common Prayer always bring theological disagreement.

have been mistaken for a renewal movement and, if Alexander Boddy had seen his vision fulfilled, this is what it would have become.

In the United States there were never any established churches because the Constitution specifically forbade any connection between religion and government. The churches were always free-standing, supported by the financial contributions of their members and able to operate as they wished without having to take account of parish boundaries. Religion, in the United States, appeared to be a commodity that was supplied by the churches and chosen by believers. If you wished to worship in the Methodist church because it suited your beliefs and sensibilities, then so be it; if you found the Baptists more in keeping with your own opinions, then there was probably a Baptist church nearby; if you found the Quakers more to your liking, then you could go there. The American population was accustomed to choose its places of worship without legal or financial pressure. Over time, many religious denominations became financially strong and intellectually respected but, as we have seen, there was always a pressure to break out of respectability and conformity into newer, more aggressive, more committed and more evangelical forms of churchmanship; the move from Methodism to the holiness churches illustrates this tendency (Chapter 2). Pentecostalism when it arrived had no established church to contend with. It was simply one more religion in the marketplace of beliefs. In saying this, it should not be thought that religion was all about finance: the notion of a 'marketplace' is simply a metaphor indicating the faith choices on offer to the population and the reality that those who worshipped in one church could not at the same time worship in another.

Outside Europe and North America the situation was more confused. Where the European empires had been in existence, Christianity had been planted all over the world.[3] Since Christianity was associated with the imperial or colonial powers, the elites of the various countries or colonies found themselves attracted to the beliefs of their overlords. It became perfectly sensible to convert to Roman Catholicism, for instance, in an African context where the rulers of your country, as in the Belgian Congo, were Roman Catholic and where they provided schools and hospitals staffed by nuns. When the imperial powers withdrew – and the 1914–18 war weakened European nations to the extent that they had

---

3 The British Empire was not specifically Christian. 'Firmly relying ourselves on the truth of Christianity, and acknowledging with gratitude the solace of religion, we disclaim alike the right and desire to impose Our convictions on any of Our subjects. We declare it to be Our Royal will and pleasure that none be in anywise favoured, none molested or disquieted by reason of their religious faith or observance, but that all shall alike enjoy the equal and impartial protection of the law ...' So proclaimed Queen Victoria: see Stephen Neill (1990), *A History of Christian Missions*, London, Penguin, p. 274.

to call resources that had previously been expended overseas back to the homeland – the African elites that came to power in the newly independent countries had often converted to the religion of their previous government.[4] There has been debate about whether this conversion was genuine or merely a matter of political convenience, but, as Jenkins has pointed out, the believers maintained their faith long after the imperial powers had gone home, and sometimes were required to demonstrate the reality of their religious commitment by martyrdom or by enduring persecution.[5] It would be misleading to suggest that African or Asian elites always converted to Christianity out of self-interest; they did not.

Yet, in countries that have traditionally been Buddhist or Hindu, the encroachments of Christianity were more limited, especially since the British Empire in India tended to work hand in glove with local rulers rather than by completely replacing them.[6] As a result, the British Empire may have facilitated the establishment of schools run by missionaries and the diffusion of the English language, without, at independence, leaving behind a government that was inclined to favour Christianity.[7] In the case of India, a tolerant government that accepted the validity of all religions – Christian, Muslim and Hindu – was formed, though this had to wait till 1947. When the revival broke out in Mukti, in India, in 1905, the British Empire was still strong and apparently impregnable. This meant that missionaries were not hampered by visa restrictions and could normally rely upon a friendly reception from the local colonial administrator. Incipient Pentecostalism, whatever its prophetic and glossolalic intensity, appeared to uninformed Indian eyes to be enthusiastic Christianity associated with special emphasis on the education and care of young women. As far as the colonial administrators were concerned, provided that the explosion of Christian life and commitment did not create a violent reaction from the majority Hindu community, there was nothing wrong in what was happening. But there were never enough Christian churches in India for Pentecostalism to challenge either the more numerous Anglicans or the great rural hinterland of ancestral Hindu or, in the north, Muslim practice.

---

4 Germany lost its colonies, and therefore its missionaries, as a condition of its defeat in 1918. Namibia, in south west Africa, still has Africans who speak German. The language has been passed through families over four generations.

5 Philip Jenkins (2002), *The Next Christendom*, Oxford and New York, Oxford University Press.

6 Korea is an unusual case. A revival there pre-dated the Azusa Street revival and it has been argued that a charismatic movement was found there before classical Pentecostalism arrived. See Jeong Chong Hee (2005), 'The Korean Charismatic Movement as Indigenous Pentecostalism', in A. Anderson and E. Tang (eds), *Asian and Pentecostal: The Charismatic Face of Christian Asia*, Baguio City, Regnum. See also Chapter 3.

7 See Niall Ferguson (2004), *Empire: How Britain Made the Modern World*, London, Penguin.

In short, when Pentecostalism burst upon the scene at the beginning of the twentieth century, few expected that it would in any way match its claims or the beliefs of its fiery practitioners. It appeared to be destined to become, at best, another renewal movement and at worst a minor sectarian irritant. The major established churches almost entirely ignored it for many years. Where Pentecostalism began to be noticed by the Nonconformist churches, friction occurred and, as we shall see, Germany put a heavy block on Pentecostal advances early on. Elsewhere in the world, in the days of the imperial powers, Pentecostalism might and did run like wildfire through missionary organizations, but even here there were missionary groups that stood firmly against Pentecostal phenomena. In the United States, the country most open to religious innovation, Pentecostalism found its most welcoming conditions.

Germany, the Berlin Declaration (1909) and the Mülheim Association

The arrival of the Pentecostal movement in Germany appeared at first glance to be likely to lead to a free-flowing spiritual movement within established churches.[8]

The Protestant churches were well organized and there were Associations by which like-minded ministers met each other. The Gnadau Evangelical Union (Gnadauer Gemeinschaftsverband) had gospel halls all over the country which were at first open to Pentecostal doctrine and experience.[9] In the spring of 1907 Jonathan Paul (1853–1931), a minister in the Lutheran Church, had, with Emil Meyer (1869–1950) of the Strandmission in Hamburg, visited T. B. Barratt in Oslo. There Meyer spoke in other tongues. Events moved quickly after that. Two young Norwegian women, Dagmar Gregersen and Agnes Thelle,[10] who had been baptized in the Holy Spirit in Barratt's meetings, went first to Hamburg and then with the evangelist Heinrich Dallmeyer (1870-1925)[11] to hold a series of meetings in Kassel between 7 July and 1 August. Initially these meetings were orderly and, although people spoke in tongues and there were healings, which were unusual at the time, other evangelical leaders were convinced that they were seeing a genuine manifestation of the Holy Spirit. At some point shortly afterwards, the meetings became disorderly

---

8 At this point I am heavily indebted to Carl Simpson's excellent article, 'Jonathan Paul and The German Pentecostal Movement: The First Seven Years, 1907–1914', *Journal of the European Pentecostal Theological Association* 1, 2008, 169–82.

9 W. J. Hollenweger (1972), *The Pentecostals*, London, SCM Press, p. 225.

10 Nils Bloch-Hoell (1964), *The Pentecostal Movement*, Oslo, Universitätsforlaget, 1964, p. 80.

11 Paul Fleisch (1957), *Die Pfingstbewegung in Deutschland*, Hannover, Heinr. Feesche Verlag, p. 392.

and there were such strange and disturbing activities in evidence that the police were called and the meetings were closed down. This, naturally, became a public scandal and appeared to have dealt the young Pentecostal movement a fatal blow.

Nevertheless, Pentecostalism spread all over Germany within the next 18 months so that in December 1908 a conference was convened in Hamburg and people from 18 different regions of Germany attended, as well as people from England, Sweden and the Netherlands. The conference decided to found a magazine, *Pfingstgrüße* (*Pentecostal Greetings*), and also took the usual step of trying to provide objective evidence for the validity of Pentecostalism by publishing accounts of the *xenolalia*, or tongues-speaking in a known language. This had no effect on other evangelicals. The Evangelical Union, after a relatively small meeting of 56 ministers, issued the infamous Berlin Declaration on 15 September 1909 in which they argued that Pentecostalism was 'from below', that is, from the devil, and therefore should be condemned unreservedly and without any further discussion. Here we see Pentecostals facing opposition from Nonconformist churches with whom they might have hoped to be in alliance.[12] The Berlin Declaration put an end to friendship. The Pentecostals were on their own.

A gathering of some 2,500 people was then convened at Mülheim from 28 September to 1 October 1909, and a counter declaration was issued. Although Pentecostalism grew in Germany and its leaders enjoyed cordial relations with other Pentecostals in other parts of Europe, the Mülheim Association formally founded in February 1914 was organized on the basis that the congregations were 'a movement' rather than a new church organization. The Mülheim Christians combined belief in charismatic gifts with many standard evangelical beliefs – indeed its ministers remained within the denominations that had ordained them – and, in this way, could be seen as the first charismatics: they were neither free-standing Pentecostals nor aloof from mainstream denominations, but rather embraced Pentecostalism for its renewing power within an existing associational structure.

The United States and the Free-Will Baptists

It is also possible to see the Free-Will Baptist churches in North and South Carolina as being early charismatics.[13] Because of their non-Calvinistic

---

12 Hollenweger, *Pentecostals*, pp. 225–8, points out that the Declaration was thought to be confirmed by the statements of a 'mentally ill girl'. What is ironical about this is that the Declaration had made a point of condemning Pentecostals for being slavishly obedient to prophetic messages given by women.

13 V. Synan (2001), 'The "Charismatics": Renewal in Major Protestant Denominations', in V. Synan (ed.), *The Century of the Holy Spirit*, Nashville, TN, Nelson, p. 186.

theology, they were already organized separately from other Southern Baptists. When in 1907 they heard the Pentecostal message from Gaston Cashwell who had received his Spirit-baptism at Azusa Street, they accepted Pentecostal doctrine and experience. Although they did not grow fast, by 1959 they comprised 135 congregations. Whether we should classify these Baptists as Pentecostals or charismatics – or simply as Baptists – their presence indicates that experiences of the Holy Spirit could leave many long-standing features of denominational church life intact.

Willis Hoover (1856–1936) and Chilean Pentecostalism

Hoover, a Methodist who chose to go as an independent missionary to Chile, read Minnie Abram's book *The Baptism of the Holy Ghost and Fire* in 1907. The book arrived at the point when Hoover was engaged in a struggle with the Methodist Episcopal Church Mission Board over control of churches founded by Chilean pastors and independent missionaries like himself (some of whom were women). The book 'gave direction to the spiritual crisis provoked by the conflict over mission praxis', and in 1909 Hoover experienced speaking in tongues, as did the congregations where he was working.[14] Towards the end of that year tongues-speaking Methodists were forced out of their churches and what had begun as a charismatic movement became a Pentecostal movement in a cycle that many early Pentecostals – T. B. Barratt for one – would have recognized.

Louis Dallière (1897–1976) and French Pentecostalism

The Protestant church in France has, for historical reasons, never been strong. At one point it was damaged by absolutist Roman Catholic kings and, at another point, by an atheistic revolutionary government. Speaking of an essay published by Louis Dallière in 1930, Bundy wrote:

> The Protestant church, he observed, was plagued by financial deficits in the parishes. These shortages resulted in similar deficits in mission programs both in France and abroad. The policymakers needed to realize that rhetoric about the obligations of the church members no longer motivated giving. It must be recognized that the financial problems were indications of internal spiritual problems.[15]

---

14 Bundy 'Chile', in S. Burgess and E. van der Maas (eds) (2002), *New International Dictionary of Pentecostal and Charismatic Movements* (*NIDPCM*), Zondervan, p. 55.

15 David Bundy (1988), 'The Making of a Pentecostal Theologian: The Writings of Louis Dallière 1922–1932', *EPTA Bulletin* VII.2, 40–68.

Dallière was a most unusual figure for his time. He was a pastor within the French Reformed Church but had philosophical expertise to the extent that he studied for a doctorate in Paris, spent a year in Harvard, and underwent a spiritual conversion that resulted in his speaking with tongues in 1932. Writing on a wide range of philosophical and theological topics from the early 1920s onwards, Dallière found himself from 1932 defending the incipient Pentecostal movement.[16] A converted English bandleader, Douglas Scott (1900–67), began to pioneer a series of new congregations all over France which eventually became the French version of Assemblies of God. He spoke appalling French but nevertheless saw amazing miracles. The French Protestants, who had a strong Calvinist streak, were dubious about the possibility of healing miracles in the modern era although they recognized that their position in French society was marginal and needed to be reinvigorated by spiritual power. Initially, Dallière saw the Pentecostal movement as a renewal movement within French Protestantism, but despite his efforts to mediate between the blunt Englishman and the French Protestants he was only partially successful. Dallière visited England to talk with the British Pentecostals and understood their beliefs and practices well. Some of the criticisms of Pentecostalism that had earlier been aired in Germany made their way to France, but, in a passionate monograph, Dallière showed that Pentecostalism could be related back to the early revivalism of Finney[17] and how it should be seen as thoroughly biblical and in line with the mainstream doctrines of the church. Dallière found himself criticized by, although not expelled from, the Reformed Church and subsequently became most famous for founding the Union of Prayer that acted as an expression of his charismatic ecumenical vision and persisted beyond his death in 1976.

Second phase

The second phase of the charismatic movement begins from about 1950. Essentially, the charismatic movement concerned the outpouring of the Holy Spirit upon the historic mainline denominations. To the surprise of Pentecostals, there was an outbreak of speaking with tongues among Anglicans, Lutherans, Presbyterians, Methodists, Baptists, Mennonites and Roman Catholics from the early 1960s onwards, though there were also a few 'early receivers' of Pentecostal experience in the 1950s.

The charismatic movement began at a time of social change.[18] When

---

16 David Bundy (1989), 'Louis Dallière (1932–1939): The Development of a Pentecostal Apologetic', *EPTA Bulletin* VIII.2, 60–93.

17 See Chapter 2.

18 A. Marwick, (1998), *The Sixties*, Oxford, Oxford University Press.

World War Two finally ended, the countries of Europe began to rebuild their shattered economies. North America had escaped relatively un-scathed from the conflict, although military casualties brought tragedy to many families. In Asia the status quo had been rebalanced after the defeat of imperialistic Japanese militarism and the installation of a demo-cratic government in that country. In the Philippines and Korea, coun-tries that had both suffered armed occupation, Western aid was welcome and Western religion appeared to have much to offer. Even in Japan, immediately after 1945, missionaries drew a ready audience.[19] By the 1960s, a new generation was growing up. All those who were born in the birth-rate boom just after 1945 reached the age of 18 in 1963 and, in democratic countries, were either able to vote or nearly so. The 1960s saw huge cultural change (think of the music of the era) brought about by a generation of anti-war young people (especially against the Vietnam war), and this was a change that was reflected in 1968 on university cam-puses as far apart as Berkeley, California, and Paris, as well as with less drama in England and Germany.[20] The old churches seemed to belong to a different era and had difficulty attracting the young. Church attendance in many countries had been disrupted by military conscription. The result of all this was to facilitate new lifestyles which, as far as charismatics were concerned, was entirely providential.

In talking about the charismatic movement it is important to distinguish three distinct although often interacting groups. First, we have the clas-sical Pentecostals in all their variety. For the purpose of this discussion, 'classical' Pentecostals are those who belong to Pentecostal denominations that specify the reality and importance of charismatic gifts – speaking with tongues, prophecy, healing and other miracles – within their foun-dation documents. So, classical Pentecostals are groups of churches that were formed specifically on the basis of their belief in the contemporary availability of spiritual gifts. They expect their ministers and members not only to believe in spiritual gifts but to exercise them; indeed, ministers of classical Pentecostal churches would not be accepted for ordination unless they did believe in spiritual gifts. Having said this, classical Pentecostals differ greatly in the nuances of their doctrines and in their interpretation of biblical prophecy. They also differ ethnically in the extent to which they are mixed black and white churches or white only or black only.

Second, there were independent Pentecostals who had often started life within the Pentecostal denominations but left as a result of disagreements or because they felt freer to work outside the parameters of denomina-

---

19 Though a renewal of Shintoism by 1952 began to reassert traditional Japanese religious values. L. Savage (1953), *Redemption Tidings* 29, 8.

20 Some of this change is reflected in David Baker, Loek Halman and Astrid Vloet (1992), *The European Values Survey*, Gordon Cook Foundation, place of publication not given.

tional life. These were often roving healing evangelists who were not tied to a local congregation that belonged within a denomination (Chapter 8).[21] The independent Pentecostal evangelists were answerable to no higher human authority than themselves, which meant that they tended to be individualistic, sometimes idiosyncratic and occasionally uncooperative with the denominational churches. The best of the independent Pentecostal evangelists were wiser than this, though. They realized that they needed to keep on friendly terms with the denominations and went out of their way to retain good working relationships; Oral Roberts was the best example.[22]

And, third, there were, as we shall see, charismatic groups and churches that sprang out of the old mainline denominations. Sometimes it became difficult to distinguish between the independent Pentecostals and the charismatics as there was traffic between the two. They might attend the same meetings, sing the same songs, believe more or less the same things and read the same books. So, to see how all this worked out, it is necessary to tell a complicated story. It is complicated not only because the charismatics came from so many different denominations, and therefore came from quite different starting points with regard to their belief in the activity of the Holy Spirit, but also because they were spread across different parts of the world. For instance, the charismatic movement among Baptists in the United States was not the same as the charismatic movement among Baptists in Russia: they had different priorities. The charismatic movement is for this reason even more complicated to describe than the Pentecostal movement itself, although, fortunately, the basic idea and fundamental experience at the heart of the movement is simple: individuals underwent a profound experience of the Holy Spirit that changed the way they lived their Christian lives individually and collectively.

We begin, though, on the West Coast of the United States since this is where the charismatic movement received its greatest initial publicity. On the scale of American churches, the Episcopalians are the most respectable, probably the most educated, and the religion of choice for the white professional elite.[23] Episcopalianism is liturgical, tends to make use of fine old buildings, a prayer book, and typically embraces a liberal Protestant outlook on life; perhaps because of this it lost 28% of its membership in the period 1965–88.[24] It came as a complete shock when Dennis Bennett (1917–91), an Episcopalian priest in Van Nuys, met tongues-speaking

---

21 A. A. Allen was one of these, as were T. L. Osborn and many others associated with the *Voice of Healing* movement.

22 Roberts went on to leave the Pentecostals and become a member of the United Methodists.

23 Synan (2001), 'The "Charismatics"', p. 151.

24 See Alister E. McGrath (1993), *The Renewal of Anglicanism*, London, SPCK, p. 39.

Christians, liked what he saw and the obvious enthusiasm they felt for their Christian faith, and asked them to pray for him. He takes up the story:

> [Someone] prayed in English, asking Jesus to baptize me in the Holy Spirit.
>
> I began to pray, as he told me, and I prayed very quietly, too. I was not about to get even a little bit excited! I was simply following instructions. I suppose I must have prayed out loud for about 20 minutes – at least it seemed to be a long time – and was just about to give up when a very strange thing happened. My tongue tripped, just as it might when you're trying to recite a tongue twister, and I began to speak in a new language!
>
> Right away I recognized several things: first, it wasn't some kind of psychological trick or compulsion. There was nothing compulsive about it. I was allowing these new words to come to my lips and was speaking them out of my own volition, without in any way being forced to do it. I wasn't 'carried away' in any sense of the word, but was fully in possession of my wits and my willpower. I spoke the new language because it was interesting to speak a language I had never learned, even though I didn't know what I was saying. I had taken quite a while to learn a small amount of German and French, but here was a language 'for free'. Secondly, it was a real language, not some kind of 'baby talk'. It had grammar and syntax; it had inflection and expression – and it was rather beautiful. I went on allowing words to come to my lips for about five minutes, then said to my friends:
>
> 'Well! That must be what you mean by "speaking in tongues" – but what is it all about? I don't feel anything!'
>
> They said joyfully:
>
> 'Praise the Lord!'
>
> This seemed a bit irrelevant and was a little strong for my constitution. It bordered on the fanatical for such a thing to be said by Episcopalians on a fine Saturday afternoon sitting right in the front room of their home![25]

More and more people within the parish began to speak in other tongues and Bennett realized his behaviour was causing consternation. He wrote to his parishioners, telling them what had happened, and during a service shared the story of his spiritual journey. A riot nearly broke out, heated insults were thrown – 'We are Episcopalians, not a bunch of wild-eyed hillbillies' – and Bennett thought it best to resign. The story reached the

---

25 Dennis J. Bennett (1971), *Nine O'clock in the Morning*, Eastbourne, Coverdale, pp. 20–1.

national press: *Time* and *Newsweek* reported that 'glossolalia seems to be on its way back in US churches – not only in the uninhibited Pentecostal sects, but even among the Episcopalians'.[26] Bennett, cast adrift, was invited by a sympathetic Episcopalian bishop to take over a rundown parish in Seattle, which he did, in the summer of 1960. A year later the congregation had been revived, new parishioners had spoken in other tongues, financial giving had increased by 50%, a new church hall was built and Bennett himself, whose book *Nine O'clock in the Morning* told the story of his life and sold widely, became an acknowledged charismatic leader.

The charismatic movement spread across the Christian world. Among those who contributed to its rapid acceptance within the mainline denominations was the extraordinary David du Plessis (1905–87). Raised in racially prejudiced South Africa within one of the old white-dominated Pentecostal denominations, the Apostolic Faith Mission, he had also imbibed a dose of anti-Catholicism. He appeared to be quite unsuited to the role of an ambassador of Pentecostalism to the rest of the church. Yet, in 1936, while du Plessis was the General Secretary of the Apostolic Faith Mission, the unconventional British healing evangelist Smith Wigglesworth had burst into du Plessis's office early one morning, pinned him to the wall, looked him straight in the eye and given him a prophecy:

'You have been in Jerusalem long enough ... I will send you to the utmost parts of the earth ... you will bring the message of Pentecost to all churches ... you will travel more than most evangelists do ... God is going to revive the churches in the last days and through them turn the world upside down ...'[27]

The prophecy lay dormant in du Plessis's brain until he became one of the team preparing for the first Pentecostal World Conference, which was held in Zürich in May of 1947. The conference, with the destructive effects of World War Two still fresh in everyone's minds, aimed to bring together Pentecostals from all over the world. Conscious of the importance of his task, du Plessis asked the leaders of his denomination for permission to extend his stay in Zürich. They refused to allow this. du Plessis then took the 'bold and prophetic' step of resigning as AFM General Secretary.[28] He had no financial support and sent a telegram to his wife telling her to come to Switzerland after selling everything they possessed. Between 1949 and 1958 he served as organizing Secretary (though with

---

26 Synan, 'The "Charismatics"', p. 153.

27 David du Plessis, (1977), *A Man Called Mr Pentecost*, Plainfield, NJ, Logos International, p. 19.

28 R. P. Spittler (2002), 'David Johannes du Plessis', in *NIDPCM*. With hindsight it was clear to du Plessis that the prophecy referred to the charismatic movement.

a break between 1952 and 1955) for the Pentecostal World Conferences. His gifts as an administrator, letter-writer, organizer, cajoler and chairman flourished and to these he brought a genuinely non-judgemental and loving attitude towards all Christians, a ready wit and an anecdotal style of preaching. His position as the Secretary of the World Pentecostal Conference gave him a unique insight into the intricacies of Pentecostalism in all its diversity. He increasingly saw himself as divinely called to carry out the commission that Wigglesworth had first relayed to him.

To their mutual amazement, du Plessis and the World Council of Churches, a liberal organization that Pentecostals traditionally shunned, found themselves friends. The story of du Plessis's invitation to the World Council Assembly in 1954 is marvellously Pentecostal. du Plessis arrived without an invitation because he believed that 'the Lord would provide', which is what happened.[29] The venerable theologians and denominational leaders of the mainline churches had, it is said, never met a rational Pentecostal, but when they met du Plessis they found someone with a sense of humour as well as a profound conviction, echoing their own, that the Holy Spirit was working to bring all the churches together. du Plessis became known as 'Mr Pentecost' and brought a message to the high-powered ecumenical functionaries of the World Council: perhaps the churches would be brought together more by the unseen power of the Spirit than by the rationalistic argumentation of numerous committees.

Once the charismatic movement had begun in the United States, it spread to other parts of the English-speaking world. This said, there were also independent Pentecostal churches or ministries that came to be influenced by the charismatic movement and eventually indistinguishable from it. This means that independent Pentecostals might look like charismatics, and charismatics, if they became detached from their denominational moorings, might look like independent Pentecostals – at least in terms of their worship practices. On top of this, when charismatics began to look at church history, they might have seen a stream of charismatic activity running down the centuries from the Montanists (second century) to the Jansenists and Quakers (seventeenth century) whereas Pentecostals would interpret the stream as being a Pentecostal one.[30] This is entirely a matter of terminology and not of substance. As an indication of their similarity, charismatics were called 'neo-Pentecostals', but quickly dropped this term in favour of 'charismatic' since it carried no connotations.

In England the charismatic movement could be said to have had a dat-

---

29 W. J. Hollenweger (1997), *Pentecostalism: Origins and Developments Worldwide*, Peabody, MA, Hendrickson, p. 352.

30 Compare the classical Pentecostal account of David Allen (1994), *The Unfailing Stream*, Lancaster, Sovereign World, and the charismatic Anglican account of Mark J. Cartledge (2006), *Encountering the Spirit*, London, Darton, Longman and Todd.

able beginning in 1964 with the formation of the Fountain Trust under the leadership of Michael Harper. Harper had been an Anglican curate in one of the showcase evangelical churches in London, but when he was baptized in the Holy Spirit and spoke in tongues in 1963 his relationship with his vicar, the distinguished John Stott who took a theological position that was critical of charismatics, cooled. Harper founded the historically important Fountain Trust without any funds at his disposal and with the intention of promoting interdenominational charismatic activity. He launched *Renewal* magazine and circulated news, analysis, teaching, book reviews and information about the conferences; in this way, he provided a clearing house whereby a growing number of charismatics could find out what was going on, meet together to reach a common mind on the dilemmas that faced them and encourage each other.[31]

One of the dilemmas that faced charismatics concerned their role within their own denominational settings. What was a charismatic to do in a church setting that traditionally forbade speaking with tongues or the laying on of hands? More generally, how should charismatic Christians relate to professional clergy? This acute question arose because charismatics found themselves part of a lay movement. In many of the traditional denominations, the ordained or professional clergy led services, preached, organized church life, and had done this for centuries. Christians within the congregations were at least acquiescent to their leaders and expected to take subservient roles. The charismatic movement, based on the belief that ordinary Christians could be filled with the Holy Spirit, speak in tongues like the apostles, manifest charismatic gifts given to them by the Holy Spirit and actively fulfil their Christian calling, raised expectations about what ordinary people could do. No longer was it necessary to go to seminary and receive extensive training in two biblical languages (Hebrew and Greek), to master the complexities of church history and the patristic debates of the first four centuries of the Christian era, understand liturgical texts with all their ambiguities and layers of meaning, but, instead, through one decisive and miraculous endowment of the Holy Spirit, everyone could talk in front of a congregation about their personal experience, indicate what they felt God had told them, and if necessary lead Bible studies or worship. The charismatic movement, for all its spirituality, was also a revolutionary movement overturning the age-long dominance of the professional clergy in favour of ordinary people with extraordinary gifts.

None of this was immediately apparent. At first it seemed that the charismatic movement would only renew the lives of individuals and congregations. Michael Harper's choice for the name of his magazine

---

31 Harper's short book introducing the Pentecostal (as he then called it) movement was widely read. See M. Harper (1965), *As at the Beginning*, London, Hodder and Stoughton.

exactly illustrates the position he took. The charismatic movement was to *renew* the church. It was not intended to reform the church and change its doctrine, nor was it intended to restore to the church all those things that had been lost down the long centuries of church history. Rather, the charismatic movement was intended to refresh individuals and parishes, and if, beyond this, revival and evangelism followed, that was all to the good, but for Anglican charismatics, after early debate, the charismatic movement must leave lines of ecclesiastical authority and the basics of Christian initiation (christening and infant baptism) untouched.

This pattern was not followed with equal smoothness elsewhere. Although Lutherans in the United States generally welcomed the charismatic movement and, like Anglicans in England, set up their own agencies for renewal, there were also much nastier confrontations. In some instances Lutheran ministers who had spoken with tongues and were suspended from their parishes responded by bringing legal actions against the denomination. When this happened, the charismatic movement was accused of being 'divisive', even though charismatics argued that they were simply tapping into a long-lost tradition within the church. Practically speaking, where churches were episcopal, that is, organized with bishops, the attitude of the local bishop was crucial. Some resisted everything to do with the charismatic movement and recoiled with horror. Others saw what was happening, appreciated the enthusiasm generated within the affected congregations, were thankful for the increased financial contributions that almost invariably followed religious enthusiasm, took heart from growing numbers in previously declining parishes and, even if they themselves did not become charismatic, nevertheless interfered little with what was going on.

The Presbyterian Church, which had no bishops, found itself with a Presbyterian Charismatic Communion in 1963 and commissioned a report on the charismatic movement so as to make a considered judgement about what should be done. This pattern was followed by almost every other denominational group.[32] When the charismatic movement began, there were those within the church opposed to what they saw and others enthusiastically in favour, and so the church hierarchy appointed theologians and practitioners to debate and weigh the matter so that a collective decision could be made. A whole series of these reports was issued, and they typically covered two types of question:

---

32 For instance there was a National Service Committee (Roman Catholic), an Episcopal Charismatic Fellowship (Episcopalian), Lutheran Charismatic Renewal Services (Lutheran), Mennonite Renewal Services (Mennonite), Service Committee for Orthodox Spiritual Renewal (Orthodox) and several Presbyterian agencies. Peter Hocken (2002), 'Charismatic Movement', in Burgess and van der Maas (eds), *NIDPCM*, p. 482.

1 Should speaking with tongues, prophecy, the seeing of visions, and other charismatic phenomena be treated as indications of psychological imbalance or are they to be understood as signs of spiritual vitality?

2 If speaking with tongues, prophecy and other charismatic gifts were accepted within the church, should charismatics approve the interpretation of these phenomena that had been worked out by Pentecostal churches?

The answers to the first question varied enormously and there were some appalling pieces of 'objective' research produced by highly biased commissions. For instance, a book by J. P. Kildahl purports to describe the psychological condition of those who speak in tongues by reference to interviews with a sample of 26 people.[33] Given that by this time there were many thousands of tongues-speakers, a sample of 26 is pitifully small and can in no way be used to generalize to the rest of the population. And in any case, as the number of people speaking with tongues grew, and as it became apparent that they were perfectly sane and balanced (as the extract from Dennis Bennett's book given earlier is at pains to show), these psychological attacks lost whatever credibility they may once have had. A Benedictine monk, Kilian McDonnell, reviewed much of the material in his book *Charismatic Renewal and the Churches* (1976), and in a direct and scholarly manner was able to provide evidence that, far from being mentally deranged, charismatics were likely to be as stable, if not more stable, than the rest of the population – a finding I replicated later.[34]

The answer to the second question was more complex and depended upon the church tradition in which the charismatic movement functioned. The issue centred on Christian initiation. Pentecostals, as we have seen, generally believed that people became Christians by an individual act of faith in Christ and that, following this, they might be baptized by immersion in water and then, following this, baptized in the Holy Spirit through the agency of Christ. This order of salvation gave little or no weight to the baptizing of infants. The argument was that infants were incapable of exercising faith in Christ and should not therefore be baptized. By contrast, many churches, including the Roman Catholic Church, the Anglican Church and the Orthodox Church, believed that infants were admitted to Christianity through water baptism and thereby received the

---

33 J. P. Kildahl (1972), *The Psychology of Speaking in Tongues*, London, Hodder and Stoughton. Kildahl actually compared 26 tongues-speakers with 13 non-tongues-speakers. For an overview of this literature, see W. K. Kay (2006), 'The Mind, Behaviour and Glossolalia: A Psychological Perspective', in M. J. Cartledge (ed.), *Speaking in Tongues: Multi-Disciplinary Perspectives*, Carlisle, Paternoster Press, pp. 174–205.

34 For replication, see W. K. Kay and L. J. Francis (1995), 'Personality, Mental Health and Glossolalia', *Pneuma* 17, 253–63. Kilian McDonnell's book was published in New York by the Seabury Press.

Holy Spirit by that rite. Consequently, they came to argue that the Holy Spirit was 'released' rather than received at the point at which people spoke in other tongues.[35] In this way it was possible to harmonize aspects of Pentecostal belief about baptism in the Holy Spirit with traditional understandings of admission to Christian churches.

Alternative concepts for ordering congregational life

If one were to look for a touchstone of the charismatic movement's teaching on congregational order it would probably be focused on words like elder or church council. This stems first of all from the study of Scripture. The role of elders figures prominently in governing structures both in the Old and New Testaments. The other side of this is the fact that charismatics have recognized some of the weaknesses inherent in a congregation that structures itself after the model of a democratic assembly. The transition from one to the other is essentially a matter of concept; it does not necessarily, or at once, involve external changes in structure, for instance, in the constitution or legal basis of a congregation.

A change in concept is sometimes described as a transition from democracy to kingdom. In explaining this transition to a group of pastors, Herbert Mirly, pastor of Resurrection Lutheran Church in Charlotte, North Carolina, said,

> We did not need to change the constitution of our congregation as this transition got under way. It was a matter of how we understood and used the existing structure. For instance, we used to come to a congregational meeting with the idea that we must 'make certain decisions.' When we began to see the congregation as an expression of 'kingdom,' we approached the whole thing differently. God makes decisions. Our business is to discern as accurately as we can what he has decided and then proceed to obey him. The so-called 'voters meeting' became a prayer meeting or a 'discernment session.' We still discuss the issues, but the attitude and approach is altogether different: instead of choosing up sides and seeing who can muster 51% of the vote, we are all standing on the same side of the line participating in the process of listening to the Lord and seeking his will in the matter.

A related concept for understanding congregational order has been that of family. The model of family tends to produce in a congregation an

---

35 S. Tugwell, (1971), *Did You Receive the Spirit?*, London, Darton Longman and Todd.

ordered set of relationships rather than simply a procedure for handling issues. The church council answers to the role of parents; the congregation, to the role of children. At first glance this seems to lead to a more centralized, authoritarian structure, but the opposite is more usually the case. Loving and sensitive parents probably listen more sympathetically to their children than an elected official does to his or her constituency. They listen because they love and seek the best for their children, not because the children have the leverage of a vote in the next election. A typical church constitution might permit a church council to do certain things with a majority or two-thirds approval of the congregation. Charismatic congregations that have developed the family concept, on the other hand, might well decide to wait if as few as 10% of the members feel uneasy about a particular action; in a family, maintaining unity is normally more important than pushing through a particular decision.

Larry Christenson (ed.), *Welcome, Holy Spirit*, Minneapolis, Augsburg Publishing House, 1987, pp. 309–12 (abridged)

All this took time and followed different patterns across the world. In Britain, responses to the charismatic movement tended not to follow such painstaking investigative procedures as occurred in the United States. In 1971 a Fountain Trust five-day gathering at Guildford Cathedral attracted more than 2,000 people and a range of speakers with different theological and denominational backgrounds.[36] Charismatic Catholics found themselves drawn into the worship and appreciated the preaching. An international conference was held at Canterbury in 1978 and the General Synod of the Church of England issued a favourable report in 1981.[37] In Finland, for example, where the charismatic movement was favourably orientated to the Lutheran Church, the movement was accepted more or less without controversy and simply classified as a renewal movement like any of the others that had occurred in the past.[38] In France, survey data showed that the charismatic movement spread among the Baptist, Reformed, Lutheran and Roman Catholic churches and expressed itself slightly differently in each, sometimes being found in residential communities as well as in local prayer groups.[39] In the United States charismatic

36 Described in *Renewal*, no. 34.

37 See, P. D. Hocken (2002), 'The Charismatic Movement', in Burgess and van der Maas (eds), *NIDPCM*, p. 491.

38 H. Heino (1988), 'Different Manifestations of the Charismatic Movement: The Charismatic Movement in Finland and America', *EPTA Bulletin* 7.4, 128–41.

39 E. Veldhuizen (1991), 'The Charismatic Renewal in Protestant and Evangelical Churches in France 1968–1988', in J. A. B. Jongeneel (ed.), *Experiences of the Spirit:*

experience was assisted by the formation of the Full Gospel Business Men's Fellowship International (FGBMFI) in 1951. Typically, its businessmen, now speaking with tongues and able to testify publicly about their own sense of the Holy Spirit's leading in their lives, held meetings in hotels across the world, jetting in and out with efficiency and speed, and attracted lay people to splendid breakfasts or sumptuous dinners. As part of its ethos, the FGBMFI forbade leadership by ordained clergy: it was by definition a lay movement. The businessmen had money, contacts, credibility and energy and helped to organize interdenominational activities. Unlike clergymen, businessmen cared very little for the church traditions or the niceties of doctrinal difference. They were pragmatists and wanted to press on with helping the church to grow. So, while professional clergy might hesitate or argue, Full Gospel businessmen published a magazine, *Voice*, which was almost entirely filled with testimonies of miraculous guidance. A man who ran an urban car dealership and who had lapsed into alcoholism found Christ, experienced the baptism of the Holy Spirit, saved his marriage and found his business prospering, had a story to tell with which other businessmen could gladly identify. This was what lay people wanted to hear rather than the 'irrelevant' preaching of uncharismatic clergy. So, in addition to being a lay movement, the charismatic movement brought into the church men who, according to most statistical studies, left church activity to their wives, sisters and mothers while, with their buddies, they pounded the golf course on a Sunday morning or sat with their feet up to relax with the weekend newspaper.

Among the other catalysts of the charismatic movement was the story of David Wilkerson, a classical Pentecostal preacher, who found himself led by the Holy Spirit to begin working among Puerto Rican drug addicts in New York. His million-selling book, *The Cross and the Switchblade* (1963), made gripping reading as the skinny preacher took on the knife and drug culture of uncontrollable teenagers. Wilkerson saw astonishing conversions following his open-air sermons and was able to set up a string of drug rehabilitation centres and farms that rescued young people from the streets. Wilkerson made it plain that his method for withdrawing young people from drugs was to make them endure 'cold turkey', during which, without any medication or attempt to cut doses down gradually, he asked addicts to abstain from drugs while they were supported by prayer. Many young people, after three days of sweating and pain, came out with their physical addiction broken. When Wilkerson then prayed for these young people to be filled the Holy Spirit, many of them experienced a fullness of joy that counteracted the allure of the needle and the pill.

Conference on Pentecostal and Charismatic Research in Europe at Utrecht University 1989, New York, Peter Lang, pp. 211–20.

Dave Wilkerson's book was read by intellectual Roman Catholics and created a spiritual hunger among them. About 25 Catholic students, a priest and two faculty members from Duquesne University (in the USA) gathered in 1967 for a student retreat. On Saturday morning two of the professors, who had been baptized in the Holy Spirit two weeks earlier, led the group in the singing of an ancient Latin hymn. One of the students asked one of the professors to pray:

> By ones and twos the small group made their way to the chapel. And as they gathered together in prayer, the Holy Spirit poured himself out upon them.
>
> There was no urging, there was no direction as to what had to be done. The individuals simply encountered the person of the Holy Spirit as others had several weeks before. Some praised God in new languages, others quietly wept for joy, others prayed and sang. They prayed from ten in the evening until five in the morning.[40]

The chapel became a holy place and the 'Duquesne weekend' eventually made a radical impact upon the Roman Catholic Church. Just over a week later Kevin and Dorothy Ranaghan, academics at the university, decided to share their experience with the local president of the FGBMFI. In spite of divergent social and theological backgrounds, they found a common bond in the Holy Spirit. At no point were the Roman Catholics willing to accept that speaking with tongues was a theological necessity indicative of being baptized in the Holy Spirit. Bit by bit, the Catholic charismatic movement spread. Its characteristics differed from those of the other churches because, by and large, the Catholics were better educated and more middle class than was common in other parts of the movement. The Catholics, because of their theology of priesthood, were inclined to defer to the official clerical authority within the churches and, as the Catholic charismatic movement progressed, it impacted parish life more readily than liturgically driven worship services. Yet, because the Roman Catholic Church was found all over the world and had internal methods of communication, news of the experience spread, priests were baptized in the Holy Spirit, as were bishops and cardinals, and the Pope himself came to welcome what was happening.[41] Indeed, the Second Vatican Council, which concluded in 1963, helped the Catholic charismatics interpret their experience as the answer to John XXIII's prayer for a new Pentecost.

---

40 Jack W. Hayford and S. David Moore (2006), *The Charismatic Century*, New York, Warner Faith, p. 219.

41 David du Plessis was received by three pontiffs, John XXIII, Paul VI and John Paul II. See Spittler, 'du Plessis', in Burgess and van der Maas (eds), *NIDPCM*, pp. 589–93.

The spreading Catholic charismatic movement encouraged other Christian groups to copy them, namely to incorporate charismatic phenomena within their own traditions. This was all a surprise to the classical Pentecostals.[42] Many of the older Pentecostals who could just about remember the origins of the movement had bitter memories of ostracism and scorn when they first raised the Pentecostal banner 50 years earlier. They had expected that the charismatics would be ejected from their own denominations and quickly beat a path to the nearest Pentecostal church. When the older churches that had been so dismissive of Pentecostalism now began to change their tune, Pentecostals were astounded. The old certainties and alliances were readjusted. Hardline Pentecostals questioned the reality and validity of the experience of charismatic Catholics while the emerging Pentecostal middle class found themselves comfortable rubbing shoulders with the tongues-speaking Episcopalians. In North America the Pentecostal churches were healthy but in Britain and in other parts of Europe Pentecostals were disappointed that they did not benefit greatly from the charismatic enduements poured on the older churches. The statistics now show that in Europe charismatics comfortably outnumber Pentecostals, a state of affairs repeated almost all over the world apart from Korea and Romania.

In the United States the first big ecumenical gathering of Pentecostals and charismatics took place in Kansas City in 1977. Although most of the American denominational charismatic renewal groups held their own annual conferences, a decision was taken to bring them all together in one place at one time. This allowed the sponsoring groups to protect their own identities while expressing unity in plenary sessions and in large evening rallies. It also allowed them to rotate key speakers so that Pentecostal, Lutheran and Roman Catholic preachers in turn all addressed the evening gatherings. At one of these a powerful prophecy was given to the conference telling delegates to mourn for the broken body of the church, and with the indication that they should do their utmost to heal rifts between Christians. About 50,000 people registered for the conference, which demonstrated as clearly as anything could how extraordinarily unifying the charismatic movement had become. Whatever accusations of divisiveness might have been thrown at it by its detractors, this vast and variegated gathering provided an unanswerable demonstration of Christian harmony (see Chapter 13).

In assessing the lasting impact of the charismatic movement, the Christian Broadcasting Network, founded by Pat Robertson, is a jewel in the crown. Robertson experienced baptism in the Holy Spirit through the ministry of the Dutch Reformed Harald Bredesen and, though Robert-

---

42 The best account of the charismatic movement as a whole is given in a long article by Peter Hocken, himself a Roman Catholic priest, in Burgess and van der Maas (eds), NIDPCM, pp. 477–519.

son was ordained with the Southern Baptists, his charismatic orientation could not be confined to allegiance to one Christian tradition.[43] The network advances trans-denominational Christian views of a conservative kind and is more flexible and adaptive than its conservative roots imply. And, if Robertson was a charismatic with connections to the Southern Baptists, Oral Roberts was a classical Pentecostal who in 1968 became a Methodist. We might say that the charismatic movement represented the attractive middle ground between the classical Pentecostals on one side and the fundamentalistically inclined evangelicals on the other.

Numbers

The extent of the Pentecostal and charismatic movements was studied through a large national sample in the United States carried out in the spring of 1992.[44] Classical Pentecostal members amounted to 3.6% of the adult population. When members of non-denominational charismatics were added, the figures rose to 5% of the population.[45] However, as many as 8.7% of the adult population claim to speak in tongues at least monthly; the figures rose again to just over 12% of the population when people were asked whether they identified with the Pentecostal and charismatic movements. The figure rose again to just under 15% if people were asked whether they felt 'close to' the Pentecostal and charismatic movement. When the figures were analysed to discover exactly how Pentecostals and charismatics were distributed among the churches, there appeared to be three clusters. One group is found within evangelical denominations, another within the Roman Catholic Church and another within historic Pentecostal denominations. The relative size of the groups reveals that the charismatic renewal movement has made greatest numerical impact among Roman Catholics – although there is evidence that some Catholics are beginning to defect to Protestant churches.[46]

---

43 Bredesen was ordained as a Lutheran but then transferred his ordination to the Dutch Reformed Church. Robertson was a Baptist who then identified with the Southern Baptists. See D. E. Harrell (1987), *Pat Robertson,* New York, Harper and Row.

44 C. E. Smidt, L. A. Kellstedt, J. C. Green and J. L. Guth (1999), 'The Spirit-Filled Movements in Contemporary America: A Survey Perspective', in E. L. Blumhofer, R. P. Spittler and G. A. Wacker (eds), *Pentecostal Currents in American Protestantism,* Chicago, University of Chicago Press, pp. 111–30. The sample comprised more than 4,000 people.

45 The words can be slippery here. I have used 'membership' instead of 'belong to'. In Pentecostal and charismatic churches membership or belonging is usually smaller than attendance. This explains why more people speak in tongues than belong to Pentecostal and charismatic churches.

46 Smidt *et al.,* 'Spirit-Filled', p. 125.

We are now in a position to make a comparison between the Pentecostal movement and the charismatic movement, though in the discussion that follows it is important to note that we are dealing with charismatics and not with neo-charismatics, a group that we will consider in the next chapter.[47] The United States, as we have said, historically offered a free market for religion. Pentecostals thrived in these conditions so that when one compares the relative size of the Pentecostal and charismatic movements, the charismatics are about three or four times as large. In most other countries the ratio between Pentecostals and charismatics is far greater. For instance, in Britain charismatics are 14 times as numerous as Pentecostals and the same ratio is found in Germany, Norway and New Zealand.[48] Another way of putting this is to say that the charismatic movement has flourished and prospered even more than the Pentecostal movement – though, of course, the Pentecostal movement started from a small base and without any institutional heritage.

The statistical comparisons suggest that where there are established churches (as in England) or majority churches (as in Germany or Switzerland), the effect is much the same. Pentecostals grew while other churches were declining, but, even so, were not able to make great headway. In France, Italy and Spain, where there was a traditionally powerful Roman Catholic Church, Pentecostals found themselves in a different position. In France, there are *relative to the population of the country* more Pentecostals than in Britain, Germany and the United States, although the absolute numbers are not high. Even so there are seven times as many French charismatics as Pentecostals. In Italy, Pentecostalism was suppressed until the post-war period by laws dating back to Mussolini. Although the Pentecostal movement has grown well, there are still 25 times as many charismatics as Pentecostals. In Spain, which had been under Franco's military dictatorship in the post-war period, the charismatic contingent is 35 times larger than the Pentecostal contingent; and in these traditionally Roman Catholic countries, the charismatic movement comprises Catholic charismatics.[49]

When we look at Romania, for many years under a strong atheistic government that expressed its nationalism through the Orthodox Church, Pentecostals outnumber charismatics. This implies that the charismatic movement has not been able to make any headway among the

---

47 All the figures in this section are taken from *NIDPCM*. The numbers of Pentecostals and charismatics in each country are given at the head of the article on each country.

48 Germany was divided from 1945 to 1989 and Eastern Germany was under a repressive atheistic regime that damaged all the churches. Statistics for the whole of Germany are therefore hard to read: the east of Germany is more comparable to Romania and the west to Britain.

49 Statistics here are deduced from Burgess and van der Maas (eds), *NIDPCM*.

Orthodox. In South Korea also, Pentecostals outnumber charismatics. Here, in a traditionally Buddhist country, Pentecostalism spread rapidly after 1945. It offered answers to human suffering, emotional and physical healing, national self-esteem and was organized by a series of exceptional leaders. Outside Pentecostal churches there were long-standing denominations (the Presbyterians and the Methodists) but these were not numerous enough to allow the charismatic movement to burgeon as it did elsewhere.

In India, a country that has never had an established or majority church, the ratio between charismatics and Pentecostals is smaller. There are about four times as many charismatics as Pentecostals, showing that the charismatic movement simply had few pre-existing churches to spread into when it arrived in the 1960s. A comparable picture is found in South Africa where the number of charismatics and Pentecostals is roughly similar, and the same is true in Singapore – though in each of these countries there are still more charismatics than Pentecostals. The explanation for the relatively small size of the charismatic movement in South Africa is likely to be similar to India's. There are not many South African churches for the charismatic movement to reach. The reason for this, however, contrasts with the situation in India. In South Africa, the African Initiated Churches are already Pentecostal in style. India has an altogether smaller segment of Indian Initiated Churches, that is, churches that combine elements of Indian religious culture and traditional Christianity.

In Central and South America the three countries of Brazil, Argentina and Guatemala have large Pentecostal churches, which, though smaller, are not dwarfed by the charismatic movement. In the rest of South America, Chile, Colombia and Ecuador, for instance, charismatics outnumber Pentecostals by at least ten to one.

Reflection

The Pentecostal movement began in a blaze of revival activity and then settled down to build up organized denominations. In the 1960s the Pentecostal experience spread across into the existing Christian denominations, which in most instances absorbed and modified it. The charismatic movement now outnumbers the classical Pentecostal movement. Although the situation has reached equilibrium in places, there are charismatics who became frustrated by the failure of ecclesiastical authorities to introduce any wholesale reforms. There were accusations that the Roman Catholic clergy simply 'sat on' the charismatic movement and that charismatic activity was never allowed into the senior echelons of the hierarchy.[50] It is difficult to judge the accuracy of these accusations

---

50 Private comments made to me by informed Roman Catholics.

and, in any event, they may be patchily true, varying from country to country. Even so, Protestant denominations were also unwilling to show bold and positive leadership. Consequently, a new brand of charismatics emerged. These were Christians who neither wanted to identify with the old classical Pentecostal churches nor with the older non-Pentecostal denominations. They wanted new churches, and they are the subject of the next chapter.

Cross-references to the SCM Reader *Pentecostal and Charismatic Studies*

8.2 Arthur Wallis, 'Apostles Today? Why not?', *Restoration*, 1981, pp. 2–5, abridged (pp. 171–4).

8.3 Larry Christenson, 'The Church: An Ordered Body', in *Welcome, Holy Spirit*, Minneapolis, Augsburg, 1987, pp. 309–12, abridged (pp. 174–7).

8.4 Derek Prince, *Discipleship, Shepherding, Commitment*, Fort Lauderdale, Derek Prince, 1976, pp. 11–15 (pp. 177–9).

8.5 David Tomlinson, 'Loyalty: Covenant Relationship', *Restoration*, March–April 1978, p. 27 (pp. 180–1).

8.7 Larry Christenson, 'The Church: A Servant', *in Welcome, Holy Spirit*, Minneapolis, Augsburg, 1987, pp. 334–9 (pp. 184–7).

Ecumenism

13.1 David J. du Plessis, *The Renewal of Christianity Must Be Both Charismatic and Ecumenical*, Oakland, CA, c. 1975 (pp. 249–50).

13.2 Michael Harper, 'Beauty or Ashes?', The Ashe Lecture, 1979 (pp. 250–4).

Prosperity

14.1 Kenneth Copeland, *Dear Partner*, Fort Worth, TX, Kenneth Copeland, 1997, pp. 115–20 (pp. 255–8).

Questions to think about

1 Has the charismatic movement made any difference to the churches in your country? What threats does the charismatic movement pose to non-charismatic denominational leaders?

2 Read what Larry Christensen, a charismatic Lutheran, says in the text box on page 184. Does he manage to 'square the circle' – to

show how the charismatic movement could exist within an existing Lutheran framework?

3 Why do you think that the charismatic movement was especially attractive to Roman Catholics?

4 How convincing do you think the explanation offered here is about the relatively small size of the charismatic movement in India?

5 How can charismatic leadership work alongside denominational leadership? Or are the two incompatible?

Further reading

Cartledge, M. J. (2006), *Encountering the Spirit*, London, Darton, Longman and Todd.

du Plessis, D. (1977), *A Man Called Mr Pentecost*, Plainfield, NJ, Logos International.

Hayford, J. W. and Moore, S. D. (2006), *The Charismatic Century*, New York, Warner Faith.

Synan, V. (2001), 'The "Charismatics": Renewal in Major Protestant Denominations', in V. Synan (ed.), *The Century of the Holy Spirit*, Nashville, TN, Nelson.

10

Beyond the Charismatic Movement

We have entered the third millennium through a gate of fire. (Kofi
Annan)

In this chapter we look at developments in Pentecostalism after the charismatic movement emerged. Our focus is on the years from about 1960
to 2009.

Emergence of networks

The charismatic movement affected long-established Christian denominations in many parts of the world. These denominations came to experience what Pentecostals had long enjoyed. This was extremely odd and
surprising. Pentecostals had spoken in tongues at the beginning of the
twentieth century and been thought mad. They had laid hands on the
sick, prayed for healing, and been prosecuted, in some cases, for practising medicine without licences. They had believed in an interventionist
God in a scientific age and had been told that they were out of date and
uneducated. Then, in the 1960s, when Pentecostals and everybody else
least expected it, the charismatic movement took place, as described in
the previous chapter. Suddenly, sophisticated and educated Christians
felt that they were in touch with the Holy Spirit and receiving charismatic
gifts.

At about the same time as this was occurring, there were social and
philosophical changes. Socially, Western societies were undergoing radical adjustments as a new generation of young people came to prominence.[1] This was most readily seen in the music and fashion businesses
but also in the election of a young American president, John F. Kennedy,
and later in refusals by young people to put on a uniform and fight in
Vietnam, something that their fathers and grandfathers would hardly

---

1 Arthur Marwick (1998), *The Sixties*, Oxford, Oxford University Press, provides
a magisterial account covering Britain, France, Italy and the USA. Paul Harvey and
Philip Goff (eds) (2005), *Religion in America Since 1945*, New York, Columbia University Press, give information about the religio-social situation in the USA.

have questioned. Riots on the campuses of Berkeley, Paris and elsewhere indicated that young people were not prepared to conform in the way that previous generations had done. This was an era of self-expression, especially in the use of drugs, art and sexuality. Sexual relationships were released from the old taboos. It is said that 'the new morality was the old immorality' and it is true that widely available contraception for women increased promiscuity.[2] Beyond these social changes, the rapidity of international communications and travel were having an effect on the absolutism of earlier belief systems. While a large part of the world was locked up under totalitarian communism, in the West juxtapositions of world views became common. Not only were there clashes in viewpoints between the generations but also clashes between Marxists and free marketeers, between existentialists and Freudians, between Eastern and Western religions, and between conventional and alternative therapies. These clashes almost certainly brought about a new acceptance of relativism. In short, the beginnings of postmodernity became visible.

The charismatic movement was greeted with great enthusiasm, and this enthusiasm remained throughout the 1960s (see Chapter 9). But, by the start of the 1970s there were charismatics who wanted more. Renewal, to their way of thinking, was all very well but it was not enough. It did not change the actual structures that governed churches. Land and buildings were still owned by the same agencies, bishops still deployed their clergy and, while an openness to the Holy Spirit affected large numbers of people, there were still those who wanted nothing to do with the new spirituality and did their best to resist any liturgical or organizational changes. The radicals felt they had no choice but to leave their churches, whether Baptist, Anglican, Pentecostal or any other, and began to meet privately in homes. Their numbers grew rapidly and the 'house churches' soon became 'new churches'. Travelling preachers took the oversight of these new congregations and appointed elders for them. Since the new churches accepted that God was restoring spiritual gifts, it was logical to assume that other kinds of gifts would also be divinely restored, particularly modern-day apostles. So the travelling preachers were recognized as apostles with an ability to teach, direct and plant churches. The new churches became apostolic networks (see also the sociological discussion in Chapter 14).[3]

At first it appeared that these networks were merely new denominations,

---

2 Oral contraception was first approved for use in the USA in 1960.

3 In Chapters 14 and 15, I have been careful to make sociological distinctions between 'churches', 'sects' and 'denominations' but elsewhere in this book it is difficult to maintain this usage precisely because the word 'church' is often used by non-sociological writers to mean 'congregation'. For more on apostolic networks see also W. K. Kay and A. E. Dyer (eds) (2004), *Pentecostal and Charismatic Studies: A Reader*, London, SCM Press.

but the radicals were determined to avoid this label.[4] They strenuously denied that they were founding denominations and they carefully avoided the practices that they believed characterized denominations. They banished any form of voting as a way of making decisions in churches. This meant that denominational conferences where appointments took place by voting were never considered. Instead, decisions remained in the hands of apostles or with an apostolic team. The new system was simple and, in the case of networks like the one set up by John Wimber of Vineyard, money from congregations to central administration was deliberately kept low so as to prevent the building up of a bureaucratic cadre. Networks attempted to model themselves as closely as they could on the biblical pattern in the book of Acts. Apostles travelled around and elders looked after local congregations. Where collective decisions had to be made, a conference was held at which everybody could speak but at which the testimony of the apostles was paramount. There were no constitutions, secretariats or lawyers dealing with property holdings.

Each apostolic network needed to be large enough to finance the apostle full-time. About 25 churches turned out to be sufficient to make up a network with one or more apostolic figures travelling around between the different congregations. Little by little, the networks grew beyond the number they originally needed for viability and so they found ways to grow larger while continuing to retain the personal touch of the apostle. There were conferences (but no voting) and spiritual gifts became part of the decision-making process in many instances. This sounds a risky procedure, but in fact spiritual gifts allowed all kinds of people – elders, local ministers, local members whether male or female – to contribute to the whole gathering of leaders. Some networks held quarterly days of prayer and fasting and others brought their people together at the beginning of the year for the same purpose.[5] At these events spiritual gifts were expected to function and the leaders were expected to weigh what was said, even to record prophetic utterances and visions, and to take them away and consider them privately or in meetings of the apostolic team. In this way the apostolic networks managed to find a way of leading that was not marked by debates and voting. Instead, charismatic gifts were used in ways that Pentecostals had rarely been willing to trust.

More importantly, the apostolic figures who led the networks were almost always active and fruitful planters of congregations. The important practical consequence of this was that apostolic figures were spearheading their networks and showing less experienced ministers what to do in order to make the network grow. This is quite the opposite of what

---

4 This was a point made to me in private correspondence.

5 See William K. Kay (2007), *Apostolic Networks in Britain*, Carlisle, Paternoster Press.

had previously occurred in denominational structures. For instance, in the nineteenth century, those in charge of the denominations, bishops or archbishops, had sent out missionaries to perform evangelism or church planting overseas.[6] While the bishops and archbishops remained comfortably at home, the missionaries suffered in distant lands. But the new networks were led by those who had a proven ability to set up congregations both at home and overseas. In many instances this is why the networks had grown. In addition, they had grown because small groups of believers had come to an apostle asking for 'covering'.[7] Occasionally, groups of congregations would break away from the apostle but, while he (or she) was providing direction that would enable the networks to grow and flourish, there was little likelihood of defection.

The apostolic networks were certainly not confined to Britain. In 1998 C. Peter Wagner published *The New Apostolic Churches*, a name that he coined in favour of 'post-denominational churches', which he felt would be offensive.[8] The new churches he identified were as far apart as Thailand, Philippines, Nigeria, South Africa, Singapore, Hawaii and the United States.[9] Their details varied but often the networks were clustered around not only an apostolic figure but a flagship megachurch. The megachurch provided the funds for associated congregations and for the implementation of the vision of the apostolic figure. Wagner believed that the churches had learned the *technical* lessons of church growth dating back to the work of Donald McGavran in the 1950s, and added to these *spiritual* principles concerned with charismatic gifts and the ministry gifts listed in Ephesians 4. This provided the new churches with new authority structures; Wagner saw 'spiritual authority delegated by the Holy Spirit to individuals'. Such authority generated new forms of ministry that were accompanied by new forms of ministry training, often taking place in church-based Bible Schools rather than in denominational seminaries. All this was connected with new styles of worship run by worship leaders who replaced musical directors. Corporate prayer or 'concert' prayer was introduced and many of the churches practised prosperity teaching, which had the effect of making them confident about repeatedly asking for money from their members. The new churches were also likely to be orientated towards power encounters of the spiritual warfare type (see Chapter 13). Moreover, as Chapter 15 points out, the new churches were sociologically mapped onto society rather differently from traditional denominations.

---

6 Kay, *Networks*, p. 265.
7 A term used to denote 'submitting to the authority of'.
8 C. Peter Wagner (1998), *The New Apostolic Churches*, Ventura, CA, Regal.
9 Again, 'church' is not used as a sociological term.

Toronto blessing and millennial expectations

Although it left no institutional legacy, the Toronto blessing made a significant impact upon the Pentecostal and charismatic movements in the 1990s.[10] The blessing was theologically described as a fresh and overwhelming encounter with the Holy Spirit that resulted in unusual behaviour similar to drunkenness (and here it was recalled that the believers in Acts 2 were mistaken for drunkards). People fell over, laughed, cried, remained silent and 'spaced out', shouted and in other ways lost their inhibitions. Those who experienced 'Toronto' testified to its soothing, calming and renewing effect. The falling over and the laughing were understood to be reactions *to* the Holy Spirit rather than manifestations *of* the Holy Spirit.[11]

The course of the spread of the Toronto blessing can be charted from reports in secular newspapers.[12] Its origins were in the ministry of independent evangelists and in their doctrine of 'anointing'. This doctrine was a variation on the belief that the Holy Spirit would gift individuals with charismatic capabilities. A man or woman who had received a special anointing was viewed as the recipient of an unusual supernatural capability and calling. The healing evangelist Benny Hinn, building his model of ministry on that of Kathryn Kuhlman, believed that he had received an anointing to carry out his special healing ministry, a ministry that was characterized by seeing people 'slain in the Spirit' or flat on their backs after being prayed for. There is dramatic TV footage of people lining up to receive prayer from Benny Hinn and of the whole line falling over as he blew on them or touched them lightly.[13] He appeared to display awesome supernatural power since wherever he directed his anointed attention people immediately collapsed. The public manifestations were also accompanied by healings, though not everybody who 'fell down under the power' got up with every physical ailment banished.

In 1992 Benny Hinn's ministry was seen and appreciated by John and

---

10 Though one result was the establishment of yet another network of churches – Partners in Harvest. See http://www.partners-in-harvest.org/toronto-christian-worship-cent/ (accessed 21.12.08).

11 Cf. M. M. Poloma (2001), 'A Reconfiguration of Pentecostalism', in David Hilborn (ed.), *'Toronto' in Perspective: Papers on the New Charismatic Wave of the Mid 1990s*, Carlisle, Acute.

12 The most rounded and historically careful account of the Toronto blessing is given by Hilborn, *'Toronto'*. The reference to *The Times* article in the next paragraph is on p. 4 of Hilborn's book. The material in this section is taken from Hilborn. A popular account of the blessing is given by Dave Roberts (1994), *The 'Toronto' Blessing*, Eastbourne, Kingsway.

13 Periodically this is held on YouTube. God Channel (UK) has hosted his programme since its inception in 1995.

Carol Arnott, pastors of the Airport Vineyard in Toronto.[14] In 1993 Rodney Howard-Browne held revival meetings in Lakeland, Florida. While conducting these meetings, 'holy laughter' broke out. The Arnotts attended a Howard-Browne meeting in Texas in 1993 and were impressed. Later that year prophecies were given about the renewal in the church. In November John Arnott attended a meeting of the Vineyard churches and heard news of the spread of unusual phenomena. Arnott received further prophecies in December. In January 1994 meetings were held at the Toronto Airport Vineyard with Randy Clarke who had just been at the Howard-Browne meetings in Florida and was booked to speak at the Airport Fellowship. About 80% of those who went forward for prayer found themselves seeing visions and undergoing spiritual transformation. The meetings were then held daily, and the same phenomena reoccurred. The Arnotts began to travel and share news of these occurrences. By the middle of that year meetings at the Airport Fellowship swelled to 1,000 (from a starting point of 250 people) and international visitors arrived by day and night. The proximity of the airport made the blessing easier to catch. Soon the Toronto Airport Fellowship had discounted hotel rates advertised on its website. People flew in, attended meetings, received their own blessing, flew out across the world and transmitted what they had received to their own denominations, congregations and fellowships. As a measure of the public profile given to these events the London *Times* (18 June 1994) printed an article by Ruth Gledhill when the phrase 'Toronto blessing' first appeared in the public domain.

Pentecostal and charismatic leaders looked with interest, excitement or alarm at the spread of the blessing through their congregations. Phenomena of the Toronto type began appearing in churches across the denominational spectrum; in London, Holy Trinity Brompton, a large Anglican evangelical church already influenced by John Wimber, began to see phenomena break out in its services. A British Assemblies of God minister, Ken Gott, warily visited, was impacted and took the blessing to his own congregation in Sunderland in north-east England. Daily meetings were established with hundreds making the journey to attend the meetings there. Denominational leaders took seriously the testimony of those who had received the blessing and, in most instances, attempted to strike a balance between embracing the blessing wholeheartedly and rejecting it unthinkingly. There were of course scathing criticisms of emotionalism and of the dangers of a false gospel.[15] For about a year until the end of 1995, when the blessing was at its height, Pentecostal and charismatic

---

14 The extent to which Benny Hinn was connected with the Toronto blessing can be disputed. It is arguable that Hinn had nothing to do with the Toronto phenomena, but in the account given here we have followed Hilborn who thinks there is a connection.

15 Hilborn documents some of these, as well as positive assessments.

Christians, and others who stood on the sidelines, attended Toronto-type meetings in churches in the English-speaking world.

Despite evidence that it had peaked, the blessing continued to surge through many congregations for the next four years. Its meaning became caught up in promises given by Paul Cain (b. 1929) about a new world revival of Christianity starting in London and spreading across the world.[16] The Toronto blessing was interpreted as a forerunner of this revival, an indication of its potency and proximity. Claims were made for the likely course of the revival on the cusp of the millennium: it would start in the church and spread out into the streets of major cities and towns. It would be bigger than any previous spiritual event. As it happened, expectations were dashed. There was neither a revival nor a meltdown of the world's computers vulnerable to the 'millennium bug'. It was to be another year before the cataclysmic events of 9/11.

When the Toronto blessing finally receded, it left behind a series of explanations.[17] The first, as we have seen, was eschatological and theological. The second was that the blessing was a revival particularly suited to late twentieth-century culture in the sense that it was highly experiential and addictive. It showed that God spoke to each generation in an appropriate way. The third was that secularization had destroyed the power of religious symbols so that it was only through direct experience that individuals might be religiously awakened. And, fourth, the Toronto blessing was understood as merely one of a number of renewals of Christianity periodically necessary to maintain spiritual momentum (see Chapter 14).

Appearance of emerging churches

There is uncertainty about the origins of the emerging church movement.[18] The outlines are clear enough, however. An analysis of contemporary culture, particularly in the West, has resulted in reshaped churches in the hands of individuals who have become disillusioned with the contemporary evangelicalism. The typical story of such individuals may be that they grew up in evangelical churches within the USA, were exposed to the certainties of their ministers, given sermons that were cut and dried, prevented from asking controversial or difficult questions and eventually became sickened by middle-class cosiness. The anguish of individu-

---

16 See Kay, *Networks, passim.* Cain was associated with earlier healing revivalists in the 1950s and was noted for his remarkable 'words of knowledge' when he would reveal personal details about strangers or make predictions.

17 More details are given in Kay, *Networks,* pp. 203–16.

18 An excellent account is given by Stephen Hunt (2008), 'The Emerging Church and its Discontents', *Journal of Beliefs and Values* 29.3, 287–96.

als like Spencer Burke is expressed in a desire for authenticity. There is a rejection of the 'linear, analytical world' and the pastor who functions like the Chief Executive Officer of the business. There is a rejection of the 'spiritual Darwinianism' that assumes bigger is always better. This mindset arises because the Pentecostal and evangelical Christian in the United States has implicitly believed that the growth of a congregation is an indication that God is blessing it. This means that large programmes and efficient churches become the template and goal to which all small churches should aim. In disillusionment, Burke moved out of his job as a pastor of a megachurch, set up his home in a beach shack and expressed his Christianity on a website with members of an online community. In his words, 'more and more, my heart is about creating safe places for leaders to ask questions and to learn from each other'.[19]

There are other narratives to introduce the emerging church.[20] They begin with the culture rather than with the individual. The analysis of the culture presumes the triumph of postmodernity. Leonard Sweet gives an example of what happens when photographic speeds increase exponentially. The first photograph simply records the scene and then the next photograph will record the scene again with whatever changes have occurred in the time between the two exposures. If photographs are taken faster and faster, eventually the still photographs turn into the motion picture. One kind of thing (the photograph that looks like a realistic painting) turns into another kind of thing (the Hollywood film). Cultural change is speeding up. The world of words and books is giving way to a visual culture. Sentences which presume a grammatical sequence of words are replaced by images without a grammar. The reality of words gives way to the hyper-reality of images, and, paradoxically, the hyper-reality is unreal. The exposure of children to computer-generated images is rewiring the human brain so that the younger generation literally lays down different cerebral connections from the older generation, and perceives a different world.[21] It is a world where human identity may be formed by the cultural icons and where body shapes may be altered by plastic surgery. It is a world in which Christianity has been drained away. In other words, the rapidity of change has been coupled with creeping secularization; Christianity has been culturally disestablished.[22]

---

19 This quotation and the story of Spencer Burke is taken from D. A. Carson (2005), *Becoming Conversant with the Emerging Church*, Grand Rapids, MI, Zondervan, p. 19.

20 Matthew Guest (2007), *Evangelical Identity and Contemporary Culture*, Milton Keynes, Paternoster Press, tells of the development of alternative worship within a large charismatic Anglican congregation. In this example the emerging church, or something very like it, coexists happily with more conventional Christianity.

21 Personal conversation with Sweet in 2006.

22 See www.leonardsweet.com.

A different master metaphor is to be found in Pete Ward's notion of the liquid church that is constantly on the move and flowing in response to the Spirit by showing imagination and creativity.[23] This is seen as matching the 'liquid nature of God' by not focusing on the Persons of the Trinity but upon their relations. In this way ontological questions about the nature of divine personhood are put aside in favour of relatedness. Since the church is related to God, the mission of the church can be a continuation of the mystical outflowing of divine love from the interrelations within the Trinity. 'The vision of the church as networks of relationship and communication suddenly takes on a powerful symbolic significance.'[24]

By common consent, the most articulate spokesperson for the emerging church is probably Brian McLaren, who emphasized that postmodernity is discontinuous with modernity.[25] The postmodern Christian should therefore be post-Protestant, post-consumerist, post-organizational and post-critical. Postmodernity of this kind stresses emotions over against philosophical thought and, in its reflections, has moved beyond debate about epistemology to reconstructions of social history. Too much confidence was placed by earlier Christians in their manifest destiny with its covert value of white supremacy. What is now needed is a philosophical pluralism because absolutism simply cannot stand. The ethnic cleansing of the Old Testament is unacceptable, and all other forms of absolute truth must be subsumed in a new kind of thinking, 'emergent thinking'.[26] This type of thinking can be understood to grow like a tree: the tree does not only grow upwards but also grows by adding one layer on another. If the alternatives of absolute truth and absolute relativism are equally impossible, we need to learn to live safely in the broken and discordant world that we occupy. We need to learn to treat the world with confidence while recognizing that every position we take may damage one section of humanity or another.

Not all emerging churches are Pentecostal or charismatic, though undoubtedly some are.[27] There are men and women who have been hurt by the authoritarianism of Christian ministers and exploited by the intransigence of ecclesiastical bureaucrats.[28] Those who have been hurt in this

23 Pete Ward (2002), *Liquid Church*, Carlisle, Paternoster Press and Peabody, MA, Hendrickson.

24 Ward, *Liquid*, p. 55.

25 Brian D. McLaren (2001), *A New Kind of Christian: A Tale of Two Friends on a Spiritual Journey*, San Francisco, Jossey-Bass; Brian D. McLaren (2004), *A Generous Orthodoxy*, Grand Rapids, MI, Youth Specialities.

26 Carson, *Conversant*, p. 31.

27 Further information is given on the web, for instance http://www.emergent-uk.org/.

28 I have met burned-out missionaries who returned home after disastrous forays to a foreign country. They were reluctant to be involved in conventional church life again. The emerging church concept gave a sense of belonging, but on a new basis.

way are reluctant to place themselves at the disposal of any authority structure or to put their trust in any vision. Yet their confidence in Christ and the desire to be related to Christ remains, and the internet with its chat rooms and websites offers a tentative intimacy without commitment or the risk of exploitation.

The internet burst onto the scene from 1990 onwards and accelerated technical and cultural change.[29] Earlier in the century, cultural change had been given a human face by population movements.

Population flows

Human population flows have occurred in waves throughout history, and reference has been made in Chapter 2 to European immigration to the USA in the nineteenth century. Since the 1930s there have been flows of refugees from Eastern to Western Europe and the USA. After 1945 at least 16 million refugees fled from communism. About the same number of people were displaced after the partitioning of British India to India and Pakistan. Later, around 4 million fled the war in Afghanistan in the 1980s. The United Nations has kept statistics charting the scale of the problem and differentiates between internal displacement (within the country) and forced displacement to another country, most frequently to the neighbouring state.[30] Asylum-seekers are a different category in that these are people who are fleeing persecution. The statistics must be read with care because migrants may move for economic reasons but be classified under another heading. In addition the statistics are by no means complete.[31]

So far as Pentecostal and charismatic churches are concerned, population flows are important in two ways. First, Pentecostals and charismatics may emigrate for religious or economic reasons but in either case they take their faith with them. The Armenian Christians who lived in Turkey at the start of the twentieth century experienced an outpouring of the Holy Spirit during which prophecies were given warning them to leave their homes and travel to new lands.[32] Many of them crossed to the United States where there is now a substantial Armenian community of at least half a million. Other Pentecostal and charismatic Christians have crossed over from West Africa to Britain under the terms of the

29 T. Friedman (2006), *The World is Flat*, Harmondsworth, Penguin.

30 http://www.unhcr.org/cgi-bin/texis/vtx/home?page=statistics (accessed 19.12.08).

31 So far as the UK is concerned net inflows of non-British EU citizens to the UK increased from 14,000 in 2003 to 74,000 in 2004. http://www.statistics.gov.uk/cci/nugget.asp?id=1311 (accessed 20.12.08).

32 Demos Shakarian (1979), *The Happiest People on Earth*, Grand Rapids, MI, Revell.

Commonwealth which imposed no visa restrictions until 1988. Many of the West African Christians came partly for job opportunities, partly to carry out evangelistic work and partly to be in a position to send money back to their country of origin. Other African Christians have moved to Germany or the Netherlands in migratory flows that have resulted in new African congregations. There are at least 600 of these, not all of them Pentecostal. The Roman Catholic Church also offers humanitarian aid to migrants. The role of the church in facilitating settlement in a foreign country is well established and many ministers act as temporary social workers, enabling migrants to find work, accommodation, education for children and healthcare. Congregations of this kind become a hub of support and a living reminder of home through the familiar music and songs of worship. Congregations will eat traditional food together and share stories of their adjustment to their new culture.

In a study of the German migrant churches, Claudia Währisch-Oblau points out that the Christians who travel from one country to live in another do not see themselves as victims.[33] They do not construct their life stories according to Western paradigms. Rather, they take the themes of Scripture to write the script of their own lives. They pray for the countries where they find themselves and ask why God has brought them to their new destinations. They see themselves as agents of revival rather than recipients of European charity. Beyond this, generalizations are problematic because of the complex ethnic and cultural mix that many of these churches have reached. Some are international or becoming so, that is, they are drawing in people of different ethnicities beyond the original core group. Others may have an African majority, with a small minority limited to another ethnic group. Asian churches, on the other hand, tend to be more ethnically cohesive, and this is because, whereas the Africans can use English and French, the Asians normally use a national or ethnic language like Korean or Tamil. Moreover, although these migrant churches are growing, they rarely attract indigenous Europeans and, despite efforts to understand each other, local pastors find that African Pentecostal theology has few points of contact with their own.

Second, population flows in one direction tend to create counterflows in the other. Those who travel from Africa to Britain often also make the journey in the other direction, even if this is only for a temporary stay. The counterflow allows the immigrant to be reimmersed in his or her native culture and religion. This may result in a reinforcement of the practices that were fading and strengthens the distinctive essence of the migrant church. In an era of global communication, counterflows also

---

33 Claudia Währisch-Oblau (2007), 'Migrants with a Mission: Pastoral Self-Understanding, Biographical Narratives, and the Conceptualization and Practice of Evangelism among Pentecostal/Charismatic Pastors in Western Germany', PhD dissertation, University of Heidelberg.

have the effect of allowing migrants to try to influence events in their countries of origin. The migrant can draw attention to abuses of power and money and attempt to advertise these in the European or other countries to which he or she has moved. In this way the migrant community can assist the religious community in the country of origin.

Conflict and persecution

Population flows across the world have resulted in the dispersion of the major world religions to the extent that, in the major Western countries, there are representatives of all world religions. Although there have been no major public disputes within the framework of Western liberal democracy between Pentecostals and Muslims, such public debate is possible. This is because Pentecostals migrating to Western democracies from countries where there are clashes between Christians and Muslims (as in Nigeria) are vigilant about their civil rights in the West.[34] So far, some of the strongest criticisms of Islam have come either from ex-Muslims or from educated female Muslims.[35] In the main, public debate has been confined to late-night discussion programmes on television. What has particularly incensed some Pentecostal Christians is that, whereas secularists appeared to tolerate strongly expressed Islamic views, less sympathy is given to Christians who speak out. Thus when the Jerry Springer show mocked Christianity, the BBC, despite complaints, permitted a broadcast but, when similar mockery of Islam was mooted, the offending programme was quickly withdrawn.[36] Clashes between secularists and religionists become increasingly likely in countries where secularism controls the media. Already there have been minor arguments between secular commentators and Islamic commentators over the issue of homosexuality, and it remains to be seen how Western democracies will handle non-negotiable and publicly expressed differences.[37] There is one area where African Christians have made their mark on Western communions and this is in the resistance to homosexual ordination: African bishops exerted pressure on the Lambeth Conference and thereby on the whole Anglican Church.[38] Given that African Anglicans are close

34 http://www.christianpersecution.info/news/nigeria-authorities-detain-500-after-violence-kills-pastors-17438/ (accessed 19.12.08).

35 Ayaan Hirsi Ali (2007), *Infidel: My Life*, London, Simon and Schuster.

36 http://news.bbc.co.uk/1/hi/entertainment/tv_and_radio/4154071.stm (accessed 19.12.08).

37 Interview between Eddie Mair and Sir Iqbal Sacranie on BBC Radio 4, 1 May 2007.

38 The conference takes place every ten years and Anglican bishops from all over the world attend.

in their theology and outlook to Pentecostal ministers, there is a sense in which these disagreements, even if they occur in a non-Pentecostal or non-charismatic context, are nevertheless expressive of Pentecostal concerns.[39]

More tragic and alarming is the harassment and persecution of Christians, many of whom are Pentecostal. Nine Elim missionaries and their four children were hacked to death in Vumba, Zimbabwe, in 1978.[40] Intermittent Hindu nationalism leads to attacks on Christians and the destruction of their property in India.[41] Christian missionaries may find their lives endangered, as when the Australian Graham Staines was burnt to death in his car in 1999.[42] Hindus who convert may be ostracized by families or lose welfare benefits.[43] In Colombia in 2007 two Pentecostal pastors were assassinated by suspected left-wing rebels after preaching at an open-air evangelistic meeting.[44] In Burundi, Christians lost whole families in the politicized gangsterism that preceded the more recent phase of peace.[45] Arrests of Christians in China have been reported and scurrilous accusations have been made against Pentecostals in Indonesia and Romania.[46] Not all these reports can be verified, but government action in some of the countries where religious attacks are alleged suggests extremist factions need to be reined in.[47]

The persecution of Pentecostal Christians must be sharply distinguished from migration. Persecution can only occur where government has a firm grip on the population and sufficient tax revenue to fund a secret police force or a complicit army. In countries where regional government has a degree of autonomy local governors can turn a blind eye to the harassment of minorities, especially if these minorities would vote for the governor's political opponents. The persecution of Pentecostal

---

39 For instance, http://www.timesonline.co.uk/tol/comment/faith/article2028610.ece (accessed 19.12.08).

40 David Maxwell (2005), '"Survival, Revival and Resistance": Continuity and Change in Zimbabwe's Post-War Religion and Politics', in Niels Kastfelt (ed.), *Religion and African Civil Wars*, London, Hurst and Co., p. 183.

41 http://www.persecutionblog.com/2008/11/hindu-extremists-attack-pentecostal-church-in-mumbai.html (accessed 19.12.08).

42 http://www.themissionsociety.org/magazines/unfinished/2008-42/128 (accessed 19.12.08).

43 Philip Jenkins (2006), *The New Faces of Christianity: Believing the Bible in the Global South*, Oxford, Oxford University Press, p. 130.

44 http://www.christianpersecution.info/news/pentecostal-pastors-shot-dead-in-colombia/ (accessed 19.12.08).

45 Conversation with Peter Kay.

46 http://www.christianpersecution.info/ (accessed 19.12.08).

47 http://dynamic.csw.org.uk/index.asp?num=6&t=press (accessed 19.12.08). For instance, the appointment of a Minister for Minorities in Pakistan suggests that minorities need protection and representation.

Christians in psychological terms appears to create extreme obstinacy and tenacity. The result of being bullied and imprisoned is to create cunning and courage in a subservient population and, when prisoners of conscience manage to survive unjust imprisonment, they can emerge with an utter determination to resist compromise. South Korean Christians told me that they have been invaded so many times that it has left them with a residual obstinacy, which, when applied within their faith, makes them very persistent in prayer. A similar obstinacy can be found among Chinese Christians who have been imprisoned for their beliefs and, as we saw in Chapter 5, engenders an unwillingness to come to doctrinal agreement with those Christians who have not been persecuted. The same psychological effect can be seen in the Donatist controversy in the fourth century.[48] If we adopt a providential reading of history (see Chapter 1), we will believe persecution is ultimately beneficial, and perhaps the Korean experience could provide an outline for a theological case that is still to be written.

Reflection

We have come to the end of our travels through Pentecostal history and have reached a point when Pentecostalism has multiplied into many varieties. In the West we see:

- denominations
- megachurches
- networks
- emergent churches.

These are different expressions of the same spiritual impulse. The denominations are organized and, where they work properly, combine the benefits of pooled resources with the freedom of ministers to take initiatives at local levels. Megachurches are sufficiently large to survive without any denominational support, though the best of them are honourable enough to remain within the denominations that nurtured them. Where megachurches exist as separate islets of Christianity, their pastors have immense authority and influence within local communities. More flexible and potentially more focused on ministry are the networks that allow congregations to react rapidly to new situations, to move people and money around, to plant congregations at home or overseas and to offer novel forms of training. Contrasting with these three types of Pentecostalism, all of which would have definite views on doctrine and practice,

---

48 David L. Edwards (1997), *Christianity: The First Two Thousand Years*, London, Cassell, p. 166f.

are emerging churches, some of which are post-Pentecostal or post-charismatic, and which are both organized and disorganized at the same time. Their long-term importance may lie in their ability to offer a standing critique of conventional Christianity.

Pentecostals survived the horrors of the twentieth century. There were Pentecostals in Soviet Russia and Pentecostals who were caught up in Nazi Germany.[49] There are Pentecostals in the Congo region with its seemingly perpetual civil war and Pentecostals who have suffered multiple bereavements through the Rwandan genocides. There are Pentecostal Christians in East Timor and others in countries dominated by militant Islam. If we can gauge the effects of the horrific attacks on New York's Twin Towers, we may conclude that tensions between Islam and Christianity have been ratcheted up. This is one of the costs of the 'war against terror' (a phrase deliberately put into quotation marks). It appears that Kofi Annan's words concerning our entrance into the third millennium through a gate of fire are correct.

It is time to move on to Pentecostal theology, for in theology as much as in experience the strength of Pentecostalism is to be found. This occupies our attention in the following three chapters.

Cross-references to the SCM Reader *Pentecostal and Charismatic Studies*

8.6 Mike Bickle with Michael Sullivant, *Growing in the Prophetic*, Eastbourne, Kingsway Publications, 1995, pp. 160–7 (pp. 181–4).

9.7 John Wimber with Kevin Springer, *Power Evangelism*, London, Hodder and Stoughton, 1985, pp. 44–7 (pp. 206–8).

Toronto Blessing

19.1 John Arnott, *The Father's Blessing*, Orlando, FL, Creation House, 1995, pp. 23–5, 88–91 (pp. 280–3).

19.2 Margaret Poloma, 'A Reconfiguration of Pentecostalism', in David Hilborn (ed.), *'Toronto' in Perspective*, Carlisle, Acute, 2001, pp. 101–4 (pp. 283–5).

Questions to think about

1 How would you compare the apostolic networks and the classical denominations? Are they essentially the same or essentially different?

---

49 B. Röckle and W. K. Kay (2003), 'Born in Difficult Times: The Founding of the Volksmission and the Work of Karl Fix', *Journal of the European Pentecostal Theological Association* 23, 72–101.

2 Is Pentecostalism compatible with the emerging church model?
3 To what extent was the Toronto blessing valuable to the Pentecostal and charismatic movements?
4 What challenges (theological or social) is the church, and Pentecostalism in particular, likely to face in the future?

Recommended reading

Hilborn, D. (ed.) (2001), *'Toronto' in Perspective: Papers on the New Charismatic Wave of the Mid 1990s*, Carlisle, Acute.

Jenkins, P. (2006), *The New Faces of Christianity: Believing the Bible in the Global South*, Oxford, Oxford University Press.

Kay, W. K. (2007), *Apostolic Networks in Britain*, Carlisle, Paternoster.

McLaren, B. D. (2001), *A New Kind of Christian: A Tale of Two Friends on a Spiritual Journey*, San Francisco, Jossey-Bass.

Ward, P. (2002), *Liquid Church*, Carlisle, Paternoster and Peabody, MA, Hendrickson.

PART 2

Theology

11

Theology 1

Introduction

In this chapter we switch from history to theology. We turn our attention from the stream of events in time to beliefs and concepts. We begin with theology itself and its purposes, and then turn to Pentecostal theology.

What is theology?

There is nowhere in the New Testament where Jesus says 'I'm going to share my theology with you'. There is nowhere in the epistles of Paul where an explicit discussion of right and wrong theology occurs. Rather, the New Testament shows us people who presumed the existence of God. Even when Paul preached to the polytheistic Greeks, he could assume his hearers believed in divine beings. What we see in the New Testament are sharp discussions over the interpretation and application of particular texts of the Old Testament. Sadducees come to Jesus and ask him about a woman married to seven different brothers in succession. Whose wife will she be at the resurrection of the dead? They believe that there is no resurrection of the dead and that their question is unanswerable: if there were resurrection, the woman would have to be married to seven men at once, which, in their thinking, is impossible. Jesus turns them to the narrative of Moses at the burning bush where God says, 'I am the God of Abraham, the God of Isaac, and the God of Jacob' (Mark 12.26). This statement comes many years after the time of Abraham, Isaac and Jacob and yet it shows that God is *still* their God. The fact that God says 'I am' (present tense) indicates that he remains their God and with the implication that they must be alive. Jesus concludes, 'He is not the God of the dead, but of the living' (Mark 12.27). Here discussion turns upon the exact meaning of a particular statement within the Old Testament and it is used to demonstrate that a philosophical belief held by the Sadducees, who were the Jewish rationalists of their day, is incorrect.

In other places in the New Testament we can see similar discussions taking place, some going back to when Jesus was a boy of 12 in the

Temple, and others in response to other questions that he was asked. Equally, the book of Acts shows us arguments Paul advances in Jewish synagogues or in other parts of the ancient world. In the case of the Jewish synagogues, Paul 'reasoned with them from the Scriptures, explaining and proving that Christ had to suffer and rise from the dead' (Acts 17.2, 3). The Pauline process was to take the Scriptures and apply rationality to them, presumably by demonstrating what they could and could not mean and how they must be understood. Later Paul speaks at the university town of Athens. Taking the Athenian willingness to worship unknown gods, Paul turns to the literary culture of the Greeks. One of the Greek poets said that we are the 'offspring of God' and another that God is all around us and that 'in him we live and move and have our being'.[1] The poets have spoken truly, says Paul, and concludes that God cannot therefore be found in idols made of metal or stone but must be alive like us. If he is alive, he can act in the world and he *has* acted in a recent miracle: he raised Christ from the dead, and Paul is a witness of this fact.

This discussion of the meaning of the text of Scripture, and its interaction with the history and culture of its day, can be called theological: it is 'theologizing' or 'doing theology'. We can define theology as 'talking logically about God', applying reason to our own spiritual experience. In a parallel way of looking at theology we can see it as 'faith seeking understanding'.[2] Whether faith predominates and is the final arbiter of meaning is another matter. 'What has Athens to do with Jerusalem?' is the impatient question of a theologian who sees Athens, the place of logic and reason, as inferior to Jerusalem, the place of faith. Even so, the theologian who asked this question (Tertullian) did use reason to propel his arguments in favour of Christianity. Luther was equally unflattering about reason, which he described as a 'whore' at the service of anyone who embraced her, whether they had faith or not.[3] Yet, on the other side of the divide, there were Christian theologians who gave reason an honourable place alongside faith. Not only Anselm of Canterbury, whom we have already quoted, but also Thomas Aquinas, the Catholic theologian of the Middle Ages who built a vast synthesis of Aristotelian logic and Christian belief. For these writers faith *and* reason reveal the mind of God.

If theology is speaking about God or – and this is not exactly the same – speaking about our experience of God, we can identify two broad categories of data that might be used in our discussion. The first concerns

---

1 Aratus and Epimenides.

2 A quotation from Anselm of Canterbury.

3 'But since the devil's bride, Reason, that pretty whore, comes in and thinks she's wise, and what she says, what she thinks, is from the Holy Spirit, who can help us, then? Not judges, not doctors, no king or emperor, because [reason] is the Devil's greatest whore' (Luther's last sermon at Wittenberg, 17 January 1546). Cf. http://www.iep.utm.edu/l/luther.htm (accessed 11.10.2008).

the canonical Scriptures that have been handed down through Judaism and early Christianity into our own hands. Here the actual words of the biblical writers have been faithfully transmitted to us. Although there is a separate department of theology that has concerned itself with textual transmission and the versions and translations of the Scripture, conservative opinion holds that the text that we have is either identical with or extremely close to the text that was given to the original recipients.[4] In the case of the New Testament, the biblical texts were rapidly circulated and copied and then translated into Syriac, Coptic, Arabic and other languages by the end of the first century. The biblical text was itself then quoted by Christian writers in the second and third centuries with the result that it would be almost possible to reassemble the text of Scripture from those quotations. The sheer volume of Christian manuscripts and their agreement with each other makes it impossible to believe that the main message of text has been altered in any substantial way during the period of transmission. Moreover, the earliest texts of the New Testament, the letters of Paul, were circulated during his lifetime and during the lifetime of those who had witnessed the ministry of Christ himself. As a result, that generation was in a position to correct the Pauline letters, had this been necessary. From these very early texts – that is, within 30 years of Jesus – we can deduce the major events of the life of Christ, his birth, aspects of ministry, death and resurrection.[5]

The second concerns the course of history, particularly the history of the people of God – what may technically be known as 'sacred history'. Here the events of the Old Testament can be read off as divine activities, as also can the astonishing events described in the New Testament itself. Alongside these historical contours, are personal religious experiences that pepper the pages of Scripture. We see the doubts and fears of the disciples prior to the crucifixion and their joy and boldness after it. We witness the dramatic conversion of Paul and hear about his own encounter with the risen Christ.

These two sources, Scripture and experience, can be seen as the raw material of Christian theology. Allied to experience is the tradition of the early church which is itself a formalized version of experience transmitted

---

4 Other opinions, of course, make other valuations of the documents we have in the New Testament, but the point to note here is that *some* kind of use must be made of these documents, which is why I take the view that Christian Scriptures are a data source for theology.

5 The case put forward in this paragraph draws upon F. F. Bruce (1960), *The New Testament Documents: Are They Reliable?*, Leicester, InterVarsity Press, and reprinted many times. J. A. T. Robinson's (1976), *Redating the New Testament*, London, SCM Press, surprisingly argued that most of the New Testament was written before AD 64. The surprise was caused by the fact that Robinson was liberal in many of his other views.

from generation to generation or else encapsulated within ritual. More-over, just as we see Scripture as a canonical text recognized by the church, so we see the church as a sacred community living in obedience to the inspired and authoritative canon. Text and church interrelate in a mutu-ally enriching manner.

Through the processes of consultation within the early church we can see Christian theology gradually being made systematic. When there is a big question in front of the church (as there was about the admission of Gentiles to what was initially a Jewish community), the church meets together to resolve the problem. This is described in Acts 15. Subsequent gatherings of the church occur in Nicaea (in AD 325), Ephesus (431) and Chalcedon (451), and at each of these doctrine is clarified or made explicit. Theology becomes the discourse of the church, the language by which it understands itself and by which it defines its boundaries, and theology rapidly makes use of the tools of Greek thought. Indeed, Christian theology can be seen as coming from both the world of Israel and the world of Greece. From the world of Israel comes the canonical text and from the world of Greece comes the armoury of philosophical thought. It is necessary to work out how the text should be interpreted, comparing one piece with another, harmonizing words in some places and in others recognizing that later statements supersede earlier ones. It is necessary to deal with the actual syntactical relationship of the words with each other and of their relationship with meaning either in Greek, the language of the New Testament, or in other languages. We can say that theology utilizes the ordinary secular tools of textual study. Equally, theology becomes coherent and systematic by calling on the resources of philosophy. As human knowledge grows, theology interacts with this expanding realm.

We can express this by saying that theology is like the trunk of a tree that constantly branches out: we now have historical theology, sacra-mental theology, biblical studies, systematic theology, Christology, the study of the church (ecclesiology), the study of the future (eschatology), the study of the way to be saved (soteriology), and others; in each case, the branches of theology will connect with the secular discipline clos-est to it. Quite early on, theology was in conversation with philosophy and history. For our purposes we note that there is no single method unique to theological discourse. Philosophy was the most important early contributor to theology simply because Greek thought raised questions about the nature of evil, the universe, human nature and God, and be-cause the strongest threat to Christianity came through heretical groups influenced by philosophical ideas. Philosophy provided terminology (like the word *persona*) that was later incorporated into Christian creeds, and Augustine, when he was converted, found that Christianity answered all the philosophical questions that had been plaguing him.

The purpose of theology

All the brightest and best theologians write with a sense of urgency and purpose. 'It is living, dying, and even being condemned which makes a theologian – not reading, speculating and understanding.' Luther's words are perplexing until one understands that theology is about wrestling with the living God in the midst of our complex human predicament.[6] Tertullian lived at a time when Christianity was spreading within the Roman Empire, but, equally, when Christians were 'living and dying and being condemned'. Born in around AD 145 he lived on until extreme old age, at least until AD 220 and possibly even longer.[7] His writings are marked by verve, logic and passion as he addresses Roman magistrates who condemn Christians out of pure laziness and malice. Why condemn Christians without investigating their alleged wrongdoings? Why say of a particular person 'he is a good man apart from the fact that he is a Christian' without taking into account that he may be a good man precisely because he is a Christian? If justice cannot be dispensed without evidence, why should Christians be condemned without even being allowed a hearing in court? The complacent prejudices of the Roman ruling elite are laid bare.

In his other writings Tertullian is equally impassioned concerning disputes between Christians and Jews over the value of Judaism (why should God give the Mosaic law to one people if it is intended for the whole world?) and the role of the Old Testament in pointing forwards to Jesus Christ as the Messiah. When he writes for Christians, he does so to elucidate the doctrines of repentance and baptism or to commend prayer.

Athanasius, born just over 100 years later than Tertullian, found himself facing a very different predicament. Christianity had been accepted within the Roman Empire and was patronized by its emperor. Yet what kind of Christianity? Disputes concerning the nature of the Trinity, which were partly disputes between Western and Eastern Christianity in disguise, centred upon the relationship of Christ to the Father. Athanasius stood for the deity and co-eternity of Christ against the Arian party that proposed a Christ who was less than God and not eternal. Here, competing theologians using the same biblical texts and similar philosophical concepts engaged in a battle that would define the future of Christianity. Athanasius defended the trinitarian position while others wobbled, a defence that resulted in his being sent into exile on several occasions.

---

6 Quoted by A. McGrath (1993), *The Renewal of Anglicanism*, London, SPCK, p. 87.

7 An excellent account of Tertullian, written with reference to modern Pentecostalism, is found in Kilian McDonnell and George T. Montague (1994), *Christian Initiation and Baptism in the Holy Spirit: Evidence from the First Eight Centuries*, 2nd rev. edn, Collegeville, MN, The Liturgical Press.

Two hundred years later the imperial capital, Rome itself, was sacked by barbarians. The psychological shock of this catastrophe was unparalleled. When the troops of Alaric swept into the streets, they burnt and destroyed as conquering armies always did, but in this case they spared men and women who took sanctuary in the churches and who claimed to be Christians. Later, when the barbarian horde had withdrawn, Roman anger turned against Christianity. Christians, so it was alleged, had infiltrated Roman life, softened military virtues and brought the wrath of the gods upon the city. Augustine (by his own testimony) was fired with a zeal for Christianity and, in a huge document entitled the *City of God*,[8] refuted the blasphemies and falsehoods that were then circulating. As he pointed out at the start of his book, those who attacked Christianity were the very same people as those who had taken refuge in Christian churches and who, to save their own lives, had claimed falsely to be Christians. In a long argument with many digressions Augustine showed that the Roman gods did not protect Rome and that, in any case, Christians suffered along with others at the onset of pagan incursions. Paganism had no moral teaching, and obscene rites were propagated in the name of Roman gods in a way that could only lead to decadence.[9] Moreover, the development of Roman theological thought based upon multiple gods produced absurdities. It was impossible to decide which god might act in any individual situation since they all had different spheres of influence and were, so it was held, really under the control of Jupiter, the supreme god.

A work that took Augustine even longer than the *City of God* was his book on the Trinity. This book begins with an examination of Scripture to show how Father, Son and Spirit interrelate and how the textual data make sense when a trinitarian account is accepted. The Father sent the Son into the world but, since this sending was by word of request or command, and since the Son is also called the Word of God, the Son complies with his own sending and, since the Holy Spirit forms the child Jesus in the womb of Mary, the Spirit is also active in the sending of the Son (book 2.9). With these and similar complicated but logical reflections Augustine shows that Scripture consistently presumes a trinitarian God and that, as a result, when human beings are made in the image of God, they are made in the image of a trinitarian God. Thus the inner nature of human beings reflects the essence of the Godhead. In the second part of this treatise Augustine compares the Trinity to the internal workings of the mind, where the mind both knows and loves itself (book 9.5) so that 'in these three, when the mind knows itself and loves itself, there remains a Trinity ... and this Trinity is not confounded together by a commingling:

---

8 Or to give its original Latin title, *Civitas Dei*.
9 Most of these points are found in book 1.

although they are each severally in themselves and mutually all in all'. By these steps he begins to show how the apparently contradictory doctrine of the Trinity makes sense. The Father, Son and Spirit can be one co-equal and co-eternal God even if the Son obeys the Father and the Spirit ministers to the Son.

A thousand years later the church was facing new dangers. Here, according to Luther, the problem lay with the tangled doctrine propagated by papal emissaries. These emissaries thought that 'letters of indulgence' could be purchased and that these letters, by drawing on the spiritual merits of dead saints, would allow the Pope to give remission from purgatory.[10] Luther, a young monk, nailed 95 points of disputation (or theses) on the door of the church at Wittenberg. He pointed out that the true treasure of the church is 'the most holy gospel of the glory and grace of God' (thesis 62) and that it made no sense for the Pope to give remission on the basis of payment rather than on the basis of contrition. As Luther's theology developed he came to view the Pope as claiming authority that was never granted to him by the early councils of the church, or by God, and through a system of subtle doctrines of obscuring the biblical truth of justification by faith. Luther's rediscovery of justification provided a divine answer to the existential angst that is fundamental to the human condition. Here was a theology that addressed not only the medieval perversions of Christianity but also the most deep-seated needs of every individual.

Each of these theological giants – Tertullian, Athanasius, Augustine and Luther – faced the crises of his own generation. For Tertullian, it was Roman persecution and pagan philosophical attack; for Athanasius, it was the nature of the Trinity and therefore the nature of salvation; for Augustine it was the evaluation of Christianity within late Roman society; and for Luther it was the dominance of Christianity by the papacy and the doctrines that supported papal power and masked the simplicity of the gospel. Each of these theologians engaged earnestly with the text of Scripture and each stood against the tide running within the culture of his day. They spoke both to the church and to their wider society. They were motivated by an intense personal devotion to Christ and they functioned within the church in one way or another, Augustine and Athanasius being bishops.

One effect of their writing was to help define the church. They formulated or clarified doctrine. Tertullian clarified the distinction between biblical Christianity and Gnosticism, Luther clarified the distinction between Roman Catholicism and what became Protestantism. Theology has a boundary-making function, which may be expressed in the formulation

---

10 A place of purgation after death to prepare the soul for heaven; a mid-point between heaven and hell.

of creeds and catechisms which, even if not verbalized in a series of short propositions, enable the church to define itself. Theology in times of crisis is bound to function as a socially divisive discourse: it shows who is inside and who is outside the church, who is in receipt of the blessing of God and who is not. This is the other side of the coin of the positive contribution of each theologian. By strengthening the church, the theologian shows what is not the church; by clarifying the nature of Christian doctrine, the theologian shows what is not Christian doctrine. In the words of Frances Young, 'Any and every attempt at doctrinal definition is bound to be divisive and also mislead limited human minds into imagining that they can encompass the mystery of the divine.'[11]

A second effect of their writing was to enable the church to understand its own faith better. Theological writing is directed outwardly towards God so that, whether in reflections upon the internal interrelations within the Trinity or in an understanding of the interaction between time and eternity during the process of prayer, Christians may appreciate more completely the extent of their relation with God. Maurice Wiles writes:

> Such variety can help theology as a whole to move beyond that which any single scheme of theology by itself could achieve in pointing to the true object of all theological study, which is inexhaustibly greater than all faltering human understanding, namely God himself.[12]

All this prepares us to think about Pentecostal theology.

Pentecostal theology

As we have seen, Pentecostalism came into existence through a combination of revivalism and pre-existing doctrine connected either with Methodism or other forms of holiness teaching (Chapter 2). There was a historical phase when Pentecostalism existed in scattered congregations or camp meetings or as a kind of doctrine preached by itinerant evangelists but before it existed in a denominational form (Chapter 4). During this intermediate phase speculative theological ideas abounded. Charles Parham, the preacher who first effectively propagated a connection between baptism in the Spirit and glossolalia, also entertained a complicated theological scheme driven by his belief in the end of history: those who had received the baptism in the Spirit were an elite group within his eschatology. But whether this could really be called Pentecostal theology

11 Frances Young (1991), *The Making of the Creeds*, London, SCM Press, p. 106.

12 Maurice Wiles (1976), *What is Theology?*, Oxford, Oxford University Press, p. 111.

is questionable. It was, to use Douglas Jacobsen's term, 'thinking in the Spirit' and belonged to the wealth of innovative ideas that sprang out of the rich experience of those who came to call themselves Pentecostals.[13] So we must distinguish between the writings of individual Pentecostals and Pentecostal theology as developed by stable Pentecostal organizations or denominations. Of course, some of the ideas of individual Pentecostals came to be adopted by larger groups of Pentecostals, but this does not invalidate the distinction.

Individualism was always possible within Pentecostalism. Individuals could walk to the front of a Pentecostal meeting and share a prayer request, a testimony to answered prayer, a vision or a verse from the Bible. If early Pentecostal theology was not written down, it lived within active congregations. It was a shared, narrative, popular, oral form of theology based on the believer's 'walk with God'. This kind of grassroots, congregational theology belonged to the whole church and has been identified by Hollenweger and Macchia as typical of Pentecostalism.[14] And they are right to do so, but this does not appear to be the whole story. For Pentecostal theology within the congregation came from the preachers who, often at great length, preached from the hot pages of their Bibles to the patient people in the pews. And preachers were those who tangled with the text of Scripture, absorbed it till they knew great chunks of it by heart, shared a common language with the authorized version of the Bible, justified their sermons and actions by reference to particular verses and came to acquire expertise in the meaning of complicated Pauline passages. Preachers of this kind produced the congregations in whose imaginations the characters of the Bible lived: 'When the roll is called up yonder, I'll be there', there with all the other saints who have lived. And preachers of this kind were well placed to write constitutional documents where nuances of meaning were savoured and appreciated.

If there was a background to the hermeneutical (or interpretative) principles of these individualistic Pentecostals it was to be found in the Methodist tradition. Wesley had held that Scripture was primary but he derived a doctrine that came to be called the 'Wesleyan quadrilateral'. This comprised the four elements of: Scripture, tradition, reason and experience. The four elements worked together so that Scripture was pre-critically interpreted in the light of experience, with an appeal to primitive tradition and using rational methods. The rational methods drew upon Scottish Common Sense philosophy, which was influential in

13 Douglas Jacobsen (2003), *Thinking in the Spirit*, Bloomington, IN, Indiana University Press.

14 F. D. Macchia (2002), 'Pentecostal Theology', in S. M. Burgess and E. van der Maas (eds), *The New International Dictionary of Pentecostal and Charismatic Movements (NIDPCM)*, Grand Rapids, MI, Zondervan. W. J. Hollenweger (1997), *Pentecostalism: Origins and Developments Worldwide*, Peabody, MA, Hendrickson.

the United States in the nineteenth century and presumed that the human mind was constructed to allow us to know the real world directly.[15] Rational methods might also be scientific in character in the sense that they made use of deduction (where one proposition was inferred from another) and induction (whereby numerous instances where collated together to infer general principles). Induction was compatible with the compiling of numerous scriptural texts in the attempt to create broadly based doctrines. Early Pentecostals, with their powerful religious experiences, came to the Scriptures with an ability to see in the text what others had missed. The New Testament was full of men and women who had been impacted by the Holy Spirit. Thus, as Kimberly Alexander points out, there were theological presuppositions underlying the emergence of a Pentecostal hermeneutic.[16]

Veli-Matti Kärkkäinen makes a similar point when he argues that the early American white Pentecostal denominations took on a form of biblical interpretation that shared epistemological roots with modernism.[17] Modernism, with its emphasis on rationality and Newtonian science, distinguishes sharply between subjectivity and objectivity, between the person who observes and the thing observed. This produced a form of biblical study that placed the believer on one side of the line and the objective text of Scripture on the other. The Scripture was fixed and unchanging; it was merely the task of the believer to read it, to take its (literal) meaning, and then to express its truths systematically. The best tool for theology was therefore a concordance. Only 50 years later, after Pentecostals had begun to engage in dialogue with other streams within Christianity, was the call for a specifically Spirit-led epistemology put.[18] Such an epistemology provides a place for 'an intuitive, non-verbal communication' between God and human beings which parallels the experience of the early apostles who wrote the New Testament Scriptures in the first place. The new approach blurs the line between the subjective believer and the objective Scripture since both participate in the work of the Holy Spirit. Interpretation of Scripture becomes 'an exercise in private reconstruction of the intentionality of the text'.[19]

---

15 George Marsen (1980), *Fundamentalism and American Culture: The Shaping of Twentieth Century Evangelicalism*, New York, Oxford University Press, p. 14.

16 Kimberley Ervin Alexander (2006), *Pentecostal Healing: Models in Theology and Practice*, Blandford Forum, Deo, pp. 28, 29. See also Robby Waddell (2008), 'The Spirit of Reviews and Response', *Journal of Pentecosal Theology* 17.1, 22–31.

17 Veli-Matti Kärkkäinen (2002), *Towards a Pneumatological Theology*, Lanham, MD, University Press of America, p. 7.

18 Especially Howard M. Ervin, as discussed by Kärkkäinen, *Pneumatological Theology*, pp. 9–14.

19 Kärkkäinen, *Pneumatological Theology*, p. 11.

Purposes of Pentecostal theology

If we return to the purpose of theology and see it as a form of discourse that defends Christianity against each new danger as it arises, while at the same time helping the church to understand itself, then Pentecostal theology begins with two urgent concerns: the state of the church during modernistic attacks upon traditional Christianity and the value of glossolalia. Pentecostal theology can be seen as another answer to the challenges identified by what was to become fundamentalism. Fundamentalism set about building an intellectual defence of historic Christian doctrines against the encroachments of modernistic assaults; the fiercest battles were fought over Scripture, miracles, fulfilled prophecy and the deity of Christ.[20]

Pentecostalism emphasized the outpouring of the Holy Spirit upon the church at the beginning of the twentieth century. Pentecostal theology starts at the point where the biblical account of the work of the Holy Spirit is transposed into the here and now. Pentecostal theology presumes that what once took place in the early church can now take place in the contemporary church. This presumption changes the old perspectives on normal Christianity and on the relationship between the church and society. If the Holy Spirit can break into today's world, then all accounts that presume that God has been relegated to the margins by rationalistic science must be rejected. We can put this another way by saying that Christianity in the 1700s had put God firmly in heaven. God was the watchmaker who had invented the world and wound up the clock but then had left it to run on its own accord following Newton's laws. Christ as the Saviour was the centre of evangelical hope and preaching, though in liberal Christianity the moral example of Christ was more welcome than the spiritual power of regeneration. By the 1800s the Protestant church was moving in the direction of becoming an institution or organization with a distinct social role. It dignified public occasions, was the guardian of morality, promoted education and was the instigator of charity, but God was still a long way away. Roman Catholic theology found the activity of God focused in the sacraments. It also attributed its authority to 'apostolic succession', to the belief that it could trace its bishops back to St Peter by an unbroken line of laying on of hands. Pentecostalism implicitly threw all this aside. God was not a long way off in heaven but active in the life of the believer and present by the Holy Spirit who made Jesus real to his followers. It was not 'apostolic succession' that gave authority to ministers but the immediate presence of the Spirit in miracles and charismatic gifts.

---

20 *The Fundamentals*, a collection of 12 books, were published in 1910 by wealthy Christians and freely distributed. They gave fundamentalism its name. The books dealt with such matters as the inerrancy of Scripture, miracles, the virgin birth, the atonement and the resurrection. They were not Pentecostal.

Conceiving the church as a body of people in direct touch with the living God set high value on the commands of Christ. Christians had long understood the church to be the agency of God upon earth but Pentecostals took this idea and narrowed it. They saw the church as a Spirit-empowered agency for missionary work across the world to prepare the nations for the end of the age in accordance with the words of Jesus in Matthew 28. If Pentecostalism could revive the 'dead' churches that made up the family of Protestantism, so much the better. As for Roman Catholicism, it appeared inconceivable that Catholics would in any way see eye to eye with Pentecostals, not least because Protestant eschatological schemes frequently saw the Roman Church as harbouring the antichrist.[21]

We have also said that Pentecostalism practised glossolalia. This is a topic that could fascinate critics and believers alike. It was the centre of controversy for a while. Arguments arose around the meaning of glossolalia, which we will consider in a moment. Yet glossolalia appeared to indicate a close and precise connection between the individual and the Spirit of God. Glossolalia were understood to be utterances inspired by the Holy Spirit but voluntarily spoken by the believer. There could hardly be a more intimate connection between the believer and God, and this opened the way for belief in contemporary prophecy or healings. For, just as the Spirit inspired incomprehensible words in other tongues, so the Spirit might also inspire comprehensible words to be uttered in the midst of the church. God became almost tangible within the congregation. It was not necessary – as with sacramental theology – to place God within a ritual or even within the bread and wine of Holy Communion but, rather, God was speaking directly to the congregation through glossolalia or prophecy, and if someone were ill it was not difficult to believe that the same Spirit who inspired words might also bring about healing in the body of the person who needed it. Glossolalia were of far more practical use than detractors realized and changed the world view of those who received the gift. No longer would believers think of themselves as inhabiting a world where the laws of physics caused events to happen mechanically while God was absent in heaven; they could think of themselves as being in the world where God was present, upholding the laws of physics certainly, but also being able to circumvent them.

Pentecostal theology as denominational theology: the nature of God

In Chapter 4 we saw how denominations were formed. One crucial step on the way to formation was to come to a 'statement of faith'. Since the formal process by which agreement was reached itself needed to be

---

21 Revelation 17.3–7.

agreed, each denomination hammered out its own constitution. The constitution defined who had the right to attend, vote, conditions of membership and so on and was drafted by the founding members. These two documents, the statement of faith and the constitution, were linked by cross-referencing in a way that ensured that the shape of the denomination grew out of its beliefs.[22] The purest theology was to be found in the statement of faith and the early Pentecostals borrowed statements of faith, used by Methodists or other evangelicals and then added in reference to spiritual gifts or the return of Christ.[23] The theology embodied in these statements was precise. There were articles on God, the Bible, how to be saved, the church and the future, the work of the Holy Spirit, and perhaps others. The wording needed to be unambiguous and supportable by Bible verses to ensure agreement. In most instances Pentecostals found it possible to agree on topics centred on the Holy Spirit because it was this consensus that drew them together in the first place.

These Pentecostals – and it was around 1910 that this name began to be used – might be thought of as 'holiness plus' Christians. They were holiness in the sense that they believed in sanctification following justification but they added on a belief in the crowning Pentecostal baptism.

We now approach a fork in the road. Bear in mind that Pentecostal theology was drawn up during exciting and unexpected changes among the churches touched by revivalism. While the fires of the Azusa Street revival (1906–12) continued to burn, William H. Durham challenged the doctrine of sanctification that was dear to the hearts of W. J. Seymour and his colleagues and which continues to be held by many Pentecostal denominatons today. This doctrine stated that there was an important phase of inner cleansing that occurred *after* salvation but *before* baptism in the Spirit. This was the classic holiness doctrine, and it had the effect of ensuring that many people who were looking for the baptism in the Spirit expected to go through a protracted period of self-examination and prayer before reaching their climactic moment of spiritual fullness. Durham taught that the work of the cross was complete and entire in itself and that those who believed and were justified did not need 'a second work of grace' to sanctify them. This controversial teaching not

22 The formation of the Church of God (Cleveland, TN) followed an analogous path when the small Christian Union of R. G. Spurling was turned into an organized church by A. J. Tomlinson. The beliefs of the Union had been codified earlier but in 1910 Tomlinson made its Pentecostal teachings explicit with the publication of its journal. See R. G. Robins (2004), *A. J. Tomlinson: Plainfolk Modernist*, Oxford, Oxford University Press. The beliefs and constitution of the church were completely interwoven. Extracts of Tomlinson's writings are given in D. Jacobsen (ed.) (2006), *A Reader in Pentecostal Theology: Voices from the First Generation*, Bloomington, IN, Indiana University Press, pp. 96–106.

23 See A. Yong (2002), 'Preface', in V.-M. Kärkkäinen (ed. A. Yong), *Towards a Pneumatological Theology*, Lanham, MD, University Press of America, p. xiv.

only offended believers who had come into Pentecostalism from holiness backgrounds but also those who worried that speaking with tongues was sometimes found among Christians whose characters were morally suspect. In short, Durham's two-stage theology confronted Seymour's three-stage theology.

Durham was causing ructions from 1910 onwards.[24] His radicalism unsettled many (but not all) early Pentecostals and made them question their beliefs. In this feverish atmosphere a fresh revelation, first publicized in 1913, proclaimed that since the baptismal formula in Acts used 'the name of the Lord' rather than the formula found in Matthew, 'in the name of the Father and of the Son and of the Holy Spirit', the two formulae could only be reconciled if the name of the Lord included the other persons of the Trinity and that this could only be so if the persons of the Trinity were not actually separate persons but one substance manifested in three different ways.[25] By this argument a group of Oneness or 'Jesus only' Pentecostals came into being. The Oneness Pentecostals emphasize that in Jesus is 'the fullness of the Godhead', so Jesus *is* the Father and the Spirit.[26] The two groups of (American) Pentecostals met together at the 1916 Assemblies of God General Council. The outline of the theological discussion would have been recognized by those who attended the Council of Nicaea more than 1,500 years earlier.

When the General Council of the Assemblies of God in the USA came down firmly in favour of a classical trinitarian understanding of God, the Oneness or 'Jesus only' Pentecostals walked out and there was, from that time onwards, a parting of the ways. The larger Trinitarian group grew through the 1920s and 1930s and started to collaborate with evangelicals in the 1940s, while the Oneness group went through an initial period of uncertainty. It developed two theologies around the practice of water baptism. The first was similar to that of the Trinitarians in its belief that a person was saved (or 'born again') in one experience and received Spirit baptism in a separate experience. The second theology argued that Christian initiation includes both new birth and Spirit baptism in one single composite event marked by water baptism.[27]

And this is where the fork in the road is visible. Those Pentecostal

---

24 David A. Reed (2008), *'In Jesus' Name': The History and Beliefs of Oneness Pentecostals*, Blandford Forum, Deo, explains: 'Within a very brief period of time, Durham's teaching of the one act of grace was transformed into a distinctive doctrine of the one name by which salvation comes, a name that is appropriated only in water baptism, and the name that reveals the nature of the true God who is one without eternal distinctions. Durham would have vigorously opposed these ideas, but it was he who forged the internal logic that demanded to be addressed', p. 135.

25 Matthew 28.19; e.g. Acts 8.16. See also Reed, *Name*, p. 137.

26 Colossians 1.19.

27 Reed, *Name*, pp. 310–13.

Christians who had been influenced by Durham were forced into making a choice by the controversy over the nature of God. All the other Christians who had been resistant to Durham and who continued to believe in sanctification as separate from Pentecostal baptism were unaffected by the Trinitarian–Oneness dispute. Great swathes of Pentecostalism, including the Church of God (Cleveland, TN) and associated denominations like the Church of God in Christ, did not undergo any of the trauma associated with the decisive 1916 General Council meeting of Assemblies of God.

Although we have needed to touch on history while examining the co-ordination of Pentecostal beliefs into coherent theological schemes, we are also attentive to the theological *method* used by Pentecostals. The method involved exposition and harmonization of biblical texts with each other and with religious experiences, and there was nothing very unusual about that; Methodists had been doing this for many years. Where Pentecostals differed was in the narrative that shaped their understandings. As we saw in Chapter 2, and as we see later in this chapter, it was their understanding of the course of church history – past, present and future – that set Pentecostals apart. Ken Archer sums it up, 'What distinguished the early Pentecostal Bible Reading Method from the Holiness folk was not a different interpretive method but a "*distinctive narrative*" which held the similar methods together in a coherent and cohesive manner' (original italics).[28]

In a formal setting, Pentecostal doctrine was hammered out by ministerial conferences where voting took place after debate according to denominational constitutions. The Trinitarian Pentecostals took their doctrine from the New Testament. The Oneness Pentecostals, who combined salvation and Spirit baptism in one theological block, also justified their scheme by reference to the New Testament. In the final statement of a Trinitarian–Oneness Dialogue published at the Society for Pentecostal Studies in 2008, the Oneness group

> identified the Holy Spirit as the Spirit of Jesus, thereby concluding that the baptism in the Holy Spirit is an integral part of receiving Christ. Based on the conversion accounts in Acts, as epitomized by Acts 2:38, they also concluded that water baptism and Spirit baptism are both part of Christian initiation. (para. 13)

We deduce that the interpretive method and underlying narrative used by Pentecostals is capable of producing several theological descriptions of the same events. And, by this means, it produces several parallel Pentecostal

---

28 Kenneth J. Archer (2004), *A Pentecostal Hermeneutic for the Twenty-First Century*, Sheffield, Sheffield Academic Press, p. 94.

denominations, often bristling with antagonism to each other, but all enjoying similar spiritual experiences and employing similar ecclesiastical practice.

Pentecostal theology as denominational theology: speaking in tongues

Charles Fox Parham is frequently identified as the man who first clinched the connection between baptism in the Spirit and speaking with tongues, though, as we have seen (Chapter 3), this connection was made earlier by Frank Sandford. In any event, Parham's understanding of tongues was missiological. He believed speaking with tongues was the miraculous enabling of Spirit-baptized individuals to speak in languages they did not understand to people who did understand them. Spirit-baptized believers would preach the gospel in foreign countries without the hard graft of language training.[29] Since Parham first publicized his views there was discussion in emerging Pentecostal circles as to the correctness of his position. While some preachers accepted it, others held back.[30] In Azusa Street and at the British Sunderland revival of 1907 the connection between tongues and baptism in the Spirit was at first upheld, though the tongues spoken on this occasion were *not* understood to be foreign languages for use on the mission field. Already, then, there is more than one opinion held about the phenomenon of glossolalia. As the Azusa Street revival progressed and as more and more people began to speak in tongues, further reflection followed and the initial leaders of the revival (W. J. Seymour at Azusa Street and Alexander Boddy in Sunderland) began to say that while the sign of baptism in the Spirit was tongues, love was the evidence of continuance.[31] Their original position was modified by pastoral concern. They saw love as being an additional sign following the sign of glossolalia. In other words, they gave prominence to Christian character alongside spiritual gifting.

Mel Robeck, in a compelling piece of scholarship, tells the story of the adoption of the doctrine of speaking with tongues as the 'initial evidence' of baptism in the Holy Spirit. The story is of a group of ministers (who

---

29 Technically this is xenolalia (*xenos* is the Greek word for 'foreign' and *lalia* is 'speech').

30 W. F. Carothers (1906), *The Baptism with the Holy Ghost and Speaking in Tongues* (Houston, privately printed), pp. 5–18, cited by C. M. Robeck (2003), 'An Emerging Magisterium: The Case of the Assemblies of God', *Pneuma* 25.2, 164–215.

31 Boddy writes in *Confidence*, 1 April 1908, of 'a baptism on the Holy Ghost with the Seal of Tongues', p. 5 (original capitals), while in *Confidence* 3, 11 November 1910, pp. 260–1, his article was entitled 'Tongues: The Pentecostal Sign; Love the Evidence of Continuance'.

became the largest Pentecostal denomination in the United States, Assemblies of God) who at first attempted to leave their doctrinal position flexible but who, after debate within their ranks, hardened their statement of faith.[32] The debate resolved the difference between speaking with tongues in Acts 2 and speaking with tongues in 1 Corinthians 12. The first occurs in Jerusalem as the apostles received the Holy Spirit on the day of Pentecost. The second refers to speaking in tongues within congregational meetings. Pentecostals drew a distinction between the sign of tongues and the gift of tongues: 'The full consummation of the baptism of believers in the Holy Ghost and fire is indicated by the initial physical sign of speaking with other tongues as the Spirit of God gives them utterance (Acts 2:4).'[33] They went on to say that 'this wonderful experience is distinct from ... the gift of tongues', which has a different purpose and use. The sign of tongues necessarily implied that anyone who had not spoken in tongues had not been baptized in the Spirit. As time went on, this position was made more dogmatic through subtle changes to the way the story of Pentecostalism was told and the suspicion with which scholars who questioned the unanimity of the founding fathers and mothers of Pentecostalism were treated.[34]

There are two forces at work here. On one side, traditionalists in a Pentecostal denomination three or four generations old are building up doctrinal defences so as to prevent the erosion of a distinctly Pentecostal form of Christianity.[35] On the other side, historians and theologians are questioning the dogmatism of this position in the light of the original intention of the ministers who first founded these denominations.[36] There

32 Robeck *Emerging Magisterium*. A more recent formulation replaces the word 'sign' with the word 'evidence', see http://ag.org/top/Beliefs/Statement_of_Fundamental_Truths/sft_short.cfm

33 Robeck, *Emerging Magisterium*, p. 186. The quotation is taken from a version of the AOG fundamental truths (article 6), as amended in 1918.

34 Robeck, *Emerging Magisterium,* cites the testimonies of J. Roswell Flower and Donald Gee, one American and the other British, who were both impeccably Pentecostal and equally respected as leaders. In each case their testimonies were reprinted by agencies within American AG without referring to the delay which occurred between their baptism in the Spirit and speaking with tongues. Accusations implying disloyalty by unnamed Pentecostal scholars were made by the General Treasurer of Assemblies of God at a seminar in 1998.

35 A range of theological data gathered from Pentecostals and charismatics is presented in W. K. Kay and A. E. Dyer (2004), *A Reader in Pentecostal and Charismatic Studies*, London, SCM Press, pp. 83–115.

36 Aaron Friesen (2009), 'The Called Out of the Called Out: Charles Parham's Doctrine of Spirit Baptism', *Journal of European Pentecostal Theological Association* (in press), argues that 'A thorough examination of Parham's theology of Spirit Baptism shows that Parham's understanding of the experience was adopted by later generations of Pentecostals only in word. Thus, Parham's contribution to Pentecostalism should be understood to reside at the level of hermeneutics, not doctrine.'

have been subsequent investigations of speaking in other tongues,[37] historically in respect of church history,[38] psychologically in respect of personality,[39] anthropologically in terms of cultural flow,[40] liturgically in terms of worship[41] and even philosophically.[42] A sociological reading of speaking in tongues as a boundary sign is also possible.[43] While none of these perspectives offers a complete account of speaking with tongues, it is important to notice the way that tongues may be used in ecumenical discourse by being reconceptualized as a kind of sacrament, an indication of the presence of the divine, and in this way drawing together hitherto separate Christian streams.[44] In other words, speaking in tongues offers a far more varied field of discussion than was first realized and should not become the site of a power struggle between Pentecostals of different kinds. If there is a division between academically orientated Pentecostals and organizationally orientated Pentecostals, this will be damaging to both since they need each other.

William H. Durham's description of speaking in tongues

On the 26th day of February, 1907, I went to the afternoon service. I was at the end of everything; and the Lord knew it. There were thirty or more people present in the prayer room. Three of God's dear children came to me, and as they stood over me, one of them said, 'Just cease trying to do anything, and surrender all to God.' I did so; when O, joy, a thrill of power went through me, followed by another. Instantly it appeared as if every one of my pores were suddenly opened and a mighty current

---

37 G. B. McGee (ed.) (1991), *Initial Evidence: Historical and Biblical Perspectives on the Pentecostal Doctrine of Spirit Baptism*, Peabody, MA, Hendrickson. This is well reviewed by Frank D. Macchia (1993) in the *Journal of Pentecosal Theology* 2, 117–27.

38 S. M. Burgess (1984), *The Holy Spirit: Ancient Christian Traditions*, Peabody, MA, Hendrickson. See also extensive articles on 'The doctrine of the Holy Spirit' by S. M. Burgess in Burgess and van der Maas (eds), *NIDPCM*.

39 W. K. Kay (2006), 'The Mind, Behaviour and Glossalalia: A Psychological Perspective', in M. J. Cartledge (ed.), *Speaking in Tongues: Multi-Disciplinary Perspectives*, Carlisle, Paternoster Press, pp. 174–205.

40 Joel Robbins (2004), 'The Globalisation of Pentecostal and Charismatic Christianity', *Annual Review of Anthropology* 233, 117–43.

41 J. H. S. Stevens (2002), *Worship in the Spirit*, Carlisle, Paternoster Press.

42 James K. A. Smith (2006), 'Tongues as "Resistance Discourse"', in Cartledge (ed.), *Speaking in Tongues*, pp. 81–110.

43 M. M. Poloma (2006), 'Glossolalia, Liminality and Empowered Kingdom Building: A Sociological Perspective', in Cartledge (ed.), *Speaking in Tongues*, pp. 147–73.

44 Frank D. Macchia (1993), 'Tongues as a Sign: Towards a Sacramental Understanding of Pentecostal Experience', *Pneuma* 15.1, 6176.

of power turned into me from every side; and so great was the infilling that it seemed as if the physical life would be crowded out of my body. I literally gasped for breath, and fell in a heap upon the floor. Strength was gone, but I was perfectly conscious of everything; so kept lifting my heart to God and earnestly entreating Him to finish the work. So intense was my longing to have the work finished, that I was reaching Heavenward with one hand all the time. God knows best how to do His work. I am glad He did not finish the work, the first time the power came upon me. My experience has been much more valuable as He gave it to me. No tongue could ever tell, what passed between God and my soul these first two hours I was under His power. It was glorious and wonderful. It was heaven. Such love, such sweetness, such a revelation of the Blood as the only remedy for sin, such a revelation of Christ as the only Savior, and many things that it is impossible for me to tell ...

The Lord permitted me to walk in this state for two days and nights. Then as I knelt before Him, the Spirit again fell on me ... This continued for some time, when finally my throat began to enlarge and I felt my vocal organs being, as it were, drawn into a different shape. O, how strange and wonderful it all was to me and how blessed it was to be thus in the hands of God. Last of all I felt my tongue begin to move and my lips begin to produce strange sounds, which did not originate in my mind. In a few moments he was speaking clearly through me in other tongues, and, then I heard Brother Seymour, the Pastor, say, 'He is through now,' etc. He said that he had retired to rest early in the evening, and that the Spirit had spoken to him and said, 'Brother Durham will get the baptism tonight,' and that he had arisen and come down. Then he lifted up his hand and prophesied that where I should preach, the Holy Spirit would fall on the people. The Lord then permitted me to rise to my feet, and He, for Whom my soul had longed, did not leave me this time, but remained, and for a long time I could not help speaking in tongues.

William H. Durham, taken from *Pentecostal Testimony* and reprinted as a booklet. See SCM Reader *Pentecostal and Charismatic Studies*, pp. 92–3.

Pentecostal theology as theology of initiation: baptism in the Spirit

If you have seen a Baptist baptismal service, you will have observed candidates going down into a tank of water. There the minister will take the candidate and say words like, 'Do you take Jesus Christ to be your Lord and Saviour?' Then, when the candidate replies 'Yes' the minister will immerse him or her in water in front of the whole congregation. In some denominations the candidate will be immersed three times in quick succession and there will be a variety of words used by the minister at this point. Most ministers will say something like, 'I now baptize you in the name of the Father and of the Son and of the Holy Spirit.' Although Oneness Pentecostals have a fixed formula relating to 'the name of the Lord' other Pentecostal groups are much more relaxed about the exact wording being used. Those who have Baptist roots will understand that baptism is 'an outward sign of an inward and spiritual grace' and, for this reason, more important for its symbolism and for the inner reality that it represents than for the actual ritual act. As a ritual it represents the burial of the individual in the ground (the water) and the resurrection of the individual into a new life (as described in Romans 6). It is administered to those who have repented of sin and embraced a new life in Christ. The old life is buried symbolically and a new life begins.

Most Pentecostals understand baptism in the Spirit analogously. Here the individual comes to Christ who is the baptizer in the Spirit. This is a description of Christ in all four of the Gospels (Matt. 3.11; Mark 1.8; Luke 3.16; John 1.33). The believer comes to Christ and is immersed by him in the river of the Holy Spirit. Only Christ can baptize in the Holy Spirit according to the biblical texts although, also according to these texts, this baptism in the Holy Spirit is often accompanied by the laying on of hands (e.g. Acts 8.17). Just as candidates for water baptism are surrounded by water, so in Spirit-baptism there is a sense of the surrounding power and presence of the Holy Spirit. But who is entitled to be baptized in the Holy Spirit? Here a variety of answers is given. One answer is that, just as water baptism is administered in the New Testament to those who have repented and believed, so Spirit baptism follows as a recognition by Christ that an individual is a member of the church. Or, to put this another way, Spirit baptism indicates the incorporation of a believer into the body of Christ (1 Cor. 12.13). There is disagreement, however, over the closeness of the Spirit baptism to initial conversion. Some Pentecostals believe that the two events are almost invariably separated by a period of time – indeed, holiness Pentecostals would anticipate a crisis experience of sanctification before Spirit baptism – while others would bring Spirit baptism and conversion very close together so that they become almost two aspects of the same initiation into the church.[45] Indeed, some Pentecostals would argue that while in principle conversion and baptism in the

---

45 Lengthy debate over whether baptism in the Spirit can be or should be separated from conversion followed the publication of James Dunn (1970), *Baptism in the Spirit*, London, SCM Press. Dunn argued, against classical Pentecostalism, that baptism in the Spirit is part of the standard New Testament pattern of initiation of Christians. A review of the main Pentecostal responses to Dunn is given by William Atkinson in two articles. Both were published in 1995 in the *Journal of Pentecostal Theology*: the first is found in the *Journal of Pentecostal Theology* 6, pp. 87–131, and entitled, 'Pentecostal Responses to Dunn's *Baptism in the Holy Spirit: Luke-Acts*'.

Spirit are separable, in practice they may be almost synchronized.[46] When one asks about the *purpose* of baptism in the Spirit, Pentecostals would turn to the writings of Luke. As far as they are concerned, the baptism of the Holy Spirit is given as an empowerment for Christian service. It is to enable Christians to be persuasive witnesses to the resurrection of Christ wherever they go (Acts 1.8). More than this, in a ground-breaking work as a starting point for a new systematic theology, Frank Macchia has broadened the concept of Spirit-baptism so as to see it as a symbol of the kingdom of God and the coming rule of Christ upon earth.[47]

In the next chapter we move to other aspects of the kingdom of God, especially to healing and eschatology.

In this chapter we have outlined early Pentecostal theology as denominational and relating to:

- the nature of God
- speaking in tongues
- baptism in the Spirit.

This theology was written in order to mark out denominational boundaries, while of course attempting to protect and encapsulate precious experiences of Jesus brought by the Holy Spirit. The contested nature of early Pentecostal theology explains its dogmatic tone.

Cross-references to the SCM Reader *Pentecostal and Charismatic Studies*

3.2 G. R. Polman, 'The Place of Tongues in the Pentecostal Movement', *Confidence*, August 1911, pp. 176–7 (pp. 29–31).

5.1 Edward Irving, *The Day of Pentecost, or, The Baptism with the Holy Ghost*, Edinburgh, John Lindsay & Co, 1830 (pp. 87–9).

5.2 William H. Durham, *Pentecostal Testimony*, 1907 (pp. 89–93).

5.3 J. Roswell Flower, *Pentecost*, untitled editorial, August 1908 (pp. 93–4).

5.4 D. Gee, 'The Initial Evidence of the Baptism of the Holy Spirit', *RedemptionTidings*, 31 May 1963, pp. 10–12 (pp. 94–8).

---

46 As J. C. Thomas points out, 'Pentecostals are not opposed to a one-stage experience so long as the Pentecostal/charismatic experience is an integral part of reception of the Spirit'. J. C. Thomas (1998), 'Max Turner's *The Holy Spirit and Spiritual Gifts: Then and Now*, (Carlisle: Paternoster Press, 1996): An Appreciation and Critique', *Journal of Pentecostal Theology*, 12, 3–22.

47 Frank D. Macchia (2006), *Baptized in the Spirit: A Global Pentecostal Theology*, Grand Rapids, MI, Zondervan.

5.5 D. Petts, 'Baptism in the Holy Spirit: The Theological Distinctive', in K. Warrington (ed.), *Pentecostal Distinctives*, Carlisle, Paternoster Press, 1998, pp. 99–119, abridged (pp. 99–102).

5.6 Dennis and Rita Bennett, *The Holy Spirit and You*, Eastbourne, Kingsway Publications, 1971, pp. 85–8 (pp. 102–4).

5.8 Frank D. Macchia, 'The Question of Tongues as Initial Evidence: A Review of *Initial Evidence*', ed. Gary B. McGee, *Initial Evidence: Historical and Biblical Perspectives on the Pentecostal Doctrine of Spirit Baptism*, Peabody, MA, Hendrickson, 1991, first published in the *Journal of Pentecostal Theology* 2, 1993, pp. 117–27, pp.110–12.

Questions to think about

1 Read the text box on p. 230 and reflect on how W. H. Durham describes speaking in tongues, noting the voluntary and involuntary aspects.
2 Reflect on the quotation from Luther: 'It is living, dying, and even being condemned which makes a theologian – not reading, speculating and understanding.' How does this shed light on Pentecostal theology?
3 Reflect on the early theological methods of Pentecostals. Was the distinction between the subjective believer and the objective Scripture drawn too sharply?
4 What might be the benefits of dogmatic theology?
5 Could the church survive without theologians?
6 Reflect on the meaning of baptism in the Spirit in the light of its parallel with water baptism.

Further reading

Dayton, D. W. (1987), *Theological Roots of Pentecostalism*, Minneapolis, MN, Hendrickson.

Jacobsen, D. (2003), *Thinking in the Spirit*, Bloomington, IN, Indiana University Press.

Jacobsen, D. (ed.) (2006), *A Reader in Pentecostal Theology: Voices from the First Generation*, Bloomington, IN, Indiana University Press.

Kärkkäinen, V.-M. (2002), *Towards a Pneumatological Theology*, Lanham, MD, University Press of America.

Kay, W. K. and Dyer, A. E. (2004), *A Reader in Pentecostal and Charismatic Studies*, London, SCM Press.

Macchia, F. D. (2006), *Baptized in the Spirit: A Global Pentecostal Theology*, Grand Rapids, MI, Zondervan.

Reed, D. A. (2008), *'In Jesus' Name': The History and Beliefs of Oneness Pentecostals*, Blandford Forum, Deo.

Yong, A. (2005), *The Spirit Poured Out On All Flesh*, Grand Rapids, MI, Baker Academic.

The *Journal of Pentecostal Theology*, which is published by Sage and goes back to 1992, is a must-read for anyone who wants to explore the best contemporary debates in Pentecostal theology. See http://jpt. sagepub.com/

The New International Dictionary of Pentecostal and Charismatic Movements, Grand Rapids, MI, Zondervan, ed. S. M. Burgess and E. van der Maas (2002), contains a wealth of original articles on Pentecostal theology.

12

Theology 2

Introduction

The first picture Pentecostalism presents to the world is often a poster about a healing meeting. People will be encouraged to bring ill people to hear the healing evangelist. There may be photographs on the poster of discarded crutches and wheelchairs. Or perhaps, in flicking through TV channels, you stumble across a large meeting showing close-ups of a singing crowd with a line of men and women standing at the front while the well-dressed evangelist moves along placing a hand on a bowed head and uttering a brief prayer or command.

Aspects of Pentecostal theology

Healing has been part of the message of Pentecostalism from its beginning and is woven into beliefs about charismatic gifts, the nature of the church and the end of history, which are the subject of this chapter.

Pentecostal theology as evangelistic and pastoral: healing and charismatic gifts

Central to healing is the figure of Jesus, either showing compassion for the physical condition of ordinary people or as the desolate figure dying on a cross. This may seem incongruous. How can the crucifixion be connected with healing when the crucifixion is a picture of unremitting suffering? Yet for many Pentecostal Christians this is exactly the point. Jesus on the cross is suffering for sin – in one form or another all Christians believe this – but Pentecostal Christians, as we have seen in Chapter 3, believe that Jesus on the cross also took human sickness. Isaiah 53.4–5 (NIV) says:

> Surely he took up our infirmities and carried our sorrows, yet we considered him stricken by God, smitten by him, and afflicted.
> But he was pierced for our transgressions, he was crushed for our iniquities; the punishment that brought us peace was upon him, and *by his wounds we are healed.*

Many Christians took the passage in Isaiah and applied it to Jesus. For instance, in the early church Philip the evangelist did so (Acts 8.35). Isaiah is understood to be speaking prophetically about the ministry and work of Jesus. Pentecostals were quick to argue that Christ atoned for sin *and* for sickness, and they did this by linking the story of the Fall in Genesis 3, when Adam sinned, with the first appearance of disease. In the Garden of Eden there was no illness, neither was there any illness in heaven. Illness arrived on earth, according to this interpretation, as a result of human sin. The effects of the Fall stretched across human history, touching both the natural world that became a place where human beings had to carve out an existence by the sweat of their brows, and the spiritual world where easy access to God was prevented by expulsion from the Garden of Eden. At the start of the twentieth century, when the story of evolution was still relatively new, many Christians believed in a literal interpretation of the opening chapters of Genesis. Today, many Pentecostals continue to believe it but, even if they do not believe literally, they will believe metaphorically. Consequently many Pentecostals believe that faith in Christ heals their bodies as certainly as it can save their souls.

For instance, the Church of God (Cleveland, TN) says in its Declaration of Faith, 'we believe divine healing is provided for all in the atonement',[1] and Assemblies of God in the United States says, 'divine healing is an integral part of the gospel. Deliverance from sickness is provided for in the atonement, and is the privilege of all believers.'[2]

As we have seen in Chapter 7, from the mid-1930s onwards the message of healing was preached by independent Pentecostal evangelists all over America and later in many parts of the world. Radio and television broadcasting gave a technological boost to their tent campaigning. In almost every case evangelists based their preaching on an exposition of the healing ministry of Jesus and, more precisely, on the connection between the miracles of Jesus and his crucifixion. To be sure, evangelists encouraged their listeners to approach healing in a positive frame of mind and to ensure that any long-term sinful habits were discarded. But preachers could also speak about 'claiming healing by faith', even encouraging the crowds who followed them that healing was a 'covenant right' to which believers were entitled in a quasi-legal way.[3] In the beginning, evangelists would personally lay hands on all the people but, as the crowds grew bigger, this became a practical impossibility. Sometimes the evangelists

---

1 http://www.churchofgod.org/about/declaration_of_faith.cfm (accessed 20.11.08).

2 http://www.ag.org/top/Beliefs/Position_Papers/pp_4184_healing.cfm (accessed 20.11.08).

3 F. F. Bosworth (1973), *Christ the Healer*, Old Tappan, NJ, Fleming H. Revel. Bosworth, who was influential on the young healing evangelists, was a respected independent healing evangelist in the USA in the 1920s and 1930s who staunchly defended the notion of 'healing in the atonement' and could write about 'the faith that takes'.

would ask their listeners to lay hands on themselves and at other times evangelists would tell people to receive healing by an act of faith where they sat or stood. If the evangelist was careful, he or she would first preach a straightforward gospel message about forgiveness of sin and then, after this but in the same meeting, offer prayer for those who were ill. Very rarely did the preacher remain in town long enough to cope with those who were not healed.

Kathryn Kuhlman (1907–79), one of several female healing evangelists, was disturbed by the emphasis on faith because this implied that if people were not healed it was because they lacked faith.[4] In this way the people who were ill were doubly condemned: they came to the evangelist burdened with an illness and were then given the impression that they had a further problem – their illness could not be removed because their faith was deficient. Kuhlman devised a different way of praying for those who were ill by employing the charismatic gift of a 'word of knowledge' by which she called out to people in a crowd some hidden personal details about their illnesses or lives. Once the people had been identified in this way, she told them that the Spirit of God would heal them, and healings often occurred. This method was based upon a theology of charismatic gifts more than on a theology of atonement. Charismatic gifts were manifestations or 'outshinings' of the Holy Spirit that were distributed both to the evangelist (in the 'word of knowledge') and to the sick person (in need of a 'gift of healing').[5]

Another ministry that combined aspects of faith teaching with spiritual gifts was exercised by A. A. Allen (1911–70). Allen was unusual, however, in his ready confrontation of evil spirits, which he saw as the real cause of human illness. So, the removal of illness also involved the expelling of demons. A cancer demon might be exorcized. And, where someone was in thrall to alcoholism, the spirit of alcoholism could be banished. The spirit of nicotine could be cast out of smokers. This kind of confrontational theology had the effect of infusing a dramatic charge into his meetings. It also shifted the blame for drug and alcohol addiction away from needy individuals, which at least solved the pastoral problem that troubled Kuhlman.

As his ministry developed, Oral Roberts (b. 1918) moved from his Pentecostal holiness origins to a wider position within the Methodist Church. His theology of healing also altered. He pressed for inner harmony of the body, soul and spirit, and sometimes worked alongside ordinary medical cures. Roberts wrote:

---

4 K. Kuhlman (1963), *I Believe in Miracles*, London, Oliphants.

5 The 'manifestation of the Spirit' (1 Cor. 12.7) is the *phanerosis* or 'outshining' of the Spirit.

What had been the most defeating to me is that doctors seem to see me as a physical and mental being only, and praying people see me as a spiritual being only. Yet they are both in the process of bringing healing to me. It was very frustrating, and God had been dealing with me about it. In fact ... He has spoken to me that He wants His healing streams of prayer and medicine merged and that His time has come for me to be a forerunner in getting it done.

And he went on:

I believe the Bible, in which God teaches He alone is the Source of our total supply: 'But my God shall supply all your need according to his riches in glory by Christ Jesus' (Phil. 4:19); and 'I am the LORD that healeth thee' (Exod. 15:26). Our total supply most certainly includes our deliverance from sickness and disease. Therefore, both healing coming through supernatural intervention, through believing the gospel and the prayer of faith, and healing coming through medicine or surgery really come through God our Source.[6]

In this way there were three generally identifiable, but interconnected, theologies of healing, being based on:

- the atonement, the cross of Christ, and emphasizing the exact parallel between forgiveness of sin and healing of the body;
- charismatic gifts, emphasizing the activity of the Holy Spirit in a sovereign way without being pinned down to exact scriptural promises;
- the authority of the believer or evangelist to confront and cast out demons causing illness and misery.

Healing is one of the gifts mentioned in 1 Corinthians 12.7–10. The text of Paul's letter reads:

Now to each one the manifestation of the Spirit is given for the common good. To one there is given through the Spirit the message of wisdom, to another the message of knowledge by means of the same Spirit, to another faith by the same Spirit, to another gifts of healing by that one Spirit, to another miraculous powers, to another prophecy, to another distinguishing between spirits, to another speaking in different kinds of tongues, and to still another the interpretation of tongues.

Belief in the power of the Spirit quickly led Pentecostals to examine these passages of Scripture and to learn from them. They concluded that there

6 Taken from O. Roberts (1995), *Expect a Miracle: My Life and Ministry. Oral Roberts an Autobiography*, London, Nelson, pp. 254–61.

were actually nine gifts mentioned here (wisdom, knowledge, faith, healing, miraculous powers, prophecy, discerning of spirits, tongues and interpretation) and that healing was only one among many. The best Pentecostal teachers examined these texts systematically and tried to work out how Christianity and especially church life would look if these gifts were prevalent. The first to do so with any success was Donald Gee (1891–1966). After consideration of the purpose of spiritual gifts and the functioning of each gift individually, Gee published his book *Concerning Spiritual Gifts*.[7] Here he tried to work out the scope of each gift and to see if he could find examples of their operation elsewhere in the Bible. For instance, on prophecy he wrote:

> As the channels of inspired utterance in the Church, true prophets fill an invaluable position, and it is an evil day when their utterances are despised (1. Thess., v, 20) and quenched by lovers of purely logical and didactic ministries, as has sometimes happened in the history of the Church with disastrous results. The office of the prophet is complemented and safeguarded by the other offices. Prophets should never become the sole guides of the Church; their limitations on the line of infallibility should be carefully noticed in 1. Cor, xiv, 29–32: and it is significant that there is not a single instance of the Church going to prophets for guidance recorded in the Scriptures. The utterances of fully recognized prophets were nevertheless treated with great respect (Acts xi, 27–29).

The second was Harold Horton (1880–1969), whose book *The Gifts of the Spirit* was first published in 1934 and then reprinted in a new edition later that year and then in a second edition in 1946.[8] Here there is an exposition of the nine gifts of the Holy Spirit as outlined in 1 Corinthians 12. This is essentially a robust exposition of the biblical text. Horton was converted from a liberal Methodist tradition and is scathing about the denial of the supernatural that was part of his training as a local preacher. The other distinctive feature of this text is that it understands the Spirit to have been present in the Old Testament, with the result that numerous illustrations are selected from there. Horton's point is that spiritual gifts are directly related to the unchanging nature of God so that, for instance,

> the Word of Knowledge is the supernatural revelation of the Holy Spirit of certain facts in the mind of God ... the Word of Knowledge

---

7 Reference is made to them in the British AOG magazine, *Redemption Tidings* 4.2, February 1928.

8 The introduction and acknowledgement make reference to Howard Carter's 'schedule of private notes'. Harold Horton (1934), *The Gifts of the Spirit*, London, privately published.

is not a God-sent amplification of human knowledge. It is a divinely given fragment of divine knowledge.[9]

This is the original insight that drives Horton's exposition and makes it credible. It also places Pentecostal understanding of charismatic gifts within the broad stream of biblical revelation.

The kind of church life envisaged by Pentecostal denominations and elaborated by Gee and Horton is of a multi-gifted congregation with a variety of charismatic gifts in operation. And this pattern can still be seen in small Pentecostal congregations today. There may be a gathering of 50 or 80 people in a room where people speak in tongues, prophesy and pray for revival. The characteristic of the gathering is that any member of the group may 'feel moved' by the Holy Spirit, and if the group grows, it may turn into a fully fledged Pentecostal congregation with plentiful participation from its membership. What is surprising to non-Pentecostals is the general sanity shown by most of those present. None of the Pentecostal gifts is involuntary and the people involved are not in trances or caught up in ecstatic mystical visions. On the contrary, they may 'feel led' by the Holy Spirit to say or do certain things without claiming to be compelled to do so and, in some congregations, people may prophesy tentatively with words like, 'I think the Lord is saying to us that we ought to ...'. If congregations grow and a revival atmosphere builds up, then claims may become more forceful and confident. A well-taught congregation, however, will appreciate the fallibility of spiritual gifts, and elders and ministers will take care to ensure that common sense coexists with heightened spirituality.

Pastoral considerations are relevant here. In ordinary Pentecostal congregations, it is common for individuals to receive prayer for healing. Here the emphasis is unlikely to be on the atonement and instead is transferred to the procedure given in James 5.14–16. The verses read:

> Is any one of you sick? He should call the elders of the church to pray over him and anoint him with oil in the name of the Lord. And the prayer offered in faith will make the sick person well; the Lord will raise him up. If he has sinned, he will be forgiven.
>
> Therefore confess your sins to each other and pray for each other so that you may be healed. The prayer of a righteous man is powerful and effective.

The text encourages those who are ill to call for the elders, and these are ordinary people of recognized stature within the congregation. They are not full-time evangelists or health professionals. These elders are

---

9 Horton, *Gifts*, pp. 48, 49.

instructed to pray for the person who has called for them and the expectation is that healing will follow. The anointing oil is presumably symbolic of the Holy Spirit. There is also a hint here that the illness of the person involved may have been brought about by wrongdoing. Forgiveness on the basis of confession is included alongside the expectation of healing. The passage provides evidence for a holistic approach in the sense that physical and spiritual healing appear to be close together.[10]

Pentecostal and charismatic Christians may also make reference to 'discernment' at this point since the causes of illness are diverse and frequently concealed.[11] As any doctor knows, diagnosis must precede treatment. As John Christopher Thomas has pointed out in a comprehensive and illuminating discussion in *The Devil, Disease and Deliverance*, it is necessary for the Christian community, sometimes represented by elders and sometimes by pastoral ministers, to discern causes for illness before getting down to prayer. It would be too simple to assume that all illness is caused by the devil (and Pentecostals do believe in the devil) or that all disease is brought about by God in order to correct human sin.[12] There may be natural causes as well, but, in any case, the most effective remedies in prayer will be brought about once 'discernment' has been utilized.

Pentecostal theology as ecclesial: the nature of the church

Gee had begun to pay attention to the shape of Pentecostal ecclesiology in the 1920s. He had early on seen the connection between ecclesiology and ministry gifts and between ecclesiology and spiritual gifts.[13] He had understood the distinctive nature of Pentecostalism by reference to a close examination of the text of the New Testament. His publications on the church began as a magazine series in January 1929[14] and continued

---

10 For a full discussion of the text from a Pentecostal and scholarly perspective, see John Christopher Thomas (1993), 'The Devil, Disease and Deliverance: James 5.14–16', *Journal of Pentecostal Theology* 2, 25–50.

11 1 Corinthians 12.10 speaks of 'discerning of spirits' as a gift of the Holy Spirit, which partly explains where the concept comes from. Further discussion is found in Stephen E. Parker (1996), *Led by the Spirit: Towards a Practical Theology of Pentecostal Discernment and Decision Making*, Sheffield, Sheffield Academic Press. A wider discussion is found in Bonnie S. Wright (2005), '"Discerning the Spirit" in the Context of Racial Integration and Conflict in Two Assemblies of God Churches', *Journal for the Theory of Social Behaviour* 35.4, 413–35.

12 John Christopher Thomas (1998), *The Devil, Disease and Deliverance: Origins of Illness*, Sheffield, Sheffield Academic Press.

13 Compare a later discussion by Benny C. Aker (2002), '*Charismata*: Gifts, Enablements, or Ministries?', *Journal of Pentecostal Theology* 11.1, 53–69.

14 *Redemption Tidings*, 5.2, February 1929.

through the rest of the year until it was published as a book in 1930.[15] *Concerning Shepherds and Sheepfolds* remained in print for at least the next 20 years.

This idea of a Pentecostal church presumed that it was a congregation of people who have put their faith in Christ, who had experienced Spirit baptism, who were looked after by a pastor and from whose numbers evangelists or other ministries might be drawn. Gee distinguished between local ministries, attached to one congregation, and trans-local ministries that involved travel. He himself was a travelling teacher for 20 or more years, with no meaningful home congregation but with a constant stream of invitations that took him from pulpit to pulpit all over the world. There were Pentecostals who attempted to make a connection between spiritual gifts and ministry gifts. Ephesians 4 spoke of the ministry gifts of apostles, prophets, evangelists, pastors and teachers, and it was easy to connect the prophet with the charismatic gift of prophecy, the evangelist with the charismatic gift of healing, the teacher with the charismatic gift of knowledge, and in this way show how a combination between calling and gifting resulted in the maximum benefit for the church as a whole. The evangelist with the charismatic gift of healing would have a far greater impact, so it was believed, than the evangelist without such a gift, and in the 1950s, when the Pentecostal evangelists got to work in the USA, this pattern was seen. Pentecostals would point to Brother So-and-So and say he was 'anointed' as an evangelist; by this they meant that the man in question had a natural aptitude for evangelism *and* that he exercised suitable charismatic gifts. Nor was it difficult to assume that ministries might develop within small local congregations before being launched out nationally and internationally.

As Pentecostalism grew it began to gain the notice and respect of other parts of Christianity. A formal dialogue between Pentecostals and Roman Catholics took place in five phases (1972–76; 1977–82; 1985–89; 1990–97; 1998–2006).[16] At the dialogue, representatives of each side met together regularly to work through a theological agenda where each side presented its own position and commented on the position of the other side. Dialogues of this kind are only successful if the two sets of people can trust each other and be honest with the other side. In the nature of things participants in dialogue tend to be academics, or attached to academic institutions, and therefore to be comfortable with lengthy discussions on points of detail or with new ideas. When the dialogues are

---

15 *Redemption Tidings*, 6.3, March 1930. Gee wrote the book during his five and a half week voyage to Australia in 1928. B. R. Ross (1974), 'Donald Gee: In Search of a Church, Sectarian in Transition', unpublished PhD, Knox College, Toronto, p. 36.

16 Jerry L. Sandidge (1987), 'Roman Catholic/Pentecostal Dialogue (1977–1982): A Study in Developing Ecumenism', *Studies in the Intercultural History of Christianity* 44, New York, Peter Lang, for summary on the early phases.

concluded, the dialogue partners issue a report which will help to guide or inform the wider bodies of which they are part.[17] Pentecostals in dialogue with Catholics were forced to consider the nature of the church and this, as might be expected, is theologically complex.[18]

At its simplest, how do we decide when a group of people is a church? Should we look at their beliefs or their characteristic practices? If we look at their beliefs and practices, are there some that are foundational and others that are optional?[19] Could a church exist without baptism, for instance? A theological inquiry of this kind will need to approach the New Testament and to take into account the intellectual traditions that have built up over 2,000 years of church history. In a discussion of the nature of the church, Kärkkäinen shows that two basic positions have been taken.[20] The church may be seen as being centred on Christ: 'Where two or three are gathered together in my name, there am I in the midst of them', said Jesus (Matt. 18.20). In technical terms Christology determines ecclesiology: such a church, historically speaking, is usually Roman Catholic and hierarchical in nature where ministers or priests gain their authority from their closeness to Christ.

An alternative model of the church focuses on the community of people and on the role of the Holy Spirit working in each of them and among them all.[21] Here the church as a body of interdependent people gathering together with a common purpose and in a common life is more likely to be found within the Orthodox tradition. In technical terms this kind of church may be *instituted* by Christ but is *constituted* by the Holy Spirit. It is the outpouring of the Spirit on the day of Pentecost that turns the gathering of 120 disciples in the city of Jerusalem from being a band of believers into a church.

These two models of the church, one christological and the other pneumatological, imply different things concerning the relationship between a local church and the universal church. This has been a consistent theological conundrum. Is a local church a microcosm of the universal church or is a local congregation only part of the universal church when it is institutionally joined to it? The pneumatological model sees a local con-

17 See a short discussion of this in Kilian McDonnell (1995), 'Improbable Conversations: The International Classical Pentecostal/Roman Catholic Dialogue, *Pneuma* 17.2, 163–74.

18 The second phase (1978–82) covered speaking in tongues, faith and experience, hermeneutics, healing, tradition, the church as communion, Mary, and ministry.

19 Assemblies of God in the USA holds that both baptism in water and Holy Communion are commanded by Christ: they are 'ordinances', and will be practised in every local congregation.

20 See A. Yong (2002), 'Preface', in V.-M. Kärkkäinen (ed. A. Yong), *Towards a Pneumatological Theology*, Lanham, MD, University Press of America, p. 67f.

21 See also Shane Clifton (2007), 'Pentecostal Ecclesiology: A Methodological Proposal for a Diverse Movement, *Journal of Pentecostal Theology* 15.2, 213–32.

gregation as formed by the Holy Spirit and manifesting the life of Christ; for these reasons it is a miniature version of the totality of the church worldwide. The other model tends to invest the functions of teaching or authority in specialist bodies like the Magisterium of the Roman Catholic Church, which are psychologically and geographically many miles away from the local church; and, to say this again, it contends that without a proper link with these bodies the local congregation is invalid – it is not a church.

Pentecostal history, and the exposition of Scripture by men like Horton and Gee as well as by the founders of Pentecostal denominations, veered towards a pneumatological understanding of the church.[22] Yet, as denominations grew and increased in strength in the 1930s, the christological, hierarchical model was also appealing because it appeared to justify denominational authority. The truth is that the early Pentecostals read their understanding of the church from the churches they had known in childhood. They did not approach ecclesiology with any theological sophistication, but rather with a practical determination to create congregations that functioned as nearly as possible like the congregations in the New Testament. And 'functioned' is the key word here.

Only later in the 1980s, when Pentecostalism was fully established and had highly educated men and women in its ranks, did the finer points of theological discourse begin to impinge upon their minds. The charismatic movement and Pentecostal–Roman Catholic dialogue brought the issue of Christian initiation to the fore. The easiest way of accessing the issue is to ask whether someone could be within the church without being baptized. Early Pentecostals would have appreciated the significance of baptism but they would, in almost every instance, have insisted that salvation is by faith in Christ alone and not by baptism. As far as nearly all Pentecostals would have been concerned, the moment of 'new birth' or justification occurred as a consequence of simple faith in Christ. They would have pointed to the thief on the cross to whom Jesus said, 'Today you will be with me in Paradise' (Luke 23.43), and would argue that this thief did not need to undergo any form of baptism for his salvation.

Yet, the New Testament unquestionably commands that those who believe should also be baptized. So baptism is indeed a gateway to the church. In the normal course of events one would expect all members of the church to have been baptized, but of course there is more than one mode of baptism practised by Christians. Could it be said that the baptism or sprinkling of babies with water had the same value as adult

22 As Dale M. Coulter (2005) has reminded us, 'One month prior to this meeting [the April 1914 meeting that led to the formation of Assemblies of God] Elizabeth Sisson called for a return to the pattern of Pentecost in which the Spirit filled all present with the love of God to create a living, breathing organism called the Church.' *Journal of Pentecostal Theology* 14.1, 81–98.

baptism by immersion? Should someone who had been baptized as an infant in an Episcopal church be rebaptized before joining a Pentecostal church? These issues were usually left to the discretion of the local pastor and resolved in a practical way. But they naturally went hand in hand with debates about the role of baptism in the Holy Spirit. All Pentecostals expected people to be baptized in water and then, sometime later, be baptized in the Holy Spirit. People might be members of Pentecostal congregations before being baptized in the Holy Spirit but full participation in the life of a Pentecostal church could not take place until they began to experience a wider range of Holy Spirit activity. Baptism in the Spirit might be a gateway to the exercise of spiritual gifts just as water baptism might be a gateway to the church itself.

Pentecostal theology as eschatological: pointing to the end of history

The realities of early Pentecostal theology are splashed across the publications that sprang up rapidly at the start of the twentieth century.[23] The *Latter Rain Evangel*, started in 1908, displays the image of the trumpet over the heading 'Voice of the Spirit'.[24] The trumpet symbolizes the arrival of a herald, a messenger with a startling announcement, and it resonates with the biblical image of 'the last trumpet' that will proclaim the return of Christ.

A scheme for interpreting the Bible divided up time until the moment when Christ would return.[25] This scheme chopped up world history into a series of dispensations or divinely ordained periods, each of which ended in judgement and each of which marked a different way by which God would deal with the inhabitants of the earth. So, for instance, the dispensational era of the law was introduced by Moses and this was followed by the era of grace introduced by Christ. The final dispensation would be that of the kingdom of God upon earth introduced by Christ on his return. The scheme was popularized by Darby and modified by Pentecostals.[26] The scheme assumed that we are all living just before the reign of Christ upon earth. The outpouring of the Holy Spirit was a sign that the period of grace is coming to an end and that cataclysmic judderings signal our passage into the new dispensation.[27]

23 This is theologically also held by those who later joined Pentecostal denominations.

24 *Latter Rain Evangel*, October 1908, p. 2. The journal was printed by the Stone Church in Chicago, Illinois, and enjoyed wide distribution.

25 See a reinterpretation of Pentecostal eschatology in Peter Althouse (2005), '"Left Behind" – Fact or Fiction: Ecumenical Dilemmas of the Fundamentalist Millenarian Tensions within Pentecostalism', *Journal of Pentecostal Theology* 13.2, 187–207.

26 See Chapter 2.

27 Relevant to the eschatological dimension of the Spirit is Blaine Charette (1996),

Yet, it would be a mistake to think that early Pentecostal eschatological schemes were cut and dried. A recent re-examination of early Pentecostal literature shows that doctrinal positions were not entirely fixed. For a start, the dispensational periods of time were thought to overlap (which meant that it was difficult to tell which dispensation we are in at the moment) and, in any case, the total number of dispensations might vary between about four and seven with the result that 'no single system of dispensations held a monopoly on the thought of early Pentecostals'.[28] What heated up speculation was the arrival of World War One. It became easy to see the catastrophic carnage of war as an indication of the tribulations that preceded the return of Christ. This implied a change in the practical function of baptism in the Spirit. The Holy Spirit was chosen to prepare the church for the rapture rather than to empower Christians for service. This eschatology, had it become dominant within the Pentecostal movement, could have turned Pentecostalism into a fervent adventist sect and destroyed its revivalistic missionary momentum.

If Pentecostals were asked how they knew they stood where they did in God's calendar, they would have answered that the outpouring of the Spirit on the original day of Pentecost was paralleled by the outpouring of the Spirit at the end of the dispensation. In both instances speaking with tongues was heard. This raised glossolalia to a level of importance way beyond its connection with an individual's baptism in the Holy Spirit.[29] So Pentecostals, when they turned their eyes to the society of which they were part, saw themselves as the bearers of the Spirit at the very end of the dispensation of grace, preaching the gospel with an urgency and power that would help to bring the church up to its full quota before impending and inevitable divine judgements.

And what of the Spirit-filled church when the judgements fell? Most Pentecostals believed that they would not be on earth when the antichrist let rip. They believed that Christ would return to 'rapture' the church by lifting it up from danger and taking believers to heaven. The rapture was a vivid reality to many Pentecostals who, as a consequence, did not expect that they would ever have to face death. Grant Wacker instances a missionary who left careful instructions about what was to be done with

---

'"Never has anything like this been seen in Israel": the Spirit as Eschatological Sign in Matthew's Gospel', *Journal of Pentecostal Theology* 8, 31–51. A best-selling presentation of this eschatology is found in Hal Lindsey (1970), *The Late Great Planet Earth*, Grand Rapids, MI, Zondervan.

28 Larry McQueen (2009), 'Early Pentecostal Eschatology in the Light of The Apostolic Faith, 1906–1908', paper presented at the 38th Annual Meeting of the Society for Pentecostal Studies, Eugene, Oregon.

29 J. H. King, leader of the Pentecostal Holiness Church, believed that tongues is the sign of the dawning of a 'Pentecostal Dispensation'. See Douglas Jacobsen (ed.) (2006), *A Reader in Pentecostal Theology: Voices from the First Generation*, Bloomington, IN, Indiana University Press, ch. 8.

her possessions if she failed to return home because she had been raptured.[30] Peculiar though it might seem to the modern reader, the rapture was in some senses a multiplication of the ascension of Christ whereby not just Christ but all believers would be lifted up from the earth. It was the ultimate demonstration of the power of the Holy Spirit since it would not only raise the church from the earth but raise the dead from previous ages. In the words of Paul:

> For the Lord himself will come down from heaven, with a loud command, with the voice of the archangel and with the trumpet call of God, and the dead in Christ will rise first. After that, we who are still alive and are left will be caught up together with them in the clouds to meet the Lord in the air. And so we will be with the Lord for ever. (1 Thess. 4.16, 17)

Although the imminence of the end of the age was strongly felt, and reflected in publications like *The Bridegroom's Messenger* and *The Midnight Cry*, the most common image used to depict the Pentecostal era was that of the 'latter rain'. Within the land of Israel rain falls at the time of planting and softens the ground and then again just before the harvest and fattens up the olives, grapes and corn. As far as Pentecostals were concerned the former rain was poured out when the church was planted at the beginning of the dispensation of grace and the latter rain is poured out at the end of the season just before the harvest. The image of harvest, like other images in the Bible, can also speak of the end of the cycle, of the end of the agricultural year and of judgement. The various images of the bridegroom returning, of the sickle being thrust into the harvest, of the Lord of the harvest returning for the fruits of his labour, were ways of saying basically the same thing and were celebrated, for example:

> Have you heard about the Latter Rain,
> God is sending on the earth again?
> On the dry and thirsty hearts to fall –
> Everyone that on the Lord doth call?
>
> CHORUS
> Fall, falling, 'tis the Latter Rain;
> Coming, coming – Pentecost again.
> Hasten, hasten, 'tis the day of power,
> Come beneath the Holy Spirit's shower.[31]

---

30 Grant Wacker (2001), *Heaven Below*, Cambridge, MA, Harvard University Press, p. 260.

31 Printed in *The Pentecost*, 1 March 1910, p. 2, and written by Clara M. Garver.

The latter rain had four implications. First, the Pentecostal church must be engaged with mission.[32] The Spirit was poured out for the sake of the harvest and Pentecostals must use the miracles and charismatic gifts that had been made available to them to bring the gospel to a darkened earth. From its earliest origins, Pentecostalism, at its best, was never a holy huddle but always concerned to look beyond the walls of the church to the great world outside. Pentecostals believed their own theology and travelled widely with almost foolish abandon, to the detriment of their health or lives. If the Holy Spirit was called 'the missionary Spirit', this summed up that aspect of their theology.[33]

Second, the church that had been filled with the Spirit was holy. The Holy Spirit burned holiness into believers. If Pentecostal 'saints' shunned the foibles of fashion and the consumer goods of the shops, it was because, so far as they were concerned, holiness meant that they were set apart for the sake of the gospel. This holiness might become legalistic, inward-looking and unhealthy, but at its best it produced individuals who were able to ignore the shallow materialism that all too often became a preoccupation of the successful church. Nearly all the veteran Pentecostal ministers, by the end of their lives, seemed remarkably old-fashioned in their attitudes. They wore the same suits, lived without ostentation and gave away large quantities of money. For instance, when Donald Gee retired he had nowhere to live.[34] Others died with almost nothing in their bank accounts.

Third, Pentecostals saw the history of the church from the time of Jesus as being a pattern of loss and restoration. They saw miracles on the pages of the New Testament, and the gradual diminishing of these miracles was not, in their view, because the Holy Spirit had been removed from the church or because the dispensational door had been closed, but simply because the church had lost its way. They saw the church in the Middle Ages as riddled with superstition and ripe for reformation. And then, in what they understood as the start of an upward trajectory, they saw the gradual renewal of the church by stages, through the recovery of the doctrine of justification by faith (in the Reformation) and mass evangelism (in the preaching of Wesley and Whitefield), to their own day. This belief could make Pentecostals seem as if they were elitist, but it was an elitism that spurred them on to dream big dreams.

---

32 The distinguished Pentecostal missionary thinking Melvin L. Hodges (1978), in *The Indigenous Church and the Missionary*, Pasadena, CA, William Carey Library, judged, 'The Church today in general suffers from a weak theology of mission. Mission, in turn, suffers from a weak theology of Church', p. 8.

33 A phrase used by J. Roswell Flower (1908) in an untitled editorial of *The Pentecost*, August 1908, p. 4.

34 See W. K. Kay (1990), *Inside Story*, Stourport-on-Seven, Mattersey Hall Publishing.

Fourth, the Holy Spirit, according to the book of Acts, is poured out upon *all* flesh (Acts 2.17). We would therefore expect to see evidence of the work of the Holy Spirit all over the world, drawing people to Christ, building communities where the grace of God is to be found and healing and reconciling diverse racial and generational groups. We might see Pentecostal churches now in existence on every continent and containing an extended range of ethnicities and ages as a sign that the Spirit has indeed been freshly outpoured. Of course, every Christian group with a wide extension might make the same claim, and each in their own way may be right to do so, but this does not stop Pentecostals from seeing the emergence of the Pentecostal/charismatic stream as a vindication of the faith vision of an earlier generation.

Pentecostal theology as a balance: elements in harmony and discord

The character of Pentecostal theology exists within the 'now and not-yet' tension brought about by the present outpouring of the Holy Spirit and the belief in a future return of Christ. Since the Holy Spirit makes Christ real he is both present now and will be present later. Since he is present now the kingdom of God is present now and yet since he will be present in the future the kingdom of God will be present to a greater extent in the future. This means that the tension between those who are not healed now despite biblical promises and charismatic gifts can be resolved by the belief that they will be healed in the future. Equally, those tragic accidents and disasters that bewilder us now will make sense when the kingdom fully comes.

The relationship between Christ and the Holy Spirit is intrinsic to Pentecostal theology. On the one hand it is Christ who receives the Spirit from the Father (Acts 2.32, 33) and pours out the Spirit, and, on the other hand, it is the Spirit who brings individuals to Christ for the glory of the Father.[35] The Spirit is both poured out and therefore distant from Christ and intimately and eternally connected with Christ since the Spirit and Christ coexist within the Godhead. Theologians attempted to describe the relationship between the persons of the Trinity by saying that they coinhere. Each person of the Godhead can only be known in relation to each of the others.[36] This relationship between the persons of the Trinity allows the Spirit to work in the hearts of men and women, building the church of which Christ is the head. It allows the Spirit to be manifested through human beings while equally and at the same time recognizing their imperfections. Indeed, Pentecostals accept that, while they may be

---

35 This reflection applies to Trinitarian Pentecostalism.

36 For a good explanation of this, see another book in this series: Mike Higton (2008), *Christian Doctrine*, London, SCM Press.

justified and sanctified, they are still capable of sin and note that there is no expectation that sin will finally be removed from the church until the end of history.

We can put all this another way by saying that the nature of God is closely connected with the nature of the church since it is through the mutual working of the Trinity that the church is being brought into being. The love that exists within the Trinity is the same love that ought to exist within the church. The love that exists within the Trinity is the same love that ought to flow out from church into mission. The Spirit sent out by the Father and the Son is the Spirit who inspires the church likewise to reach out. It is the Spirit who reaches out to bring back to Christ those who are distant from him. It is the church that shares in the life of God in a fellowship or *koinonia*, which mirrors and partakes of the eternal life of the Godhead. It is the church that represents the future as pointing towards the end of history while, at the same time, being indicative of the 'now' aspect of the kingdom of God upon earth.

Equally, we may say that the love relationship within the Trinity is also a relationship that permits human liberty: 'Where the Spirit of the Lord is, there is liberty' (2 Cor. 3.17). There is in Pentecostalism a constant interchange between the authority of God and of Scripture and the liberty of the Spirit. There is perfect liberty where the Spirit of the Lord is at work and this liberty in no way contradicts the authority of the Godhead since it is a liberty created by the Godhead. So authority and liberty, while they may appear to be in tension in human situations, can be reconciled from a divine perspective. And, just as the Spirit creates liberty with the authority of the Godhead, so the Bible is seen as both a book that is written, fixed and containing the commands and promises of God, and, at the same time, a book that is in harmony with the spiritual utterances of those who are currently filled with the Holy Spirit. So the Bible is canonical, recognized as such by the apostles and the early church, and yet the same Spirit that inspired the Bible also inspires the church. Pentecostal theology, because of its sense of narrative and drama, is also a theology in which there is an interplay between the written word and the preached and prophesied word.

Cross-references to the SCM Reader *Pentecostal and Charismatic Studies*

3.1 A Report of the Address at the Sunderland Convention by the Revd A. A. Boddy, Tuesday Night 2 June, *Confidence*, June 1914, pp. 116–17 (pp. 28–9).

3.2 G. R. Polman, 'The Place of Tongues in the Pentecostal Movement', *Confidence*, August 1911, pp. 176–7 (pp. 29–31).

3.3 Elizabeth Sisson, 'Want any help?' *Confidence*, October–December 1921, p. 52 (pp. 31–2).

3.4 Aimee Semple McPherson, 'Pre-millennial Signal Towers', from 'The Bridal Call Foursquare', delivered at Angelus Temple, 24 August 1924, abridged (pp. 32–4).

3.5 David Allen, 'The Millennium: An Embarrassment or a Fundamental of the Faith?' Paper delivered at the European Pentecostal Theological Association Conference, Brussels, 16 April 1987, abridged (pp. 35–7).

3.6 J. Rodman Williams, *Renewal Theology*, vol. 3: *The Millennium*, Grand Rapids, MI, Zondervan, 1988, pp. 428–31, abridged (pp. 38–41).

3.7 Dave Wilkerson, *The Vision*, Old Tappan, NJ, Spire Books, 1974, pp. 31, 32, 91, 92, abridged (pp. 41–3).

3.8 Peter Hocken, 'The Holy Spirit Makes the Church more Eschatological', in P. Hocken, *Blazing the Trail*, Guildford, Eagle Publishing, 1994, (pp. 43–6).

4.1 A. A. Boddy, 'Health in Christ', *Confidence*, March 1910, pp. 175–9, abridged (pp. 52–6).

4.2 Smith Wigglesworth (1922), 'Filled with God' (Hebrews 2, August 1922), in R. Liardon (ed.), *Smith Wigglesworth: The Complete Collection of His Life Teachings*, Tulsa, Oklahoma, Albury, 1996, pp. 143–6 (pp. 56–9).

4.3 H. Horton, *The Gifts of the Spirit,* Luton, Redemption Tidings Bookroom, 1934, pp. 106–18 (pp. 60–3).

4.4 G. Jeffreys, *Healing Rays*, Worthing, H. E. Walter Ltd, 1985, first published 1932, pp. 32–3 (pp. 64–5).

4.5 F. F. Bosworth, *Christ the Healer,* Old Tappan, New Jersey, Fleming H. Revel Company, 1924 (abridged from the edition in 1973), pp. 24–31 (pp. 65–6).

4.6 C. L. Parker, 'Gifts of Healing', *Redemption Tidings*, 2 December 1960, pp. 5, 6, 3 (pp. 67–70).

4.7 T. L. Osborn, *Healing the Sick,* Oklahoma, T. L. Osborn Evangelistic Association, 1992 edn, pp. 83–4 (pp. 70–3).

4.8 K. Kuhlman, *I Believe in Miracles,* London, Oliphants, 1963, pp. 196–200 (pp. 73–6).

4.9 O. Roberts, *Expect a Miracle: My Life and Ministry. Oral Roberts, an Autobiography*, London, Nelson, 1995, pp. 254–61 (pp. 77–80).

4.10 J. Wimber with K. Springer, *Power Healing,* London, Hodder and Stoughton, 1985, pp. 84–6 (pp. 81–2).

5.9 Peter Hocken, *The Glory and the Shame*, Guildford, Eagle Publishing, 1994, pp. 46–50, abridged (pp. 113–15).

5.10 T. B. Barratt, *In The Days of the Latter Rain*, London, Elim Publishing House, 1928, pp. 108–9, 112–14, abridged (pp. 116–17).

5.11 Mike Bickle with Michael Sullivant, *Growing in the Prophetic*, Florida, Strang Publications, 1996, pp. 178–81 (pp. 118–20).

8.1 *The Constitution of the Apostolic Church UK*, 3rd edn revised, originally published in 1937, abridged (pp. 168–70).

8.2 Arthur Wallis, 'Apostles Today? Why Not?', *Restoration*, November–December 1981, pp. 2–5, abridged (pp. 171–4).

8.3 Larry Christenson, 'The Church: An Ordered Body', in *Welcome, Holy Spirit*, Minneapolis, Augsburg, 1987, pp. 309–12, abridged (pp. 174–7).

8.4 Derek Prince, *Discipleship, Shepherding, Commitment*, Fort Lauderdale, Derek Prince, 1976, pp. 11–15 (pp. 177–9).

8.5 David Tomlinson, 'Loyalty: Covenant Relationship', *Restoration*, March–April 1978, p. 27 (pp. 180–1).

8.6 Mike Bickle with Michael Sullivant, *Growing in the Prophetic*, Eastbourne, Kingsway Publications, 1995, pp. 160–7, abridged (pp. 181–4).

8.7 Larry Christenson, 'The Church: A Servant', in *Welcome, Holy Spirit*, Minneapolis, Augsburg, 1987, pp. 334–9, abridged (pp. 184–7).

Community

20.2 Mother of God Community, Gaithersburg http://www.motherof god.org/ (2003) (pp. 287–8).

20.3 Cardinal Suenens, 'An Evaluation of the Charismatic Movement', *Renewal* 76, 1978, pp. 24, 25 (pp. 288–90).

Megachurches

21.1 Colin Dye, 'Kensington Temple: London City Church', http://www.kt.org/g12/london.php (2004) (pp. 291–3).

Questions to think about

1 Reflect on healing as (i) a physical event and (ii) an event affecting the whole of a person – body and mind, past and future, as an individual and as someone in relationship with others. Does it make sense to expect healing in the light of the kind of God the Bible shows God to be?

2 If the church is a place where the Holy Spirit is at work, what kind of place would we expect the church to be?

3 Can we reasonably think of the church as pointing towards the end of history? Can we think reasonably of the world ending?

Further reading

Alexander, K. E. (2006), *Pentecostal Healing: Models in Theology and Practice*, Blandford Forum, Deo.

Jacobsen, D. (ed.) (2006), *A Reader in Pentecostal Theology: Voices from the First Generation*, Bloomington, IN, Indiana University Press.

Kärkkäinen, V.-M. (2002), *Towards a Pneumatological Theology*, Lanham, MD, University Press of America.

Kay, W. K. and Dyer, A. E. (2004), *A Reader in Pentecostal and Charismatic Studies*, London, SCM Press.

Macchia, F. D. (2006), *Baptized in the Spirit: A Global Pentecostal Theology*, Grand Rapids, MI, Zondervan.

Reed, D. A. (2008), *'In Jesus' Name': The History and Beliefs of Oneness Pentecostals*, Blandford Forum, Deo.

Thomas, J. C. (1998), *The Devil, Disease and Deliverance: Origins of Illness*, Sheffield, Sheffield Academic Press.

Yong, A. (2005), *The Spirit Poured Out on All Flesh*, Grand Rapids, MI, Baker Academic.

The *Journal of Pentecostal Theology*, which is published by Brill and goes back to 1992, is a must-read for anyone who wants to explore the best contemporary debates in Pentecostal theology. See www.brill.nl

The journal *Pneuma*, published by Brill, goes back to 1979 and contains a wide range of articles on all aspects of Pentecostal scholarship including theology. See www.brill.nl/pneu

The New International Dictionary of Pentecostal and Charismatic Movements, Grand Rapids, MI, Zondervan, edited by S. M. Burgess and E. van der Maas in 2002, contains a wealth of original articles on Pentecostal theology.

13

Theology 3

Introduction

As Pentecostalism has grown during the course of a century, it has diversified. The beginnings of Pentecostalism were simple and practical. Over time, Pentecostal denominations came into existence and then Bible schools, colleges and even universities were built. Many of these educational institutions sprang up in the West initially, but, as Pentecostalism has been established in almost every part of the world, these institutions have been planted in many cultures so that there are now notable Pentecostal institutions in Asia, Africa and Latin America. By and large, Pentecostal scholars read each other's writings and meet at international conferences. As a consequence, there is a layer of Pentecostal scholarship that is interdenominational and international and which is quite separate from Pentecostalism as it is practised by ordinary members of Pentecostal congregations. There are three main groups of Pentecostals who travel widely and have an overview of the movement to which they belong. These are denominational officials, itinerant preachers belonging to independent ministries loosely affiliated with several denominations, and academics. The group that we are concerned with in this chapter is Pentecostal academics, some of whom are working in Bible colleges and focus on the training of ministers, as well as those who work in universities or other higher education institutions and interact with academics from other backgrounds in other parts of the world. Pentecostal biblical scholars will meet biblical scholars from other denominations and other countries. Pentecostal systematic theologians will do the same. The result of this is that Pentecostal theology as a discipline, with its own methods, conventions and history, may be detached from church life. I say 'may be' because Pentecostal theologians will also attempt to ground their work within the life of the worshipping community and not simply within the life of the academic community; but there is a constant tension between the demands of the academy and the needs of the church, and theologians have to be careful to attend to each.

We can put this in a different way by saying that there is a distinction between the academy and the church. The academy has a life of its own and relates to national culture. The academy (by which we mean the collection of higher education institutions of each country) routinely comments on the implications of government policy, educational theory, law, scientific advance, ethical dilemmas, and in a host of other ways drives the intellectual life of a nation. The academy is the place of scientific research, new ideas, invention and learning, and stands quite separate from the church. The relationship between the academy and the church goes back into the roots of Christian civilization but, for our purposes, we need to notice that the relationship between Pentecostal churches and the academy is containable within the last hundred years. At the beginning, at Azusa Street, Mukti and the Korean revivals, there was no relationship at all between Pentecostalism and academy. Pentecostalism was a cultural phenomenon belonging to people who had in almost every case never enjoyed university education or high culture. As the century progressed, however, Pentecostals began to interact with the academy and even to form academies of their own – these were the Bible schools and later the universities that they founded – and there inevitably came to be dialogue between the academy and the Pentecostal churches. We could say that the academy and the church were rival centres of authority. Sometimes the Pentecostal churches, either the pastors or the denominational leaders, would criticize their own educational institutions for being 'out of touch' or obsessed with irrelevant impracticalities. At other times the academy might criticize the churches for embracing unthinkingly ideas that had no place in Pentecostalism.

For this reason we will step back from the historically based theology of the previous two chapters and attempt a more general reflection on Pentecostal theology as a whole, whether it comes from the academy or from the church. It will be convenient to divide the material into the academic and the popular.

Academic perspectives

We look first at the starting points for Pentecostal theology, since these are rationally prior to anything else, and then move on to current concerns in the field.

Starting points for Pentecostal theology

When it turns its powers of analysis upon starting points for Pentecostal theology, the academy can begin by examining the historically established doctrines of Pentecostalism. In this book we have followed this line (Chapters 2 and 3) to see how Pentecostal theology came to be configured at the beginning of the twentieth century. As we shall see in the next section, Pentecostal theology of this kind is a series of interconnected themes. Yet, if we ask a more fundamental question about Pentecostal theology and try to probe not only how it actually came into existence but the conditions for its existence, we shall come to different answers. When we do this we look at Pentecostal theology theoretically by detaching it from its historical moorings and consider it as abstractly as we can.

Here the starting point for Pentecostal theology may be seen as the distinctive experience of the baptism in the Holy Spirit.[1] This is the point of difference between Pentecostal Christians and non-Pentecostal Christians, especially if we insist that baptism in the Holy Spirit is accompanied by speaking with other tongues. Although non-Pentecostal Christians would claim an encounter with God in prayer or by sacraments, Pentecostals would characteristically insist that a greater revelation of God is available through the life-changing impact of Pentecostal baptism.

When we come to construct a Pentecostal theology, this experience can be analysed into its component parts and related to biblical, historical or systematic theology. The Pentecostal baptism is primarily an experience of the Holy Spirit and can be analysed by reference to the wider work of the Holy Spirit in the individual, the church and the world. Equally the Holy Spirit is related to Christ and so the baptism is also an experience of Christ in some way that needs to be clarified and understood. At the same time, Spirit baptism is related to the church and the function of Christians within the church. All these different components can be unpacked and understood either separately or in conjunction. Yet if we are looking at this experience in order to work out what a distinctive Pentecostal theology is, then beginning with experience may prove unsatisfactory. Dale Coulter, in a perceptive and important article, shows that the experience of baptism in the Spirit, if enjoyed by a Baptist, Methodist or Roman Catholic, does not immediately turn them into a Pentecostal.[2] As he asks:

> if one begins with only an experience of the Spirit, theologically what separates a Pentecostal who happens to be part of the classical Pentecostal denomination from a non-Pentecostal – charismatic or otherwise – who does not happen to be part of that same denomination?[3]

His pointed question is addressed to Terry Cross (and perhaps Simon Chan) who may be in danger of suggesting that only the distinctive Pentecostal experience of God results in a distinctive Pentecostal theology.[4]

---

1 Though it would also be possible to start from the doctrine and experience of healing and then build across to Spirit-baptism.

2 Dale M. Coulter (2001), 'What Meaneth This? Pentecostals and Theological Inquiry, *Journal of Pentecostal Theology* 10.1, 38–64.

3 Coulter, 'What Meaneth This?', 43.

4 Referring to Simon Chan (2000), *Pentecostal Theology and the Christian Spiritual Tradition*, Sheffield, Sheffield Academic Press, and to Terry Cross, *The Church: A People of God's Presence* (forthcoming).

While the Pentecostal baptism does indeed hold together thought and emotion and, in theological terms, the transcendence and immanence of God, it does not, in his view, provide sufficient leverage to allow for the construction of complete Pentecostal theology.

An alternative approach by Amos Yong attempts to explore Pentecostal experience of the Spirit communally.[5] In Coulter's words, 'Yong proposes to examine what the collective experience of Pentecostal community tells us about Pentecostal distinctives.'[6] This experience of the Spirit is examined through a phenomenological analysis of rituals which leads to what Yong describes as the 'pneumatological imagination'. One of the elements of this imagination is to call into question the 'duality between the material and the non-material worlds'. In other words, Pentecostals and charismatics inhabit a world that may not conform to the conventional Cartesian distinction between subject and object or observer and external world. This results in an analysis of the world views of Pentecostals and charismatics and shows that normal post-Enlightenment categories do not operate in the same way for them. For instance, Pentecostals and charismatics may believe that spiritual causes produce material effects, whereas many post-Enlightenment individuals would rule out the possibility of non-material causes; they would not believe that angels could move stones in front of empty tombs. Yet, and this is Coulter's analysis, world views do not take us any closer to the core of Pentecostal theology.

His own proposal is that what distinguishes the theological core of Pentecostals from the theological core of other Christian groups is *'not any individual doctrine per se but the entirety of those doctrines and their interaction with one another'*.[7] This is an entirely reasonable suggestion because it enables us to see how Pentecostal Christians are part of the historic vision of the church and of the church today. It is not that Pentecostals hold different beliefs from others but that they configure these beliefs to produce a new normative pattern. Indeed, the interaction between Scripture, revelation and experience of the Spirit leads Pentecostals into new territory. It allows them to take the view that they are being 'led by the Spirit' (Rom. 8.14) into new understandings. In a more radical continuation of this motion, it is possible to argue that Pentecostals could and should take a view of the canonical Scriptures that would distinguish them very sharply from other evangelical Christians. Evangelicals hold fast to the Scriptures as the final and complete revelation of the will and purpose of God which cannot be added to or altered. But, in a more radical suggestion, it is arguable that Pentecostals may listen to the voice of the Spirit today and find ways to interpret Scripture that have been

---

5 A. Yong (2000), *Discerning the Spirit(s)*, Sheffield, Continuum.
6 Coulter, 'What Meaneth This?', 47.
7 Coulter, 'What Meaneth This?', 56.

hitherto avoided or unknown. So Pentecostals may construct a theology that is dependent upon a dynamic revelation which provokes imaginative interpretations of Scripture. This is in line with a proposal made some years before by J. K. A. Smith who had condemned 'textualism' as the hallmark of evangelicalism and argued for its replacement by listening to the voice of the Holy Spirit.[8]

There is also another starting or 'foundational' (as he calls it) point for Pentecostal theology. Yong turns to the work of the Roman Catholic charismatic Donald Gelpi.[9] Gelpi's writings have drawn on the philosophical thought of three writers whose ideas he has brought together into a new synthesis. Taking the work of C. S. Peirce (1839–1914), who founded American pragmatism as well as elements of a scientific method, Josiah Royce (1855–1916), who advocated absolute idealism,[10] and A. N. Whitehead (1861–1947), whose 'process theology' was formulated because of an inability of the scientific process to deal with the universe as a whole, Gelpi explores many theological topics. For instance, he argues that human beings can experience grace because reality consists of 'three irreducible types of experiential feelings which Peirce calls qualities'.[11] So far it has to be said that Pentecostals have not taken up these ideas with any vigour. Yet, undoubtedly Pentecostals will attempt to bring their insights to bear in numerous intellectual realms as the twenty-first century progresses.[12] Naive Biblicism or an appeal to private experience will not cut ice with convinced secularists and only a sophisticated philosophical apparatus can be expected to rebut rationalistic dismissals. Gelpi's intellectual achievements may prove invaluable in years to come.

Pentecostal systematics

An original way of systematizing Pentecostal theology is to be found in Stephen J. Land's *Pentecostal Spirituality: A Passion for the Kingdom*.[13] Land gives attention to the mutual interaction between orthodoxy (right belief), orthopraxy (right practice) and orthopathy (right affection). By

8 J. K. A. Smith (1997), 'The Closing of the Book: Pentecostals, Evangelicals and the Sacred Writings', *Journal of Pentecostal Theology* 11, 49–71.

9 A. Yong (2002), 'In Search of Foundations: The Oeuvre of Donald L. Gelpi, SJ, and its Significance for Pentecostal Theology and Philosophy', *Journal of Pentecostal Theology* 11.1, 3–26.

10 'The metaphysical view (also maintained by G. W. F. Hegel and F. H. Bradley) that all aspects of reality, including those we experience as disconnected or contradictory, are ultimately unified in the thought of a single all-encompassing consciousness.' http://plato.stanford.edu/entries/royce/ (accessed 29.11.08).

11 Yong, 'In Search of', 15.

12 For instance, philosophy in J. K. A. Smith (2003), 'Advice to Pentecostal Philosophers', *Journal of Pentecostal Theology* 11.2, 235–47.

13 Published in 1993 in Sheffield by Sheffield Academic Press.

these terms he means to show how belief, praxis and affection may all be integrated within Pentecostalism. What is interesting about his proposal is that he includes affection within the realm of the theological discourse. He wishes to show how praise, joy and thanksgiving, which are themes of much Pentecostal testimony, can be found within Pentecostal tradition and he takes time to analyse Pentecostal songs of worship to show how deeply these affections run within Pentecostal churches. The subtitle of his book, 'a passion for the kingdom', demonstrates that these affections drive motivation and are not merely feeling-drenched reactions to spiritual experiences. Pentecostals are those who are waiting for the return of Christ, and, in an illuminating phrase, 'theology, for Pentecostals, is a discerning reflection by the eschatological missionary community upon lived reality'.[14]

In a complicated and schematic argument Land discerns a profound integration between the theological logic in the roles of Christ (as saviour, sanctifier and Spirit baptizer) and the blessings of righteousness, peace and joy enjoyed by the redeemed community, and these are held together against a background of a knowledge of God as righteous, loving and powerful.[15] In a final section Land pushes forward to examine how Pentecostal spirituality can be re-visioned by what he calls 'the eschatological Trinity', that is, the work of the Godhead in bringing about the consummation of the kingdom of God.

John Christopher Thomas, in a presidential address to the Society for Pentecostal Studies in 1998, mapped out a possible programme for Pentecostal theology in the twenty-first century.[16] He argued that this kind of theology would:

- stem from the Pentecostal community (rather than isolated individual scholars)
- integrate reason and emotion, or, in his words, 'head and heart'
- dialogue with the traditions outside Pentecostalism
- bear the marks of accountability (to the church and to other scholars)
- be contextualized (resulting in cultural diversity) and
- be confessional (in that it would be avowedly Pentecostal).

In giving examples of the way that this kind of theology might work he drew attention to the fivefold gospel of Jesus as (1) Saviour, (2) Sanctifier, (3) Baptizer in the Holy Ghost, (4) Healer and (5) Coming King.[17] This

---

14 Land, *Pentecostal Spirituality*, p. 192.

15 Land, *Pentecostal Spirituality*, p. 125.

16 John Christopher Thomas (1998), 'Pentecostal Theology in the Twenty-First Century', *Pneuma* 20.1, 3–19.

17 Thomas gives an initial capital to each of these roles as I have done here. Pente-

fivefold delineation of the gospel demonstrates how Pentecostalism is both similar to and dissimilar from other groups within Christianity: 'To mention but two examples, when the fivefold gospel paradigm is used as the main point of reference, the near kinship to the holiness tradition is obvious, as is the fundamental difference with many of those within the evangelical tradition.'[18]

The fivefold gospel is the hub of a systematic theological approach to Pentecostalism.[19] It is based on the work and role of Jesus Christ. Pentecostalism does not begin with proofs for the existence of God or a consideration of God as Creator. Nor does it start in 'holy history' with the historic pilgrimage of the church. Rather, each aspect of the fivefold gospel can be related to the progress of an individual from a state outside the church to a state inside the church, and then, once inside the church, to being made holy and empowered in preparation for a new role preparing the way for the return of Christ. The fivefold gospel parallels standard evangelicalism with its stress upon Jesus as saviour while being quite distinct in highlighting the role of Jesus as a baptizer in the Spirit. Equally, the role of Jesus as healer is distinct, while, as Thomas says, the role of Jesus as the sanctifier, the one who makes the Christian holy, parallels that same function within the Wesleyan holiness tradition.

Implicit within his address, and at times explicitly stated, Thomas contends for a *constructive* theology. This is a theology that is not merely based on critical examination of the biblical text and Christian tradition using the standard tools of scholarship, but rather a theology that *imaginatively* explores how Christian tradition, and specifically Pentecostal tradition, can fulfil the purposes of God.

A third scheme for presenting Pentecostal theology systematically has been advanced by the Korean pastor Yonggi Cho whose enormous prestige is based on the huge size of Yoido Full Gospel Church and its associated university that he has helped to build in Seoul, South Korea.[20] Cho's extraordinary ministry began in the period after the Korean War (1950–53) when Seoul was in a wretched condition and the lives of South Koreans were poverty-stricken. Over a period of about 50 years this church has grown until it became the largest congregation in the world.

---

costals commonly do this to indicate how closely the roles are associated with Christ himself.

18 Thomas, 'Theology', 17.

19 Mark Cartledge has shown that the fivefold pattern also applies to early British Pentecostalism as found in the pages of *Confidence*. See M. J. Cartledge (2008), 'The Early Pentecostal Theology of *Confidence* Magazine (1908–1926): A Version of the Five-Fold Gospel?', *Journal of the European Pentecostal Theological Association* 28.2, 117–30.

20 An examination of Cho's work is given in Wonsuk Ma, William W. Menzies and H.-S. Bae (eds), *David Yongghi Cho: A Close Look at this Theology and Ministry*, Baguio, APTS Press.

Cho has a slightly different analysis of the fivefold gospel. In his teaching the gospel comprises:

• rebirth (salvation or regeneration)
• fullness of the Holy Spirit
• divine healing
• blessing
• kingdom of heaven and second coming.

The fourth aspect is centred on a text in Galatians and the words, 'He [God] redeemed us in order that the blessing given to Abraham might come to the Gentiles through Christ Jesus, so that by faith we might receive the promise of the Spirit' (Gal. 3.14). This provision is seen as the answer to 'the problems of poverty and the curse'.

In addition to this, Cho speaks of the threefold blessing on Christians. This is:

• spiritual blessing (restoring a fresh relationship between human beings and God)
• environmental blessing (of our circumstances)
• physical blessing of health.

Here Pentecostal theology is directed at the ability of God to meet basic human needs.[21] At the beginning of his ministry when he was preaching to malnourished and desperately poor Koreans, Cho's message was that God can make a difference to our lives here and now. Christianity, in this preaching, was not 'pie in the sky when you die' but the promise of a better life, through a living relationship with Christ in the power of the Holy Spirit, now. This promise applied regardless of the fact that Koreans were struggling to survive in their war-damaged city. God could bring apparent impossibilities into existence; the eye of faith could see beyond immediate circumstances to a more prosperous future. This theology is taught in both the university and seminary linked with Cho's congregation.

The fourth and final starting point for a systematic Pentecostal theology has been drawn out by Terry Cross in an address to the 2007 meeting of the Society for Pentecostal Studies. After considering the fragmentation of the intellectual landscape through postmodernism,[22] Cross has argued

---

21 This account is taken from David Yonggi Cho (1997), *A Bible Study for New Christians*, Seoul, Seoul Logos.

22 In an earlier dissection of the damage that might have been done to systematics by the incursions of postmodernism, Amos Yong (1998), 'Whither Systematic Theology? A Systematician Chimes in on a Scandalous Conversation', *Pneuma* 20.1, 85–93, defends the possibility of systematics and casts it, among other things, as an enterprise that correlates diverse narratives.

that the only proper starting point for such a theology is reflection on the Trinity because

> all aspects of life in the Spirit – of salvation, sanctification, Spirit baptism, healing, experience of the age to come in this present age – can be 'read' through the prism of the triune God. The nature of God (triune, societal, relational) becomes the paradigm for theological reflection for every possible doctrine.[23]

The fifth and final starting point for systematic Pentecostal theology has been offered by Keith Warrington who begins with the notion of 'encounter ... of a radical experience of the Spirit' that is 'self-authenticating' and cannot be 'circumscribed by the Bible', so that God can 'radiate his presence in fresh ways'.[24] In practice Warrington works through what Pentecostals believe about God, the church, the Bible, ethics, mission, healing, exorcism, suffering and eschatology.

If the starting points of Thomas, Land and Cho carry echoes of the preaching of Pentecostal pastors, this is because even academic Pentecostal theology begins in church and in the proclamations of the pulpit. A fully fledged, multi-volume systematic theology of Pentecostalism could take the elements of the fivefold gospel (or fourfold if sanctification is removed as a separate item) and start to weave them into a coherent discourse covering the whole of Christian theology.[25] If Cross is right, however, this scheme will need to be expanded so as to draw more explicitly on the rich and extensive resources of trinitarian theology. No one has yet accomplished that task.[26] If Warrington is correct, then we can expect a contextualized theology growing out of the praxis of Pentecostal churches.

---

23 Terry Cross (2007), 'Can there be a Pentecostal Systematic Theology? An Essay on Theological Method in a Postmodern World', presented at the 30th Annual Meeting of the Society for Pentecostal Studies, Lee University, Cleveland, TN.

24 Keith Warrington (2008), *Pentecostal Theology*, London, T & T Clark, pp. 20–4.

25 David Bundy (1993), 'The Genre of Systematic Theology in Pentecostalism', *Pneuma* 15, 89–107, provides a bibliographical overview of Pentecostal systematic theologies.

26 Although E. S. Williams (1885–1980), an early Assemblies of God General Superintendent, wrote three volumes entitled *Systematic Theology*, their coverage is relatively limited. J. Rodman Williams (1988), *Systematic Theology*, Grand Rapids, MI, Zondervan, gives systematic theology from a renewal perspective. S. M. Horton (ed.) (1995), *Systematic Theology*, Springfield, MO, Logion, offers a multi-authored text with chapters on topics often included in systematics. Wayne Grudem (1999), *Systematic Theology*, Leicester, InterVarsity Press, is written by a charismatic for an evangelical publishing house but nevertheless provides a fine discussion of spiritual gifts in addition to its other concerns.

Pentecostal ecumenics[27]

In a previous chapter we have referred to the Pentecostal–Roman Catholic dialogue and to dialogue between Trinitarian Pentecostals and Oneness Pentecostals. A dialogue between Pentecostals and the World Alliance of Reformed Churches started in 1995, and another between Pentecostals and the World Council of Churches (WCC) through its Joint Consultative Group authorized at the Harare assembly in 1998. A new dialogue was established with members from the Lutheran World Federation in 2005.[28] Dialogue is a form of ecumenical engagement designed to clear away misunderstandings, to reaffirm common ground and to make plausible collaborative efforts between hitherto disparate Christian groups. Dialogue involves sitting around a table talking. It is essentially intellectual rather than practical. If it is successful, dialogue will eventually result in changes of attitude and practice within the dialogue partners but this is not guaranteed since the responsibility for changing practice lies with ecclesiastical leaders who usually refrain from participating in face-to-face talks.

For Christians, the unity of the church is of great importance because in John 17 Jesus prayed 'that they may be one'. It is also vital because the great historic chasms between Orthodoxy and Catholicism (in the Great Schism of 1054) and between Catholicism and Protestantism (as a result of the Reformation from about 1523 onwards) have given rise to political animosities that have, in their worst manifestations, stood behind armed conflict (as in the Thirty Years War in Germany, 1618–48). Thinking Christians applaud any effort to bring churches together but, equally, most Christians recognize that the unification of churches is far more than any rebranding of buildings or the issuing of ambiguous joint statements by people in ceremonial robes. Many Pentecostals would argue that one of the gifts of the Pentecostal movement to the whole church is an emphasis on the experience of the Holy Spirit coupled with the freedom in worship that such an experience brings. The ecumenicism of the Spirit appears to be spontaneous, enjoyable and centred on Christ, whereas the ecumenicism of painstaking committee work appears to move the churches forward only an inch at a time.

Irrespective of their concerns about committee-led and institutionally shaped forms of ecumenical activity, Pentecostals have attempted to work out ways to allow greater co-operation between the churches. The forum for such activity is the World Council of Churches, which con-

---

27 The English word 'ecumenical' has roots in the Greek *oikos* or house and, by extension, its semantic range is stretched to the inhabited world, that is, where we live. The ecumenical movement is concerned with promoting Christian unity.

28 http://www.oikoumene.org/en/member-churches/church-families/pentecostal-churches.html (accessed 3.12.08).

vened its first meeting in Amsterdam in 1948 and holds meetings roughly every seven years to discuss matters of common interest. As Donald Gee, a British Pentecostal, pointed out, for all their laborious conferring the Amsterdam delegates (with 60 typewriters generating 20 tons of paper) reached no nearer to a Pentecostal outpouring than any other big committee working through a heavily loaded agenda.[29] Additionally, the World Council of Churches has always been hampered by the failure of the Roman Catholic Church to join. Logically enough, the Roman Catholic Church, which officially takes the view that it is the 'true' church, believes that other churches should join it rather than it should join on an equal basis with other churches.[30] For many years Pentecostals, probably foolishly, avoided the World Council of Churches with the result that the Council became a more theologically liberal body than Pentecostals wanted.[31] However, when the first Pentecostal churches began to join, as some of the Latin American Pentecostal churches did in 1961, the situation changed.[32] By and large, Pentecostal church leaders still do not respond enthusiastically to invitations from the World Council of Churches but Pentecostal theologians now find themselves at least welcomed and interested in the agenda under discussion.

In a discussion of Pentecostal involvement in ecumenism, Yong starts by examining the ecumenical dimensions of the famous day of Pentecost when the Holy Spirit fell and Peter preached the gospel at the start of the church era.[33] People drawn from all over the Roman Empire were among the 3,000 converts. Nearly all of these people were Jews; nevertheless, they came to Jerusalem from provinces hundreds of miles apart and they comprised a sample of what would become a worldwide church. Only a few years afterwards Gentiles were added to their numbers with the result that there was ecumenical unity-in-diversity growing out of those early Pentecostal outpourings.[34]

In the last century, ecumenical tradition was 'more about affirming differences than it was about making churches the world over fit into one mould'.[35] Consequently, Yong argues that Pentecostals have nothing to

---

29 *Pentecost* 6. This was a journal edited by Gee, at the request of the World Conference of Pentecostal Churches, from 1947 until his death in 1966.

30 The Roman Catholic Church has never been a member of the World Council of Churches but does participate in various ways. See http://www.oikoumene.org/en/member-churches/church-families/the-catholic-church.html (accessed 3.12.08).

31 C. M. Robeck (1997), 'The Assemblies of God and Ecumenical Cooperation: 1920–1965', in Wonsuk Ma and Robert P. Menzies (eds), *Pentecostalism in Context: Essays in Honour of William W. Menzies*, Sheffield, Sheffield Academic Press.

32 http://www.pctii.org/news/wcc-news.html (accessed 3.12.08).

33 Amos Yong (2005), *The Spirit Poured Out on All Flesh*, Grand Rapids, MI, Baker Academic. See Acts 2.

34 Acts 10, when Peter visits the household of Cornelius.

35 Yong, *The Spirit Poured Out*, p. 174.

fear from the ecumenical movement because its frequent aim is to affirm their identities while expecting them to affirm the identities of others. In any case, and looking at Pentecostalism from another angle, we can say that it is well suited to respecting a variety of Christian traditions because of its own history. Pentecostalism grew out of Wesleyan, holiness, Zionist and other doctrinal stances, and it can be seen as a fresh expression of Christian unity made by melting together metals hewn from the rocks of many traditions. The Azusa Street revival itself illustrates this reality: people came from all over the world to receive their spiritual experience and, while they were on their knees together, they were united in a great but disorganized event. Its visitors were struck by the racial diversity in the revival. Black, white and Hispanic were all present and race was ignored. Such harmony overturned established social conventions and, in the minds of the revivalists, pointed to the church in heaven worshipping from every tribe and language and nation (Rev. 5.9). Later, and sadly, Pentecostalism divided along racial lines with some denominations becoming almost entirely white and others almost entirely black. But for those first few years there was unity, and Pentecostalism can at least point to the temporary fulfilment of an ecumenical ideal, an ideal that carried with it an implication for social justice. For, where the colour of a person's skin was ignored, grounds for discrimination were removed. And, where discrimination was removed, social justice could flourish.

Pentecostals and other religions

In the immediate post-Azusa Street era Pentecostals travelled far and wide in missionary work. They inevitably crossed into new cultures and countries and confronted what were then exotic new religions. Tony Richie has argued that this early phase of Pentecostalism was infused with optimism and that at least one denominational leader, J. H. King, took the benign view that 'not all non-Christian religions are entirely bereft of true divine presence'.[36] This conviction arose out of considering the stories of Hindus and Mongolians who had become Christians. The seeds of their Christian faith had been planted in their pre-Christian days. In theological terms the crucial issue for Christians concerns the scope of the forgiveness available through Christ's death. If it is argued that Christ suffered for the sins of the whole world and offered atonement for all the sins of everyone who has ever been born, then it may also be arguable that non-Christians benefit from this sacrifice. J. H. King certainly believed that the atonement was universally necessary for salvation while drawing a distinction between the objective and subjective aspects of the

---

36 Tony Richie (2006), 'Azusa-Era Optimism: Bishop J. H. King's Pentecostal Theology of Religions as a Possible Paradigm for Today', *Journal of Pentecostal Theology* 14.2, 247–60.

cross. So, while King believed that infants who die go to heaven because the benefits of the atonement cover their sin, he also extended this argument to the original sin of all non-Christians.

This interpretation of King's theology has been contested by other scholars who argue that, although there may be elements in his belief that include non-Christians, the main thrust of his belief is no different from that of other classical Pentecostals.[37] In other words, it is an overstatement to put King forward as a champion of theological inclusivism. Whether or not this is so, later Pentecostals and charismatics certainly faced up to the competing claims and world views of major religions.[38]

In 1996 Clark Pinnock, writing as a charismatic Christian, confronted the thorny theological problem of who is going to heaven. 'Does God love the whole world or not?'[39] He proposes that the particularity of the gospel is focused in Christ, the only mediator between God and humanity, while the Spirit, present everywhere, upholds the universality of God's action. 'Spirit is not confined to the church but is present everywhere, giving life and creating community ... the Spirit is in a position to offer grace to every person.'[40] This division between the work of the Son and the Spirit may be ripe for further theological development but, in any case, Pentecostals would agree that the Spirit is at work all over the world in all situations and circumstances. By their apprehension of the powerful function of the Spirit, Pentecostals have catapulted themselves into the most pressing theological debate of the twenty-first century.

Where does the wind of the Spirit blow? Yong noted three basic positions regarding religions: exclusivism, inclusivism and pluralism.[41] Exclusivists hold that salvation is only available through Jesus Christ and that those who have never heard the gospel are eternally lost, whatever their religious disposition. Inclusivists hold that salvation is founded upon the person and work of Christ and that its benefits have been made universally available through the revelation of God in creation, or by prevenient grace or by the activity of the Holy Spirit. Pluralists, who usually represent the liberal face of the major religious traditions, hold that all the main religions offer a different path to ultimate reality or God.

---

37 Tony G. Moon (2007), 'J. H. King's Theology of Religions: "Magnanimous Optimism"?', *Journal of Pentecostal Theology* 16.1, 112–32.

38 Tony Richie has continued to raise the subject within the Society for Pentecostal Studies. See Tony Richie (2006), 'God's Fairness to People of All Faiths: A Respectful Proposal for Discussion Regarding World Religions', *Pneuma* 26.1, 105–19.

39 Clark H. Pinnock (1996), *Flame of Love*, Downers Grove, IL, InterVarsity Press, p. 192.

40 Pinnock, *Flame*, p. 192.

41 Amos Yong (1999), '"Not Knowing Where the Wind Blows ..." On Envisioning a Pentecostal-Charismatic Theology of Religions', *Journal of Pentecostal Theology* 14, April, 81–112.

In an extensive and thoughtful discussion Yong argues that Pentecostals will need to work out a theology of religions by taking note of the resources of empirical theology. They will need to examine religions carefully to see where phenomenological similarities exist and they will need to create adequate descriptive categories to allow theological and doctrinal comparisons. Beyond this is the matter of truth. At this point, and immediately, we pass into philosophical territory. According to Yong, most Pentecostals have been influenced by Scottish common-sense philosophy that results in foundationalism. In short, this is the view that knowledge is built up from sense perceptions that are the foundation of the great superstructure that constitutes what we know. He argues that this epistemology is being challenged by the global expansion of the Pentecostal and charismatic movements and by postmodern critique of foundationalist assumptions. Consequently, a search for truth among religiously diverse groups will depend upon inter-religious dialogue (presumably of a kind that includes epistemology as well as theology). Fresh agreements must be hammered out between opposing religions, but this does not prevent Pentecostals continuing to witness to the reality of their own story.[42]

Pentecostalism and Christology

We can approach this topic by asking the old theological question, 'Was it not possible for Christ to sin or was it possible for Christ not to sin?' The issue is to do with the exact human nature of Jesus.[43] If it is argued that Jesus became human and was tempted exactly as we are and yet remained without sin so that he could be a perfect sacrifice for sin, then we are likely to wonder exactly what sort of human nature Jesus had. The question arises in an acute form because, if Jesus is God, it is impossible for him to sin since, by definition, sin is an offence against God. So we are left with the theological conundrum that Jesus, in order to redeem humanity, must be exactly like humanity yet, equally, in order to redeem humanity, he must be quite unlike us with regard to his perfection. This theological puzzle was gradually resolved by the church in the great early ecumenical councils. The understanding of Christ's life in the hands of some of the earliest theologians, before the ecumenical councils

---

42 The encounter between Christianity and religions at the non-academic level is expressed most sharply in countries like Nigeria, where Pentecostals and Muslims both attempt to convert the other.

43 These four states, which are derived from Scripture, correspond to the four states of humanity in relation to sin enumerated by Augustine of Hippo: (a) able to sin, able not to sin (*posse peccare, posse non peccare*); (b) not able not to sin (*non posse non peccare*); (c) able not to sin (*posse non peccare*); and (d) unable to sin (*non posse peccare*). http://www.monergism.com/thethreshold/articles/onsite/four-fold.html

had deliberated, saw Jesus Christ as the man anointed by the Holy Spirit. In other words, questions about the precise nature of Christ's humanity were not asked. Rather, Christ was the Messiah, or man anointed by God with an unrestrained measure of the Holy Spirit. Subsequent theological reflection, particularly drawing on the Gospel of John, emphasized that Jesus is the *Logos*, or Word. 'In the beginning was the Word and the Word was with God and the Word was God' (John 1.1), and this is how his divinity should be understood.

Recent understandings of the person of Christ have led to discussion of Spirit Christology.[44] In a precise account Del Colle has stated:

> Rather than accounting for the incarnation as the assumption of a human nature by a pre-existent divine person (Son/*logos*) this view attempts to account for the mediating activity of Jesus as a human being inspired by God whose agency is best described as Spirit.[45]

Although Spirit Christology has emerged within Pentecostal theology, it did not start there. Yet it is certainly important to acknowledge that theologizing about the person of Christ goes a long way back into Protestant thought. As Habets pointed out, the Puritan John Owen (1616–83) developed an understanding of Christ as the God-Man who was as human as we are though conscious of God through the agency of the Holy Spirit, as we may be.[46] Two centuries later Edward Irving (1792–1834) gave us a theology of Christ as the Son of God who carried out his ministry and performed miracles through the operation of the Holy Spirit rather than through the indwelling power of the *logos*. So, Jesus was like us and, in Irving's account, Jesus took on himself sinful human flesh even if he himself did not sin. In this respect Jesus was just like us but possessed the ability, through the operation of the Holy Spirit, not to sin. We have here a very human Jesus, one who is no longer an impassive icon or untouchable stained-glass picture, but the man who received the Spirit and then, after his ascension, poured this gift out upon the church and, ultimately, the human race.

Pentecostal theologians are beginning to grapple with theological issues raised by Spirit Christology but they are doing so with care. As Del Colle goes on, 'The primary issue is how to acknowledge the pneumatological

---

44 The first on the contemporary scene was Harold D. Hunter (1983), 'Spirit Christology: Dilemma and Promise', *Heythrop Journal* 24.2 and 24.3; Harold D. Hunter (1983), *Spirit Baptism: A Pentecostal Alternative*, Lanham, University Press of America.

45 Ralph Del Colle (1993), 'Spirit-Christology: Dogmatic Foundations for Pentecostal-Charismatic Spirituality', *Journal of Pentecostal Theology* 3, 91–112.

46 Myk Habets (2003), 'Spirit Christology: Seeing in Stereo', *Journal of Pentecostal Theology* 11.2, 199–234.

dimension of Christology without utilising it to displace logos-Christologies and their Trinitarian outcome.'

Edward Irving and the nature of Christ

The point at issue is simply this; whether Christ's flesh had the grace of sinlessness and incorruption from its proper nature, or from the indwelling of the Holy Ghost. I say the latter. I assert, that in its proper nature it was as the flesh of his mother, but, by virtue of the Holy Ghost's quickening and inhabiting of it, it was preserved sinless and incorruptible. This work of the Holy Ghost, I further assert, was done in consequence of the Son's humbling himself to be made flesh. The Son said, 'I come:' the Father said, 'I prepare thee a body to come in:' and the Holy Ghost prepared that body out of the Virgin's substance. And so, by the three-fold acting of the Trinity, was the Christ constituted a Divine and human nature, joined in personal union for ever.

Edward Irving, from the Preface to his Sermon on the Incarnation, and quoted by Gordon Strachan (1973), *The Pentecostal Theology of Edward Irving*, London, Darton, Longman and Todd, p. 30.

Popular perspectives

In this section we look at two facets of Pentecostal theology found in some congregations, which have grown up in the churches rather than the academy.

Prosperity spirituality

Prosperity spirituality has been found in North America, South Africa and parts of Asia and Africa. It is a doctrine that originates in the pages of the Old Testament: 'God will make you most prosperous in all the work of your hands' (Deut. 30.9). The doctrine holds that God wishes to make Christians prosper and, although it has also made much of 3 John 2,[47] is largely exemplified by the blessings God promised to Abraham and the abundant material well-being of Israel in its golden epoch.[48] In

---

47 The text is in the doorpost of Cho's church in Seoul and Oral Roberts claimed that it changed his life.

48 See also David R. McConnell (1990), *The Promise of Health and Wealth*, London, Hodder and Stoughton; Andrew Perriman (ed.) (2003), *Faith, Health and Prosperity*, Carlisle, Paternoster Press; Simon Coleman (2000), *The Globalisation of Charismatic Christianity: Spreading the Gospel of Prosperity*, Cambridge, Cambridge University Press. A survey of interpretations of 3 John 2 is given by Heather L.

order to apply the doctrine to the church it is necessary to ignore major differences between the Old and New Testaments and to presume that the blessings promised Israel in the days of Moses are directly transferable to the church despite the biblical warnings that the church will face persecution, for example, 'We must go through many hardships to enter the kingdom of God' (Acts 14.22).

When the Pentecostal movement started, many adherents were poor. Even after they had begun to worship as Pentecostals in fine churches, those in the Western world faced the financial consequences of the stock-market crash of 1929 and the economic depression of the 1930s. Prosperity teaching took off in the 1950s and undoubtedly appealed to believers who had grown up in grinding poverty. In addition, Pentecostalism began in an atmosphere of eschatological fervour and expectation of the return of Christ. By the 1950s, this fervour was evaporating and the attractions of consumer society were glittering before Western eyes. Pentecostals found it easy to believe that God wanted them to be prosperous as the post-war world climbed to new economic heights.

The Oral Roberts Evangelistic Association published *God's Formula for Success and Prosperity* in 1956. It was essentially a series of life histories or testimonies of individuals who, by maintaining Christian standards in business and by giving generously to Christian causes, had prospered. Here were wealthy American businessmen explaining that the secret of their success was to be found in giving to others and receiving back new wealth by the power of God working in the market.[49] In 1970 Oral Roberts published *Miracle of Seed-Faith* and printed over half a million copies that year. There were three principles of seed-faith:

1 God is your source of supply, not your job or your business;
2 you should 'give that it may be given to you' (Luke 6.38) so that your giving becomes in effect the planting of seeds that will generate a harvest of financial abundance; and
3 you should expect a miracle and live daily with confidence in God.

Although there were critics of the prosperity gospel, it spread rapidly.[50] The message was taken up by other televangelists including T. L. Osborn. Critics argued that the 'Madison Avenue lifestyle' of the evangelists was inappropriate for Christians and that the motivation of giving in order to

---

Landrus (2002), 'Hearing 3 John 2 in the Voices of History', *Journal of Pentecostal Theology* 11. 1, 70–88.

49 L. Braxton (1966), 'God's Banker', in Abundant Life Magazine, *God's Formula for Success and Prosperity*, Oral Roberts Evangelistic Association. First published in 1955 and copyrighted by America's Healing Magazine.

50 Milmon F. Harrison (2005), *Righteous Riches: The Word of Faith Movement in Contemporary African American Religion*, Oxford, Oxford University Press.

receive was corrupt.[51] Indeed, it was argued that the televangelists were on a treadmill whereby they required enormous income to allow them to broadcast and that they could only receive this income by appealing to their audiences. So the audiences were asked to give and the only inducement that the evangelist could offer was that donors would receive extra money back from other sources. It sounded like the spiel of a conman, though many Christians affirmed that it was not.

Prosperity spirituality has become complicated in other ways. It is distinct from 'redemption lift', which has been noticed at least since the time of John Wesley. The lift occurs as formerly ill-disciplined and dissolute individuals become Christians, apply themselves to their jobs, are honest in their dealings and so, gradually, by hard work become wealthy. This upward social mobility is a function of sustained individual effort in a society that is open to a market economy. In at least one African form prosperity spirituality has turned into a complicated 'trading with God' variant. Here wealth is generated in a precise way by giving to God, receiving back from God, giving from the new wealth and, in this way, moving up in a spiral. 'Trading with God' can have its downside as well because, if people fail to give to God, then punishments fall upon them. In its worst form the doctrine results in millionaire pastors who rule over relatively poor congregations.[52] But, of course, the pastor can point to himself as evidence that the doctrine of giving is true since he was once as poor as his congregation and is now rich.

Other variants in the subculture of prosperity spirituality are likely to be associated with Word of Faith proponents like Kenneth Hagin (1917–2003) and Kenneth Copeland (b. 1936), who have developed prosperity teaching in parallel with teaching about faith for healing.[53] Wealth becomes a right that Christians may claim in prayer or by 'positive confession'. Positive confession occurs when people 'claim in faith' wealth or goals that they do not presently possess but which they expect they will in future possess. This kind of confession can sound strange because those who practise it will begin to speak in what appears to be a delusory fashion about objects that they do not possess or are not in existence. Nevertheless, such teaching has been refined by Yonggi Cho, who teaches that Christians can use their sanctified imaginations to stimulate prayer and achieve the eventual existence of what is currently beyond them.[54]

---

51 Valentine Cunningham (1972), 'Eratosthenes Butterscotch', *Redemption Tidings*, 20 July.

52 Paul Gifford (1998), *African Christianity: Its Public Role*, London, Hurst and Co.

53 Teaching about prosperity is also given by Joyce Meyer (b. 1943) and Creflo Dollar (b. 1962), both of whom have TV ministries in the USA.

54 Paul Yonggi Cho with R. Whitney Manzano (1983), *The Fourth Dimension: More Secrets for a Successful Life*, vol. 2, Plainfield, NJ, Bridge Publishing Inc.

The practice of prosperity spirituality, despite its critics, results in positive expectations about the future and is an antidote to financial and psychological depression. Undoubtedly there have been Christians who have risen out of appalling circumstances by the exercise of this kind of faith. Equally, and unfortunately, there are individuals who have fallen flat on their faces by naming and claiming objects that they were unable to obtain and by ending in debt or disgrace.

Paul Yonggi Cho and the fourth dimension

The Holy Spirit came on the day of Pentecost not only to cause men to be able to prophesy (speak forth the Word of God), but also to give the ability to have visions and dreams.

In the Old Testament we often see God giving visions and dreams concerning future events. In fact, Samuel was called a seer (1 Sam. 9:9). Daniel was able to see from Babylon the development of successive kingdoms and looked into the Church age and beyond. Ezekiel could see beyond his land into a foreign land.

This phenomenon was not limited to the Old Testament. In the New Testament, Ananias, Paul and even a Roman, Cornelius, had prophetic visions and dreamed dreams.

This does not necessarily mean that we should all remain in ecstatic states. However, it does mean that we are to participate in God fulfilling His will in our lives by first envisioning His purpose and then filling our imagination with it through dreaming.

Consequently, the believer should not be limited to the three-dimension plane, but should go beyond that into the fourth-dimensional plane of reality. We should live in the Spirit. We should guard our minds from all negative and foolish thinking. This keeps the canvas clean for the artwork of the Holy Spirit to be painted on our imaginations. Creativity, perception, intelligence, and spiritual motivation will be by-products of an imagination which has been activated by the Holy Spirit.

Paul Yonggi Cho with R. Whitney Manzano (1983), *The Fourth Dimension: More Secrets for a Successful Life*, vol. 2, Plainfield, NJ, Bridge Publishing Inc., p. 55.

Spiritual warfare

In the words of Paul:

For our struggle is not against flesh and blood, but against the rulers, against the authorities, against the powers of this dark world and against the spiritual forces of evil in the heavenly realms. (Eph. 6.12)

The implication of this sentence is that Christians must live in opposition to 'the powers of this dark world' that dominate centres of authority. There appears to be a contrast between invisible spiritual forces and the present world order. As a result of reading these words there are Christians who have conceptualized Christianity as a perpetual titanic battle between the forces of light and darkness. This contrast can turn every event and circumstance into a victory for God or the devil.

It is difficult to pinpoint exactly when spiritual warfare became prevalent in some sections of the Pentecostal and charismatic movements. From around the 1970s, when travelling teachers could circulate tape recordings of their preaching, expositions of the book of Daniel began to explain that there were angelic beings assigned to particular territories.[55] It is revealed that the help needed by God's people is delivered by Michael (traditionally the archangel who protected Israel) who is resisted by 'the Prince of the kingdom of Persia' (Dan. 10.13). This angelic struggle is interpreted in the context of a supposed hierarchy of spiritual beings with archangels at the top and demons at the bottom. The bad angels control the demons and the demons harass human beings. What is necessary for spiritual progress, therefore, is the defeat or binding of these wicked angels so that the regions they control can be liberated by Christians.[56]

The notion of spiritual warfare results in a form of prayer that is addressed to evil angels. In other words, it is not a conventional form of prayer addressed by the Christian to God as a Father, but rather a form of prayer that attempts to converse with personified evil. This produces Christians who will declaim and proclaim defeat for satanic powers and declaim and proclaim victory for God. This is essentially a verbal exercise which, in philosophical terms, is thought to be performative, that is, to have an effect on the material world.

The practice has led to attempts to identify the particular spiritual forces that might be controlling cities or countries and to defeat them. The process is seen as being supported by the words of Jesus about 'the binding of the strongman' and by its practical effectiveness in evangelism.[57] Those who practise this form of prayer argue that amazing results have occurred as whole regions have been transformed by the grace of God: drug dealers have been sent packing, addicts have been liberated, families reconciled, prosperity gained.[58] Moreover, practitioners of spirit-

---

55 One of the most clear and persuasive of these preachers was Derek Prince (1915–2003), who travelled widely.

56 Further details are given in C. Peter Wagner and Fredrick D. Pennoyer (1996), *Wrestling with Dark Angels: Towards a Deeper Understanding of the Supernatural Forces in Spiritual Warfare*, Ventura, CA, Regal Books.

57 Matthew 12.29.

58 The first *Transformations* video presented by George Otis Jr shows dramatic changes in Colombia, Kenya, Mexico and California.

ual warfare will argue that it is only by 'power encounters' with the Holy Spirit that the gospel can be effectively preached in areas of entrenched resistance to Christianity. It is the 'power encounters' of healing, deliverance from demons or setting free from curses that brings people to Christ. It is not ceremonial Christianity or ethical example but rather a demonstration of the dynamic power of God.

The practice of spiritual warfare therefore has two distinct spheres of operation: first, the binding of angelic powers, and, second, exorcism of demons. These two spheres are not to be confused with each other, but success in the demonic sphere is seen as evidence for invisible success in the angelic sphere. Descriptions of exorcisms have been given by observers who note what appear to be multiple personality disorders and their cures, or claimed cures.[59]

This explanation of the world is heavily dualistic. Moreover, dualism cuts across Wesleyan teaching on sanctification, which traditionally has explained why honest believers may sometimes do bad things or why they struggle against bad habits. The Wesleyan position is that sanctification is achieved only after one or more crises, and even relapses. Consequently the advocates of spiritual warfare tend not to be those who construct their lives around the fivefold gospel.

Where poverty is conceived of as devilish, spiritual warfare may be combined with health and prosperity teaching. For many centuries the ascetic tradition of monastic self-denial elevated poverty to a virtue. Francis of Assisi gave up his luxuries for the sake of a mendicant lifestyle following in the footsteps of Jesus. Yet poverty voluntarily embraced is quite different from poverty that brings about the deaths of children and pitiful adult life expectancy. If one believes that the devil 'comes to steal, to kill and to destroy' (John 10.10), it makes sense to view poverty as the consequence of spiritual attack rather than of economic laws. Spiritual warfare may turn its fire upon the slums of African cities and Latin American ghettos in an attempt to remedy these situations.[60]

The difficulty for any analyst is to decide whether changes that occur as a result of the preaching of the gospel and of the setting up of vibrant churches have anything to do with spiritual warfare, even if those churches practise spiritual warfare. The difficulty arises because there is no evidence, for instance, that the Methodist revival of the eighteenth century practised any spiritual warfare and yet its results brought changes to the poor of England's burgeoning towns. In other words, the preaching of the message of Jesus *by itself* transforms societies without any

---

59 Wonsuk Ma (1997), 'A "First Waver" looks at the "Third Wave": A Pentecostal Reflection on Charles Kraft's Power Encounter Terminology', *Pneuma* 19.2, 189–206.

60 See also William K. Kay (1998), 'A Demonised Worldview: Dangers, Benefits and Explanations', *Journal of Empirical Theology* 11.1, 17–29.

accompanying prayer of the spiritual warfare type. Moreover, the New Testament provides no example of spiritual warfare in action. We look in vain at the missionary journeys of Paul to try to find any of the favoured practices of modern spiritual warriors. What we see is Paul preaching a gospel that is validated by miracles of healing while being guided by the Holy Spirit.[61]

With this we conclude our exploration of Pentecostal theology. We attempted to limit this discussion to the theology of Pentecostal denominations and have avoided gathering up and classifying all the theological ideas that individual Pentecostal theologians have floated. We have taken the purpose of theology as being to address the challenges of the day, and for this reason we have considered the ecumenical movement and other religions. We have looked at how Pentecostalism understands itself in the congregations it creates, that is, in its ecclesiology and in its defining doctrine experience. Finally, we have distinguished between Pentecostal theology in the churches and in the academy.

Cross-references to the SCM Reader *Pentecostal and Charismatic Studies*

5.12 Paul Yonggi Cho with R. Whitney Manzano, *The Fourth Dimension: More Secrets for a Successful Life*, vol. 2, Plainfield, NJ, Bridge Publishing, 1983, pp. 50–5 (pp. 120–3).

Ecumenism

13.1 David J. du Plessis, *The Renewal of Christianity Must Be Both Charismatic and Ecumenical*, Oakland, CA, *c.* 1975 (pp. 249–50).
13.2 Michael Harper, 'Beauty or Ashes?' The Ashe Lecture, 1979 (pp. 250–4).

Prosperity

14.1 Kenneth Copeland, *Dear Partner*, Fort Worth, TX, Kenneth Copeland, 1997, pp. 115–20 (pp. 255–8).

Exorcism

18.1 David du Plessis, *Simple and Profound*, Orleans, Paraclete Press, 1986, pp. 61–3 (pp. 269–70).
18.2 Don Basham, *Deliver us from Evil*, London, Hodder and Stoughton, 1979, pp. 61–4 (pp. 271–2).

---

61 E.g. Acts 14.8; 16.7.

Spiritual Warfare

18.3 Terry Law, 'The Power of Praise and Worship', in *Principles of Praise*, Tulsa, Victory House, 1985, pp. 145–56 (pp. 273–4).

18.4 G. Otis, Jr, *The Twilight Labyrinth*, Grand Rapids, MI, Chosen Books, 1998, pp. 281–3 (pp. 275–6).

18.5 Andrew Walker, 'The Devil you Think you Know', in Tom Smail, Andrew Walker and Nigel Wright (eds), *Charismatic Renewal*, London, SPCK, 1995, pp. 86–105 (pp. 277–9).

Questions to think about

1 To what extent might academic Pentecostal theology and popular Pentecostal theology find themselves disagreeing?
2 What is dialogue between religions or between different streams within the same religion likely to achieve?
3 What difference does it make to your understanding of Jesus if his humanity is emphasized by Spirit Christologies (i.e. by seeing him as a Spirit-inspired man)?
4 Does it matter to God whether you are rich or poor?

Further reading

Coleman, S. (2000), *The Globalisation of Charismatic Christianity: Spreading the Gospel of Prosperity*, Cambridge, Cambridge University Press.

Grudem, W. (1999), *Systematic Theology*, Leicester, InterVarsity Press.

Perriman, A. (ed.) (2003), *Faith, Health and Prosperity*, Carlisle, Paternoster Press.

Roberts, O. (1995), *Expect a Miracle: My Life and Ministry*, London, Thomas Nelson Publishers.

Warrington, K. (2008), *Pentecostal Theology*, London, T & T Clark.

PART 3

Sociology

14

Sociology 1

Introduction

In this chapter we switch from theology to sociology. We turn our attention from beliefs and concepts about God to beliefs and concepts about society. We begin with sociology itself and then turn to the sociology of the Pentecostal and charismatic movements.

What is sociology?

Sociology is a relatively new academic discipline. The word was first coined in 1838 by the Frenchman Auguste Comte (1798–1857).[1] The discipline is essentially the application of scientific methods to the study of society. After the Enlightenment of the seventeenth century when human rationality was directed at a new series of targets, it was inevitable that someone would think of attempting to understand society itself by probing it with logic or describing it with new concepts. Comte made use of historical information and thought that he could detect three distinct stages through which society had progressed up until his own time. The first age was theological: social explanations were provided by attributing causation to the will of God. The second stage was metaphysical: society was understood by attributing causation to abstract impersonal forces like those found in economics. The third stage was positive: society was understood by the connection between theory and sense data. Each social stage was also matched with preferred methods of government. The third and final stage was matched with republicanism, leaving behind monarchy and the rule of a priesthood. Thus sociology discovered the direction of social change. Politically, societies would in future distribute power on the basis of elections and merit rather than birth and privilege. Scientifically, sociology as the newest science was able to reveal the true logic of the human mind. Since each science depended upon earlier sciences (physics can only be carried out after astronomy has made its observations, and astronomy can only properly function when mathematics has

---

1 In French, *La sociologie*.

been refined, and so on), sociology builds on and includes the insights of all the other sciences; it is the master science. In practice it can be divided into two parts: statics and dynamics. Statics is concerned with the study of socio-political systems and dynamics enquires into the process of social change.

Later, sociology became less schematic and dogmatic. Comte's positivism fell out of favour, but his notion that scientific methods should be applied to the study of society remains.

Sociology of religion

Karl Marx (1818–83) started from a political position derived from the philosopher Hegel but ended up with a description of society that could be put alongside Comte's. Both Marx and Comte understood human history to be divisible into stages and, though their stages were different, they had in common that they understood the trajectory of human history to be fixed. Whereas Comte had a place of a sort for religion, Marx displayed an unremitting hostility to all forms of religion because he believed them to be essentially conservative. For Comte, religion had to be reformed but for Marx it had to be abolished.

One way of viewing the outcome of Comte's and Marx's thought is that they believed they had discovered 'laws' of social change in the same way that laws of physics had been discovered. If physics could predict the movement of objects within the solar system, sociology could predict the movement of society. The overall pattern was from simple and primitive communities to segmented societies. But what of religion? In terms of its function, it was usually a cohesive force providing the basis for morality. Yet, when sociologists began to look more closely, they faced theoretical problems.

Religion is large and multi-dimensional. Religion covers both beliefs and rituals. It is concerned with moral beliefs about interpersonal relations and rituals for birth, marriage and death. It will offer grand explanations of the purpose of existence and singular explanations for special events. Since religion is situated within society, and society itself, as sociologists readily admit, is perpetually changing, we have two moving targets. Sociological explanation has to keep pace with a series of transformations. Social transformations between one kind of society and another will include transformations of religion. But this leads to the question: does social change produce religious change or does religious change produce social change? For Comte, the driving force was to be found within society itself and religion needed to adapt to whatever social stage had been reached. A more subtle analysis was provided by Max Weber (1864–1920).

Weber analysed the interactive relationship between religion and society, and in his book *The Protestant Ethic and the Spirit of Capitalism* he offered an account of the emergence of capitalism from post-Reformation Europe.[2] Weber asked why it was that capitalism had emerged in Europe rather than elsewhere in the world. Other countries had attained similar degrees of sophistication both philosophically and technologically. Yet it was in Europe that the engine of social change that can be called capitalism came into being. In his extensive discussion Weber noted that the lending of money for interest had been ethically questionable for many centuries. Biblical support for this position might be found in such texts as: 'If one of your countrymen becomes poor and is unable to support himself among you, help him ... Do not take interest of any kind from him ... You must not lend him money at interest or sell him food at a profit' (Lev. 25.35–37). Just prior to the Reformation, lending money for charitable purposes was sanctioned, but after the Reformation there was a radical change.[3] To simplify a lengthy argument, we can say that Weber also noted that the Reformers broadened the concept of 'vocation' to include secular employment.[4] A man might be a blacksmith, ploughman or magistrate and this might be his calling within society, and he should give himself to what he did just as rigorously as any priest. When the Protestant Reformers re-examined the biblical texts they judged that the lending of money for interest was no longer sinful. The removal of the sin of usury, combined with secular vocation, delivered an unexpected benefit. Hard-working people generated surplus finance (or capital) which they were able to bank. The banks were now able to lend money at interest and this created conditions for small businesses to thrive. Capitalism began to take off.

Weber offered another crucial insight into religion. In his analysis of different types of authority he pointed out that religious authority, in the first instance, is often charismatic. By this he meant something very similar to what any Pentecostal might mean. Religious authority, in its early stages, consisted in the gifted individual whose life and teachings became authoritative for disciples, followers, congregations or admirers. The authority did not stem, as might happen later, from legal-rational sources or from tradition. Rather, the charismatic individual was a living source of authority, often with prophetic insight, and standing, in

---

2 This was published in English in 1930.

3 '... the church itself was virtually compelled to permit undisguised usury in the charity funds (*montes pietatis*) when the loans were in the interests of the poor; this became definitively established after Pope Leo X (1513–21).' These are the words of Max Weber (1922), *The Sociology of Religion*, Boston, MA, Beacon Press, p. 219. First published in English in 1964.

4 Max Weber (1904–05), *The Protestant Ethic and the Spirit of Capitalism*, reprinted by Mineola, NY, Dover in 2003. Reference to vocation is given in ch. 3.

many cases, at the margins of society. Subsequently the authority of the charismatic individual would be transferred into or seized on by a religious bureaucracy attempting to sustain the original religious impulses embodied by the charismatic founder. The two-stage process of religious development could be seen in Christianity, to be sure, but also in other religions.[5] Whereas the original charismatic figure is simple, visionary and unconventional, the later bureaucratic establishment has exactly the opposite characteristics. It is complicated, cautious and conventional. Religious history may be seen as a series of cycles from the prophetic founder through a period of bureaucratic deadness and decline and then through a new prophetic individual to another slow decline, and so on. In Christianity the cycle might historically result in a sequence of renewal movements attempting to recapture Christianity's first ethos.

In Weber's analysis there is a recognition that charismata may also be routinized. Charismatic gifts may be turned into ritual equivalents that only symbolically represent the benefits they are supposed to bring. For instance, the charismatic gift of healing according to the New Testament actually brought healing to people who were sick, whereas, in its ritual form, anointing with oil as a symbol of the Holy Spirit may bring nothing more than a reminder of how Christianity once was. The routinization of charismata goes hand in hand with the growth of bureaucratic labyrinths and in this way transforms the face of a once-vital religion.

Partly as a way to renew Christianity, fresh splinter groups come into existence. Weber's distinction between the churches and *sects* belongs more fully to the work of Troeltsch, though Weber was aware of it. Ernst Troeltsch (1865–1923), writing almost entirely within a German Christian tradition, understood the emergence of sects as stemming from original themes within the Gospels.[6] The Gospels show the fellowship of disciples with Jesus and the small group who gathered around him at the beginning of his ministry. This desire for simplicity of life and intimacy of relation with Christ is part of the attraction of the sect. It offers to serious individuals the opportunity to be close to each other and God, even if they have to pay a high psychological price for this privilege. It is set against the great claims of the church, which may embrace all the people of a nation, and, by public rituals and ceremonies, authenticate the great occasions of state. Troeltsch contends that the New Testament reveals Christianity both in its form as the universal church crossing national and international boundaries and in its form as a sect offering fellowship

---

5 Weber notes that the first systematization of the teaching of a charismatic leader may be taken up by a rationalistic priesthood – see *Sociology*, p. 79 – but the transition to bureaucracy is not far behind.

6 Published in English as *The Social Teaching of the Christian Churches*. Extracts are conveniently given by Robin Gill (ed.) (1987), *Theology and Sociology: A Reader*, London, Geoffrey Chapman.

to a few. The sect is therefore not an evil aberration but a valid expression of Christian life. And, in terms of the cycle of renewal, the sect has an important part to play. It may be the vehicle by which renewal is carried to the larger body of the church.

In sociological inquiry the classification of different religious subgroups becomes complicated. The church may be a large inclusive grouping that is coterminus with a nation. The nation's spiritual life may be displayed by the church, which, because it is on public display and has recognizable social functions (by offering sanctioned ceremonies for birth, marriage and death), is easily distinguishable from the sect. Yet as social theory attempted to grapple with increasingly varied social organizations, and as society itself changed, sociologists found themselves having to refine their terminology and conceptual systems. There might be different types of church.[7] For instance, the church might be only identified with the ruling group or, in another period, there might be a church within a church as in the case of monastic forms within Catholicism or, in its early stage, Methodism within the Church of England. And then sects might be of different kinds depending on their starting point. There might be Catholic sects or Protestant sects and, as Protestantism developed non-traditional forms, there might be Mormon sects or Adventist groups that were only remotely related to traditional Protestant congregations. As a result of these complications Bryan Wilson (1926–2004) argued that sects should be defined not by their doctrines but by their attitude to society.[8] The sect should be contrasted with church. In short:

- a sect was opposed to society and exclusive;
- a church was merged into society and inclusive.

If churches are large and inclusive and sects are small and exclusive, they can be placed at opposite ends of a continuum.[9] In the middle can be placed the denomination, which is neither as large as the church nor as small as the sect. More importantly, the denomination acknowledges the doctrinal validity of other similar religious groups. A Baptist will acknowledge the equal validity of Methodists or Presbyterians. From the

---

7 Y. M. Yinger (1957), *Religion, Society and the Individual*, New York, Macmillan.

8 Bryan R. Wilson (1963), 'A Typology of Sects in a Dramatic and Comparative Perspective', *Archives de Sociologie de Religion* 16, pp. 49–63.

9 Roy Wallis (1976), *The Road to Total Freedom: A Sociological Analysis of Scientology*, London, Heinemann, p. 13, provides a fourfold classification around respectability, deviance, inclusive (pluralistically legitimate) and exclusive (uniquely legitimate). The sect is deviant and exclusive, the denomination is respectable and inclusive, and so on. I have not used this scheme since it is not easily applicable to Pentecostalism.

sociological point of view it is observable that sects may become denominations over several generations. What begins as a tiny cluster of people, sheltered against the world, who hold doctrines by which they identify themselves as the spiritual elite, may become, as the group grows, friendlier to the world and less hostile to other religious groups which they now recognize may have a similar salvation to their own. In the same way, the church that identifies itself as being universally valid and applicable to all the members of a particular society may, with the arrival of new religious expressions, come to view itself as a denomination. The Anglican Church in Britain accepts the religious validity of Baptists – something that was unthinkable in the seventeenth century, and there may be similar softening of attitude among established churches in Scandinavia and elsewhere. In this way sects and churches, once they turn into denominations, can meet on middle ground.[10]

One of the differences between the church and the sect concerns class. The church is usually middle class whereas the sect is often either working class or belongs to the layer of self-taught shopkeepers and small manufacturers who have traditionally lacked higher education.[11] As the sect becomes a denomination, it also becomes more middle class. In this way we can understand religious change as riding on a shifting wave rippling through broad social structures. Part of the transformation of religious groups is driven by economic improvement, especially if economic improvement is connected with educational opportunities. The relevance of this to Pentecostalism lies in the alternative method of analysis, which uses race rather than class as the key category. If we see race as being fundamental to Pentecostalism – and the division of Pentecostal denominations in the United States along racial lines points in this direction – sociological analysis will need to be refocused. If, on the other hand, race and class are tied together, then the original analysis will hold true. In practice, the most complete analysis will utilize racial and class variables and attempt to separate out the contribution of each to changes in attitude by Pentecostals. There is some indication that in the USA class supersedes race.[12] In other words, if white middle-class and black middle-class people are more like each other than they are like white working-class and black working-class people, it will be evident that race has diminishing importance.

We need also to give attention to *secularization* as a social process characterized by a decline in religious observance, a lessening of the political power of the church and its associated symbols and a rejection

---

10 See also H. Richard Niebuhr (1929), *The Social Sources of Denominationalism*, New York, Holt, for an account of the transition from sect to denomination.

11 Weber, *Sociology*, ch. 7.

12 See Alistair Kee (2006), *The Rise and Demise of Black Theology*, Aldershot, Ashgate, and the discussion in *Pneuma* 30, 291–8.

of its world view. In essence, religion is thought to retreat before the advance of modernity. No single definition of modernity can be offered. It is normally connected with *enlightenment*, which is a philosophical and intellectual shift that can be marked most easily by Kant's essay advocating the dismissal of ancient authorities in favour of the primacy of human reason.[13] 'That is why', in Owen Chadwick's words, 'the problem of secularization is not the same as the problem of enlightenment. Enlightenment was of the few. Secularization is of the many.'[14] And, because it is 'of the many' it has become one of the master themes of the contemporary sociology of religion.[15]

Max Weber helps in understanding what is happening because he attributes to religion the capacity to create social forms and organizations. Any decline in religion for whatever reason will lead to visible institutional and social change. The arrival of modernity, as an expression of rationality in technology and bureaucracy, disenchants the world and drives religion into the private sphere. Religion survives because life's contingencies stimulate religious explanations and meanings even though the advance of rationality removes mystery from nature. The result of all this is that religion, as a source of ideas and meanings, may once have shaped the whole of life but modernity and secularization signal the end of a culture unified in this way.

Religious symbols persist although secular culture, with its autonomous and irreconcilable value domains, reduces the possibility of community. Rationality coupled with technology spawns vast bureaucratic entanglements that inhibit human freedom.[16] At the start of the Reformation, the radical individualism of Protestantism legitimated the idea of human rights and sowed the seeds of extended enfranchisement. Subsequently, sixteenth-century Puritanism may have been seen as one type of rationalization designed to order the whole of human life according to religious belief through an ability to conceive of human law as being an instrument of divine purpose.[17] Looser, more evangelical expressions

13 I. Kant (1784), 'An Answer to the Question: What is Enlightenment?' A copy can be found on http://www.english.upenn.edu/~mgamer/Etexts/kant.html

14 O. Chadwick (1975), *The Secularisation of the European Mind in the 19th Century*, Cambridge, Cambridge University Press, p. 9.

15 See for instance Peter L. Berger (1969), *The Sacred Canopy: Elements of a Sociological Theory of Religion*, New York, Anchor Books; Grace Davie (1994), *Religion in Britain since 1945*, Oxford, Blackwell; Alan Aldridge (2000), *Religion in the Contemporary World: A Sociological Introduction*, Cambridge, Polity Press; Callum G. Brown (2001), *The Death of Christian Britain*, London, Routledge; Steve Bruce (2002), *God is Dead: Secularization in the West*, Oxford, Blackwell.

16 S. Seidman (1985), 'Modernity and the Problem of Meaning: the Durkheim Tradition', *Sociological Analysis* 46.2, 109–30.

17 D. Zaret (1989), 'Religion and the Rise of Liberal-Democratic Ideology in 17th Century England', *American Sociological Review* 54.2, 163–79.

of Christianity gave more inward, and perhaps more Arminian, accounts of faith that issued less in law and more in charity. Protestantism itself, by demystifying the sacraments, could be a force for secularization: this is secularization from within the church. And, once the sacraments are devalued, the material world of nature becomes less holy.[18]

Secularization is one of the themes of twentieth-century sociology. It is also contested.[19] The nub of the argument concerns high levels of church attendance within the United States. If secularization is a consequence of modernity, then we would expect church attendance to be low in the United States, but the reverse is true: the figures are higher than in Europe. One explanation for variations in levels of secularization in different countries and between the USA and Europe may be to do with the church's relationship to government.[20] Where the church is close to government, it has a form of religious monopoly. Religion will then decline if high church attendance brings no political benefits with it. In Europe, established churches are vulnerable to this effect. In the United States a religious free market operates, and has done for more than two centuries. Competition between churches for members keeps attendance high – that, at least, is one plausible explanation.[21]

In the next section we apply these ideas to Pentecostal churches, with one caveat: classical sociological theory developed in Europe may not easily fit Asian, African or Latin American countries.

Sociology of Pentecostalism

Sects, denominations or churches?

We can ask how to classify Pentecostal churches. More specifically, is the standard trajectory from sect to denomination visible? The answer to this question must be a general, though hesitant, 'Yes'. Early Pentecostalism shared with the holiness movement a reaction against social norms. It avoided the fashions of the day, had a low opinion of sport and other recreational activities, and tended to be apolitical. Where healing doctrine was excessively emphasized, medical practitioners were shunned.

---

18 Berger, *Sacred Canopy*, e.g. p. 111.

19 For instance, see Charles Taylor, *A Secular Age*, The Belknap Press of Harvard University Press. Taylor questions the notion that the society's journey from pre-modernity to postmodernity can be described in 'culture neutral' terms. See also Grace Davie (2007), *The Sociology of Religion*, London, Sage.

20 David Martin (1978), *A General Theory of Secularization*, Oxford, Blackwell.

21 I. R. Iannoccone (1992), 'Religious Markets and the Economics of Religion', *Social Compass* 39, 123–31. However, note the searching comments of Bernice Martin (2006), 'Pentecostal Conversion and the Limits of the Market Metaphor', *Exchange: Journal of Missiological and Ecumenical Research* 35.1, 60–91.

Where theological education was available, many Pentecostals prided themselves on their lack of it. In all these areas Pentecostals displayed sectarian tendencies. Occasionally they deemed themselves to be a spiritual elite. For instance, Charles Fox Parham's doctrine of the man-child put proto-Pentecostals into a class of their own.[22] Only those who were filled with the Spirit would escape the tribulation and be safe from the clutches of the antichrist. Similar exclusiveness was found among Oneness Pentecostals. Yet, to balance this tendency there was an inclusiveness at Azusa Street itself where races mingled freely and social concern was expressed through charitable acts. In the same way, the calling together of the original council that led to the formation of the Assemblies of God in the United States was an inclusive invitation that welcomed black and white as well as proto-Pentecostals who had come from Wesleyan holiness backgrounds and from interdenominational groups like the Christian and Missionary Alliance.

In Britain the same opposing tendencies were also noticeable. Alexander Boddy wanted to spread the Pentecostal message across to Christian denominations and his invitations to the conferences at Sunderland were public. He thought that the young Pentecostal movement was given by God to renew the churches rather than to bring new sectarian organizations into existence. If there was sectarianism in the early Elim churches, this resulted from the dominance of George Jeffreys rather than from any doctrine. This was the exclusiveness of an alpha male rather than the exclusiveness of a self-designating elect. Jeffreys held public meetings up and down Britain and everybody was welcome to attend. On the other hand, the Apostolic Faith congregations associated with William Hutchinson did become sectarian in their attitudes as a result of the man-child doctrine and the cold shoulder given to Hutchinson by other Pentecostals once these doctrinal disputes came out into the open.

In Norway also there was a tension between the attempts of T. B. Barratt to usher in Pentecostalism as a spiritual movement for the whole church which, after disputes over water baptism, became more closed. Similarly, in Germany and the Netherlands the polarities of openness and exclusiveness could be found. This leads to the conclusion that in the West, at any rate, Pentecostalism was never fully sectarian. Its evangelistic and missionary activities prevented it from insulating itself. If Pentecostalism *did* become exclusive, this tended to occur in the 1920s after Pentecostal groups had been established and when the early spiritual fire had died down.

---

22 Charles F. Parham (1944), *A Voice Crying in the Wilderness*, 4th edn, Baxter Springs, Kansas: 'the man-child will rule all nations in the thousand years reign of Christ. The man-child is the raptured saints and are called the first fruits unto God, being 144,000 in number', p. 90.

In Asia the situation is harder to read. Christianity was the religion of foreigners who looked different and often dressed differently from the rest of the population. In any of the countries where Pentecostal missionaries began to make inroads, they did so among poor people, people a long way from the centres of power and money. In India, Pentecostals reached out to young women whose social status often depended upon that of their husbands, though if they were widowed their status was rarely high.[23] In China and Korea, Pentecostals worked among the people who were keen to receive education and medical help that Christian missionaries might offer (Chapter 5). This implies that they were not the wealthiest people within the population, since, if they had been wealthy, they would have their own access to education. In any event, there do not appear to be any accounts of the conversion of ruling families or government ministers. In Africa, by contrast, where tribal societies were found, there are records of chieftains who were converted.[24] Nevertheless it is doubtful whether classifications of social class can properly be made in these situations and, in addition, it was difficult for individuals living in such close-knit interdependent groupings to adopt an antisocial attitude. In other words, the classic symptoms of sectarianism were much more difficult to display in traditional African settings. Finally, in Latin America many of the wealthier landowners had been Catholic for generations and this left the Pentecostal converts at the bottom of the social ladder (Chapter 6). Only Pentecostals who came out of Methodism might be exceptions to this generalization.

Having said that early Pentecostals were both open and sectarian in their mentality, the building of denominations is significant. This is why we have emphasized (Chapter 4) the transition from the disorganized revival to the organized denominations. Denominations had a place in society, leaders, magazines, a headquarters; and the ordination of ministers could be expected to raise the social status of those who were ordained. At the same time the emergence of denominations inevitably leads to a relativization of Pentecostal self-understanding. This probably happened most quickly in the United States where several substantial Pentecostal denominations were quickly built. Although there was disagreement between Pentecostal denominations, there was also a gradual willingness to accept alternative formulations of the same Pentecostal

---

23 As in Pandita Ramabai's ministry at Mukti. Discussion of Indian society at the turn of the century can be found in Horace A. Rose (1911–19), *A Glossary of the Tribes and Castes of the Punjab and the North-West Frontier Province*, published in Lahore in three volumes. See also H. A. Rose (1908), 'On Caste in India', *Man 8*, 98–103.

24 W. F. P. Burton (1937), *When God Changes a Man*, London, Victory Press. A similar account is also given in W. F. P. Burton (1947), *Mudishi: The Congo Hunter*, published privately.

truths. The building of denominations is not merely a matter of organizational stability: it also implies a more positive attitude to society.

Further adaptation

The charismatic movement began to flow over the churches in the 1960s (Chapter 9). What is significant about this spiritual movement in sociological terms is that the charismatics belonged to long-standing denominations. At a stroke Pentecostalism found itself alongside sympathetic people in middle-class congregations. The charismatic movement challenged whatever vestiges of sectarianism might have been remaining within the hearts and minds of older Pentecostals. At interdenominational gatherings Pentecostals found themselves listening to preachers from Anglican or Roman Catholic churches. They found themselves singing worship songs together and gradually imbibing new social attitudes. This showed itself in many ways, including in the belief that ministers ought to be treated as professional people with proper remuneration. But it showed itself also in a willingness to become involved in social causes whether these were related to public morality on television or debate about abortion. It also had an impact on the value that Pentecostals began to give to all forms of education. In short, the charismatic movement accelerated Pentecostalism's move from the margins of society to the mainstream.

Resisting secularization in the charismatic movement and the third wave

The charismatic movement took place within Baptist, Episcopalian, Catholic, Anglican and other churches or denominations (see Chapter 10). By the beginning of the 1970s, however, there were preachers who were becoming impatient with renewal. This is because the renewal touched spiritual life and worship without altering ecclesiastical structures. Congregations entered into freedom in worship and new joy when the Spirit was outpoured in the 1960s, but ten years later the more radical preachers felt that the Spirit wanted to do something new. Instead of 'a charismatic roundabout' these preachers wanted to redesign church structures and practices so that a complete overhaul of congregational life could occur. Beyond this they wanted to reorganize the relations between congregations so as to get rid of the non-charismatic hierarchy that often oversaw development at parish level. By the 1970s 'house churches' were coming into existence, but very soon these were far too large for houses. They migrated to hired halls in schools and community centres and became 'new churches' under the supervision of travelling preachers who came to be designated 'apostles'. The new churches became 'apostolic networks', and the networks were seen as the 'third wave' following Pentecostalism (first wave) and the charismatic movement (second wave).[25]

Sociologically, the apostolic networks could be interpreted as a reversion to sectarianism. The networks differed according to the distinctive doctrines of the apostolic figure and according to his (usually it was a man) personality. Some of the networks were exclusive and sectarian, even aggressively so, to the extent that they dismissed all denominations of every kind, including Pentecostal ones: 'God has finished with denominations because he is bringing in his kingdom.'[26] This theological cry was intended to indicate that the kingdom was a larger concept than any denomination, and that denominations should dismantle themselves to reassemble on common ground. Other networks were more inclusive and far less sectarian in their theology and attitudes. They wanted to co-operate with each other and with other Christians, especially those in the Pentecostal and charismatic movement. In Britain, summer gatherings of Christians in camps like those held by Spring Harvest were specifically charismatic and specifically interdenominational. John Wimber (1937–97), who began his ministry as an interdenominational church growth consultant in California, was instrumental in spreading the message of healing within the charismatic movement but, in a later phase of his ministry, he started to construct his own network, the Vineyard.[27] Even so, his interdenominational or ecumenical attitude was felt within his new grouping. Similar willingness to work with others occurred when the networks found themselves unable to change the landscape in the way that they had at first hoped. A few of the networks reconceived of themselves as service organizations for the whole body of Christ. Others, more focused and tenacious in their goals, continued to grow congregations both in their country of origin and in other parts of the world.

When a practical assessment of networks is made, it appears that the more sectarian ones were likely to be more stable, more capable of growth and more able to retain their vibrant spirituality. In short, they were able to buck the trend of secularization. Some, but by no means all, of the less sectarian networks were more disorganized. The disorganized ones had always refused to adopt the hallmarks of denominationalism because this was the style of church from which they were trying to escape. As a result, they never established the routines, both financial and organ-

---

25 The most complete account of these networks in Britain is to be found in William K. Kay (2007), *Apostolic Networks in Britain*, Carlisle, Paternoster Press. This book should be consulted for details about the more and less sectarian networks mentioned here.

26 Cf. John Noble (1971), *Forgive Us Our Denominations*, London, Team Spirit.

27 Bill Jackson (1999), *The Quest for the Radical Middle: A History of the Vineyard*, Cape Town, Vineyard International Publishing.

izational, which would have enabled them to sustain themselves. Within 30 years they had almost vanished apart from within a few independent congregations.

Resisting secularization with cells

Pentecostal groups had always been willing to meet in homes. They had no belief about sacred buildings. Before the Azusa Street revival broke out William J. Seymour held home prayer meetings in Bonnie Brae Street. In the current era it was probably Yonggi Cho in Korea who first reintroduced home meetings, and he did so for the purpose of building up a big congregation. Cho's approach was systematic and purposeful. The city of Seoul was divided up into districts, and home groups were planted to allow people to meet for prayer and mid-week Bible study without having to make long journeys. At some point home groups were redesignated 'cell' groups. The guiding metaphor here came from the New Testament which saw the church as 'the body of Christ'. Since all living things are made up of cells, the church could legitimately become cellular. The cell had the advantage of providing meaningful pastoral care together with opportunities to make close personal friendships, something that was particularly important when congregations became vast and individuals were in danger of feeling swallowed up in a crowd. Cho preached to the World Pentecostal Conference in Rio de Janeiro in 1967 and this is probably when the concept of cells was transferred to Latin America.

The route by which the home groups for prayer and Bible study became evangelistic groups and then, eventually, discipleship groups is impossible to trace exactly. At some point the cell groups, especially in Latin America, became a control method for monitoring lifestyle and maintaining church discipline. The cell group, in this form, was sectarian. More than this, the cell group was in danger of taking over the lives of those who belonged to it. Members might be expected to socialize mainly with those in their own cells. Cell group leaders, in the Latin American post-1986 G12 format, were given considerable authority over their members. In this it was similar in style to the 'shepherding movement' that appeared in the USA in the 1970s.[28] In the shepherding movement each member was expected to be under the direct authority of somebody else, whether a pastor or cell group leader. Suffice it to say that this regimented sectarianism was open to abuse and was rapidly criticized and modified. From a sociological viewpoint we can interpret hardline cells as an extreme response to secularization.

---

28 S. D. Moore (2003), *The Shepherding Movement*, London, T & T Clark.

Resisting secularization with megachurches and politics

There are two other ways Pentecostals resist secular values. The first, now to be found on every continent, is in the megachurch. This is the church of 5,000 or more with the capacity to create a Christian micro-climate that protects members from the influences of atheistic or immoral culture. In the megachurch it is possible to use the restaurant to dine, to borrow books from the library, to use the sports hall, to take your children for organized games, to make use of the educational facilities and to find friends with whom to go on holiday. The pastor may broadcast sermons that members can listen to at home and the choir will sell music to play in the car or kitchen. Within the megachurch, the Christian is living in a community that attempts to meet all needs. In at least one megachurch there is a special pastor who visits those who are hospitalized with heart attacks and others who specialize in bereavement counselling. Nor is this microclimate entirely protective. Teams from the church may go out to reach homeless people and there may be a drug rehabilitation programme or a care centre for single mothers.

The second way of resisting secular culture is to attack it or attempt to transform it. In attack mode, Pentecostals may broadcast their views on political, economic and social issues and provide an alternative commentary on world events. Outside the United States most secular media organizations are controlled by relatively small numbers of people whose views are constantly reinforced and, in Europe, almost entirely irreligious. Anybody travelling backwards and forwards between Europe and the USA and watching television on both continents is quickly aware of the contrast between the way that religion is treated. What is viewed as moderately conservative in America may be castigated in Europe for its fundamentalism. In transformative mode, Pentecostals may wish to argue that their faith can change society by bringing in new values. At least one of the apostolic networks has attempted to enable its members to gain success in business and commerce. This is another form of the Protestant work ethic but it is driven by an amillennial theology focused on the kingdom of God.[29] We can put this in another way by reversing Weber's insight: instead of letting modernity disenchant the world and drive religion into private space, religion is trying to reconceive modernity and invade public space.

Cross-references to the SCM Reader *Pentecostal and Charismatic Studies*

5.12 Paul Yonggi Cho with R. Whitney Manzano, *The Fourth Dimension: More Secrets for a Successful Life*, vol. 2, Plainfield, NJ, Bridge Publishing, 1983, pp. 50–5 (pp. 120–3).

---

29 Kay, *Networks*, p. 285.

8.2 Arthur Wallis, 'Apostles for Today? Why Not?', *Restoration*, November–December 1981, pp. 2–5 (pp. 171–4).

8.3 Larry Christenson, 'The Church: An Ordered Body', in *Welcome, Holy Spirit*, Minneapolis, Augsburg, 1987, pp. 309–12, abridged (pp. 174–7).

8.4 Derek Prince, *Discipleship, Shepherding, Commitment*, Fort Lauderdale, Derek Prince, 1976, pp. 11–15 (pp. 177–9).

8.5 Dave Tomlinson, 'Loyalty: Covenant Relationship', *Restoration*, March–April 1978, p. 27 (pp. 180–1).

Questions to think about

1 Do the insights of sociology ring true for you?
2 What is happening to religion where you live? Is it flourishing, or being challenged by secularization, or being transformed?
3 If you attend a Pentecostal or charismatic church, is it sectarian in its attitudes?
4 If people buy more because more goods are available, will they become more religious if more religions are available?

Further reading

Bruce, Steve (2002), *God is Dead: Secularization in the West*, Oxford, Blackwell.

Kay, William K. (2007), *Apostolic Networks in Britain*, Carlisle, Paternoster Press.

Davie, Grace (2007), *The Sociology of Religion*, London, Sage.

15

Sociology 2

In many respects RCT [Rational Choice Theory] is to America what secularization theory is to Europe. (Grace Davie)[1]

The ethos of modern society (individual autonomy, social and cultural diversity, practical relativism) is a uniquely hostile environment for any minority belief-system. (Steve Bruce)[2]

The subject of practical theology as a practical science is situated within the historical context of the practical character of theology in general. (Johannes van der Ven)[3]

Introduction

In this final chapter, we continue to reflect sociologically on Pentecostalism. We do so, first, by considering Rational Choice Theory (RCT) as an alternative to secularization theory – though there is no reason why the two theories should not work in tandem. Second, we look at practical theology which, for present purposes, can be categorized as a discipline in a close relationship with sociology. Lastly, we consider seven main areas of Pentecostalism.

Rational Choice Theory

If we assume that there are fixed parameters to the human condition – we are born with the risk of perinatal injury, we face an uncertain universe full of painful accidents and we must come to terms with the darkness of death – it is not surprising that religion exists. All the major religions provide well-tested responses to these features of our lives. As a result,

---

1 Grace Davie (2007), *The Sociology of Religion*, London, Sage, p. 67.
2 Steve Bruce (2002), *God is Dead*, Oxford, Blackwell, p. 160.
3 Johannes van der Ven (1993), *Practical Theology: An Empirical Approach*, Kampen, Netherlands, p. 33.

religion is bound up with the perpetual struggles of humanity. Rational Choice Theory presumes that, in every society, there is a fixed quota of religion that finds expression in our choices.[4] These choices balance out benefits and costs, in the same way as economic choices do. High costs are paid if we accede to rigorous religious demands, but these demands allow us to gain high benefits in the form of strong personal and psychological security. Life seems less uncertain, we have an explanation for accidents and, most of all, we have an answer to death itself. Low costs come in the form of weak religious demands but these only deliver limited benefits.

A logical consequence of the theory is that religious life will flourish where there are many providers of religion. Or, to put this another way, in societies where religious choice is limited, secularization will be most evident. Rational Choice Theory has been used to explain the vitality of religiosity in the United States. Where there are lots of religious providers, there is a religion for everybody to suit every need. The beauty of this explanation is that it handles the contrasting levels of religiosity in North America and in Europe. Rather than explaining the decline of religion in the Western world by the advance of scientific modernity – and then having to offer a supplementary hypothesis for the different levels of religiosity in North America and Europe – the theory covers both continents. Where there is choice, religion flourishes; where there is no choice, religion declines. Indeed, one scholar goes further and argues that 'religious supply generates an increase in demand, not the other way round'.[5]

Debates between rational choice and secularization theorists have at times been strongly worded, and it is not necessary for us to choose between the two theories. It may well be, for instance, that secularization explains an overall trend, while RTC explains micro-trends. It may be that the two theories function differently with respect to men and women[6] or within different historical or geographical settings.[7]

Sociological explanation

We need to be clear what sociological explanation does. The struggle by Durkheim to establish sociology independent of psychology revolved around his care to maximize the contribution of 'social facts' and to

---

4 'We argue that the sources of religion are shifting constantly in societies but that the amount of religion remains constant.' R. Stark and W. S. Bainbridge (1985), *A Theory of Religion*, New York, Peter Lang, pp. 2, 3.

5 Davie, *Sociology*, p. 73, quoting Fink.

6 Davie, *Sociology*, p. 83.

7 Davie, *Sociology*, p. 77.

minimize the contribution of individual psychological differences.[8] In his study of suicide he examined the social conditions within Protestant and Roman Catholic countries and argued that Protestant religion tended to enhance individual decision-making whereas Catholicism tended to diminish it. For this reason, and because Protestant religious communities might be less supportive than Catholic or Jewish ones, suicide would be more frequent in Protestant countries as, indeed, it proved to be.[9] The reasoning adopted by Durkheim is classically sociological. Social factors predominate because society shapes the very concepts by which we think.

The danger of secularization theory is that it appears to minimize the role of human agency and to leave us with a sense of inevitability about the decline of belief systems and their institutional correlates. As religious beliefs decline, so the institutions that express and support these beliefs also decline. Since these institutions are social and public, religion declines in public consciousness. The danger of RTC is that it overplays the role of human rationality by ignoring the force of habit and emotion. It envisages large numbers of autonomous individuals constantly calculating how to achieve their ends with the minimum of psychological or economic cost. It neglects the durability of institutions (which minimize behavioural variation) and the function of education in shaping our perception of choice.

Practical theology

Theology, like most intellectual fields, has a practical department; there is a theoretical dimension and a practical application. Initially, practical theology was concerned with the pastoral training of ministers but, more recently, it has diverged into separate approaches.[10] In the approach recommended here, practical theology makes use of social science methods to explore theological questions. Social science methods may

8 E. Durkheim (1938), *The Rules of Sociological Method*, New York, Free Press, e.g. pp. xxxix, xlviif; Gianfranco Poggi (2000), *Durkheim*, Oxford, Oxford University Press, pp. 29–31.

9 E. Durkheim (1897), *Le Suicide: étude de sociology*, Paris, Alcan.

10 Duncan B. Forrester (2000), *Truthful Action: Explorations in Practical Theology*, Edinburgh, T & T Clark. See also the extended discussion in Mary E. Moore (2004), 'Purposes of Practical Theology: A Comparative Analysis between United States Practical Theologians and Johannes van der Ven', in Chris A. M. Hermans and Mary E. Moore (eds), *Hermeneutics and Empirical Research in Practical Theology*, Leiden, Brill, pp. 169–95; Richard R. Osmer (2008), *Practical Theology: An Introduction*, Grand Rapids, MI, Eerdmans; John Reader (2008), *Reconstructing Practical Theology*, Aldershot, Ashgate; Pete Ward (2008), *Participation and Mediation: A Practical Theology for the Liquid Church*, London, SCM Press.

be qualitative (using words) or quantitative (using numbers). In one of the most sophisticated attempts to combine theology and social sciences, we begin with an enquiry that is theologically driven because the focus of its investigation is brought to attention by theological discourse.[11] For instance, we may be concerned with the best way to plant churches or train ministers or lead worship or relate congregations to their surrounding culture. We may be concerned with interpretations of human suffering in parallel Christian traditions. What matters is that the preliminary concern is theological. This is followed by a reflection on the theological concepts involved, and these concepts may then be translated into social science variables that can be tested in a real setting. The testing can occur through the established methods of the social sciences. The results of this empirical testing are returned to the hands of theologians who will reflect theologically upon what has been found. In this way the solution to a problem or the answering of a question begins in theology, switches into social science methods and then concludes in theology. We will use the perspectives of practical theology to illuminate several of the areas that follow.

Seven areas of Pentecostalism

These areas are presented in roughly historical order. It has to be emphasized that each of these areas merits copious study and that the abbreviated versions given below are only intended to illustrate the breadth of Pentecostalism and the general possibilities opened up by sociological theory and practical theology.

Education

Here we look at the burgeoning of Pentecostal educational programmes and institutions and see these as a means by which religion reproduces itself in socially acceptable ways. We presuppose a distinction between education, which respects the rights and rationality of learners, and indoctrination which does not.[12] In sociological terms it is unclear whether Rational Choice Theory or secularization theory better explains the growth of educational institutions. The founding of an educational institution represents a *choice* to examine and perpetuate the religious outlook. Equally, we could say that educational institutions are formed as a *defence* against secularization. And this may be so even if secularization and education grow from the same intellectual root, that is, the desire to

---

11 Van der Ven, *Practical Theology*.

12 I. A. Snook (1972), *Indoctrination and Education*, London, Routledge and Keegan Paul.

demystify the world by extending knowledge. In any case, neither of these two sociological theories can account for the diversity of Pentecostal education. There are now Pentecostal liberal arts colleges, distance learning programmes of great professionalism and well-endowed Pentecostal universities. We are better seeing Pentecostal education as being generated by a sequence of historical factors: first, the protection of doctrine, then the formation of denominations with accredited ministers, and then the training of such ministers in line with denominational norms, and finally the flourishing of genuine higher education.[13]

Women

Pentecostals recognized that the Spirit was poured out on women as much as on men and that charismatic gifts can operate as freely through women as men. The passage in Acts 2, which describes the initial arrival of the Holy Spirit, specifies the occurrence of glossolalia and also refers back to Joel's prophecy when it was said that the Spirit would be poured out on 'your sons *and daughters*' (Acts 2.17).

The role of women within Pentecostalism has been much studied.[14] In the beginning, women were active and important carriers of Pentecostalism.[15] This can be seen in the Welsh revival, in the Azusa Street revival, in the outpouring of the Spirit at Mukti, India, and later in the many Spirit-filled female missionaries who went out all over the world. In the United States, Aimee Semple McPherson became a cultural icon and left a lasting legacy. As denominational regulation grew in complexity and rigidity, Pentecostal women found themselves hemmed in and unable to com-

---

13 For further discussion, see William K. Kay (2004), 'Pentecostal Education', *Journal of Beliefs and Values* 25.2, 229–39.

14 E.g. E. C. Lehman Jr (1981), 'Patterns of Lay Resistance to Women in Ministry', *Sociological Analysis* 41, 317–38; S. D. Rose (1987), 'Women Warriors: The Negotiation of Gender in a Charismatic Community', *Sociological Analysis* 48, 245–58; E. Blumhofer (1993), *Aimee Semple McPherson: Everybody's Sister*, Grand Rapids, MI, Eerdmans; D. M. Gill (1995), 'The Contemporary State of Women in Ministry in Assemblies of God', *Pneuma* 17.1, 33–6; W. K. Kay and M. Robbins (1999), 'A Woman's Place is on her Knees: The Pastor's View of the Role of Women in Assemblies of God', *Journal of the European Pentecostal Theological Association* 18, 64–75; G. B. McGee (2004), *People of the Spirit: The Assemblies of God*, Springfield, MO, Gospel Publishing House; Philip Jenkins (2006), *The New Faces of Christianity*, Oxford, Oxford University Press, ch. 7; E. Alexander and A. Yong (eds) (2008), *Philip's Daughters: Women in Pentecostal-Charismatic Leadership*, Princeton Theological Monograph.

15 Indeed, Bernice Martin argues persuasively that Pentecostalism is still 'a modernizing egalitarian impulse'. See B. Martin (2001), 'The Pentecostal Gender Paradox: A Cautionary Tale for the Sociology of Religion', in R. K. Fenn (ed.), *The Blackwell Companion to the Sociology of Religion*, Oxford, Blackwell.

mand the influence they held in earlier days.[16] Gradually denominations became male-dominated and women found themselves pushed overseas to the less desirable posts and to the more sacrificial callings. While it is true that several Pentecostal denominations were open to the ministry of women long before the 1960s, it is equally true that many denominations in practice closed the door to women. British Assemblies of God always theoretically made room for female ministry but few congregations chose women pastors. This was not a matter of denominational policy but a consequence of congregational autonomy, and congregations reflected the preferences of their age.

From the 1960s women became important within the charismatic movement, especially among independent television evangelists (like Marilyn Hickey and Joyce Meyer from the 1990s), and in the home groups run by large Korean churches.[17] Sociologically, there was the tension between the traditional role of women in families and the freedom they found in Christ through the Spirit.[18] Any reduction in the role of women, any failure to mobilize their talents, led, in the long term, to religious decline. In this respect, it was in the interests of Pentecostals to make room for women and thereby to combat secularization. Too often, churches failed to find a balance, and women, particularly after the 1960s when financially rewarding careers opened up, were apt to devote their energies to the job market.[19] If they were attempting to maintain a Christian marriage, the couple might become a double-income pair with two careers to pursue.

The role of women within Pentecostalism also fits an explanation taken from Rational Choice Theory. Where there were many options for women in ministry, they became writers, editors, evangelists, pastors, and in other ways fulfilled their callings. In 1925, two-thirds of missionaries in American Assemblies of God were women.[20] When options for women were closed down by denominational protocols, women were forced to work in whatever limited niches were available. Some became

16 Relevant was the example of Assemblies of God in North America. Its first constitutional statement in 1914 affirmed that women are called 'to prophesy and preach the Gospel', though not to act as elders. However, in 1935 the prohibition on female elders was reversed. Gill, 'Contemporary State'. Although women could act as elders, their opportunities for full-time ministry were still limited.

17 Scott Billingsley (2008), *It's a New Day: Race and Gender in the Modern Charismatic Movement*, Tuscaloosa, AL, University of Alabama Press.

18 A point made by Billingsley, *New Day, passim*.

19 For instance, in Britain between 1971 and 1976 a further 1 million married women moved into paid employment. See Arthur Marwick (1982), *British Society Since 1945*, Harmondsworth, Penguin, p. 190.

20 Barbara Cavaness (2006), 'God Calling: Women in Pentecostal Missions', in Grant McClung (ed.), *Azusa Street and Beyond: 100 Years*, Gainsville, FL, Bridge Logos, p. 59.

musical directors and Sunday school teachers and others went overseas. When Pentecostal churches dampened down the free flow of spiritual gifts, there were even fewer opportunities for women since they could no longer prophesy in congregational worship. When women found themselves shunned by the church, they turned to the world of commerce or business and the churches were the poorer for it.[21] The rational choice made by women was this, 'where there is room for me to exercise my gifts, I will go', whether this was in the church (as many preferred) or in secular employment (which had the advantage of being paid).

Social concern

For all its eschatological fervour, Pentecostals had their feet firmly planted on the ground. While it is true that many of the early Pentecostal denominations in the West were frightened of preaching a 'social gospel' because of its associations with liberal theology, Pentecostals in the rest of the world were keen to ameliorate the societies where they lived. Before too long Pentecostals began to set up homes for old people and orphanages, and to provide food for the hungry. Aimee Semple McPherson is an early example of this compassionate ministry. In the 1960s, David Wilkerson launched his teen challenge ministry to rehabilitate young drug addicts. The startling characteristic of his work was his insistence that young people could find a way out of drug dependency by 'cold turkey' (immediate withdrawal of all drugs) and baptism in the Holy Spirit.[22] More recently, Donald Miller and Tetsunao Yamamori have investigated global Pentecostalism from the angle of Christian social engagement. They look at social ministries among children and youth in South Africa, Egypt and Kenya, drug rehabilitation programmes in Hong Kong, and outreach work in Nairobi and Brazil among street children. They see this 'progressive Pentecostalism' as an example of holistic ministry and write that the thesis of their book 'is that some of the most innovative social programs in the world are being initiated by the fast-growing Pentecostal churches'.[23]

Many of these activities flow out of the lives of big, booming Pente-

---

21 Keith Warrington (2008), *Pentecostal Theology*, London, T & T Clark, p. 145, quoting David Roebuck and K. C. Mundy, says that in the Church of God male leaders circumscribed the roles of women to protect family values. Between 1950 and 1990 the percentage of women ministers in this denomination declined from 18.2 to 7.7.

22 David Wilkerson (1964), *The Cross and the Switchblade*, New York, Pyramid Books. See also W. K. Kay and A. E. Dyer (eds), (2004), *A Reader in Pentecostal and Charismatic Studies*, London, SCM Press, ch. 16.

23 Donald E. Miller and Tetsunao Yamamori (2007), *Global Pentecostalism: The New Face of Christian Social Engagement*, Los Angeles, University of California Press, p. 6.

costal congregations, as well as through the parachurch agencies. The activism and energy of Pentecostals may be stimulated by the narratives of their own lives (if they have been 'saved' from crime or addiction) or by reading the Gospels with fresh eyes. It is difficult to explain the range of social concerns tackled in so many different countries of the world using sociological theory. This work is not undertaken as an antidote to secularism or in response to a calculus of meritorious behaviour. The best way to understand what is happening is through the application of practical theological methods, something that Miller and Yamamori sketch out in their introductory chapter. Altruistic behaviour has attracted a variety of explanations, some of which unconvincingly attempt to translate it into a form of selfishness.[24] The best explanation begins with the notion that Pentecostals feel empowered to the extent that they wish to tackle the most difficult social problems by the most direct methods. It is empowerment that is a starting point, as earlier research has indicated[25] – but this empowerment must be linked with compassion.

Democratic/undemocratic governance

Pentecostal denominations could, from the beginning, be positioned on a continuum ranging from democratic to undemocratic. The earliest lightweight organizations were designed to enhance the position of a particular leader (e.g. Charles Fox Parham) or, in the constitution of Assemblies of God, to set in place a scaffolding that was fundamentally democratic. Although there were no general debates on the topic, Pentecostals were aware that the organizations that they were creating vested power either in the few or the many. This contrast arose partly out of the range of biblical models of leadership on offer. Israel during the time of the judges was ruled by an almost random series of charismatic individuals who were specially gifted to meet national emergencies. During the time of Israel's monarchy a dynastic system was in operation so that the throne passed from father to son. The earlier system required no court or formal apparatus of state, and tribal elders attended to the affairs of their people. The later system required a centre of government, a palace, a court, a system of taxation and strict rules of accession. In the early church, the apostles had authority and their opinions were important in the taking of major decisions but, in local churches in far-flung provinces, elders governed congregations. One might think that the Old Testament governmental systems were irrelevant to Pentecostalism – and so they

---

24 Richard Dawkins (2006), *The Selfish Gene*, Oxford, Oxford University Press.

25 L. J. Francis and W. K. Kay (1995), *Teenage Religion and Values*, Leominster, Gracewing. In a survey of more than 13,000 young people we found that theists were much more likely than atheists to reject the proposition, 'There is nothing I can do to solve the world's problems', p. 75.

should have been – but it was all too easy for careless readers of Scripture to overlook fundamental distinctions between Israel and the church.

In democratic systems, authority was recognized by vote. Hands were raised at conferences or slips of paper were put into ballot boxes. Shared collective decisions could be made about electing individuals to positions of power and responsibility. This was completely in line with Western democratic tradition but, it has to be said, completely absent from the New Testament. There appears to be no voting in the Bible. Nevertheless, the Assemblies of God denominations, in the different countries of the world where this style of Pentecostalism was found, almost invariably chose their Executive Councils or their superintendents by vote. Before any vote, there was debate. The result of this lengthy, and sometimes mind-numbingly boring procedure, was to allow every minister to express an opinion. As the denominations grew larger and larger, conferences became more and more bogged down in lengthy agendas, and discussions could drift away from substantive issues to the minutiae of business procedure. Propositions were made, amended, voted on, re-amended and voted on again until a majority was eventually obtained. As a result, both in the early days of Pentecostalism and from the 1970s onwards, more radical Pentecostals began to question the value of any voting system. One of its weaknesses was that it gave as much weight to the opinion of the newest and youngest member of any conference as to the oldest and wisest. Several of the democratic Pentecostal denominations (e.g. in Britain and Australia) were persuaded to transition into the undemocratic format.[26]

In sociological terms we could argue that the drift away from democracy was a response to the pressure of secular culture. The churches needed to be effective and decisive to survive. They wanted greater authority to be given to the most successful ministers. By recognizing these ministers as in some sense apostolic, it became easier to give them authority and to let decision-making be carried out away from the conference floor. The individuals who were given authority within previously democratic Pentecostal denominations were often pastors of megachurches who, for the most part, ran their churches without any in-built consultative machinery. As a result, it became easy for megachurch pastors to hand their congregations on to their sons or sons-in-law or for an entire denomination to come under the control of a very small group of people.[27] Here, if we are to apply Rational Choice Theory, it must be that the choices that were made rested upon insufficient information. No doubt the ministers who voted to give additional authority to their leaders assumed that they were going to gain from 'better leadership', and in this sense

26 Shane Clifton (2009), *Pentecostal Churches in Transition*, Leiden, Brill.
27 Evidence could be provided but will be withheld to avoid offence or litigation.

their decisions were rational. Unfortunately, if they then found that the leadership they were receiving was no better than the leadership they had been receiving during the days when the denomination was democratic, there was no way they could turn the clock back. They were stuck with a new system.

Race

Race has been implicated in Pentecostalism from its inception. Not only were the different races involved in the earliest Pentecostal outpourings but, within the Azusa Street revival, multi-racialism was a feature of the meetings. Within the United States this early conjunction of races was shattered by doctrinal disputes and by residual prejudice, with the result that most Pentecostal denominations emerged as mono-racial entities. There were honourable exceptions to this rule (for example, the Church of God (Cleveland, TN)), and even the largely white denominations became more racially integrated as the century proceeded. In 1994 representatives of black and white Pentecostal denominations gathered in Memphis and issued a 'racial reconciliation' manifesto.[28] In a moving and apparently unplanned demonstration of repentance a white pastor, Donald Evans, washed the feet of a black leader, Bishop Clemmons. This was reciprocated when Bishop Blake washed the feet of the Assemblies of God General Superintendent, Thomas Trask.[29]

The development of Pentecostalism and race in the United States is well documented and more salient than elsewhere because of the multiplicity of races within the North American population.[30] In other parts of the world nations tend to be more racially homogeneous with the result that racial issues attract less public attention. As we have seen, in India race is bound up with caste to produce forms of prejudice that can be disguised under the covering of Hindu culture. In Malaysia, the political constitution presumes Malays are Muslim and forbids them from converting to any other faith. Consequently, the Christian community is largely Chinese and of Indian extraction. Even so, the discrimination against Christians may be seen as a form of racism. In the United Kingdom, racism has been connected with multiculturalism in the sense that the cultural practices of some religious groups have given rise to racist

---

28 Signed by Ithiel Clemmons, Leonard Lovett, Cecil M. Robeck and Harold D. Hunter. See Paul Harvey and Philip Goff (eds), *Religion in America Since 1945*, New York, Columbia University Press, pp. 388–9.

29 Harvey and Goff (eds), *Religion*, pp. 389–91, quoting Vinson Synan.

30 Charles Fox Parham justified racial discrimination on theological grounds. Brief sociological discussion can be found in George Lundskow (2008), *The Sociology of Religion: A Substantive and Transdisciplinary Approach*, London, Pine Forge, p. 350.

responses. The practice of arranged marriage conflicts with Western concepts of human rights, with the result that those religious groups that prevent their children from choosing their own spouses may be discriminated against.[31] Even so, Pentecostals in the United Kingdom with Caribbean ancestry may find themselves disadvantaged socially. In Europe, Pentecostalism is concerned with race by virtue of its connection with migrant churches. Here, migrant Africans within German or Dutch culture (as we have seen in Chapter 10) may be welcomed by liberal theological traditions but shunned elsewhere. Given that these Africans are often in receipt of welfare payments, their treatment in the press or on the streets appears to depend upon their willingness to comply with the majority culture.

The debate about race in the United States and Europe has periodically been highly charged. The civil rights movement of the 1960s was suffused by African American grievances and inspired by rhetoric that had its origins in African American preaching.[32] It is impossible to do justice to the many aspects of the debate but it is true to say that at the heart of the civil rights movement biblical conceptions of justice informed the aspirations and influenced the non-violent strategy of its greatest leader, Martin Luther King.[33] Only later did other activists move the debate in a different direction. James Cone, for instance, contended that 'black theology is not prepared to accept any doctrine of God, man, Christ, or Scripture which contradicts the black demand for freedom now'.[34] Indeed, he could argue that 'God is black' by which he meant that God's identification with the poor and oppressed made blacks a latter-day chosen people.[35] Thus the debate about race impacted theology and produced a new theology forged in the fire of racial conflict and adapted to enable black pride to replace black humility, and black intellectual constructions to knock down long-standing European traditions.[36] Even so, we should note, in the words of Barack Obama, that African American churches in the mainstream served

As the centre of the community's political, economic, and social as well as spiritual life; it understood in an intimate way the biblical call

---

31 This can be seen by some press coverage in the UK and by national or local elections where race is more salient than party in determining the outcome.

32 Martin Luther King, Jr is a prime exemplar of the power of this rhetoric.

33 Harvey and Goff (eds), *Religion*, pp. 139–49, which quotes King's letter from Birmingham City jail in 1963. See also Michael Battle (2006), *The Black Church in America*, Oxford, Blackwell, ch. 6.

34 James H. Cone (2006), *Black Theology and Black Power*, Maryknoll, NY, Orbis Books, p. 120.

35 Harvey and Goff (eds), *Religion*, pp. 170–4.

36 Robert Beckford (2000), *Dread and Pentecostal*, London, SPCK, is informative here.

to feed the hungry and clothe the naked and challenge powers and principalities.[37]

The most high-profile black Pentecostal proclamations were made through the television programmes of a new generation of media ministers. Frederick K. C. Price, T. D. Jakes and Creflo Dollar have built megachurches that reflect the strength of the African American Pentecostal constituency.[38] Much of their theology has been infused with health and prosperity doctrine though, more recently, they have focused on lifestyle and family issues. The arrival of a black middle class has been followed by the typical failings of middle-class professional people: overwork, broken marriages, heart problems caused by overweight, unruly children and recreational drug abuse. In the United States the influential black middle class has an abundance of material possessions bought at the cost of long hours of demanding professional work.[39] The interpretation of race in North America has been informed by sociological enquiry but largely unclouded by sociological theory.

Church growth

As we have already seen, Pentecostal churches have grown throughout the course of the twentieth century. Yet the reasons for their growth have been a matter of sociological speculation. It has been suggested in Chapters 5, 6 and 7 that they grow because there is a compatibility between a Pentecostal world view (one with miracles, spirits and an interventionist God) and the default world view of a continent (e.g. Africa or Asia). Yet the compatibility of world views cannot be the whole answer. This is because congregations grow at different speeds even when the dominant cultural world view is sympathetic to Pentecostalism. Could it be that Pentecostal churches grow precisely because they are Pentecostal?

This question was raised by Margaret Poloma in a study of American Assemblies of God.[40] My own questionnaire-based survey of four classical Pentecostal denominations in a British context replicated and extended her study.[41] In a nutshell, Poloma proposed that Pentecostal churches in which an abundance of charismatic gifts is manifested tend also to be evangelistic and attractive to newcomers. Congregations

---

37 Barack Obama (2007), *The Audacity of Hope*, New York, Canongate, p. 207.

38 Scott Billingsley (2008), *New Day*, ch. 4.

39 Milmon F. Harrison (2005), *Righteous Riches: The Word of Faith Movement in Contemporary African American Religion*, Oxford, Oxford University Press.

40 Margaret M. Poloma (1989), *The Assemblies of God at the Crossroads: Charisma and Institutional Dilemmas*, Knoxville, TN, University of Tennessee Press.

41 William K. Kay (2000), *Pentecostals in Britain*, Carlisle, Paternoster Press, ch. 9.

become charismatic and evangelistic as a result of the example and teaching of their ministers. These deductive steps can be made by following a series of statistically significant correlations. In the British data there is a correlation between ministerial charismatic activity and ministerial evangelistic activity. There is also a correlation between ministerial charismatic activity and congregational charismatic activity and, finally, there is a correlation between church growth and congregational charismatic activity. Consequently, we can envisage a small congregation being gradually transformed by the impact of a successful Pentecostal minister. He or she moves to the congregation and begins to encourage evangelism and charismata. Gradually the group responds and, once it reaches about 200 people, the congregation becomes outgoing and conscious of its varied spiritual capabilities. Newcomers receive help from the body of the congregation rather than from a single professional member of the clergy. In short, the successful Pentecostal minister has mobilized, enlarged and empowered the congregation to meet human need. Charismatic gifts sensitively operated bring people spiritual, psychological and physical help, and people helped in this way are glad to join Pentecostal churches.

There are other methods by which congregations can be mobilized, most notably by the 'home group' principle. Here the church is energized by numerous small groups and the dozens of leaders of these groups who are given responsibility for attending to the well-being of the families in their care. Again, the congregation is not simply a passive collection of spectators listening to the preaching of a minister from afar but, instead, is expected to take part in prayer, local projects and evangelism.

This analysis of the multifaceted activity of Pentecostal congregations has been achieved by applying practical theological methods to large-scale studies of Pentecostal denominations. The questionnaire survey observes the academic criteria of quantitative social sciences while the focus of attention upon charismatic gifts is derived from theological study of the text of the New Testament and the descriptions given there of the workings of first-century congregations.

Networks

As we saw in Chapter 10, some Pentecostal or charismatic churches from the 1970s onwards began to take on a reticular structure. They became networks linked together by apostolic ministry. They were flatter than hierarchical denominations in the sense that there was a shorter distance between the bottom of the communal structure and the top. In sociological terms it is important to note that the old denominations were founded at a time when the social order was heavily stratified. Whereas Europeans knew about an old landed aristocracy, even the United States in the late nineteenth century began to observe the arrival of a new ostentatiously rich plutocracy. In a markedly stratified society the upper echelons of a church would map onto the highest social echelons. So, in Europe bishops consorted with the ruling classes, and lower ranks of ecclesiastical clergy consorted with appropriate points lower down the social scale. In the USA and elsewhere the connection between the highest ecclesiastical ranks and the highest levels of society were less obvious but they were there all the same. However, when Western society began to evolve rapidly after 1945, social differences were eroded. In a society without big class barriers, the networks of the 1970s were able to follow natural social contours much more easily than the old denominations. We can see this form of adaptation as one reason for the ability of networks to resist secularization, and it is a phenomenon open to study by practical theology.[42]

Conclusion

Pentecostalism exists within many different societies, all of which are developing at different speeds. The application of sociological theory to the study of Pentecostalism may shed light on particular national contexts but cannot be guaranteed to illuminate every place equally. Moreover, few sociological commentators would now claim that their investigations were capable of uncovering predictive laws similar to those customarily utilized by the physical sciences. Sociological inquiry can show how Pentecostalism has adapted to changing social conditions and, in this way, begin to distinguish between essential and non-essential elements. In the earlier historical chapters of this book our assumption is that ultimately it is the marriage between theology and experience that makes Pentecostalism what it is. We can put this another way by saying that the driving aims of Pentecostalism are supplied by its theology whereas the social forms of Pentecostalism result from its context. If, as Pentecostals believe, the Holy Spirit continues to be poured out in the twenty-first century, we will see yet more innovations in the years to come.

Cross-references to the SCM Reader *Pentecostal and Charismatic Studies*

Women

15.1 E. N. Bell, 'Women Elders', *The Christian Evangel*, 15 August 1914, p. 2 (pp. 259–60).
15.2 Arthur Wallis, 'Women in the Church', *Restoration*, September–October 1979, pp. 28–9 (pp. 260–2).

---

42 W. K. Kay (2007), *Apostolic Networks in Britain*, Carlisle, Paternoster Press

Social concern

16.1 David Wilkerson, *The Cross and the Switchblade*, New York, Pyramid Books, 1964, pp. 153–7 (pp. 263–6).

Prosperity

14.1 Kenneth Copeland, *Dear Partner*, Fort Worth, TX, Kenneth Copeland, 1997, pp. 115–20 (pp. 255–8).

Megachurches

21.1 C. Dye, 'Kensington Temple: London City Church', http://www.kt.org/g12/london.php (2003) (pp. 291–3).

Questions to think about

1 Which of the seven areas outlined in this chapter does Rational Choice Theory offer most help in understanding?
2 Could practical theology help us understand the areas of race or education?
3 Can Pentecostalism help to heal the effects of racialism?
4 Has Pentecostalism treated women well?

Further reading

Billingsley, S. (2008), *It's a New Day: Race and Gender in the Modern Charismatic Movement*, Tuscaloosa, AL, University of Alabama Press.

Davie, G. (2007), *The Sociology of Religion*, London, Sage.

Harvey, P. and Goff, P. (eds), *Religion in America Since 1945*, New York, Columbia University Press.

Miller, D. E. and Yamamori, T. (2007), *Global Pentecostalism: The New Face of Christian Social Engagement*, Los Angeles, University of California Press.

Stark. R. and Bainbridge, W. S. (1985), *A Theory of Religion*, New York, Peter Lang.

Time Line of Events of the Pentecostal and Charismatic Movements in Britain and USA

Europe/UK	Influences from the rest of the world	USA
1740–80s John Wesley and John Fletcher's ideas on perfection and holiness and the use of the term 'baptism in the Holy Spirit'.		
1807 Primitive Methodism revived Methodism with various phenomena accompanying much evangelistic fervour. Camp/tent Meetings developed in USA.		
1831 Edward Irving and the Catholic Apostolic Church – glossolalia evidenced.		
	1860s onwards: Holiness Movements used terminology like Baptism in the Holy Ghost, later adopted with new meaning by the Pentecostal Movement. *continued*	

Europe/UK	Influences from the rest of the world	USA
	Various streams from these American or British Keswick Higher Life teachings were instrumental in building a platform for the Pentecostals.	
		Charles Finney's revival meetings and altar calls – anxious seat 1823–1870s. W. E. Boardman formed a 'reformed line' to sanctification.
1850s–80s John Nelson Darby – Dispensationalist approach to Scripture and eschatology.		
	1857–58 revival spread to Ireland, Wales, England ...	
		Phoebe Palmer and altar calls – crisis sanctification 1839 onwards and by 1859 equated sanctification with baptism in the Holy Ghost.
		IPHC National Holiness Association formed in Vineland, NJ (IPHC[1]) 1867
1875 Keswick Conferences started in UK (holiness by faith, power for service).		
		1870s onwards D. L. Moody – similar to Keswick teaching.
		1879 Iowa Holiness Association formed.

Europe/UK	Influences from the rest of the world	USA
		1886 Barney Creek meetings became the proto-**Church of God**.[2]
		1894–1905 Charles Dowie and Zion City Healing rooms.
		1895 1898 First Pentecostal Holiness congregation organized in Goldsboro, NC.
		1899 Fire Baptized Holiness Association (national) formed; B. H. Irwin elected general overseer.
		1862–1948 Frank Sandford.
		1901 Charles Parham at Topeka, Kansas. **Agnes Ozman** received the gift of tongues and that began to become a sign of receiving the baptism of the Holy Ghost.
		1902 First Church of God is formed.
1904 The Welsh Revival became a catalyst for furthering hunger for God in Britain, India, France and California.		
		1905 **W. J. Seymour** accepts Parham's doctrine.
		1906–07 First General Assembly of the Church of God, Cleveland, Tennessee.

Europe/UK	Influences from the rest of the world	USA
		1906–09 Azusa Street Revival, Los Angeles, became the centre of Pentecostal experience with W. J. Seymour at the centre after events of 9 April 1906 at Bonnie Brae Street. Joseph Smale and Frank Bartleman became involved.
	1906 Korean Revival.	
	1906 T. B. Barratt visits Los Angeles, and returns to Norway to commence Pentecostal meetings there.	
1907 T. B. Barratt visits Sunderland Parish Church.		
1907 Kassel Meetings – German Pentecostalism begins with Jonathan Paul and Emil Meyer.		
		1907 G. Cashwell led Free-Will Baptists of Carolinas into Pentecostalism.
		1908 W. H. Durham visits Azusa Street from Chicago.
	1909 Willis C. Hoover founds Pentecostal Methodist Church of Chile.	
1909 Confidence Paper published from Sunderland.		

Europe/UK	Influences from the rest of the world	USA
1909 Pentecostal Missionary Union formed through the auspices of Sunderland's Revd Alexander A. Boddy and Cecil Polhill. India and China form the initial destinations; Belgian Congo later. **1909 Apostolic Church UK** formed by D. P. Williams as Apostle, and Brother W. J. Williams as Prophet at Penygroes. **1909 Berlin Declaration** opposes incipient Pentecostalism in Germany.	**1909 Argentina** **– Alice Wood** leads congregations to Pentecostalism. Italian missionaries Louis Fracesconi, Giacomo Lombardi and Lucia Menna also arrive.	**1910 W. H. Durham** begins **Finished Work** movement in Chicago. **1910** David Wesley Myland wrote his book *The Latter Rain Covenant*. **1911 Fire Baptized Holiness and Pentecostal Holiness Church** merged in Falcon, NC; S. D. Page elected first general superintendent.

Europe/UK	Influences from the rest of the world	USA
		1911 A second visit of W. H. Durham to Azusa Street led to Seymour expelling him for his teaching the Spirit's coming as a two-stage event, not three. Controversy ensued.
		1911 onwards 'Jesus only' Doctrine controversy; rejected by **1915** by Assemblies of God, USA.
	1913 onwards Liberia, Ivory Coast & Ghana – William Wade Harris (1865–1929) promoting the gospel with miraculous signs, contextualized and persecuted.	
1914 Mülheim Association founded for German Pentecostalism.		
		1914 Assemblies of God, USA formed in Hot Springs, Arkansas.
	1914 Bulawayo, Rhodesia (now **Zimbabwe**) had a Pentecostal mission from this date.	
1915 Elim Pentecostal Churches UK formed by George Jeffreys in Ireland; spread to Britain especially over 1920s–30s with evangelistic campaigns planting new churches.		

Europe/UK	Influences from the rest of the world	USA
	1915 W. F. P. Burton forms the Congo Evangelistic Mission, which would accept Pentecostal workers from various Pentecostal denominations.	
1919–30s George and Stephen Jeffreys' campaigns in Britain create many Pentecostal churches.		
1919 Hampstead Heath Bible School, London, formed with Howard Carter as Principal, continuing the PMU's training schemes.		
1922–24 Negotiations in Britain among independent Pentecostal Assemblies.		
1924 The Assemblies of God Great Britain and N. Ireland formed, unrelated to the American one.		
		1918 Aimee Semple McPherson began preaching and in 1923 established the 5,300-seat Angelus Temple⁵ which became the centre of her revival, healing and benevolent ministries. She was the first woman to receive a FCC radio licence and was a pioneer religious broadcaster.

Europe/UK	Influences from the rest of the world	USA
		1928 700 stations broadcast various Christian teachings in USA. **1930 Kathryn Kuhlman** gains recognition by opening Denver Revival Tabernacle.
1932 Louis Dallière defended the Pentecostal experience in **France** and later founded the **Union of Prayer,** significant in later French ecumenical charismatic movement. **Douglas Scott** itinerates in France creating **French Assemblies of God.**		
	1936 Smith Wigglesworth prophesied to David du Plessis in South Africa of a coming worldwide movement.	
1939 European Pentecostal Conference in Stockholm, Sweden.		
	1939–45 World War Two intervenes. **1947 First World Pentecostal Conference.** **1947–62 David du Plessis** from South Africa became General Secretary for the World Pentecostal Conferences. Donald Gee became editor of the conference's paper, *Pentecost,* until he died.	

318

Europe/UK	Influences from the rest of the world	USA
		1948 Latter Rain Movement[4] resurfaced in North Battleford Saskatchewan by Brother Hawtin and P. G. Hunt after meeting William Branham (b. 1909).
		20 April 1949 Opposed by Assemblies of God, USA.
		1948 onwards Healing Evangelists like T. L. Osborn, W. Branham, Oral Roberts, A. A. Allen, A. C. Valdez, Katherine Kuhlman roam the world. *Voice of Healing* promotes these from Gordon Lindsay's Christ for All Nations.
		1951 Full Gospel Business Men's Fellowship International was started in California by Demos Shakarian;[5] now led by Richard Shakarian, it is in 132 nations, reaching Businessmen for Christ from a 'lay' perspective.
		1953 Jack Coe founded Fundamental Assemblies of God, on being expelled from AG.
		1954 onwards Oral Roberts broadcasted TV programmes. Others like Benny Hinn and Marilyn Hickey follow suit during **1980s**.

Europe/UK	Influences from the rest of the world	USA
		1958 T. L. Osborn ceased broadcasting to do more foreign healing ministry.
1950s Early signs of the Charismatic Movement in Britain.		
	1950s Brazil Manoel de Mello founds house churches, and Irgeja do Evangelho Quadrangular is launched through mass evangelism.	
	1954 Tommy Hicks held large meetings in Argentina.	
	1954 Ecumenical moves by David du Plessis, World Council Assembly, and by mid-1960s he introduced Pentecostal teaching to Roman Catholics at Notre Dame.	
	1958 Yonggi Cho commenced ministry in Seoul, South Korea. Great growth by later 1960s onwards. By 2008 Yoido Full Gospel Church claimed 760,000 members.	

Europe/UK	Influences from the rest of the world	USA
		c. 1959 Dennis Bennett, an Episcopalian priest at Van Nuys, California, experienced tongues; moved to St Luke's, Seattle, and wrote *Nine O'clock in the Morning*, promoting charismatic experience across the world. Followed by David Wilkerson's *The Cross and the Switchblade* (1963), which had great effect across denominations.
		1962 du Plessis disfellowshipped from Assemblies of God USA for contact with World Council of Churches.
		1963 Presbyterian Charismatic Communion began. Other denominations in USA followed suit.
1964 The Fountain Trust established as an organ for charismatic renewal among mainline churches, especially Anglicans; Michael Harper became its Director.		
		1965 Oral Roberts University chartered.

Europe/UK	Influences from the rest of the world	USA
1965 David Watson came to York and by 1973 built up the small congregation at St Michael le Belfry (although he died in 1984). Much evangelism resulted from renewal at this congregation, continuing with John Wimber's ministry visits in the 1990s.		
1966 Donald Gee died.		
	1960s Ezekiel Guti planted churches in **Zimbabwe:** Assemblies of God, African, founded 1968. Travelling ministry through Africa and to USA, growth through 1990s.	
		1967 Catholic Charismatic Renewal begins in Pittsburg, Pennsylvania – the 'Duquesne weekend'.
		1970s–1990s Communities like Mother of God, Gaithersburg, Maryland began.
Late 1960s/early 1970s Pioneer network of churches begins under **Gerald Coates** in UK.		
1971 Fountain Trust gathered 2000 charismatic leaders at Guildford Cathedral in the UK.		

Europe/UK	Influences from the rest of the world	USA
	In the same decade the Universal Church of the Kingdom of God was founded in **Brazil.**	
Early 1970s British Apostolic Networks are founded – Terry Virgo begins New Frontiers International from Brighton.		
1974 Roger Forster begins **Ichthus** in Forest Hill, London, as a holistic evangelistic training ministry.		
1975 Noel Stanton forms The Jesus Fellowship.		
1975 Bryn Jones formed the Bradford Church, which becomes the headquarters for **Restoration/Harvest Time,** mainly in the north of UK.		
		1975 *Charisma* **magazine** begins publication.
Late 1970s Gerald Coates forms **Pioneer** also London based.		
		1978 CBN university (now Regent University) founded by Pat Robertson, and broadcasts 700 club on TV.
		1981 Third Wave begins at Fuller Theological Seminary in California under **John Wimber.**

Europe/UK	Influences from the rest of the world	USA
1981 Ground Level network begins in Lincolnshire, UK. **Mid-1980s**, John Wimber's influence reaches UK. By 1990s Vineyard UK is formed and New Wine Bible week/network among Baptist and Anglican denominations grows stronger by late 1990s.		
	Since 1960s Ghana – Charismatic growth; great 'Pentecostal' growth according to two surveys in 1987 and 1992. Finance into broadcasting, promoting prosperity.	
	1985 Nicholas Bhengu, Zulu Pentecostal evangelist, in **South Africa,** died.	
	1992 Argentina Carlos Annacondia begins his ministry (spiritual warfare emphasis).	
	1990s Argentina – Omar Cabrera promoted prosperity ideas; Foundación Visión de Futuro which is linked with Asociación Iglesia de Dios Argentina; Hector Gimin also plants many churches.	

Europe/UK	Influences from the rest of the world	USA
		January 1994 Toronto blessing begins in Toronto Vineyard, Canada under John Arnott; visitors arrive from all over the world.[6]
		1994 Pensacola Revival, Florida, with Steve Hill.
		1994 Memphis Miracle of racial reconciliation.
1994/95 Sunderland Revival with Ken Gott creates UK centre for Toronto blessing.		
	1990s Cell church movement gets under way in Singapore and spread under Lawrence Kong, Ralph Neighbour and Lawrence Singlehurst (YWAM). Rapid church growth, missional output from Asia. Ideas spread across the world.	
	1991 onwards G12 system of cell church growth develops under Cesar Castellanos, Colombia. By 2000 this had influenced the biggest Pentecostal church in the UK – Kensington Temple, London City Church, under Colin Dye,[7] and from that to its own version of G12 c. 2005.	
	Late 1990s onwards emergent church noted.	

Europe/UK	Influences from the rest of the world	USA
	Massive population flows after 1945 and 1989 affected Pentecostal/charismatic growth, globalizing it further while greater persecution also spread.	

Notes

1 http://www.IPHC.org
2 http://www.chofgod.org/history.cfm
3 http://www.angelustemple.org/history1.shtml
4 http://www.discernment.org/restorat.htm#The%20Early%20Roots%20of%20 Latter%20Rain%20Theology/
5 http://www.fgbmfi.org/
6 http://www.tacf.org/
7 http://www.kt.org and http://www.elim.org.uk/

Bibliography

Abbreviations

NIDPCM = *New International Dictionary of Pentecostal and Charismatic Movements*, Grand Rapids, MI, Zondervan.

Abrams, M. (1909), 'How the Recent Revival was Brought About in India', *Latter Rain Evangel* July, 6–13.

Aker, B. C. (2002), '*Charismata*: Gifts, Enablements, or Ministries?', *Journal of Pentecostal Theology* 11.1, 53–69.

Aldridge, A. (2000), *Religion in the Contemporary World: A Sociological Introduction*, Cambridge, Polity Press.

Alexander, E. and Yong, A. (eds) (2008), *Philip's Daughters: Women in Pentecostal-Charismatic Leadership*, Princeton Theological Monograph.

Alexander, K. E. (2006), *Pentecostal Healing: Models in Theology and Practice*, Blandford Forum, Deo.

Ali, A. H. (2007), *Infidel: My Life*, London, Simon and Schuster.

Allen, D. (1994), *The Unfailing Stream*, Lancaster, Sovereign World.

Althouse, P. (2005), '"Left Behind" – Fact or Fiction: Ecumenical Dilemmas of the Fundamentalist Millenarian Tensions within Pentecostalism', *Journal of Pentecostal Theology* 13.2, 187–207.

Anderson, A. H. (2000), *Zion and Pentecost: The Spirituality and Experience of Pentecostal and Zionist/Apostolic Churches in South Africa*, Pretoria, University of South Africa Press.

—— (2004), *An Introduction to Global Pentecostalism*, Cambridge, Cambridge University Press.

—— (2007), *Spreading Fires: The Missionary Nature of Early Pentecostalism*, London, SCM Press.

Anderson, A. H. and Hollenweger, W. J. (eds) (1999), *Pentecostals after a Century*, Sheffield, Sheffield Academic Press.

Anderson, A. and Tang, E. (eds) (2005), *Asian and Pentecostal: The Charismatic Face of Christian Asia*, Oxford, Regnum, and Baguio City, APTS.

Anderson, R. M. (1979), *Vision of the Disinherited*, Oxford, Oxford University Press.

Andrews, J. (2003), 'The Regions Beyond', unpublished PhD thesis, University of Wales, Bangor.

Archer, K. J. (2004), *A Pentecostal Hermeneutic for the Twenty-First Century*, Sheffield, Sheffield Academic Press.

Baker, D., Halman, L. and Vloet, A. (1992), *The European Values Survey*, Gordon Cook Foundation, place of publication not given.

Barratt, T. B. (1927), *When the Fire Fell and an Outline of My Life*, Oslo, Alfons Hansen and Sonner.

Barrett, D. B. and Johnson, T. (2002), 'Global Statistics', in S. M. Burgess and E. M. van der Maas, *NIDPCM*, Grand Rapids, MI, Zondervan.

Bartleman, F. (1925), *How 'Pentecost' Came to Los Angeles – As It Was in the Beginning*, reprinted in 1980 under the title *Azusa Street: The Roots of Modern Day Pentecost*, Plainfield, NJ, Logos International.

Battle, M. (2006), *The Black Church in America*, Oxford, Blackwell.

Baxter, S., 'Apostolic Faith' (2 July 1926), in J. R. Goff (1988), *Fields White Unto Harvest: Charles F. Parham and the Missionary Origins of Pentecostalism*, Fayetteville, University of Arkansas Press.

Bays, D. H. (2002), 'China', in Burgess and van der Maas (eds), *NIDPCM*, 59.

Beckford, R. (2000), *Dread and Pentecostal*, London, SPCK.

Beeson, T. (1974), *Discretion and Valour*, London, Fount.

Bennett, D. J. (1971), *Nine O'clock in the Morning*, Eastbourne, Coverdale.

Berger, P. L. (1969), *The Sacred Canopy: Elements of a Sociological Theory of Religion*, New York, Anchor Books.

Bergunder, M. (2002), 'The Pentecostal Movement and Basic Ecclesial Communities in Latin America: Sociological Theories and Theological Debates', *International Review of Missions*, XCI, no. 361, 163–86.

——— (2005), 'Constructing Indian Pentecostalism: On Issues of Methodology and Representation', in Anderson and Tang (eds), *Asian and Pentecostal*, pp. 177–213.

——— (2007), 'Constructing Pentecostalism: On Issues of Methodology and Representation', *Journal of the European Pentecostal Theological Association* 27.1, 55–73.

Billingsley, S. (2008), *It's a New Day: Race and Gender in the Modern Charismatic Movement*, Tuscaloosa, AL, University of Alabama Press.

Bloch-Hoell, N. (1964), *The Pentecostal Movement*, London, Allen and Unwin.

——— (1964), *The Pentecostal Movement*, Oslo, Universitätsforlaget.

Blumhofer, E. L. (1985), *The Assemblies of God: A Popular History*, Springfield, MO, Radiant Books.

——— (1993), *Restoring the Faith*, Chicago, University of Illinois Press.

——— (1993), *Aimee Semple McPherson: Everybody's Sister*, Grand Rapids, MI, Eerdmans.

Blumhofer E. L., Spittler, R. P. and Wacker, G. A. (eds) (1999), *Pentecostal Currents in American Protestantism*, Chicago, University of Chicago Press.

Boddy, A. A. (1908), 'A Baptism on the Holy Ghost with the Seal of Tongues', *Confidence*, 1 April 1908, 5.

Boddy, A. A. (1910), 'Tongues: The Pentecostal Sign; Love the Evidence of Continuance', *Confidence* 3, 11 November, 260–1.

Bosworth, F. F. (1973), *Christ the Healer*, Old Tappan, NJ, Fleming H. Revel.

Boulton, E. C. W. (1928), *George Jeffreys: A Ministry of the Miraculous*, London, Elim Publishing House.

Bourdieu, Pierre (1977), *Outline of a Theory of Practice*, Cambridge, Cambridge University Press.

Braxton, L. (1966), 'God's Banker', in Abundant Life Magazine, *God's Formula for Success and Prosperity*, Oral Roberts Evangelistic Association.

Brown, C. G. (2001), *The Death of Christian Britain*, London, Routledge.

Bruce, F. F. (1960), *The New Testament Documents: Are They Reliable?*, Leicester, InterVarsity Press.

Bruce, S. (2002), *God is Dead: Secularization in the West*, Oxford, Blackwell.

Bundy, D. (1988), 'The Making of a Pentecostal Theologian: The Writings of Louis Dallière 1922–1932', *EPTA Bulletin* VII.2, 40–68.

———— (1989), 'Louis Dallière (1932–1939): The Development of a Pentecostal Apologetic', *EPTA Bulletin* VIII.2, 60–93.

———— (1992), 'Spiritual Advice to a Seeker: Letters to T. B. Barratt from Azusa St', 1906, *Pneuma* 14.2, 159–70.

———— (1993), 'The Genre of Systematic Theology in Pentecostalism', *Pneuma* 15, 89–107.

———— (1998), 'Pentecostalism in Argentina', *Pneuma* 20.1, 95–109.

———— (2002), 'Argentina', in Burgess and van der Maas (eds), *NIDPCM*, pp. 23–5.

———— (2002), 'Chile', in Burgess and van der Maas (eds), *NIDPCM*, pp. 55–8.

———— (2002), 'Colombia', in Burgess and van der Maas (eds), *NIDPCM*, pp. 65–6.

Burgess, S. M. (1984), *The Holy Spirit: Ancient Christian Traditions*, Peabody, MA, Hendrickson.

———— (2002), 'The Doctrine of the Holy Spirit', in Burgess and van der Maas (eds), *NIDPCM*.

Burton, W. F. P. (1933), *God Working with Them*, London, Victory Press.

———— (1937), *When God Changes a Man*, London, Victory Press.

———— (1947), *Mudishi: The Congo Hunter*, published privately.

Carothers, W. F. (1906), *The Baptism with the Holy Ghost and Speaking in Tongues*, Houston, privately printed, pp. 5–18, cited by Robeck, 'An Emerging Magisterium'.

Carson, D. A. (2005), *Becoming Conversant with the Emerging Church*, Grand Rapids, MI, Zondervan.

Cartledge, M. J. (2006), *Encountering the Spirit*, London, Darton, Longman and Todd.

———— (ed.) (2006), *Speaking in Tongues: Multi-Disciplinary Perspectives*, Carlisle, Paternoster Press.

———— (2008), 'The Early Pentecostal Theology of *Confidence* Magazine (1908–1926): A Version of the Five-Fold Gospel?' *Journal of the European Pentecostal Theological Association* 28.2, 117–30.

Cartwright, D. W. (1986), *The Great Evangelists: The Lives of George and Stephen Jeffreys*, Basingstoke, Marshall Pickering.

Cavaness, B. (2006), 'God Calling: Women in Pentecostal Missions', in G. McClung (ed.), *Azusa Street and Beyond: 100 years*, Gainsville, FL, Bridge Logos.

Cerillo Jr, A. (1997), 'Interpretive Approaches to the History of American Pentecostal Origins', *Pneuma* 19.1, 29–52.

———— (2002), 'Frank Bartleman: Pentecostal "Lone Ranger" and Critic', in J. R.

Goff and G. Wacker (eds), *Portraits of a Generation*, Fayetteville, University of Arkansas Press, pp. 105–22.

Chadwick, O. (1975), *The Secularization of the European Mind in the 19th Century*, Cambridge, Cambridge University Press.

Chan, S. (2000), *Pentecostal Theology and the Christian Spiritual Tradition*, Sheffield, Sheffield Academic Press.

Charette, B. (1996), '"Never has anything like this been seen in Israel": The Spirit as Eschatological Sign in Matthew's Gospel', *Journal of Pentecostal Theology* 8, 31–51.

Charisma Magazine (September 2003), 'Church-Growth Strategy Goes Global'.

Clark, A. D. (1971), *A History of the Church in Korea*, Seoul, The Christian Literature Society of Korea.

Clark, M. (2001), 'Asian Pentecostal Theology: A Perspective from Africa', *Asian Journal of Pentecostal Studies* 4.2, 181–99.

Cleary, E. L. and Stewart-Gambino, H. (eds) (1992), *Conflict and Competition: The Latin American Church in a Changing Environment*, London, Lynne Rienner.

Clifton, S. (2007), 'Pentecostal Ecclesiology: A Methodological Proposal for a Diverse Movement', *Journal of Pentecostal Theology* 15.2, 213–32.

——— (2009), *Pentecostal Churches in Transition*, Leiden, Brill.

Coleman, S. (2000), *The Globalisation of Charismatic Christianity: Spreading the Gospel of Prosperity*, Cambridge, Cambridge University Press.

Colle, R. D. (1993), 'Spirit-Christology: Dogmatic Foundations for Pentecostal-Charismatic Spirituality', *Journal of Pentecostal Theology* 3, 91–112.

Collingwood, R. G. (1980), *The Idea of History*, Oxford, Oxford University Press.

Cone, J. H. (2006), *Black Theology and Black Power*, Maryknoll, NY, Orbis Books.

Coulter, D. M. (2001), 'What Meaneth this? Pentecostals and Theological Inquiry', *Journal of Pentecostal Theology* 10.1, 38–64.

——— (2005), 'Pentecostal Visions of the End: Eschatology, Ecclesiology and the Fascination of the *Left-Behind* Series', *Journal of Pentecostal Theology* 14.1, 81–98.

Cox, H. (1996), *Fire from Heaven*, London, Cassell.

Cross, T. (2007), 'Can there be a Pentecostal Systematic Theology? An Essay on Theological Method in a Postmodern World', presented at the 30th Annual Meeting of the Society for Pentecostal Studies, Lee University, Cleveland, TN.

——— *The Church: A People of God's Presence* (forthcoming).

Cunningham, V. (1972), 'Eratosthenes Butterscotch', *Redemption Tidings*, 20 July.

d'Epinay, C. L. (1969), *Haven of the Masses: A Study of the Pentecostal Movement in Chile*, London, Lutterworth Press.

Davie, G. (1994), *Religion in Britain since 1945*, Oxford, Blackwell.

——— (2007), *The Sociology of Religion*, London, Sage.

Dawkins, R. (2006), *The Selfish Gene*, Oxford, Oxford University Press.

Dayton D. W. (1976), *Discovering an Evangelical Heritage*, Peabody, MA, Hendrickson.

———— (1987), *Theological Roots of Pentecostalism*, Peabody, MA, Hendrickson.

———— (2005), 'Rejoinder to Lawrence Wood', *Pneuma* 27.2, 367–75.

Dempster, M. W., Klaus, B. D., Petersen, D. (eds) (1999), *The Globalization of Pentecostalism: A Religion Made to Travel*, Carlisle, Paternoster Press.

Divine, R. A., Breen, T. H., Fredrickson, G. M. and Williams, R. H. (1995), *America Past and Present*, 4th edn, New York, HarperCollins College Publishers.

Dorrien, G. (1998), *The Remaking of Evangelical Theology*, Louisville, KY, Westminster John Knox Press.

Dowie, J. A. (1902), 'If It Be Thy Will', *Leaves of Healing* X.20, 8 March.

du Plessis, D. (1977), *A Man Called Mr Pentecost*, Plainfield, NJ, Logos International.

Dunn, J. D. G. (1970), *Baptism in the Spirit*, London, SCM Press.

———— (1995), 'Pentecostal Responses to Dunn's *Baptism in the Holy Spirit: Luke-Acts*', *Journal of Pentecostal Theology* 6, 87–131.

Durkheim, E. (1897), *Le Suicide: étude de sociology*, Paris, Alcan.

———— (1938), *The Rules of Sociological Method*, New York, Free Press.

———— (1951 [1897]), *Suicide*, New York, Free Press.

Edsor, A. W. (1989), '*Set Your House in Order*', Chichester, New Wine Ministries

Edwards, D. L. (1997), *Christianity: The First Two Thousand Years*, London, Cassell.

Eim, Y. S. (2002), 'South Korea', in Burgess and van der Maas (eds), *NIDPCM*, p. 240.

Eusebius of Caesarea (c. 324), *The History of the Church from Christ to Constantine*, Introduction by G. A. Williamson, London, Penguin Classics, 1980.

Faupel, D. W. (1996), *The Everlasting Gospel*, Sheffield, Sheffield Academic Press.

———— (2007), 'Theological Influences on the Teachings and Practices of John Alexander Dowie', *Pneuma* 29.2, 226–53.

Ferguson, N. (2004), *Empire: How Britain Made the Modern World*, London, Penguin.

Finney, C. G. (1846), *Reflections on Revival*, comp. D. W. Dayton (1979), Minneapolis, MN, Bethany Fellowship.

Fleisch, P. (1957), *Die Pfingstbewegung in Deutschland*, Hannover, Heinr, Feesche Verlag.

Flora, C. B. (1976), *Pentecostalism in Colombia: Baptism by Fire and Spirit*, London, Associated University Presses.

Fonseca, A. B. (2008), 'Religion and Democracy in Brazil: A Study of the Leading Evangelical Politicians', in P. Freston (ed.), *Evangelical Christianity and Democracy in Latin America,* Oxford, Oxford University Press.

Forrester, D. B. (2000), *Truthful Action: Explorations in Practical Theology*, Edinburgh, T & T Clark.

Francis, L. J. and Kay, W. K. (1995), *Teenage Religion and Values*, Leominster, Gracewing.

Freston, P. (1998), 'Pentecostalism in Latin America: Characteristics and Controversies', *Social Compass* 45.3, 335–58.

———— (2004), 'Contours of Latin American Pentecostalism', in Donald M. Lewis (ed.), *Christianity Reborn: The Global Expansion of Evangelicalism in the Twentieth Century*, Grand Rapids, MI and Cambridge, Eerdmans, pp. 221–70.

Friedman, T. (2006), *The World is Flat*, Harmondsworth, Penguin.

Friesen, A. (2009), 'The Called Out of the Called Out: Charles Parham's Doctrine of Spirit Baptism', *Journal of European Pentecostal Theological Association* 1, 43–55.

Frodsham, S. H. (1926), *With Signs Following*, Springfield, MO, Gospel Publishing House.

Garrard, D. J. (2002), 'Democratic Republic of Congo', in Burgess and van der Maas (eds), *NIDPCM*, pp. 67–76.

Garver, C. M. (1910), *The Pentecost*, 1 March, 2.

Gaxiola-Gaxiola, M. J. (1991), 'Latin American Pentecostalism: A Mosaic within a Mosaic', *Pneuma* 13.2, 107–29.

Gee, D. (1941), *The Pentecostal Movement*, London, Elim Publishing House.

—— (1967), *Wind and Flame*, Nottingham, Croydon, Assemblies of God Publishing House.

—— (1980), *These Men I Knew*, Nottingham, Assemblies of God Publishing House.

Gifford, P. (1998), *African Christianity: Its Public Role*, London, Hurst and Co.

—— (2004), *Ghana's New Christianity: Pentecostalism in a Globalising African Economy*, Bloomington and Indianapolis, Indiana University Press.

Gilbert, M. (1999), *A History of the Twentieth Century (vol. 3)*, London, HarperCollins.

Gill, D. M. (1995), 'The Contemporary State of Women in Ministry in Assemblies of God', *Pneuma* 17.1, 33–6.

Gill, R. (ed.) (1987), *Theology and Sociology: A Reader*, London, Geoffrey Chapman.

Goff, J. R. (1988), *Fields White Unto Harvest: Charles F. Parham and the Missionary Origins of Pentecostalism*, Fayetteville, University of Arkansas Press.

Goff Jr, J. R. and Wacker, G. (eds) (2002), *Portraits of a Generation: Early Pentecostal Leaders*, Fayetteville, University of Arkansas Press.

Gordon, A. J. G. (1882), *The Ministry of Healing: Miracles of Cure in All Ages*, Boston, H. Gannett.

Graham, B., (1988), *Just as I Am*, London, HarperCollins.

Grass, T. (2006), *Gathering in his Name*, Milton Keynes, Paternoster Press.

Grudem, W. (1999), *Systematic Theology*, Leicester, InterVarsity Press.

Guest, M. (2007), *Evangelical Identity and Contemporary Culture*, Milton Keynes, Paternoster Press.

Habets, M. (2003), 'Spirit Christology: Seeing in Stereo', *Journal of Pentecostal Theology* 11.2, 199–234.

Harper, M. (1965), *As at the Beginning*, London, Hodder and Stoughton.

Harrell, D. E. (1975), *All Things are Possible*, Bloomington, Indiana University Press.

—— (1985), *Oral Roberts: An American Life*, Bloomington, Indiana University Press.

—— (1987), *Pat Robertson: A Personal, Political and Religious Portrait*, San Francisco, Harper and Row.

——— (2001), 'Healers and Televangelists after World War II', in V. Synan (ed.), *The Century of the Holy Spirit*, Nashville, TN, Thomas Nelson.

Harrison, M. F. (2005), *Righteous Riches: The Word of Faith Movement in Contemporary African American Religion*, Oxford, Oxford University Press.

Harvey, P. and Goff, P. (eds) (2005), *Religion in America Since 1945*, New York, Columbia University Press.

Hathaway, M. R. (1998), 'The Elim Pentecostal Church: Origins, Development and Distinctives', in K. Warrington (ed.), *Pentecostal Perspectives*, Carlisle, Paternoster Press, p. 10.

Hayford, J. W. and Moore, S. D. (2006), *The Charismatic Century*, New York, Warner Faith.

Hee, J. C. (2005), 'The Korean Charismatic Movement as Indigenous Pentecostalism', in Anderson and Tang (eds), *Asian and Pentecostal*.

Heino, H. (1988), 'Different Manifestations of the Charismatic Movement: The Charismatic Movement in Finland and America', *EPTA Bulletin* 7.4, 128–41.

Hempton, D. (2005), *Methodism: Empire of the Spirit*, New Haven, Yale University Press.

Higton, M. (2008), *Christian Doctrine*, London, SCM Press.

Hilborn, D. (2001), *'Toronto' in Perspective: Papers on the New Charismatic Wave of the Mid 1990s*, Carlisle, Acute.

Hinchliff, P. (1964), *John William Colenso*, London, Nelson.

——— (1990), 'Africa', in J. McManners (ed.), *The Oxford Illustrated History of Christianity*, Oxford, Oxford University Press.

Hocken, P. D. (2002), 'The Charismatic Movement', in Burgess and van der Maas (eds), *NIDPCM*.

Hodges, M. L. (1978), *The Indigenous Church and the Missionary*, Pasadena, CA, William Carey Library.

Hollenweger, W. J. (1972), *The Pentecostals*, London, SCM Press.

——— (1997), *Pentecostalism: Origins and Developments Worldwide*, Peabody, MA, Hendrickson.

Horton, H. (1934), *The Gifts of the Spirit*, London, privately published.

Horton, S. M. (ed.) (1995), *Systematic Theology*, Springfield, MO, Logion.

Huber, S. (2008), 'Leading Tone or Background Music: A Comparative Analysis of the Public Significance of Religion in 21 Nations', paper given at the ISERT meeting at the University of Würzburg.

——— (2007), 'Are Religious Beliefs Relevant in Daily Life?', in H. Streib (ed.), *Religion Inside and Outside Traditional Institutions*, Leiden, Brill.

Hudson, D. N. (1999), 'A Schism and its Aftermath: An Historical Analysis of Denominational Discerption in the Elim Pentecostal Church, 1939–1940', PhD dissertation, King's College, London.

Hunt, S. (2008), 'The Emerging Church and its Discontents', *Journal of Beliefs and Values* 29.3, 287–96.

Hunter, H. D. (1983), 'Spirit Christology: Dilemma and Promise', *Heythrop Journal* 24.2 and 24.3.

——— (1983), *Spirit Baptism: A Pentecostal Alternative*, Lanham, University Press of America.

Iannoccone, I. R. (1992), 'Religious Markets and the Economics of Religion', *Social Compass* 39, 123–31.

Irvin, D. T. (2005), 'Pentecostal Historiography and Global Christianity: Rethinking the Question of Origins', *Pneuma* 27.1, 35–50.

Jackson, B. (1999), *The Quest for the Radical Middle: A History of the Vineyard*, Cape Town, Vineyard International Publishing.

Jacobsen, D. (2003), *Thinking in the Spirit*, Bloomington, Indiana University Press.

—— (ed.) (2006), *A Reader in Pentecostal Theology: Voices from the First Generation*, Bloomington, Indiana University Press.

Jenkins, P. (2002), The Next Christendom, Oxford and New York, Oxford University Press.

—— (2006), *The New Faces of Christianity: Believing the Bible in the Global South*, Oxford, Oxford University Press.

Jones, C. E. (1974), *Perfectionist Persuasion: The Holiness Movement and American Methodism, 1867–1936*, Metuchen, NJ, Scarecrow Press.

Jones J. R. (2007), 'Diving Healing in British Pentecostalism from 1900–1939', unpublished MPhil dissertation, University of Wales, Bangor.

Jones, R. T. (2004), *Faith and the Crisis of a Nation: Wales 1890–1914*, Cardiff, University of Wales Press.

Kärkkäinen, Veli-Matti (2002), *Towards a Pneumatological Theology*, Lanham, MD, University Press of America.

Kay, P. K. (1995), 'The Four-Fold Gospel in the Formation, Policy and Practice of the Pentecostal Missionary Union (PMU) (1909–1925)', unpublished MA thesis, University of Gloucester.

Kay, W. K. (1989), 'A History of British Assemblies of God', PhD dissertation, Nottingham University.

—— (1990) *Inside Story*, Stourport-on-Severn, Mattersey Hall Publishing

—— (1992), 'Three Generations On: The Methodology of Pentecostal History', *EPTA Bulletin* X.1 and 2, 58–70.

—— and Francis, L. J. (1995), 'Personality, Mental Health and Glossolalia', *Pneuma* 17, 253–63.

—— (1997), 'Phenomenology, Religious Education, and Piaget', *Religion* 27, 275–83.

—— (1998), 'A Demonised World View: Dangers, Benefits and Explanations', *Journal of Empirical Theology* 11.1, 17–29.

—— and Robbins, M. (1999), 'A Woman's Place is on Her Knees: The Pastor's View of the Role of Women in Assemblies of God', *Journal of the European Pentecostal Theological Association* 18, 64–75.

—— (2000), *Pentecostals in Britain*, Carlisle, Paternoster Press.

—— (2003), 'Revival: Empirical Aspects', in A. Walker and K. Aune (eds), *On Revival: A Critical Examination*, Carlisle, Paternoster Press, pp. 185–204.

—— (2004), 'Pentecostal Education', *Journal of Beliefs and Values* 25.2, 229–39.

—— and Dyer, A. E. (eds) (2004), *Pentecostal and Charismatic Studies: A Reader*, London, SCM Press.

—— (2006), 'The Mind, Behaviour and Glossolalia: A Psychological Perspective', in M. J. Cartledge (ed.), *Speaking in Tongues: Multi-Disciplinary Perspectives*, Carlisle, Paternoster Press, pp. 174–205.

—— (2007), *Apostolic Networks in Britain*, Carlisle, Paternoster Press.

—— (2009), 'Karl Popper and Pentecostal Historiography', *Pneuma* (in press).

Kee, A. (2006), *The Rise and Demise of Black Theology*, Aldershot, Ashgate.

—— (2008), 'Time to Move On from the Rhetoric of Race: A Response by Alistair Kee, *Pneuma* 30, 308–14.

Kildahl, J. P. (1972), *The Psychology of Speaking in Tongues*, London, Hodder and Stoughton.

Kim, I.-J. (2005), 'History and Theology of Korean Pentecostalism: Sunbogeum (pure Gospel) Pentecostalism', doctoral dissertation, University of Utrecht.

King, P. L. (2006), *Genuine Gold: The Cautiously Charismatic Story of the Early Christian and Missionary Alliance*, Tulsa, OK, Word and Spirit Press.

Kuhlman, K. (1963), *I Believe in Miracles*, London, Oliphants.

Land, S. (1993), *Pentecostal Spirituality: A Passion for the Kingdom*, Sheffield, Sheffield Academic Press.

Landrus, H. L. (2002), 'Hearing 3 John 2 in the Voices of History', *Journal of Pentecostal Theology* 11.1, 70–88.

LaPoorta, J. (1999), 'Unity of Division: A Case Study of the Apostolic Faith Mission of South Africa', in M. W. Dempster, B. D. Klaus and D. Petersen (eds), *The Globalization of Pentecostalism: A Religion Made to Travel*, Carlisle, Paternoster Press.

Larbi, K. E. (2001), *Pentecostalism: The Eddies of Ghanaian Christianity*, Accra, Ghana, Centre for Pentecostalism and Charismatic Studies.

Lee, Y.-H. (2001), 'Korean Pentecost: The Great Revival of 1907', *Asian Journal of Pentecostal Studies* 4.1, 73–83.

Lehman Jr, E. C. (1981), 'Patterns of Lay Resistance to Women in Ministry', *Sociological Analysis* 41, 317–38.

Lewis, D. K. (2001), *The History of Argentina*, Basingstoke, Palgrave Macmillan.

Lindsey, H. (1970), *The Late Great Planet Earth*, Grand Rapids, MI, Zondervan.

Lundskow, G. (2008), *The Sociology of Religion: A Substantive and Transdisciplinary Approach*, London, Pine Forge.

Ma, W. (1997), 'A "First Waver" looks at the "Third Wave": A Pentecostal Reflection on Charles Kraft's Power Encounter Terminology', *Pneuma* 19.2, 189–206.

—— (2002), 'Philippines', in Burgess and van der Maas (eds) (2002), *NIDPCM*, pp. 201–7.

—— (2002), 'Pentecostal Theology', in Burgess and van der Maas (eds), *NIDPCM*.

—— (2005), 'Asian (Classical) Pentecostal Theology in Context', in Anderson and Tang (eds), *Asian and Pentecostal*.

Ma, W., Menzies, W. W. and Bae, H.-S. (eds) (2004), *David Yonggi Cho: A Close Look at His Theology and Ministry*, Baguio City, APTS.

Macchia, F. D. (1993), 'Tongues as a Sign: Towards a Sacramental Understanding of Pentecostal Experience, *Pneuma* 15.1, 61–76.

—— (2002), 'Pentecostal Theology', in Burgess and van der Maas (eds), *NIDPCM*.

—— (2006), *Baptized in the Spirit: A Global Pentecostal Theology*, Grand Rapids, MI, Zondervan.

Mackenzie, R. (1993), *David Livingstone: The Truth Behind the Legend*, Eastbourne, Kingsway.

Mariz, C. L. (1994), *Coping with Poverty: Pentecostals and Christian Base Communities in Brazil*, Philadelphia, Temple University Press.

Marsen, G. (1980), *Fundamentalism and American Culture: The Shaping of Twentieth Century Evangelicalism*, New York, Oxford University Press.

Martin, B. (2001), 'The Pentecostal Gender Paradox: A Cautionary Tale for the Sociology of Religion', in R. K. Fenn (ed.), *The Blackwell Companion to Sociology of Religion,* Oxford, Blackwell, 52–66.

—— (2006), 'Pentecostal Conversion and the Limits of the Market Metaphor', *Exchange: Journal of Missiological and Ecumenical Research* 35.1 60–91.

Martin, D. (1978), *A General Theory of Secularization*, Oxford, Blackwell.

—— (1990), *Tongues of Fire: The Explosion of Pentecostalism in Latin America*, Oxford, Blackwell.

—— (2002), *Pentecostalism: The World their Parish*, Oxford, Blackwell.

Marwick, A. (1982), *British Society Since 1945*, Harmondsworth, Penguin.

—— (1998), *The Sixties*, Oxford, Oxford University Press.

Maxwell, D. (1999), 'Historicizing Christian Independency: The Southern African Pentecostal Movement c 1908–60', *Journal of African History* 40, 243–69.

—— (2005), '"Survival, Revival and Resistance": Continuity and Change in Zimbabwe's Post-War Religion and Politics', in Niels Kastfelt (ed.), *Religion and African Civil Wars*, London, Hurst and Co.

—— (2006), *African Gifts of the Spirit: Pentecostalism and the Rise of a Zimbabwean Transnational Religious Movement*, Oxford, James Currey.

McConnell, D. R. (1990), *The Promise of Health and Wealth*, London, Hodder and Stoughton.

McDonnell, K. and Montague, G. T. (1994), *Christian Initiation and Baptism in the Holy Spirit: Evidence from the First Eight Centuries*, 2nd rev. edn, Collegeville, MN, The Liturgical Press.

McDonnell, K. (1995), 'Improbable Conversations: the International Classical Pentecostal/Roman Catholic Dialogue', *Pneuma* 17.2, 163–74.

McGee, G. B. (ed.) (1991), *Initial Evidence: Historical and Biblical Perspectives on the Pentecostal Doctrine of Spirit Baptism*, Peabody, MA, Hendrickson.

—— (2002), 'Minnie F. Abrams: Another Context, Another Founder', in J. R. Goff and G. Wacker (eds), *Portraits of a Generation*, Fayetteville, University of Arkansas Press, pp. 87–104.

—— (2004), *People of the Spirit: The Assemblies of God*, Springfield, MO, Gospel Publishing House.

McGrath, A. E. (1993), *The Renewal of Anglicanism*, London, SPCK.

McLaren, B. D. (2001), *A New Kind of Christian: A Tale of Two Friends on a Spiritual Journey*, San Francisco, Jossey-Bass.

—— (2004), *A Generous Orthodoxy*, Grand Rapids, MI, Youth Specialities.

McManners, J. (1990), 'The Expansion of Christianity', in J. McManners (ed.), *The Oxford Illustrated History of Christianity*, London, Guild Publishing, pp. 304–5.

McQueen, L. (2009), 'Early Pentecostal Eschatology in the Light of the Apostolic Faith, 1906–1908', paper presented at the 38th Annual Meeting of the Society for Pentecostal Studies, Eugene, Oregon.

Menzies, W. W. (1971), *Anointed to Serve*, Springfield, MO, Gospel Publishing House.

—— (1975), 'The Non-Wesleyan Origins of the Pentecostal Movement', in V. Synan (ed.), *Aspects of Pentecostal-Charismatic Origins*, Plainfield, NJ, Logos International, pp. 81–98.

—— (2006), 'The Reformed Roots of Pentecostalism', *Asian Journal of Pentecostal Studies* 9.2, 260–82.

Meredith, M. (2006), *The State of Africa*, London, Free Press.

Meyer, B. (2003), 'Ghanaian Popular Cinema and the Magic in and of Film', in Birgit Meyer and Peter Pels (eds), *Magic and Modernity*, Stanford, Stanford University Press.

Miller D. E. and Yamamori, T. (2007), *Global Pentecostalism: The New Face of Christian Social Engagement*, California, University of California Press.

Miller, J. (2003), *Missionary Zeal and Institutional Control: Organizational Contradictions in the Basel Mission on the Gold Coast, 1828–1917*, Grand Rapids, MI, Eerdmans.

Moon, T. G. (2007), 'J. H. King's Theology of Religions: "Magnanimous Optimism"?', *Journal of Pentecostal Theology* 16.1, 112–32.

Moore, M. E. (2004), 'Purposes of Practical Theology: A Comparative Analysis between United States Practical Theologians and Johannes van der Ven', in C. A. M. Hermans and M. E. Moore (eds), *Hermeneutics and Empirical Research in Practical Theology*, Leiden, Brill, pp. 169–95.

Moore, S. D. (2003), *The Shepherding Movement*, London, T & T Clark.

Murray, I. H. (1996), *The Puritan Hope: Revival and the Interpretation of Prophecy*, Edinburgh, Banner of Truth.

Neill, S. (1990), *A History of Christian Missions*, Harmondsworth, Penguin.

Nelson, S. and R. (2002), 'Frank Sandford: Tongues of Fire in Shiloh, Maine', in J. R. Goff Jr. and G. Wacker (eds) (2002), *Portraits of a Generation*, Fayetteville, University of Arkansas Press.

Niebuhr, H. R. (1929), *The Social Sources of Denominationalism*, New York, Holt.

Noble, J. (1971), *Forgive Us Our Denominations*, London, Team Spirit.

Noll, M. A. (1997), *Turning Points*, Grand Rapids, MI, Baker Books.

Obama, B. (2007), *The Audacity of Hope*, New York, Canongate.

Oblau, G. (2005), 'Pentecostal by Default? Contemporary Christianity in China', in Anderson and Tang (eds), *Asian and Pentecostal*, p. 428ff.

Osmer, R. R. (2008), *Practical Theology: An Introduction*, Grand Rapids, MI, Eerdmans.

Parham, C. F. (1944), *A Voice Crying in the Wilderness*, 4th edn, Baxter Springs, Kansas.

Parker, S. E. (1996), *Led by the Spirit: Towards a Practical Theology of Pentecostal Discernment and Decision Making*, Sheffield, Sheffield Academic Press.

Pastor, G. S., Stone, W. J. and Rapoport, R. B. (1999), 'Candidate-centred Sources of Party Change: The Case of Pat Robertson, 1988', *The Journal of Politics* 61.2, 423–44.

Perriman, A. (ed.) (2003), *Faith, Health and Prosperity*, Carlisle, Paternoster Press.

Pinnock, C. H. (1996), *Flame of Love*, Downers Grove, IL, InterVarsity Press.

Poggi, G. (2000), *Durkheim*, Oxford, Oxford University Press.

Poloma M. M. (1989), *The Assemblies of God at the Crossroads: Charisma and Institutional Dilemmas*, Knoxville, TN, University of Tennessee Press.

—— (2001), 'A Reconfiguration of Pentecostalism', in Hilborn (ed.), *'Toronto' in Perspective*.

—— (2006), 'Glossolalia, Liminality and Empowered Kingdom Building: A Sociological Perspective', in Cartledge (ed.), *Speaking in Tongues*, pp. 147–73.

Pope, R. (2006), 'Demythologising the Evan Roberts Revival, 1904–1905', *Journal of Ecclesiastical History* 57.3, 515–34.

Price, C. and Randall, I. (2000), *Transforming Keswick*, Carlisle, OM Publishing.

Pulikottil, P. (2005), 'Ramankutty Paul: A Dalit Contribution to Pentecostalism', in Anderson and Tang, *Asian and Pentecostal*, pp. 245–57.

Reader, J. (2008), *Reconstructing Practical Theology*, Aldershot, Ashgate.

Reed, D. A. (2008), *'In Jesus' Name': The History and Beliefs of Oneness Pentecostals*, Blandford Forum, Deo.

Richards, W. (2005), 'An Examination of Common Factors in the Growth of Global Pentecostalism', *Journal of Asian Mission* 7.1, 85–106.

Richie, T. (2006), 'Azusa-Era Optimism: Bishop J. H. King's Pentecostal Theology of Religions as a Possible Paradigm for Today', *Journal of Pentecostal Theology* 14.2, 247–60.

—— (2006), 'God's Fairness to People of All Faiths: A Respectful Proposal for Discussion Regarding World Religions', *Pneuma* 26.1, 105–19.

Riss, R. M. (2002), 'Osborn, Tommy Lee', in Burgess and van der Maas, *NIDPCM*, p. 950.

Robbins, J. (2004), 'The Globalisation of Pentecostal and Charismatic Christianity', *Annual Review of Anthropology* 233, 117–43.

Robeck Jr, C. M. (1997), 'The Assemblies of God and Ecumenical Co-operation: 1920–1965', in Wonsuk Ma and Robert P. Menzies (eds), *Pentecostalism in Context: Essays in Honour of William W. Menzies*, Sheffield, Sheffield Academic Press.

—— (2002), 'Florence Crawford: Apostolic Faith Pioneer', in Goff and Wacker (eds), *Portraits*, pp. 219–35.

—— (2002), 'National Association of Evangelicals', in Burgess and van der Maas (eds), *NIDPCM*, p. 923.

—— (2003), 'An Emerging Magisterium: The Case of the Assemblies of God', *Pneuma* 25.2, 164–215.

—— (2006), *The Azusa Street Mission and Revival*, Nashville, TN, Nelson Reference and Electronic.

Roberts, D. (1994), *The 'Toronto' Blessing*, Eastbourne, Kingsway.

Roberts, O. (1995), *Expect a Miracle: My Life and Ministry. Oral Roberts an Autobiography*, London, Nelson.

Robins, R. G. (2004), *A. J. Tomlinson: Plainfolk Modernist*, Oxford, Oxford University Press.

Robinson, J. (2005), *Pentecostal Origins*, Milton Keynes, Paternoster Press.

Robinson, J. A. T. (1976), *Redating the New Testament*, London, SCM Press.

Robinson M. (2005), 'The Growth of Indonesian Pentecostalism', in Anderson and Tang, *Asian and Pentecostal*, p. 335.

Röckle, B. and Kay, W. K. (2003), 'Born in Difficult Times: The Founding of the Volksmission and the Work of Karl Fix', *Journal of the European Pentecostal Theological Association* 23, 72–101.

Rose, H. A, (1908), 'On Caste in India', *Man* 8, 98–103.

——— (1911–19), *A Glossary of the Tribes and Castes of the Punjab and the North-West Frontier Province*, published in Lahore in three volumes.

Rose, S. D. (1987), 'Women Warriors: The Negotiation of Gender in a Charismatic Community', *Sociological Analysis* 48, 245–58.

Rosen, P. T. (1979), 'The Marvel of Radio: Review Essay', *American Quarterly* 31.4, 572–81.

Ross, B. R. (1974), 'Donald Gee: In Search of a Church, Sectarian in Transition', unpublished PhD, Knox College, Toronto.

Russell, B. (1918), 'On the Notion of Cause', in *Mysticism and Logic*, reprinted by Penguin, 1953.

Sandidge, J. L. (1987), 'Roman Catholic/Pentecostal Dialogue (1977–1982): A Study in Developing Ecumenism', *Studies in the Intercultural History of Christianity* 44, New York, Peter Lang.

Savage, L. (1953), 'Japan', *Redemption Tidings* 29, 8.

Savage, M. and Burrows, R. (2007), 'The Coming Crisis of Empirical Sociology', *Sociology* 41.5, 885–99.

Seidman, S. (1985), 'Modernity and the Problem of Meaning: The Durkheim Tradition', *Sociological Analysis* 46.2, 109–30.

Sepúlveda, J. (1999), 'Indigenous Pentecostalism and the Chilean Experience', in Anderson and Hollenweger (eds), *Pentecostals after a Century*, p. 114.

Shakarian, D. (1979), *The Happiest People on Earth*, Grand Rapids, MI, Revell.

Simpson, A. B. (1885), 'How to Receive Divine Healing', *The Word, The Work, and The World* 20, July–August.

Simpson, C. (2008), 'Jonathan Paul and the German Pentecostal Movement: The First Seven Years, 1907–1914', *Journal of the European Pentecostal Theological Association* 1, 169–82.

Smidt, C. E., Kellstedt, L. A., Green, J. C. and Guth, J. L. (1999), 'The Spirit-Filled Movements in Contemporary America: A Survey Perspective', in Blumhofer, Spittler and Wacker (eds), *Pentecostal Currents in American Protestantism*, Chicago, University of Chicago Press, p. 189., pp. 111–30.

Smit, A. (1945), *After Two Hundred Years*, Cape Town, UCT Publications,

Smith, C. L. (2007), *Revolution, Revival and Religious Conflict in Sandinista Nicaragua*, Leiden, Brill.

Smith, J. K. A. (1997), 'The Closing of the Book: Pentecostals, Evangelicals and the Sacred Writings', *Journal of Pentecostal Theology* 11, 49–71.

Smith, J. K. A. (2003), 'Advice to Pentecostal Philosophers', *Journal of Pentecostal Theology* 11.2, 235–47.

—— (2006), 'Tongues as "Resistance Discourse"', in Cartledge (ed.), *Speaking in Tongues*, pp. 81–110.

Snook, I. A. (1972), *Indoctrination and Education*, London, Routledge and Keegan Paul.

Spittler, R. P. (2002), 'David Johannes du Plessis', in Burgess and van der Maas (eds), *NIDPCM*, pp. 589–93.

Stark, R. and Bainbridge, W. S. (1985), *A Theory of Religion*, New York, Peter Lang.

Stevens, J. H. S. (2002), *Worship in the Spirit*, Carlisle, Paternoster Press.

Stevenson, J. (1984), *British Society 1914–45*, Harmondsworth, Penguin.

'Stone Church in Chicago, Illinois', *Latter Rain Evangel*, October 1908, 2.

Strachan, G. (1973), *The Pentecostal Theology of Edward Irving*, London, Darton, Longman and Todd.

Suico, J. (2005), 'Pentecostals in the Philippines', in Anderson and Tang (eds), *Asian and Pentecostal*, pp. 345–62.

Sutton, M. A. (2007), *Aimee Semple McPherson and the Resurrection of Christian America*, London, Harvard University Press.

Synan, V. (1971/1997), *The Holiness-Pentecostal Tradition*, Grand Rapids, MI, Eerdmans.

—— (2001), 'The "Charismatics": Renewal in Major Protestant Denominations', in V. Synan (ed.), *The Century of the Holy Spirit*, Nashville, TN, Nelson.

Tang, E. (2005), '"Yellers" and Healers: Pentecostalism and the Study of Grassroots Christianity in China', in Anderson and Tang, *Asian and Pentecostal*, pp. 467–69.

Taylor, C. (2007), *A Secular Age*, Cambridge, MA, Belknap Press.

Taylor, S. (2000), *Livingstone's Tribe: A Journey from Zanzibar to the Cape*, London, Flamingo.

Thomas, J. C. (1993), 'The Devil, Disease and Deliverance: James 5.14–16', *Journal of Pentecostal Theology* 2, 25–50.

—— (1998), 'Max Turner's *The Holy Spirit and Spiritual Gifts: Then and Now*' Carlisle, Paternoster Press, 1996: An Appreciation and Critique', *Journal of Pentecostal Theology* 12, 3–22.

—— (1998), 'Pentecostal Theology in the Twenty-First Century', *Pneuma* 20.1, 3–19.

—— (1998), *The Devil, Disease and Deliverance: Origins of Illness*, Sheffield, Sheffield Academic Press.

Trevor-Roper, H. (1967), *The Rise of Christian Europe*, London, Book Club.

Tugwell, S. (1971), *Did You Receive the Spirit?*, London, Darton Longman and Todd.

Van der Ven, J. (1993), *Practical Theology: An Empirical Approach*, Kampen, Netherlands.

Veldhuizen, E. (1991), 'The Charismatic Renewal in Protestant and Evangelical Churches in France 1968–1988', in J. A. B. Jongeneel (ed.), *Experiences of the Spirit: Conference on Pentecostal and Charismatic Research in Europe at Utrecht University 1989*, New York, Peter Lang, pp. 211–20.

Wacker, G. (2001), *Heaven Below: Early Pentecostals and American Culture*, Cambridge, MA, Harvard University Press.

Wacker, G. with Armstrong, Chris R. and Blossom, J. S. F. (2002), 'John Alexander Dowie: Harbinger of Pentecostal Power', in Goff Jr and Wacker (eds), *Portraits*.

Waddell, R. (2008), 'The Spirit of Reviews and Response', *Journal of Pentecostal Theology* 17.1, 22–31.

Wagner, C. P. (1998), *The New Apostolic Churches*, Ventura, CA, Regal.

Wagner, C. P. and Pennoyer, F. D. (1996), *Wrestling with Dark Angels: Towards a Deeper Understanding of the Supernatural Forces in Spiritual Warfare*, Ventura, CA, Regal Books.

Währisch-Oblau, C. (2007), 'Migrants with a Mission: Pastoral Self-Understanding, Biographical Narratives, and the Conceptualization and Practice of Evangelism among Pentecostal/Charismatic Pastors in Western Germany', PhD dissertation, University of Heidelberg.

Wallis, A. (1985), *China Miracle*, Eastbourne, Kingsway.

Wallis, R. (1976), *The Road to Total Freedom: A Sociological Analysis of Scientology*, London, Heinemann.

Ward, P. (2002), *Liquid Church*, Carlisle, Paternoster Press and Peabody, MA, Hendrickson.

—— (2008), *Participation and Mediation: A Practical Theology for the Liquid Church*, London, SCM Press.

Warrington, K. (2008), *Pentecostal Theology*, London, T & T Clark.

Weber, Max (1904–05), *The Protestant Ethic and the Spirit of Capitalism*, reprinted Mineola, NY, Dover, 2003.

—— (1922), *The Sociology of Religion*, Boston, MA, Beacon Press.

Wesley, J. (1703–1777), 'A Plain Account of Christian Perfection', in *The Works of John Wesley* (1872), ed. T. Jackson, 11.29, pp. 366–446. http://www.whatsaiththescripture.com/Fellowship/Wesley.Christian.Perfectio.html

Wesley, L. (2007), Letter to the editor, *Pneuma* 29.1, 365–6.

Wiles, M. (1976), *What is Theology?*, Oxford, Oxford University Press.

Wilkerson, D. (1964), *The Cross and the Switchblade*, New York, Pyramid Books.

Willems, E. (1967), *Followers of the New Faith: Culture Change and the Rise of Protestantism in Brazil and Chile*, Nashville, TN, Vanderbilt University Press.

Williams, J. R. (1988), *Systematic Theology*, Grand Rapids, MI, Zondervan.

Wilson, B. R. (1961), *Sects and Society: The Sociology of Three Religious Groups in Britain*, London, Heinemann.

—— (1963), 'A Typology of Sects in a Dramatic and Comparative Perspective', *Archives de Sociologie de Religion* 16, 49–63.

—— (1966), *Religion in a Secular Society*, London, Watts and Co.

Wilson, E. A. (1994), 'Who Speaks for Latin American Pentecostals?', *Pneuma* 16.1, 143–50.

—— (2002), 'Brazil', in Burgess and van der Maas (eds), *NIDPCM*, p. 36.

Wiyono, G. (2005), 'Pentecostalism in Indonesia', in Anderson and Tang (eds), *Asian and Pentecostal*, p. 320.

Wolfe, K. M. (1984), *The Churches and the British Broadcasting Corporation 1922–1956*, London, SCM Press.

Womersley, D. (1973), *Wm. F. P. Burton: Congo Pioneer*, Eastbourne, Victory Press.

Wood, L. (2006), 'Can Pentecostals be Wesleyans? My Reply to Don Dayton's Rejoinder', *Pneuma* 28.1, 120–30.

World Council of Churches (2004), 'Consultation on Faith, Healing and Mission, Santiago de Chile, 28–30 October 2004', *International Review of Mission* 93, 407–12.

Wright, B. S. (2005), '"Discerning the Spirit" in the Context of Racial Integration and Conflict in Two Assemblies of God Churches', *Journal for the Theory of Social Behaviour* 35.4, 413–35.

Yao, X. and Badham, P. (eds) (2007), *Religious Experience in Contemporary China*, Cardiff, University of Wales Press.

Yinger, Y. M. (1957), *Religion, Society and the Individual*, New York, Macmillan.

Yong, A. (1998), 'Whither Systematic Theology? A Systematician Chimes in on a Scandalous Conversation', *Pneuma* 20.1, 85–93.

—— (1999), '"Not Knowing Where the Wind Blows ..." On Envisioning a Pentecostal-Charismatic Theology of Religions', *Journal of Pentecostal Theology* 14, April, 81–112.

—— (2000), *Discerning the Spirit(s)*, Sheffield, Continuum.

—— (2002), 'In Search of Foundations: The Oeuvre of Donald L. Gelpi, SJ, and Its Significance for Pentecostal Theology and Philosophy', *Journal of Pentecostal Theology* 11.1, 3–26.

—— (2002), 'Preface', in V.-M. Kärkkäinen, *Towards a Pneumatological Theology*, ed. A. Yong, Lanham, MD, University Press of America.

—— (2005), *The Spirit Poured Out on All Flesh*, Grand Rapids, MI, Baker Academic.

—— (2006), 'Justice Deprived, Justice Demanded: Afropentecostalisms and the Task of World Pentecostal Theology Today', *Journal of Pentecostal Theology* 15.1, 127–47.

Yonggi Cho, D. (1997), *A Bible Study for New Christians*, Seoul, Seoul Logos.

Yonggi Cho, P. with Manzano, R. W. (1983), *The Fourth Dimension: More Secrets for a Successful Life*, vol. 2, Plainfield, NJ, Bridge Publishing Inc.

Young, F. (1991), *The Making of the Creeds*, London, SCM Press.

Yun, B. (2004), *The Heavenly Man*, London, Monarch.

Zaret, D. (1989), 'Religion and the Rise of Liberal-Democratic Ideology in 17th Century England', *American Sociological Review* 54.2, 163–79.

Zhaoming, D. (2005), 'Indigenous Chinese Pentecostal Denominations', in Anderson and Tang (eds), *Asian and Pentecostal*, p. 444.

Websites

Annacondia, C. (2008)
http://www.godtube.com/view_video.php?viewkey=345d20e9287be1b6d7e0
(accessed 25.07.08)

Anon (editorial staff) (1989)
http://forerunner.com/forerunner/X0274_Revival_Surges_in_Ar.html
(accessed 25.07.08)

Assemblies of God
http://ag.org/top/Beliefs/Statement_of_Fundamental_Truths/sft_short.cfm
http://www.ag.org/top/Beliefs/Position_Papers/pp_4184_healing.cfm (accessed
20.11.08)

DeBorst, R. P.
http://www.christianvisionproject.com/2007/08/liberate_my_people.html
(accessed 25.07.08)

G12
http://www.g12europe.com/about-g12/ (accessed 29.07.08)

Goode, W. (1934) in *Gifts of the Spirit Stated and Examined*, see
http://books.google.co.uk/books?hl=en&id=pprGxmz5SfQC&dq=william+
goode+gifts+of+the+spirit+stated&printsec=frontcover&source=web&ots=
TMs4vgWWV5&sig=Pna_Rw-mehBVnPC8CwjbqKxNMDg&sa=X&oi=
book_result&resnum=1&ct=result#PPA11,M1

http://wordpress.com/tag/african-cultural-heritage/

http://archaeology.about.com/od/tterms/qt/timbuktu.htm

http://mizoramsynod.org/synfo.php?article&read_article&article_id=16
(accessed 3.04.08)

http://books.google.co.uk/books?hl=en&id=pprGxmz5SfQC&dq=william+
goode+gifts+of+the+spirit+stated&printsec=frontcover&source=web&ots=
TMs4vgWWV5&sig=Pna_Rw-mehBVnPC8CwjbqKxNMDg&sa=X&oi=
book_result&resnum=1&ct=result#PPA11,M1.

http://dynamic.csw.org.uk/index.asp?num=6&t=press (accessed 19.12.08)

http://news.bbc.co.uk/1/hi/entertainment/tv_and_radio/4154071.stm (accessed
19.12.08)

http://plato.stanford.edu/entries/royce/ (accessed 29.11.08)

http://www.christianpersecution.info/ (accessed 19.12.08)

http://www.christianpersecution.info/news/nigeria-authorities-detain-500-after-
violence-kills-pastors-17438/ (accessed 19.12.08)

http://www.christianpersecution.info/news/pentecostal-pastors-shot-dead-in-
colombia/ (accessed 19.12.08)

http://www.churchofgod.org/about/declaration_of_faith.cfm (accessed
20.11.08)

http://www.monergism.com/thethreshold/articles/onsite/four-fold.html

http://www.necf.org.my/berita/berita_nov_dec1999/argentine.htm (accessed
25.07.08)

http://www.oikoumene.org/en/member-churches/church-families/pentecostal-
churches.html (accessed 3.12.08).

http://www.pctii.org/news/wcc-news.html (accessed 3.12.08)

http://www.persecutionblog.com/2008/11/hindu-extremists-attack-pentecostal-
church-in-mumbai.html (accessed 19.12.08)

http://www.statistics.gov.uk/cci/nugget.asp?id=1311 (accessed 20.12.08)

http://www.themissionsociety.org/magazines/unfinished/2008-42/128 (accessed 19.12.08).

Jones, R. T. (1905), *Faith*, letter dated 31 January 1905. CD-ROM, *The Welsh Revival*, published by The Revival Library (see www.revival-library.org) in the history written by J. V. Morgan.

Kant, I. (1784), 'An Answer to the Question: What is Enlightenment?' A copy can be found on http://www.english.upenn.edu/~mgamer/Etexts/kant.html

Luther, M., 'Wittenberg', 17 January 1546. Cf. http://www.iep.utm.edu/l/luther.htm (accessed 11.10.2008)

Martinez, H. http://ipsnews.net/news.asp?idnews=37295 (accessed 29.07.08)

Memmi, A. http://www.english.emory.edu/Bahri/Memmi.html

National Association of Evangelicals http://www.nae.net/index.cfm?FUSEACTION=nae.history (accessed 15.04.08)

Partners in Harvest http://www.partners-in-harvest.org/toronto-christian-worship-cent/ (accessed 21.12.08)

Pew Forum statistics http://pewforum.org/surveys/pentecostal/

Palmer, P. (1845) *The Way of Holiness*, New York, Lane and Tippett, pp. 17–18, cited at http://wesley.nnu.edu/wesleyan_theology/theojrnl/21-25/23-13.htm (accessed 13.04.07)

Riss, R. http://www.grmi.org/Richard_Riss/history/argentina2.html (accessed 25.07.08)

Sweet, L. http://www.leonardsweet.com

Times On line http://www.timesonline.co.uk/tol/comment/faith/article2028610.ece (accessed 19.12.08)

UN Refugee Agency http://www.unhcr.org/cgi-bin/texis/vtx/home?page=statistics (accessed 19.12.08)

World Council of Churches http://www.oikoumene.org/en/member-churches/church-families/the-catholic-church.html (accessed 3.12.08)

http://www.oikoumene.org/en/member-churches/regions/latin-america/rgentina.html (accessed 25.07.08).

http://www.oikoumene.org/en/member-churches/regions/latin-america/cepla.html

http://www.oikoumene.org/en/member-churches/regions/latin-america/colombia.html (accessed 29.07.08)

Index